D0141405

The War on Welfare

POLITICS AND CULTURE IN MODERN AMERICA

Series Editors: Glenda Gilmore, Michael Kazin, and Thomas J. Sugrue

Volumes in the series narrate and analyze political and social change in the broadest dimensions from 1865 to the present, including ideas about the ways people have sought and wielded power in the public sphere and the language and institutions of politics at all levels—local, national, and transnational. The series is motivated by a desire to reverse the fragmentation of modern U.S. history and to encourage synthetic perspectives on social movements and the state, on gender, race, and labor, and on intellectual history and popular culture.

The War on Welfare

Family, Poverty, and Politics
in Modern America

Marisa Chappell

PENN

University of Pennsylvania Press
Philadelphia

Copyright © 2010 University of Pennsylvania Press

All rights reserved. Except for brief quotations used for purposes of review or scholarly citation, none of this book may be reproduced in any form by any means without written permission from the publisher.

Published by
University of Pennsylvania Press
Philadelphia, Pennsylvania 19104-4112

Printed in the United States of America on acid-free paper
10 9 8 7 6 5 4 3 2 1

Library of Congress Cataloging-in-Publication Data

Chappell, Marisa.
    The war on welfare : family, poverty, and politics in modern America / Marisa Chappell.
        p.   cm. — (Politics and Culture in Modern America)
    ISBN 978-0-8122-4204-1 (alk. paper)
    Includes bibliographical references and index.
    1. Public welfare—United States—History—20th century. 2. Poor women—Government policy—United States. 3. Welfare recipients—Employment—United States. 4. Aid to families with dependent children programs—United States—History—20th century. I. Title.
HV91 .C4513   2009
362.5/560973—dc22   2009033289

For Pat

Contents

Acronyms

AB: Aid to the Blind
ACLU: American Civil Liberties Union
AFDC: Aid to Families with Dependent Children
AFDC-UP: Aid to Families with Dependent Children-Unemployed Parent
AFL-CIO: American Federation of Labor-Congress of Industrial
    Organizations
AFSCME: American Federation of State, County, and Municipal Employees
AJC: American Jewish Committee
APTD: Aid to the Permanently and Totally Disabled
APWA: American Public Welfare Association
BLS: Bureau of Labor Statistics
BWWH: Black Women for Wages for Housework
CAA: Community Action Agency
CBC: Congressional Black Caucus
CCAP: Citizens' Crusade Against Poverty
CDF: Children's Defense Fund
CED: Committee on Economic Development
CHN&BP: Coalition for Human Needs and Budget Priorities
CLUW: Coalition of Labor Union Women
CORE: Congress of Racial Equality
CSWP&L: Center for Social Welfare Policy and Law
DOL: Department of Labor
DPS: Domestic Policy Staff
DWAC: Downtown Welfare Advocacy Center
EEOC: Equal Employment Opportunities Commission
EITC: Earned Income Tax Credit
EOA: Economic Opportunity Act
FAP: Family Assistance Plan
FEAC: Full Employment Action Council
FLSA: Fair Labor Standards Act
FRAC: Food Research and Action Center

FSA: Family Support Act
HEW: Department of Health, Education, and Welfare
HHS: Department of Health and Human Services
LCCR: Leadership Conference on Civil Rights
LWV: League of Women Voters
MEJ: Movement for Economic Justice
MIND: Methods of Intellectual Development
NAACP: National Association for the Advancement of Colored People
NAB: National Alliance of Businessmen
NAM: National Association of Manufacturers
NASW: National Association of Social Workers
NBER: National Bureau of Economic Research
NCC: National Council of Churches of Christ
NCCW: National Council of Catholic Women
NCFE: National Committee for Full Employment
NCHE: National Committee on Household Employment
NCJW: National Council of Jewish Women
NCNW: National Council of Negro Women
NCNW: National Congress of Neighborhood Women
NCSW: National Conference on Social Welfare
NCWWW: National Council on Women, Work, and Welfare
NFS: National Federation of Settlements and Neighborhood Centers
NIT: Negative Income Tax
NOW: National Organization for Women
NOW-LDEF: NOW Legal Defense and Education Fund
NSWA: National Social Welfare Assembly
NUL: National Urban League
NWPC: National Women's Political Caucus
NWRO: National Welfare Rights Organization
NYT: *New York Times*
OAA: Old Age Assistance
OASDI: Old Age, Survivors, and Disability Insurance
OBRA: Omnibus Budget Reconciliation Act
OEO: Office of Economic Opportunity
OMB: Office of Management and Budget
PBJI: Program for Better Jobs and Income
PRWORA: Personal Responsibility and Work Opportunity
    Reconciliation Act
PSID: Panel Study of Income Dynamics

RAM: Redistribute America Movement
SCLC: Southern Christian Leadership Conference
SIP: System Improvement Plan
SSI: Supplemental Security Income
STEP: Solutions to Employment Problems
TANF: Temporary Aid to Needy Families
UAW: United Auto Workers
VISTA: Volunteers in Service to America
WEAL: Women's Equity Action League
WHCF: White House Conference on Families
WICS: Women in Community Service
WIN: Work Incentive Program
WOW: Wider Opportunities for Women
YWCA: Young Women's Christian Association

Introduction

In 1996, President Bill Clinton fulfilled his promise to "end welfare as we know it." After vetoing two similar bills, Clinton signed the Personal Responsibility and Work Opportunity Reconciliation Act (PRWORA), which abolished the nation's most controversial welfare program, Aid to Families with Dependent Children (AFDC). Since 1935, poor single mothers and their children had at least a statutory entitlement to cash aid through the AFDC program.[1] The PRWORA explicitly ended that entitlement, froze federal welfare funding, denied benefits to legal immigrants, and mandated strict work requirements and time limits for welfare receipt.[2] The bill's principal goal was not to alleviate or eradicate poverty; its target was a supposedly failed federal program. To the nation's political elites—from Democrat Bill Clinton to conservative Congressional Republicans to the plethora of scholars and pundits debating the country's welfare "problem"—AFDC symbolized the failures of the Johnson administration's War on Poverty. While AFDC originated in 1935 as part of the Social Security Act, most Americans associate it with the 1960s, in part because that decade saw tremendous increases in AFDC caseloads and a number of new federal antipoverty programs. AFDC's abolition was to put an end, once and for all, to the moribund policies of a discredited 1960s liberalism.[3]

According to conventional wisdom, the policies of that discredited liberalism encouraged poor mothers to forgo both marriage and employment and to depend instead on government aid. With the PRWORA, Congress explicitly set out to "end the dependence of needy parents on government by promoting job preparation, work, and marriage." When the law came up for reauthorization in 2002, Republican President George W. Bush proposed stricter work requirements, while Congressional Democrats sought more funding for child care and job training, but both agreed that poor single mothers should support their children through wage labor rather than government aid. Both also agreed that single motherhood itself—along with teen pregnancy and out-of-wedlock births—represented a "crisis in our nation" for which AFDC had been largely responsible. The

PRWORA declared marriage "the foundation of a successful society" and "an essential institution . . . which promotes the interests of children," and Bush requested an additional $300 million for programs to encourage welfare mothers to marry. Few Americans were likely to disagree with Bush's proclamation that "children from two-parent families are less likely to end up in poverty, drop out of school, become addicted to drugs, have a child out of wedlock, suffer abuse, or become a violent criminal and end up in prison." By 2002, welfare reformers across the spectrum had reached a consensus that creation and maintenance of "stable families" should finally become a "central goal of American welfare policy."[4]

Ironically, the promoters of the apparently discredited 1960s liberalism would have agreed completely. In fact, concern about family dysfunction among the poor was central to liberal antipoverty efforts in the 1960s. Despite the controversy it generated, the infamous "Moynihan Report"—a 1965 Labor Department document that blamed African American poverty largely on the "deterioration of the Negro family"—expressed a broad consensus on the American left, subscribed to by liberals, social democrats, and grassroots antipoverty activists alike.[5] Like more recent welfare reformers, 1960s antipoverty advocates saw single motherhood as a significant social problem. But what I am calling the 1960s antipoverty coalition—members of the League of Women Voters, the National Council of Churches, the National Urban League, and dozens of other mainstream and respectable middle-class organizations, along with union leaders, welfare rights activists, and liberals in both political parties—offered a much different solution than their Reagan-era successors. The coalition's concern about family dysfunction among the poor did not lead its members to demand a contraction of federal redistributive policies. Instead, they lobbied for "fundamental income redistribution," full employment, and a guaranteed income for all American families.[6] How did the same preoccupation with "fixing" poor families produce a campaign to expand federal income support in the 1960s and a more successful crusade to contract it by the 1990s?

It is doubly ironic that contemporary critics blast 1960s liberals for ignoring—or even encouraging—family dysfunction among the poor. In reality, it was the antipoverty coalition's very commitment to promoting family stability that prevented it from designing effective solutions to children's poverty. While waging a War on Poverty, campaigning for a guaranteed income, and designing a full employment policy, the antipoverty coalition remained wedded to a particular model of the family that was already unrealistic by the 1960s: the male-breadwinner, female-homemaker ideal. Though the model had long informed employers' and policymakers' assumptions and actions, it never accurately described many poor and working-class families whose breadwinners could not earn a "family wage," an income high enough to support a nonworking wife and children. Even during the cultural heyday of the "traditional family"—the post-World War II decades—wives entered the labor market in large numbers, enabling many families to attain a standard of living that could not be sustained on a single income.[7]

This trend continued in the 1960s and the 1970s. By then, deindustrialization, stagnating wages, and a host of public policy decisions, combined with rising rates of divorce and out-of-wedlock births, meant that by the 1980s, only a small percentage of American families conformed to the male-breadwinner model.[8] If feminist activism and sexual revolution undermined that model's cultural foundation, economic transformation destroyed its financial viability. As corporations sought cheaper labor outside the United States, American workers lost access to the well-paid, unionized manufacturing jobs that had allowed men with little formal education to support families; declining union membership, an eroding social safety net, and the growth of part-time, temporary, and contingent service sector labor increased economic insecurity. "The idea of the traditional family was never realizable for most families in the industrial era," noted political scientist Sanford Schram: "with postindustrialism, it is no longer sustainable as an ideal."[9] But that ideal continued to shape the antipoverty coalition's political strategies and policy proposals well into the 1970s, and it persists as a powerful ideological touchstone in many quarters up to the present.

The antipoverty coalition's commitment to the family wage ideal highlights yet another irony in the story of welfare's end. Even as it demanded a much broader and deeper federal commitment to eradicating poverty, the antipoverty coalition elaborated an intellectually respectable and politically appealing critique of the AFDC program. During the second half of the 1960s, poverty lawyers, liberal foundations, and religious organizations helped poor single mothers organize and demand more generous welfare grants, but at the same time the antipoverty coalition sought to replace AFDC with a more comprehensive income support system. Its case for that broader system rested, in large measure, on a critique of AFDC. By providing aid to single mothers and not male-headed families, they argued, AFDC drove unemployed and low-earning fathers to desert their children and thereby perpetuated family dysfunction in America's inner cities. By the late 1960s, this indictment of AFDC became central to liberal proposals for expanded social provision, and by the late 1970s it had become central to a conservative crusade to restrict or even abolish cash grants for poor single mothers and their children. The antipoverty coalition's commitment to an increasingly obsolete family wage system not only blinded it to alternative solutions to children's poverty offered by some welfare rights activists and feminists, from paid motherhood proposals to comprehensive plans to enable poor single mothers to earn adequate wages; it also contributed to an antiwelfare ideology that ultimately undermined popular and political support for federal social welfare programs of all sorts, from AFDC and food stamps to Unemployment and Disability Insurance.[10]

This book's analysis of the antipoverty coalition offers a rethinking of American liberalism in the 1960s and 1970s. The prevailing picture in the scholarship portrays Great Society liberals as economically conservative but culturally radical. Although liberals were much more willing than self-described conservatives to address social problems with federal dollars, the Democratic Party, organized labor, and other liberals had largely made peace with corporate America. Derided by radicals as "corporate liberals," they certainly rejected proposals from the left to replace capitalist ownership with socialism, to decouple income from wage labor, or to devote massive resources to "empower" the nation's poor and minority communities.[11] But to characterize liberals, in general, as economic conservatives, as radicals did at the time and as a majority of scholarship continues to do, collapses important distinctions between Great Society Democrats and Goldwater Republicans by portraying liberals too homogeneously. In fact, as I will argue, by the second half of the 1960s, a broad coalition of liberals had joined grassroots antipoverty activists to demand massive federal redistribution in the form of guaranteed jobs and a guaranteed income. It wasn't a socialist revolution, to be sure, but it was a great deal more radical than anything a mainstream politician might offer today.

If historians portray Great Society liberals as economic conservatives, many academic and popular treatments paint them as cultural radicals. Though few would argue that Hubert Humphrey, Walter Reuther, or Martin Luther King, Jr., embraced countercultural values, many analysts link middle-class liberals with the youth-led cultural rebellions of the late 1960s and 1970s that embraced illegal drugs, rejected the hegemony of marriage and heterosexual monogamy, and encouraged young people to "question authority" in politics and society as well as in their everyday lives. If not the primary movers and shakers of this upheaval, liberals were at least permissive apologists of the moral relativism of the counterculture and of a seemingly rapid shift in American values more generally, as political conservatives repeatedly argued.[12] However, the antipoverty coalition's welfare reform and full employment campaigns reveal an underlying cultural conservatism that valued social order and promoted traditional gender roles and family structure. Thus, though the prevailing narrative portrays Great Society liberals as economically conservative and culturally radical, the reverse is more apt; indeed, I will argue that it was liberals' cultural conservatism with respect to gender and family structure that fatally undermined their generous social-democratic economic vision.

This book argues that traditional assumptions about appropriate family structure and family economics were as central to welfare politics in the 1960s and 1970s as they are today. I analyze the history of welfare politics by tracing those assumptions and their consequences, not through a detailed policy analysis or in-depth social history, but as political history with ideas at its center. I explore the ways in which various groups of Americans interpreted the connections among poverty, family structure, and racial inequality; the programs that policymakers and lawmakers adopted and the alternatives they rejected; and the ways in which unexamined assumptions about families, gender roles, and racial order structured the terms in which policymakers, activists, and advocates talked about welfare and economic justice. Above all, this book argues that both liberal and conservative welfare reformers failed to acknowledge the collapse of the family wage system. That failure made AFDC an increasingly despised program, stifled a potentially liberating vision of economic citizenship, and continues to leave hundreds of thousands of single mothers and their children in poverty.

Welfare and the Family Wage

In the past twenty years, historians' attention to race and gender ideology has revolutionized our understanding of American welfare state development. Until the 1980s, class served as the primary category of analysis in the field, as scholars engaged primarily with the work of political scientists Frances Fox Piven and Richard A. Cloward, who argued that twentieth-century social programs in the United States—whether old age insurance and unemployment compensation or public assistance—served the needs of capitalist employers and political elites to preserve social order and "regulate labor."[13] Scholars then began to delineate the racial fault lines in the nation's social safety net, while women's and gender historians demonstrated the importance of gender ideologies in determining both the structure and administration of welfare state programs.[14] As scholars continue to debate the relative weight of these factors, and a new wave of scholarship highlights the importance of "state structures" and "policy feedback," few analysts would deny that racism and racial inequalities, class and labor market relations, and deeply rooted gender assumptions have all played important roles in the development and structure of American social citizenship.[15] So, too, does the family. In fact, the family—or more specifically, the family wage system—served as a key concept through which political elites structured racial, class, and gender relations throughout the twentieth century.[16]

Though often referred to as "traditional," the male-breadwinner, female-homemaker family—and the family wage on which it relied—was a nineteenth-century development. The domestic economy of the preindustrial period rested centrally on women's productive and reproductive labor, whether in field, household, or workshop. Gradually, as a wage labor economy reshaped family economics in the decades between the Revolution and the Civil War, the male-breadwinner family model became a symbol of status and respectability for a new middle class of merchants, manufacturers, and professionals who adopted a "domestic ideology" that redefined household labor as nonproductive. The nineteenth-century doctrine of "separate spheres" justified woman's relegation to the private, domestic sphere as both natural and socially necessary.[17]

At the same time, as working-class families continued to rely on the productive labor of women and children, a new breadwinner pride compensated some wage-earning men for their loss of economic independence in the burgeoning free labor market. By the early twentieth century, both labor unions and middle-class reformers demanded that employers pay skilled male workers a "living wage" or "family wage" that would buy them the respectability that came with supporting a nonworking wife and children.[18] Meanwhile, employers used the family wage ideal to justify low wages for women, who were presumed to be "secondary" workers earning "pin money" rather than family breadwinners.[19] Racial and class boundaries characterized the family wage system from the outset. Well into the twentieth century, primarily white, native-born, skilled male workers earned enough to adopt the middle-class family model, leaving the vast majority of European immigrants and Mexican, Asian, and African Americans to pool several family members' earnings in order to survive.[20]

Like 1960s antipoverty liberals, Progressive Era reformers saw the male-breadwinner family as a prerequisite for social stability and upward mobility and incorporated this family model into their various efforts to humanize capitalism and provide economic protection to workers and their families.[21] As scholars employing "state-centered" approaches have argued, the focus on women and children in early American welfare state development reflected, in part, the tremendous obstacles in the way of broader protections for all workers and citizens. Unable to convince legislators, employers, or judges to interfere with men's "freedom of contract" by regulating working conditions or providing old age pensions or unemployment compensation, reformers relied instead on "maternalist" approaches. In the name of protecting mothers and children, middle-class women's clubs, trade union women, and settlement house reformers won protective labor laws for women and children, mothers' aid programs for fatherless families, and a federal maternal and infant health program. If male workers were left to the mercy of an unregulated labor market, at least women and children would fall under the protective arm of government.[22]

The architects of the nation's nascent welfare system sought quite explicitly to promote male-breadwinning and female-homemaking in poor immigrant communities. Nearly every state in the nation passed "mothers' aid" or "mothers' pension" legislation in the two decades before 1935 in response to new theories of childhood emphasizing the importance of home life and to pressure from middle-class women's clubs, which launched broad-based grassroots lobbying campaigns on behalf of mothers' aid. These statutes authorized local governments to provide cash aid to families left destitute by the death or incapacity of a male breadwinner. A handful of advocates saw mothers' pensions as a step toward broader state endowment of motherhood, while many supporters justified the program as payment for mothers' valuable service to the nation. To most reformers, though, the small cash grants would merely allow poor widows to keep their children at home rather than send them to an institution. In theory, the grants would also enable mothers to devote themselves full-time to childrearing—for no woman, as the New York State Commission on Relief for Widowed Mothers declared in 1914, "can be both the home-maker and the breadwinner of her family." Though African American clubwomen developed day nurseries to help poor mothers combine wage labor and parenting, white clubwomen and reformers sought to preserve single mothers' status as homemakers.[23] Sounding much like welfare reformers of our own day, mothers' pension advocates insisted that "normal family life" was "the foundation of the state and its conservation an inherent duty of government."[24]

The case of mothers' pensions—AFDC's forerunners—reveals the racial exclusion at the heart of the early American welfare state and of the family wage ideal upon which it was built. As a number of historians have shown, white middle-class reformers employed social welfare programs like mothers' pensions to impose a normative family model on a largely immigrant working class in need of "Americanization" while ignoring the problems of poverty and single motherhood among African Americans.[25] Fiscal constraints combined with administrators' attitudes to limit receipt of mothers' pensions to white women with dead or disabled husbands; deserted, divorced, and never-married mothers, along with nonwhite women, rarely received aid.[26] As historian S. J. Kleinberg noted, "the prevailing ethos took for granted that all people of color, including women and children, should be economically active," so "the absence of a paternal wage earner in their households did not provoke much public concern among white reformers."[27] In practice, even white widows who received aid were usually expected to supplement their small grants by taking in washing or sewing or otherwise earning wages—poor single mothers, no matter how "worthy," would not gain access to stay-at-home motherhood after all. "Rather than a policy that universalized the status of motherhood and paid mothers to raise their children at home," then, "the first public policy for single mothers required able-bodied women to earn and reinforced exclusionary practices based on race and family status."

These "exclusionary practices," and the family wage model that justified them, made their way into the nation's federal welfare system. The Social Security Act of 1935 established the welfare state's basic framework by setting up a number of federal and federal-state programs including Old Age Insurance and Unemployment Insurance as well as Old Age Assistance (OAA), Aid to the Blind (AB), and Aid to Dependent Children (ADC, renamed Aid to Families with Dependent Children in 1961). As a plethora of scholarship has detailed, this framework helped to establish a hierarchy of social citizenship. Employee contributions gave Old Age and Unemployment Insurance an aura of respectability and entitlement, as did federal funding, federal eligibility standards, and a largely white and male clientele. Meanwhile, OAA, AB, and ADC, the noncontributory public assistance programs often labeled "public welfare" or simply "welfare," relied on partial state funding and left eligibility and administration largely in the hands of state and local authorities. The different program structures affected recipients directly, of course, but they also shaped the way Americans thought about social provision. By the 1950s, the Social Security Administration had convinced Americans that social insurance programs were earned entitlements while public assistance programs, which retained the label "welfare," were mere charity.[28]

American social protection, then, depended upon participation in the labor market rather than on citizenship or residence, and the jobs that bought the most protection were those reserved for white men. Steadily employed industrial workers won maximum hour and minimum wage protections, the right to organize and bargain collectively, and access to social insurance programs to shield them from poverty during old age or unemployment. By virtue of the kinds of jobs they performed and their typical work patterns, most women did not have direct access to social insurance protection. While a number of left-leaning critics challenged various aspects of the Social Security Act, the vast majority of Americans in the 1930s shared the "gendered imagination" of federal policymakers, who assumed that by protecting male breadwinners from falling into poverty they were, in turn, protecting women and children.[29]

White women found themselves incorporated into the new welfare state as dependents rather than direct beneficiaries, but African American women lacked even that protection. Powerful Southern congressmen ensured the exclusion of domestic and agricultural laborers, three-fifths of African American workers, from Old Age Insurance, Unemployment Insurance, and the Fair Labor Standards Act. In the end, seasonal and marginal workers, along with most African Americans and the poorest white women were left to rely on public assistance programs, including ADC, which added federal dollars to state-level mothers' aid. Lawmakers also ensured that state and local governments retained control over these programs, leaving potential recipients subject to local racial and moral prejudices, labor market demands, and fiscal pressures.[30] Until the late 1960s, state lawmakers and local administrators encountered few obstacles in their efforts to restrict access to "welfare" and minimize caseloads and costs.[31]

The Social Security Amendments of 1939 deepened the welfare state's racial and class divisions. Instead of incorporating agricultural and domestic laborers into the social insurance programs, federal policymakers and Congressional lawmakers "enhanc[ed] the benefits of already covered (mostly white) males" by offering pensions to the widows and children of deceased beneficiaries. White male workers could henceforth act as breadwinners even in death, while federal funds would enable their widows to devote themselves to childrearing full time. Black fathers, shut out of good jobs by employer and labor union discrimination, could rarely act as sole breadwinners even in their prime working years. Survivors' benefits thus removed most white widows from the AFDC rolls, which were increasingly the last resort for nonwhite mothers and unmarried, divorced, and deserted mothers of all colors.[32] State legislators and local officials saw little benefit in letting these mothers remain at home with their children. An early federal survey of welfare administration in one Southern state, for example, attributed black women's exclusion from the AFDC rolls to a "unanimous feeling on the part of the staff and board that there are more work opportunities for Negro women," an "intense desire not to interfere with local labor conditions," and a feeling that "the Negro mother should . . . continue her usually sketchy seasonal labor or indefinite domestic service rather than receive a public assistance grant."[33] To most white Americans, full-time motherhood was one more piece of a system of white privilege.

Postwar developments only sharpened the family wage system's racial boundaries. Anticommunist fervor and the celebration of free enterprise amidst unprecedented economic expansion dashed New Dealers' hopes for a "Third New Deal," which might have expanded access to employment and social protections.[34] Instead, veterans' benefits and union victories helped millions of white men gain the economic security of good wages and home ownership. For the first time, a majority of white men earned a "family wage," a paycheck large enough to support non-wage-earning dependents, even as more of their wives entered the expanding service-based labor market to feed growing consumption standards. African American men remained largely shut out of union jobs and suburban housing developments. Just as millions of African Americans abandoned a crumbling Southern agricultural labor market for opportunities in industrial cities, those cities were beginning to suffer from deindustrialization and declining tax bases.[35] Excluded from stable, well-paid jobs and social insurance protections, African Americans experienced higher rates of poverty, marital dissolution, and unwed motherhood than whites.[36] By 1960, black families made up 40 percent of AFDC rolls, and a majority of adult recipients were divorced, deserted, or never-married mothers rather than widows.[37]

In the 1960s, mothers began to organize and demand their "right" to welfare, a massive civil rights movement demanded attention to racial disadvantage, and white liberals launched an antipoverty crusade. This new broadened antipoverty coalition targeted the family wage system's racial boundaries as a fundamental barrier in the way of racial equality, economic security, and social order. Thus 1960s liberals differed sharply from the New Deal's architects, but in their commitment to the male-breadwinner family structure, they shared much with them. Depression-era policymakers "built New Deal social welfare policy on the values of a bygone era" when they "ignored the fact that growing numbers of mothers were gainfully employed outside the home," and the antipoverty coalition of the 1960s made the same mistake.[38] By putting family structure at the center of its demand for a more generous and comprehensive welfare state, the coalition limited its repertoire of antipoverty strategies and prepared the way for a popular and ultimately successful political attack on AFDC.

Explaining the End of Welfare as We Knew It

This book offers an explanation for AFDC's declining political viability in the last three decades of the twentieth century. It is not the first to do so. Since the 1970s the study of welfare's "failure" has been a virtual cottage industry among poverty analysts, journalists, and both conservative and liberal pundits. The prevailing explanation for the increasingly successful political attack on AFDC is that Americans quite justifiably began to reject a failed program that caused dependence and family dysfunction among the poor. However, sociologists, poverty analysts, and ethnographers have demonstrated that AFDC itself had little impact on women's marital or childbearing decisions and the program acted for most recipients as a supplement to earnings or as a temporary source of support between periods of employment.[39] Thus, it is the *perception* that the AFDC program produces undesirable family and work behaviors among the poor that needs explaining. The development of that perception is, in large part, what this book seeks to explain.

By focusing on the period between 1964 and 1984, this book locates AFDC's fate in a longer political and intellectual history than many contemporary treatments acknowledge. A number of recent analyses explain the PRWORA, the 1996 law that abolished AFDC, primarily in terms of 1990s partisan politics or, more broadly, political elites' recent shift to "neo-liberalism."[40] The latest incarnation of a long-standing American commitment to free market economics, neoliberalism prescribes a vast reduction in government regulation of the marketplace, including tax reductions, deregulation, privatization, and significant retrenchment in social welfare programs. The "conventional wisdom," as one scholar described this economic and political philosophy, "holds that governments must reduce the tax burden and the public provision of social welfare in order to be able to attract capital and maintain (or regain) competitiveness in the global economy of the twenty-first century."[41] As the foregoing description suggests, both its enthusiasts and many less partisan observers attribute neoliberalism and its policies to the unrelenting and irresistible demands of an increasingly global marketplace. Even scholars who contest the inevitability of neoliberal policies explain welfare state retrenchment, including AFDC's demise, as a result of a political and economic consensus.[42]

The neoliberal explanation complements other arguments that explain AFDC's fate as part of a larger conservative shift in American politics after the 1960s. Scholars have pointed to "changes in the balance of class power" that began in the 1970s: demographic and economic shifts that increased the political power of conservative suburban and "Sunbelt" regions, electoral and technological changes that increased the costs of political campaigns, the declining power and influence of organized labor, and a well-funded and politically savvy corporate mobilization aimed at restoring business profitability. AFDC, in this narrative, was merely the most vulnerable of a whole host of social policies targeted by an increasingly powerful conservative political elite seeking to lower tax rates and reduce workers' bargaining power.[43] These analyses provide a more uniquely American story than broader treatments of the global turn to neoliberalism. If the American welfare state has long been relatively weak and fragmented compared to those of other industrialized nations, after all, the politics of retrenchment have also been peculiarly powerful here.[44] No doubt, PRWORA and the various efforts to restrict AFDC in the two previous decades were part of a larger political and economic agenda—reducing social supports in order to "regulate labor," maintain global competitiveness, and enrich corporate shareholders.

However, the symbolic centrality of the AFDC program to American antiwelfare politics, along with the language of family that dominates welfare reform debates, suggests a more complex story. Neoliberal policymakers have been much less successful in attacking social insurance programs like Old Age, Survivors, and Disability Insurance (OASDI, or "Social Security"), which enjoy broad popular support. That support stems, in part, from the public perception that social insurance payments are "earned" benefits—a perception encouraged by federal administrators seeking to legitimate payroll deductions in the programs' early days. It stems, as well, from the programs' targeted beneficiaries. Initially, powerful Southerners in Congress ensured that social insurance programs excluded agricultural and

domestic workers, along with temporary, seasonal, and many service workers. Most nonwhites, by virtue of the kinds of jobs they held, found themselves outside the social insurance safety net, reliant instead on locally
controlled public assistance or welfare programs. And while Unemployment Insurance found defenders in organized labor, and OASDI created its
own powerful old age lobby, AFDC's clients, poor single mothers, had little
political power or support.[45] This was all the more true as the rolls became
increasingly nonwhite in the post-World War II decades. Few Americans
quibbled with Survivors Insurance, which enabled mostly white widows to
avoid wage labor while they raised children, but many began to question
AFDC, which sought to provide the same privilege to a group of mothers
that was increasingly nonwhite and non-widowed.[46]

Those who argue that women's increasing presence in the labor market undermined support for AFDC must attend to this racial history. Certainly, as the family wage system collapsed after the 1960s and fewer
mothers could afford to remain outside the labor market, AFDC appeared
increasingly anachronistic. The argument that "times have changed" rever-
berates through welfare reform debates in the 1970s and 1980s. "A program
that was designed to pay mothers to stay home with their children," one
veteran welfare reformer noted in the mid-1980s, "cannot succeed when we
now observe most mothers going out to work."[47] And certainly, "long-term
shifts in expectations about women's employment" undermined popular
and political support for programs that funded some women's caregiving
labor.[48] But the women most likely to enroll in AFDC—poor single mothers, many of them nonwhite—had long been excluded from American society's family wage bargain. Only in the 1960s, at a high point of federal
activism to combat poverty and racial inequality, did an influential group
of reformers propose to include them—through federal job creation, a
guaranteed income, and a genuine full employment policy. The predominantly liberal reformers who proposed and campaigned for these policies
hoped to create male-breadwinner families among poor African Americans
and to restore public support for federal redistribution.

Tragically, they attempted to do so as the foundation upon which the
postwar family wage system was built crumbled. That foundation was built
in part on the nation's global economic dominance in the wake of World
War II and on federal policies that fueled both economic growth and broad
consumption. The Cold War fueled a massive military-industrial complex,
and federal contracts sustained many older industries, created brand new
ones, and fueled a phenomenal expansion of higher education. Federal

housing and educational policies, the G.I. Bill in particular, bought millions of veterans a middle-class lifestyle, while powerful industrial unions did the same for millions of blue-collar workers. By the beginning of the 1970s, though, the economic foundations of the family wage system had begun to collapse. Deindustrialization, declining union strength, and increasing assaults on labor and federal social spending created a drastically altered economy. The family wage system became increasingly anachronistic and unattainable, even for its onetime beneficiaries (white, blue-collar men in major unionized industries), precisely at the moment that the antipoverty coalition sought to extend that system to encompass African American families.

Other options were available. The growing expectation that mothers support their children by wage earning has led several nations to adopt a collection of social supports to help women combine parenting and wage labor and to ensure that families with a working parent can climb out of poverty.[49] In the late 1960s and early 1970s, when the American political system was significantly more open to expansive redistributive programs than it is in the early twenty-first century, a handful of activists offered just such a program. Some liberals proposed family allowances, which would have provided additional income to all families with children. Social democrats demanded massive federal job creation and universal health care. Antipoverty feminists agreed, adding that affirmative action plans and universal child care would be necessary to ensure that women could take advantage of public jobs. And welfare rights activists continued to insist on a nonstigmatized income support program that would empower parents to make decisions about work and childrearing, improve workers' bargaining power, and ensure that no child would continue to live in poverty. This book seeks to explain how and why these voices were marginalized and these alternatives rejected.

The policy preferences, political strategies, and philosophical debates at the center of this book reflect broadly contested notions of citizenship, work, and family. Welfare reform attracted discussion and input from a broad range of Americans, not simply administrators and legislators. Policymakers did not work in isolation; they encountered organizations, advocates, and activists who offered their own perspectives on welfare and economic justice. None of these participants in welfare reform debates worked in an ideological vacuum. In fact, assumptions about race, gender, and class profoundly shaped welfare programs, policies, and politics. But while the central participants in welfare debates often shared ideas and assumptions with the wider public, they also helped shape public opinion about welfare. Careful attention to the ideas, strategies, and rhetoric employed by presidential advisors, legislators, activists, and advocacy groups provides a clearer explanation of welfare politics than focusing on popular opinion alone.[50]

The book is roughly chronological. Chapter 1 introduces the 1960s antipoverty coalition and traces its fairly rapid acceptance of a guaranteed income as the solution to poverty and racial disadvantage. Recent attention to the welfare rights movement has expanded our understanding of left-leaning politics in this period, but welfare recipient activists often worked in coalition with middle-class organizations and activists.[51] While contact with AFDC recipients and poor youth helped radicalize the members of mainstream liberal organizations, the guaranteed income campaign had its roots in the coalition's interpretation of black urban poverty. In the midst of several summers of urban rioting and rapidly growing AFDC rolls, the antipoverty coalition insisted that racial discrimination, high unemployment, and low wages available to African American men prevented them from becoming viable family breadwinners. Convinced that the male-breadwinner family was a prerequisite for upward mobility and social order, the coalition hoped to use federal redistributive policies—large-scale job creation and a federally guaranteed income—to extend that signal middle-class privilege, the family wage system, to poor and working-class African Americans. Although most scholars insist that controversy over the 1965 Moynihan Report banished discussion of the black family from leftist and liberal debate, Chapter 1 demonstrates that the subject dominated antipoverty discussions in the late 1960s.[52]

The coalition's efforts to extend the family wage system ran up against a conservative interpretation of welfare, poverty, and racial inequality. Antiwelfare conservatives—Southern Democratic and conservative Republican lawmakers, business lobbyists, and private citizens who sought to restrict, contract, or even abolish income support programs—were committed to a free market ideology that rejected federal social spending. But their antipathy to AFDC also stemmed from their allegiance to a racially and economically exclusive family wage system. Even as they celebrated the male-breadwinner family, antiwelfare conservatives drew sharp boundaries around it: the family wage was at once a sign of respectability and a reward for appropriate work and sexual behavior—a duty and a privilege, in other words, reserved primarily for working- and middle-class whites. Southern lawmakers sought to maintain a racial caste system and business leaders saw in welfare mothers an "untapped source of manpower."[53]

Because they were convinced that a guaranteed income would eradicate poverty, ensure racial equality, and ease social disorder, antipoverty liberals within the Nixon administration persuaded the president to offer a radical kind of welfare reform. The Family Assistance Plan (FAP), the subject of Chapter 2, would have replaced AFDC with a guaranteed income for all American families. In designing and selling the FAP, liberal policymakers in the Nixon administration and antipoverty coalition members sharpened their critique of AFDC as a program that destroyed black families and alienated the "working poor"—a term that referred to two-parent white families who were excluded from the welfare system's benefits. The FAP, they promised Nixon, would *produce* two-parent families among African Americans and *reward* two-parent families among the white "working poor." It would also redistribute the financial and symbolic rewards of the federal welfare system away from African American single mothers and toward white male breadwinners. The male-breadwinner ideology thus convinced a Republican president to propose a vast expansion in the nation's social safety net.

Although Congress twice failed to implement the FAP, debate over the program profoundly shaped the future of welfare politics. While a guaranteed income might well have revolutionized the nation's social safety net, the FAP relied on an outmoded family model that would have limited its effectiveness in combating poverty. It would certainly have provided a welcome financial boost to the poorest two-parent families, but a few hundred dollars a year would not have saved the male-breadwinner family structure, and the plan did little to help poor single mothers or alter the labor market conditions that perpetuated poverty even among many full-time workers; by the 1970s it was hardly the answer to women's and children's poverty. The FAP would have done little to help poor single mothers, but its advocates further undermined support for the only program that did, AFDC. To sell the program, liberal policymakers honed their critique of AFDC as a destructive program that drove poor fathers away, an argument that became central to an increasingly successful antiwelfare conservatism. At the same time, the FAP's structure, which seemed to pit the interests of AFDC mothers against those of two-parent "working poor" families, shattered the antipoverty coalition consensus and convinced many on the political left that "welfare"—associated with African Americans and single motherhood—was a losing political issue.

Chapter 3 describes the fallout by tracing the evolution of both liberal and conservative positions on welfare and economic justice in the mid-1970s. That decade saw a significant expansion of the nation's social safety net for the aged, blind, and disabled and even for low-income workers who became eligible for an expanded Food Stamp Program and an Earned Income Tax Credit (EITC). But AFDC rolls leveled off and the program faced repeated administrative and political attacks. I argue that this trend was the result of political choices on both the left and the right. Scholars have long criticized liberals for ceding poverty and welfare issues during the 1970s and allowing conservatives to set the terms of debate.[54] My exploration of liberal strategy offers an explanation for that shift. After the FAP, the antipoverty coalition—both middle-class liberals and grassroots antipoverty activists—consciously neglected defending AFDC in its effort to keep white, working-class voters in the Democratic fold and build a new progressive majority. AFDC's public image as a black program made it a risky issue, but so, too, did its association with "broken families." AFDC recipients seemed to flout the male-breadwinner family ideal so central to the value system of white, working-class voters and to the liberal lobbyists and reformers who sought their support. As they mobilized on behalf of federal full employment legislation, liberals' continued allegiance to a rapidly eroding family wage ideal left AFDC mothers with few allies.

Chapter 3's analysis of economic justice campaigns during the 1970s challenges prevailing interpretations of liberal politics after the 1960s. Most scholars insist that liberals and the left more generally not only ignored the plight of the white working class in the 1960s but also shifted wholeheartedly to "identity politics" during the 1970s. In doing so, the argument goes, wayward liberals rejected a politics of class that might bring Americans of different races together to tackle socioeconomic problems and pursue "common dreams."[55] In fact, while feminism flourished and colleges instituted programs in women's, African American, and Chicano studies, the liberal reformers and grassroots activists of the antipoverty coalition—including the most prominent and powerful national voices of liberalism in civil rights and religious organizations, labor unions, and the Democratic Party—pursued a politics and policies designed to bring various poor, working- and middle-class constituencies together. But in the context of a deeply sex- and race-segregated labor market and in the face of a continued allegiance to male breadwinning, feminists and welfare recipient activists found that poor single mothers would never gain access to resources without attention to the specific needs of women.

If the left ignored AFDC in the 1970s, conservatives placed it front and

center in a well-funded campaign to discredit federal social welfare programs, a development I describe in Chapter 3. The antipoverty coalition's
indictment of AFDC proved particularly useful in this effort. Conservative
scholars and pundits joined business lobbyists in arguing that the welfare
system created an "underclass" culture by providing "perverse incentives"
that discouraged wage labor and marriage among the poor. Antipoverty liberals had employed much the same argument during the guaranteed income campaign; they had offered broader income support programs as the
answer to AFDC's "perverse incentives." But the emerging conservative
consensus insisted that any and all public assistance would undermine
breadwinning among poor men and discourage marital stability. Liberals
and activists seeking to expand federal income support found their own arguments used against them and were increasingly unable to articulate an
effective rationale for "welfare."

By the time President Jimmy Carter proposed his welfare reform plan,
anxiety about family transformation reached well beyond antipoverty activists. Chapter 4 reconstructs the widespread public discussion about "family
crisis" that engaged journalists, politicians, activists, and social science "experts" in the second half of the 1970s. Americans, it seems, finally noticed
the collapse of the male-breadwinner family system but, I argue, most de-
baters blamed cultural changes, from feminist ideology to a "culture of nar-
cissism," while ignoring the more fundamental economic change—the
continued erosion of the family wage bargain. Some former liberals even
joined conservative activists in constructing a "New Right" and defending
the "traditional" family and the free market. Others expressed profound
ambivalence about family change, an ambivalence reflected during events
such as the White House Conference on Families but also in the Carter
administration's welfare reform proposals.

The Program for Better Jobs and Income (PBJI) looked much like
Nixon's Family Assistance Plan in its assumptions about family structure
and male breadwinning. The Carter administration's fiscal conservatism
combined with its lingering family wage ideology led to a program that, like
the FAP, promised additional income to two-parent families but less to
poor single mothers. The PBJI also failed to deliver on its promise to help
welfare mothers gain access to the training, jobs, and services that might
make employment a viable antipoverty strategy. But, as Chapter 4 argues,
by the second half of the 1970s, an emerging network of antipoverty feminists—including welfare rights activists and members of traditional wom-
en's organizations—challenged not only the "pro-family" policies of an

increasingly powerful "New Right" but also the male-breadwinner assumptions of their liberal allies. While the national feminist organizations are often taken to task for ignoring the plight of poor women and welfare recipients, this chapter demonstrates that despite significant class and racial tensions, feminist activists and organizations did respond to the eroding family wage system and the so-called "feminization of poverty."[56] In fact, while the antipoverty coalition in general failed to offer a coherent response to the PBJI, this feminist network offered a comprehensive alternative framework for welfare reform: education, jobs, training, and support services that would provide women with the income necessary to raise children out of poverty. Their call for a degendered family wage, though, met with little success in an increasingly conservative political climate.[57]

During the 1980s, as Chapter 5 argues, the antipoverty coalition's 1960s ideology bore fruit, but not in the way liberal advocates had intended. The antiwelfare conservatives in and around the Reagan administration marshaled charges that AFDC destroyed poor families and fostered social disorder in the nation's cities to demand a contraction of the program in the Omnibus Budget Reconciliation Act (OBRA). Even as the administration offered minor tax and social security reforms to help middle- and upper-class mothers to choose paid labor in the marketplace or unpaid labor in their own homes, it insisted that poor single mothers (and, of course, poor fathers) fend for themselves in the low-wage labor market. Liberal Democrats, organized labor, and the organizations of the increasingly fragmented antipoverty coalition opposed Reagan's spending cuts but offered no coherent vision for AFDC or welfare reform. The coalition's commitment to extending the male-breadwinner family to the urban poor had largely disappeared, as had its related defense of poor women's caregiving labor and the welfare rights movement's larger insistence on a "right to live." Few on the left even uttered the phrase "guaranteed income" anymore.

Yet Reagan's welfare cuts offered the antipoverty coalition a chance to redefine AFDC for a new economy, an approach that we can glimpse in the responses of recipient activists and some of their liberal allies. By focusing its cuts on recipients with earned income, OBRA finally pushed some liberals to talk about poor single mothers as part of the "working poor" and, along with recipient activists, to see AFDC as a tool to survive and ideally to escape the low-wage labor market. This is how a majority of AFDC recipients had always used the program anyway, and it had the potential to garner broad public support, given the widespread entry of women of all classes into the labor market.[58] While this new vision of AFDC sparked occasional grassroots coalitions and campaigns among welfare recipients, labor unions, and community activists, though, it did not save AFDC. By the late 1980s, as recipient activists and their allies continued to articulate this argument, many nationally prominent liberals and advocacy organizations joined antiwelfare conservatives in forging a "new consensus" on welfare. Antipoverty liberals' long-standing concern with AFDC's damaging effect on poor African American families, now married to antiwelfare conservatives' long-standing insistence that poor and nonwhite mothers participate in the labor market, led, by 1996, to the "end of welfare as we know it."

Chapter 1
Reconstructing the Black Family: The Liberal Antipoverty Coalition in the 1960s

Our men, once deliberately emasculated as the only way to enforce their servile status, might easily be tempted by a family structure which by making them the financial head of the household, seemed to make them its actual head. In our desperation to escape so many suffering decades, we might trip down the worn path taken by so many in America before us.

—Eleanor Holmes Norton, 1971

In 1963, United Auto Workers (UAW) president Walter Reuther launched a "Citizens' Crusade Against Poverty" (CCAP), an effort to harness the energies of a "unique coalition of church, civic, fraternal, labor and business groups" toward a "national issue of conscience." That "unique coalition" was in the thick of another issue of conscience in 1963, of course—the struggle for African American civil rights. Coupled with massive civil disobedience among African Americans throughout the nation, pressure from organized liberal America would result in the landmark Civil Rights Act of 1964, which effectively dismantled the legal framework of racial segregation in the American South, and the Voting Rights Act of 1965, which at long last ensured basic political rights to black Southerners. If response to Reuther's CCAP invitation is any indication, the liberal civil rights coalition brought a similar moral energy to the issue of poverty. Liberals exhibited "overwhelming interest and support," and by 1966, Reuther had convinced over 125 organizations to join his crusade to "eradicat[e] . . . poverty in our times." With labor, religious, and foundation funding, CCAP saw itself as a civilian counterpart to the federal government's War on Poverty, the embodiment of middle-class Americans' "special responsibility to help those who have not been so fortunate, who have been left behind."[1]

The list of individuals and organizations that responded to Reuther's call reads like a Who's Who of the liberal-labor lobby. The CCAP attracted civil rights luminaries Martin Luther King, Jr., Bayard Rustin, A. Philip Randolph, Whitney Young, Jr., Dorothy Height, and John Lewis. On the labor front, the American Federation of Labor-Congress of Industrial Organizations (AFL-CIO), the UAW, and a number of individual unions joined, as did major religious organizations like the Anti-Defamation League of B'nai B'rith, the American Jewish Committee (AJC), the National Council of Churches of Christ (NCC), and the National Catholic Conference. Social workers and social welfare advocates—organizations like the Young Women's Christian Association (YWCA) and the National Social Welfare Assembly (NSWA)—also participated. The CCAP scope reached from America's most famous contemporary socialist Michael Harrington to a handful of corporate leaders, reflecting the breadth of this 1960s antipoverty coalition.[2]

The CCAP's leaders were not alone in calling for "immediate bold and vigorous action" against poverty. In his 1964 inaugural address, President Lyndon Johnson turned his predecessor's call for federal action on behalf of the poor into a battle cry, launching a "War on Poverty." The resulting Economic Opportunity Act (EOA), an eclectic collection of programs to channel resources and services into poor communities, epitomized the constraints of liberal ideology and political reality. By the time national decision-makers discovered what Michael Harrington called "the other America," the country was in the midst of its longest economic boom in history.[3] Two decades of Cold War repression and general affluence had decimated the socialist left and made major structural reforms like industrial democracy, economic planning, or national health care infeasible. Meanwhile, the post-World War II triumph of therapeutic culture popularized behavioral explanations of poverty. So while some federal antipoverty planners revived the World War II-era call for a "Third New Deal," the governing elite—the "Vital Center" of corporate leadership and the moderates who dominated both political parties—eschewed structural solutions to unemployment and poverty. They were convinced that priming the economic pump through government spending and tax cuts, augmented by efforts to improve "opportunity" and rehabilitate the poor, would ensure that all worthy citizens could live the "American Dream." As historian Michael Katz noted, "no approach to poverty could be more conventional, or more American."[4]

The CCAP strayed little from this centrist liberalism.[5] It called for an enlarged federal role in ensuring high levels of employment and moderate redistribution through progressive tax policies and expanded minimum wage legislation. These were hardly radical. Nor, necessarily, was the CCAP's pledge to mobilize poor people.[6] Reuther insisted that the poverty war "must not develop along the lines of a well-intentioned social welfare program of the rich doing favors for the poor."[7] He hoped that the CCAP could serve as a "national network" for the thousands of grassroots poor people's organizations already forming across the country, and he won a Ford Foundation grant to train one thousand "community workers" to help organize the poor into "community unions."[8] A handful of radicals hoped that grassroots organizing would enable the poor to force fundamental reforms, but the CCAP viewed it as an antidote to psychological deficiencies among the poor. As "aliens in their native land," both "materially and psychologically outcast," the poor would surely benefit by participating in the design and implementation of antipoverty programs, action which would "break . . . through the apathy of the poor" and instill "the will to help themselves."[9] Above all, the CCAP sought "to bring the disadvantaged back into the mainstream of American life."[10]

A mere half decade later, the liberal members and supporters of the CCAP had moved well to the political left. Several summers of urban riots and growing militancy among young African American activists suggested to many of them that federal antipoverty efforts were not only too late, but too little. National opinion-makers declared that violence and discontent among poor African Americans, rising welfare rolls, and other signs of "social disorder" in the country's ghettos amounted to an "urban crisis." While conservatives responded by seeking to curtail antipoverty spending and institute "law and order," organized liberal America offered a much different solution. Through antipoverty activism, many middle-class liberals had developed relationships with poor people that challenged individualistic interpretations of disadvantage and strengthened their commitment to eradicating poverty. In 1965, the CCAP's James Patton had called for a "national dialogue" to generate "a few really big ideas" for solving poverty; by the end of the decade, his call came to fruition as a wide spectrum of liberals joined radicals and welfare rights activists in demanding a federally guaranteed income.

The antipoverty coalition might have responded to the urban crisis and the politicization of poverty in a variety of ways. Its decision to demand a radical kind of welfare reform, the replacement of AFDC and other public assistance programs with a guaranteed income, emerged from its interpretation of African American disadvantage and the urban crisis. This interpretation was shaped by the coalition's gender, race, and class ideology: it saw the urban crisis as a crisis of the Black family. Antipoverty liberals and left-ists blamed structural factors—racial discrimination, unemployment, low wages, inadequate education and training programs, and a perverse and stigmatizing welfare system—for breaking up African American families and promoting the intergenerational transmission of poverty and disadvantage. Only by massive federal efforts to shore up male-breadwinner family structure among urban African Americans, they came to believe, could the country solve the interrelated problems of racial inequality, poverty, and social disorder.

By exploring the sources and the ideology of the guaranteed income campaign, this chapter provides a new picture of Great Society liberalism. Middle-class liberals in the late 1960s offered much bolder solutions to poverty and racial disadvantage than most scholars acknowledge. But their turn to a guaranteed income was not an "aggressive attempt by shaken liberals to win back the support and trust" of increasingly radical black activists, as Gareth Davies argues in the only book-length historical analysis of the campaign. Instead, interactions with poor people, frustration with political resistance to job creation and other big-ticket antipoverty programs, and above all a commitment to allowing African Americans the benefits of male breadwinning and female homemaking pushed middle-class liberals to break from the War on Poverty's "opportunity liberalism" and embrace the guaranteed income. But, for the vast majority, that support was hardly "predicated on the radical—not to mention unpopular—notion that individual behavior and status were not proper standards by which entitlement should be judged."[11] On the contrary, it was an effort to overcome poverty and racial disadvantage and ensure that African Americans could take advantage of educational and economic opportunities by including them, once and for all, in the nation's family wage bargain.

A "Quiet Revolution": The Antipoverty Coalition

America has the resources to meet the challenge of poverty. Men and women of good will from all groups must act together to demonstrate the sense of national purpose and the will to square America's promise with practical performance in this vital area. (Walter Reuther, 1966)[12]

In 1965, Sargent Shriver told Congress that the "most important and exciting thing about the war on poverty" was "that all America is joining in . . . religious groups, professional groups, labor groups, civic and patriot groups are all rallying to the call."[13] That same year, *New York Times* columnist James Reston celebrated the "group of leaders" in "every city and community" who "believe this job can be done and who are helping."[14] Shriver and Reston each had good reason to act as cheerleader for federal antipoverty programs. Shriver ran the Office of Economic Opportunity (OEO), which administered the War on Poverty. A scion of the Eastern establishment and brother-in-law to John F. Kennedy, he represented the Democratic Party's intellectual elite: those who took offense at overt racial discrimination and drastic economic inequality but maintained faith that enlightened federal leadership could promote a fairer, more humane capitalism. Reston, for his part, wrote for the official organ of the liberal center, a newspaper whose editorial staff promoted the integrationist, Cold War liberalism that dominated national politics in the early 1960s.

Shriver and Reston also described something very real: many Americans *were* becoming personally involved in antipoverty activity. Through their affiliations with civic, religious, and labor groups and in response to stirring political rhetoric, ordinary citizens helped to wage the War on Poverty. Federal policy provided some direct means for participation; citizens signed on as Volunteers in Service to America (VISTA) or as board members for local Community Action Agencies (CAAs). At the same time, a number of organizations researched poverty in their communities and set up their own programs. In a three-year action study, for example, Church Women United, the women's wing of the NCC, provided thousands of volunteers for literacy and tutoring programs, migrant ministries, Headstart programs, and CAAs throughout the country.[15] Federal attention and resources did indeed fuel the process Shriver hoped it would, "of arousing, of mobilizing, of harnessing the moral energies of the American people." Vice President Hubert Humphrey pronounced this mobilization "A Quiet Revolution."[16]

At the center of that revolution were civil rights organizations and activists. The mobilization of hundreds of thousands of African Americans contributed much of the energy that fueled reform in the 1960s. White liberal America enlisted in the movement, lending support to campaigns to dismantle the legal foundations of segregation and discrimination in the South. But the Black freedom struggle had always been about more than "civil rights." Grassroots activists and national leaders alike understood that, as A. Philip Randolph put it, "economic and civil rights are inseparable."[17] With the passage of civil rights and voting rights legislation in 1964 and 1965, the same years that witnessed the beginnings of annual explosions of violence in the nation's African American "ghettos," movement leaders and their white liberal and radical allies increasingly turned their attention to the economic foundations of black disadvantage. While presidents Kennedy and Johnson had a variety of reasons for declaring war on poverty, by 1965 that war had everything to do with racial politics.[18]

As African American communities throughout the country battled both political and economic exclusion, national civil rights organizations developed programs for institutional change. Even outside the South, African Americans found themselves confined to an unstable, low-wage labor market and to crowded neighborhoods with substandard housing. In the 1960s, social worker Whitney Young, Jr., transformed the National Urban League (NUL) from a rather staid social welfare organization into a vigorous proponent of federal efforts to equalize opportunity for African Americans. In 1964, Young presented the Urban League's "Domestic Marshall Plan" which called for massive investment in America's cities—an influx of federal money for education, jobs, housing, and social services designed to produce a "social revolution" that would "broaden the application of the American Dream to our Negro citizens at last."[19] Longtime labor and civil rights leader A. Philip Randolph and his protégé Bayard Rustin developed their own plan in 1966. A blueprint for federal commitment to eliminating poverty among Americans of all colors, their Freedom Budget called for federal investment in job creation, income support, housing, health care, transportation, and urban renewal. Both plans envisioned "a far different kind of capitalism from that American had known," one "more democratically controlled, socially beneficial, and egalitarian in its outcomes."[20] Both also attracted widespread liberal support, expressing the antipoverty coalition's consensus that it was the federal government's responsibility to provide the jobs, income, and infrastructure necessary to banish poverty and racial disadvantage.

Organized labor joined these calls for vigorous federal action. In the 1960s, the leaders of the nation's major unions began to remind their members that workers who had "been able, through our collective efforts, to improve our lot in life" had a "special responsibility" to help others "who had been left behind."[21] AFL-CIO president George Meany and other labor leaders criticized federal antipoverty legislation as "hardly a first, small step" and called for the kinds of massive investments spelled out in the Freedom Budget.[22] Reuther and Meany vigorously defended federal antipoverty budgets against Congressional axes and lent their imprimatur to coalitions fighting for more generous appropriations. They also made "special efforts . . . to involve rank-and-file union members" in antipoverty activities. National union offices ran leadership training programs, nagged regional councils to recruit volunteers, and sent films, discussion outlines, and pamphlets to local unions, dispelling negative stereotypes about poor people, reminding members that they were "natural allies" of the poor, and providing instructions about how to get involved.[23] Among those who answered the call was Dorothy Haener, who headed the UAW Women's Department. Haener helped the Wayne County (Michigan) AFL-CIO set up a Labor Conference to Mobilize Against Poverty and took a leading role in a number of antipoverty coalitions.[24] Haener's commitment was unusual, but Julius Rothman of the AFL-CIO Department of Urban Affairs bragged in 1967 about "hundreds of instances of informal cooperation by unions and union members with anti-poverty programs and agencies."[25]

Antipoverty work was so popular in the 1960s it even attracted some corporate participation. Given business's long-standing hostility to government social welfare programs, its participation in antipoverty activism, however tepid, is a testament to the sense of crisis that plagued Americans in the late 1960s. Business antipoverty efforts expressed both a sincere philanthropic impulse and a healthy dose of self-interest, as American Business Press president John Babcock revealed in a letter to the nation's business press. The riots, the "crisis in social welfare," and the general "agony our cities are undergoing" all provided American businessmen with the "EDITORIAL OPPORTUNITY OF THE CENTURY," Babcock insisted, a way to burnish their image as benevolent capitalists. He advised that business take a "leadership role" in promoting antipoverty activities, which would help their communities and, at the same time, bring them positive publicity. Both "self-interest" and "public-spirited[ness]" would thereby be served.[26]

Some capitalists responded to the call. In 1968, five hundred corporate executives formed the National Alliance of Businessmen (NAB) to promote private efforts to train and employ the poor.[27] That same year, National Association of Manufacturers (NAM) head W. P. Gullander called for private industry's "own all-out war on poverty," the kind of "galvanic effort that, a quarter century ago, sent Liberty ships coursing down the ways day after day, with the armed and invincible might of American military production." But while federal dollars had fueled World War II's productive power, NAM consistently opposed federal spending and promoted private-sector antipoverty programs as part of a "fresh vision of the social responsibility of business."[28] *Fortune* magazine profiled the NAM Solutions to Employment Problems (STEP) program, designed to help companies initiate minority hiring programs, and Methods of Intellectual Development (MIND) program, a basic education effort for "unskilled and inexperienced workers"—"captives of a cultural pathology" who were mired in a "ghetto subculture."[29] NAM touted business efforts in various cities to train and recruit minorities, rehabilitate slum housing, and encourage "ghetto owned and controlled companies" as corporate America's very own "Quiet Revolution."[30]

The violence of the 1967 Detroit riot, marking a "third summer of widespread civil disorder," brought reform-minded businessmen more fully into the antipoverty fold through a new organization, the Urban Coalition. Executives from major corporations joined the usual suspects from civil rights, labor, religious, and women's organizations and local governments, 1,000 strong, at an "Emergency Convocation" at the Shoreham Hotel in Washington, D.C., in August. The group sought to "create a sense of national urgency" to "meet the crisis of our cities."[31] While the group sought an end to racial discrimination, social order as much as social justice informed its priorities. The Coalition's articles of incorporation exhibited little of the activist flavor that was increasingly prevalent in liberal circles, defining its mission as "charitable, educational, and scientific," dedicated to a "reduction in neighborhood tensions, community deterioration and juvenile delinquency."[32] At root, Urban Coalition members sought "a greater commitment" among the country's private citizens not to ensure social or economic justice but rather to help improve "the conditions of urban life which had bred civil disorder."[33] To this end, local coalitions developed low-income housing and held public forums on issues like school policies and police-community relations.

In early 1970, members of the Newark (New Jersey) Urban Coalition, representing the conservative pole of the antipoverty coalition, met some women from the opposite pole. Organizers of an all-day welfare seminar paired the one hundred business leaders and government officials with hostesses from the Newark Welfare Rights Organization, one of thousands of grassroots poor people's groups that had developed across the country during the previous decade.[34] Consisting primarily of single mothers receiving AFDC, welfare rights groups advocated for fellow recipients, publicized regulations (making recipients aware, for example, that they were entitled to special grants for furniture, winter coats, and school clothing), pressured case workers for better treatment, and lobbied elected officials to increase welfare grants and eliminate restrictions on recipients' rights to privacy and personal dignity. In 1966, representatives from welfare rights groups across the country met in Detroit to form the National Welfare Rights Organization (NWRO). Over the next several years, the mostly African American, mostly female membership grew to nearly 25,000, opened access to welfare for hundreds of thousands of eligible families, and influenced national debate over government responsibility for citizens' economic well-being.[35]

CCAP's 1966 conference reveals some of the tensions within the antipoverty coalition between welfare rights activists and middle-class liberals. CCAP leaders dubbed their second annual meeting a "poor people's convention" and invited members of neighborhood and tenant associations, welfare rights groups, and other grassroots poor people's organizations, many of whom were profoundly disappointed with both the structure and tone of the meeting. Above all, they complained that "experts" dominated the major sessions and leaders kept tight control over discussion. The dissatisfaction erupted when Sargent Shriver appeared and delivered what critics called "a 'Chamber of Commerce' address," emphasizing the War on Poverty's successes by "reeling off a lot of statistics in a typical public relations performance designed to make everyone happy."[36] The "disaffected poor people" shouted Shriver off stage, bypassing what editors of the *New Republic* called "their professional 'brokers'—the coalition of labor, church, civil rights, and Democratic leaders who have been acting as their middlemen in social conflicts for the last twenty years."[37] The *Nation*'s editors concluded that the CCAP, "a group drawn from the prosperous," was "unable to speak for the poor," and that "for all its excellent intentions and sponsorship . . . does not have a program and a strategy to deal with today's festering poverty."[38]

The conflict was about who should direct the antipoverty coalition and how much that coalition should demand. George Wiley, former chemistry professor and leader in the Congress of Racial Equality (CORE), pushed CCAP to bring poor people into leadership positions and to lobby for significant income redistribution. A week before the contentious meeting, Wiley had submitted to CCAP a "Proposal for the Establishment of an Anti-Poverty Action Center." Frustrated by "always having to tone down statements to keep from offending divergent elements of a tenuous coalition," Wiley hoped to "press for radical change" on behalf of his "true constituents . . . the great mass of deprived Negroes at the bottom of the social and economic ladder."[39] But, he complained, CCAP leaders' "initial interest cooled off, particularly after the episode when poor people expressed themselves in their own way to Sargent Shriver."[40] Wiley promptly resigned from

CCAP and launched the Poverty/Rights Action Center. Impressed by welfare rights mobilization and influenced by activist academics Frances Fox Piven and Richard Cloward, who saw welfare as a fruitful tool for mobilizing the poor, Wiley helped to coordinate the formation of the NWRO. He served as the organization's executive director and major fundraiser until 1972.[41]

As the only national organization of poor people, the NWRO had a measure of credibility within the antipoverty coalition. The group sought middle-class support through Wiley's fundraising efforts, a "Friends of Welfare Rights" network, "Live on a Welfare Budget" campaigns, and outreach to liberal organizations. Wiley was in constant demand as a speaker and advisor, while recipient leaders like Johnnie Tillmon, Beulah Sanders, and Ruby Duncan, all African American single mothers and AFDC recipients, represented the NWRO to liberal organizations and before Congress.[42] Wiley's contacts with middle-class and wealthy supporters proved invaluable, but the recipients themselves sometimes proved the group's best ambassadors, as the UAW's Mildred Jeffrey discovered when the NWRO met in Detroit in 1969. A volunteer chauffeur for four women ("two white, two black") from "back-country . . . Louisiana" and a group of Mexican American women from Colorado, Jeffrey found them all to be "great people— dignified, moderate, determined." She subsequently urged Reuther to provide financial support to the NWRO and tried to arrange an "exploratory meeting" between the groups' leaders. There is no evidence that such a meeting ever took place, but Jeffrey's personal contact with welfare recipient activists reinforced her conviction that the NWRO represented "one of the really significant groups effectively organizing poor blacks, whites, Mexican-Americans and Indians."[43]

Jeffrey's interest in welfare rights was unusual within organized labor; she would have had more company in one of the many women's organizations that committed themselves to antipoverty work in the 1960s. It was here, as well as in liberal Protestant religious organizations, that welfare rights activists found some of their best middle-class allies. A long history of social service provision and promotion of women's and children's welfare made women's groups a natural source for antipoverty activism, as did their pool of educated and motivated volunteers. By the 1960s, leaders of women's groups were self-conscious about class and race differences and sought to "work with—not for—people different from ourselves."[44] At the same time, boosters for women's voluntary activity drew on the long-standing image of women as uniquely suited to altruistic endeavors.

Figure 1. Johnnie Tillmon of the National Welfare Rights Organization addresses a Mother's Day March on Washington in 1968, with NWRO Executive Director George Wiley looking on. Behind Wiley sits Ethel Kennedy, wife of Senator Robert Kennedy. Courtesy Wisconsin Historical Society (WHS Image ID 8771).

"Women have a special mandate to help fight and win the war on poverty," Women's Bureau head Mary Dublin Keyserling told a Home Economics Workshop at the University of Maryland in 1965. "Traditionally they have been entrusted with the health and welfare of the family," and "their talents, their deep concern for human happiness are needed now to help make America the rich and powerful, the good and beautiful as well."[45]

The work of women's organizations might well be labeled a "significant moral reawakening," as Keyserling dubbed it.[46] The National Council of Jewish Women (NCJW), with more than 100,000 members, established preschool programs in over thirty cities, pressed employers and local governments to offer education and vocational training to poor women, and ran "schools for community action" to educate its members about "the particular problems facing women in poverty."[47] The YWCA housed female Job Corps participants; the General Federation of Women's Clubs developed preschool and adult literacy programs; B'nai B'rith members tutored children and distributed free school lunches; and League of Women Voters members—over 1,700 of them—served on local antipoverty boards and commissions.[48] The League also researched public welfare, giving members "a chance to meet low-income families and to realize their desperation." Becoming "deeply involved" in welfare politics and antipoverty programs led leagues in nearly every state to lobby for more generous welfare grants.[49] Meanwhile, the NCJW joined the National Council of Catholic Women (NCCW), Church Women United, and the National Council of Negro Women to form Women in Community Service (WICS), which provided 10,000 volunteers to solicit and support Women's Job Corps recruits.[50] By 1967, one hundred and ten women's organizations participated in the first national Conference on Women in the War on Poverty. That same year, participants in a Citizens' Advisory Council on the Status of Women meeting referred to women's organizations as "social change agents," and federal welfare official Ellen Winston gave speeches on "The New Volunteerism," a trend in which middle-class women championed the cause of their poor sisters.[51] Leaders of women's organizations assured Congress that antipoverty activity had proven "a revelation" to thousands of white, middle-class, civically active women across the country.[52]

Both women's and religious organizations encouraged their members to commit personally to fighting poverty. Christian and Jewish leaders sermonized on the obligation of each individual to work against poverty and to promote social justice. "It is time to stop paying maids the legal pittance known as minimum wage," lectured one contributor to the lay Catholic journal *Commonweal*. "It is time not to buy color TV's and to send checks to organizations the poor run themselves to solve their own needs. It is time to stop playing bridge and start tutoring kids."[53] Likewise, the Women's Advisory Council on Poverty urged "individual responsibility." "Let each one ask herself, 'What will I do to win the war against poverty?' "[54] The two hundred participants in an NCJW School for Community Action in Virginia took such admonitions seriously. After discussing the plight of maids who earned poverty-level wages, each pledged to pay no less than $1.25 per hour for domestic help, thirty-five cents below the minimum wage—a small step, but a commitment nonetheless.[55]

As the rhetoric of Black Power made participation in African American organizations less inviting to all but the most radical whites, interracial antipoverty work provided an increasingly attractive outlet for socially conscious middle-class white Americans. A nearly full-page advertisement in a 1967 issue of the *New York Times* suggests just what these opportunities meant, especially to women. Fifty-five women—leaders of religious and civic organizations, civil rights activists, celebrities, and wives of national political figures—countered Congressional attacks on the OEO in strong language. "American women have responded to the challenge of the War on Poverty in greater numbers than any other national effort except in time of war," they insisted, and that service had "moved us, changed us . . . inspired us."[56] One of the signatories, LaDonna Harris—a social justice activist, wife of liberal Democratic Senator Fred Harris, and chair of the National Women's Advisory Council of the War on Poverty—urged Congress to recognize just how much the OEO's opportunities for "meaningful service" meant to Americans who were "no longer satisfied with dropping our money into the poor box, or making baskets for the poor at Christmastime, or giving our 'fair share' to the united funds."[57]

The NCJW's Schools for Community Action epitomize the combination of education and action practiced by 1960s women's organizations. The explicit intent of the 1964–65 program, "The Immovable Middle Class," was to help "sympathetic white liberals who . . . are puzzled, hurt or angered by increasing Negro militancy" answer the question: "Am I personally involved? Am I to blame? What can I do?" Through lectures, readings, and discussions, participants were to examine "with painful honesty, the way our selfish interests as privileged members of the middle class are keeping millions of fellow Americans entrapped in a vicious circle of poverty."[58] The next step was obvious in the 1966 program title, "Women on the Move."

The women that the NCJW hoped to see "on the move" were both middle-class members and poor women with whom they sought alliances. A critical part of these "soul-stretching" experiences was hearing from poor women themselves, replacing "the old concept of working 'for' people with the more acceptable and inevitably more productive approach of working 'with' people to solve social problems."[59] Denver's Council invited leaders of local women's organizations to meet with "Mrs. Esterline Stephen, a 'Headstart' Mother; Mrs. Joyce Keel, a Job Corps Girl; Mrs. Helen Martinez, An ADC Mother; [and] Mrs. Eumiye Tsuchiya, A Domestic and a Mother." These women, the invitation urged, "have a story to tell— something you'll want to hear!"[60] Councils in forty-eight cities conducted "Women on the Move" programs, convincing national leaders that "a real and meaningful dialogue is possible between poor and middle-class women."[61] Other groups established dialogue in less formal ways. When Philadelphia League members helped poor parents prepare for a school board meeting, for example, they were "developing communication with ghetto areas," according to one participant. "This is not a means of saying, 'We know how to get things and we will tell you'," she assured, "but, rather, sitting down and asking, 'What are your problems and how should we go about them?'"[62]

Women's organizations' desire to establish connections with poor women intensified in the late 1960s as urban rioting signaled to many "the imminent danger of America becoming a nation divided." In response, the NCJW developed its most ambitious school yet, bringing leaders to Baltimore, Maryland, in 1969 in order to "increase their knowledge of poverty and their sensitivity to conditions of life within the inner city."[63] On a "brief visit with a family in Baltimore's inner city," participants experienced "the flaking paint, the sagging steps, the dimly lit airless hallways, the stench— and then the tired faces of the family living in the second floor apartment." As an official report concluded, "no statistical survey, no sociological study, no impassioned speech could convey the meaning of poverty as did that brief visit." But participants were not merely voyeurs who viewed poor people as objects of pity. Instead, planners brought in members of the Baltimore affiliate of the NWRO to act as tour guides and host an evening with participants. Without a transcript or detailed report of this meeting, we can only speculate at the information exchanged, but some participants decided that evening to raise funds for the NWRO. Evaluation forms suggest that the experience intensified participants' commitment to antipoverty activism. "Whether long-lasting bonds and connections [between NCJW and NWRO members] were forged only time will tell," noted an official report, but "undoubtedly understanding and insight into the plight of the welfare mother were broadened through this particular exposure."[64]

The first Conference on Women in the War on Poverty in May 1967 marked formal recognition of women's antipoverty efforts. The four hundred delegates who attended the federally sponsored event asked Sargent Shriver to appoint an Ad Hoc Committee of the Women's Council on Poverty as a more permanent vehicle for mobilizing and coordinating women's efforts.[65] President Johnson addressed the conference, noting that "long before" the War on Poverty or even the New Deal, "women's groups were fighting poverty in the neighborhoods and legislative halls."[66] Shriver, too, lauded women's activism. He explained the "unprecedented outpouring of activity and compassionate interest on the part of American women" by equating antipoverty work with efforts "to nourish, reshape, reinspire, almost recreate life [which] is what being a woman is all about."[67] And, indeed, Shriver and his audience along with other members of the antipoverty coalition would rely on very particular ideas of what being a woman was all about—and what being a man was all about—as they confronted an urban crisis and a related "welfare crisis" in the last three years of the decade.

The Antipoverty Consensus on Black Family Crisis

The root of the problem, I submit, is . . . the fact that white Americans have never treated Negroes as men—have never permitted them to be men—to feel (in their bones as well as their heads) that they are men, able to stand on their own two feet, able to control their own destinies. Asked what it is that Negroes want, spokesmen from Frederick Douglass to W. E. B. DuBois to Martin Luther King have answered in identical terms. Negroes want to be treated like men. (Charles E. Silberman, 1965)[68]

In the summer of 1965, members of the antipoverty coalition heard tantalizing bits of information about a provocative new government report. Written by Assistant Secretary of Labor Daniel P. Moynihan, *The Negro Family: A Case for National Action* would become the basis for President Lyndon Johnson's Howard University address, "To Fulfill These Rights," which called for a "next and more profound era in civil rights" dedicated to achieving "not just equality as a right and a theory but equality as a fact and as a result."[69] At long last, the nation's highest official seemed poised to tackle the socioeconomic foundation of racial disadvantage. Yet the Moynihan Report provoked a firestorm of controversy among those most likely to support such an effort, the liberal and radical members of the antipoverty coalition. The vitriol was so great, with charges of racism and bad social science on the one side and accusations of demagoguery and denial on the other, that two liberal sociologists used the report and its reception as a book-length case study of "the politics of controversy."

To this day, scholars and pundits across the political spectrum blame the Moynihan controversy for pushing discussion of the black family off the liberal agenda.[70] In 1967, Moynihan accused his critics of undermining his effort to convince lawmakers that only federal intervention could reverse black economic disadvantage. The result, claimed journalist Nicholas Lemann, was that "all public discussions in mainstream liberal circles of

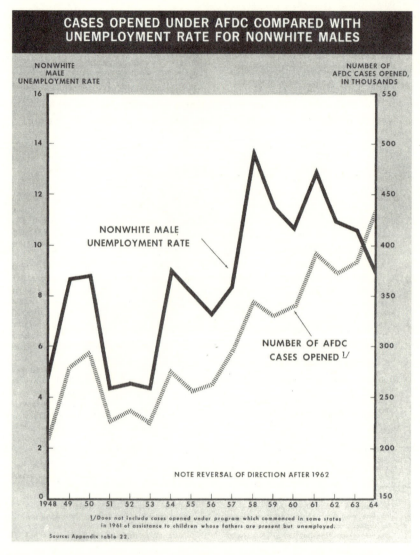

Source: Appendix table 22.

Figure 2. Graph from Daniel Moynihan's 1965 *The Negro Family: A Case for National Action*. Here, Moynihan demonstrates that until recently the AFDC caseload and nonwhite male unemployment rose and fell together. The decoupling of those trends suggested to Moynihan that the problem of single motherhood and AFDC may have become part of a self-perpetuating "tangle of pathology."

issues like the state of the black family and the culture of poverty simply ceased."[71] Indeed, at the conference Johnson called for in his Howard University address, executive director Berl Bernhard proclaimed to the amusement of his audience: "I want you to know that I have been reliably informed that no such person as Daniel Patrick Moynihan exists."[72] Yet Moynihan most certainly did exist, and the premises behind his report would profoundly shape welfare and poverty politics for the next two decades and beyond. In fact, the controversy over his report has blinded historians to the larger consensus on the importance of family structure to black economic disadvantage. No doubt, the Moynihan controversy exposed some very real philosophical and strategic divisions within the antipoverty coalition. But virtually all participants in the debate agreed that racial poverty and disadvantage would disappear only when African Americans formed "traditional," male-breadwinner families.

It is not surprising that a clear expression of this consensus came from Moynihan, a central figure in the antipoverty coalition. A poster boy for American opportunity, Moynihan had pulled himself up from a poor, single-mother, Irish Catholic upbringing on New York's Lower East Side to a G.I. Bill-assisted Ivy League education and a rising career in both academia and Democratic politics. One of the original architects of the Economic Opportunity Act, he put his social science training (he held a doctorate in political science) to the service of solving social problems. Distrustful of radicals who sought to organize the poor into a class-conscious political force, he nonetheless pushed the Johnson administration to move beyond a services strategy and devote considerable resources to jobs and income programs. Moynihan thus represented the center of the 1960s antipoverty coalition; he was a racial liberal seeking to use federal policies to ensure economic opportunity, upward mobility, social stability, and a more humane capitalism.

In the service of those goals, Moynihan produced *The Negro Family*, a brief to convince his boss President Johnson to embark on an unprecedented jobs and income policy. Moynihan used a plethora of statistics showing high and rising rates of divorce, separation, desertion, out-of-wedlock births, and welfare "dependence" to argue that "the Negro family in the urban ghettos is crumbling," even "approaching complete breakdown." He located the source of that deterioration in the position of black men. Drawing on a well-established social science literature, he argued that centuries of "unimaginable treatment" toward African Americans—from the slavery and segregation of the past to the rapid urbanization, discrimination, and unemployment of the present—had undermined family stability. Unable to support their families, black men abandoned them, leaving a "matriarchal structure" and its attendant "aberrant, inadequate, or anti-social behavior" which then "perpetuate[d] the cycle of poverty and deprivation." This "tangle of pathology," Moynihan argued, left many, if not most, African Americans unable to take advantage of the legal and political rights they had recently won and necessitated a new phase of federal efforts to ensure "equality of results." That new phase, Moynihan insisted, should be "directed to a new kind of national goal: the establishment of a stable Negro family structure."[73]

As scholars recognized even at the time, the report "presented little that was new or startling."[74] The historian Daryl Michael Scott has traced the contested use of the "image of the damaged black psyche" throughout the twentieth century and demonstrated the centrality of family structure in that imagery. As early as 1899, W. E. B. Du Bois argued that slavery and black men's inability to find jobs promoted weak families, "breeders of idleness and extravagance and complaint." In the 1920s and 1930s, Chicago School sociologists identified "matriarchy" as a sign of disorganization among urban black families. And in the postwar era, an increasingly powerful therapeutic ethos prompted social scientists and other racial liberals to place damage imagery at the center of their calls to dismantle segregation. As part of this effort, scholars attributed "the large amount of juvenile delinquency and crime among Negroes" to urban "matriarchies," in which boys grew without male role models or male discipline, emasculated by aggressive mothers and unable to enter mainstream society. From African American sociologists like E. Franklin Frazier and Kenneth Clark to white liberal scholars like Abram Kardiner and Lionel Ovesey, the notion of a pathological "matriarchal" family structure among urban African Americans had by the 1960s "the stamp of social science consensus."[75]

How did a document that simply reiterated social science orthodoxy provoke such controversy? Written for an internal audience, the report was leaked piecemeal to the antipoverty community and, more importantly, to journalists who played up its more sensational aspects. Quotations about illegitimacy, juvenile delinquency, and slavery's destruction of the black family made better copy than recital of more prosaic information like unemployment statistics. Further, despite general agreement about the problem, liberals and radicals were divided about the wisdom of airing issues like high rates of delinquency and nonmarital births that might serve as "fuel for a new racism."[76] Lee Rainwater and William Yancey also blamed Moynihan's writing style. Calculated to instill a sense of urgency, the report's freewheel-ing use of the term "fundamental" promoted confusion as to the root prob-lem—was the "fundamental" problem family structure, as Moynihan twice stated, or was it the broader social and economic factors that kept African Americans in poverty? The issue was not merely semantic. As an influential policymaker with the ear of the president, Moynihan's interpretation of the problem was bound to affect federal response. To many on the left, the mere suggestion that black disadvantage stemmed from a problem seemingly in-ternal to the black community raised a red flag, particularly when it came from an administration in which they were rapidly losing trust.

Above all, Moynihan's critics feared that the report would be used to dismiss poor urban African Americans as unsalvageable. In the report's final chapter, Moynihan included a graph showing that unemployment and welfare rates no longer rose and fell together; rather, in the early 1960s, AFDC rates continued to climb even as unemployment fell. The numbers suggested, Moynihan argued, that policymakers must at least "acknowl-edge" the "view, held by a number of responsible persons, that [the] prob-lem [of family dysfunction] may in fact be out of control."[77] Perhaps, for all the blame Moynihan placed on slavery, discrimination, and unemploy-ment, the black family would be viewed as not only undeserving but also as beyond help. This is what Moynihan's critics meant when they called the report "a massive academic cop-out for the white conscience."[78]

Initially, though, mainstream African American leaders supported Moynihan's interpretation. King, Roy Wilkins, and Whitney Young, Jr., all preapproved a draft of the Howard University address, which drew gener-ously from Moynihan's report, and King drew on the report in a number of speeches he made in late 1965. He called "the statistics" Moynihan provided "alarming," lamented the rise of "matriarchy," and characterized such fam-ilies as "fragile, deprived, and often psychopathetic."[79] Young was even more enthusiastic; he had made the identical argument in his 1964 book *To Be Equal*, where he described the Domestic Marshall Plan's goal as counter-ing the "damage inflicted upon the Negro by generations of injustice and neglect" and "rehabilitat[ing] urban Negro families" by "transform[ing] the dependent man into the independent man." To justify his unabashed call for social engineering, Young partook of the same damage imagery Moynihan used, citing "matriarchal" families and bemoaning the "emascu-lated . . . Negro male." Little wonder Young initially welcomed the Moyni-han Report for making the position of the Negro male "the key to the future of the Negro poor."[80]

In fact, the African American *man's* economic and social position was central to discussions of black disadvantage in virtually all major 1960s antipoverty proposals. *Ebony* magazine's photo editorial "A Man Around the House" quoted liberally from the Moynihan Report, for example, and labeled the "heritage of matriarchy" in African American culture "one of the most destructive forces in the life of the Negro family." *Ebony*'s editors called on government and private industry to provide "job retraining and other special consideration . . . to the Negro man," for "if the Negro is ever to win his rightful place in American society, something must be done, and done soon, to build a strong and stable family structure among Negro ghetto dwellers."[81] Several civil rights leaders had more specific plans for that "something." "The Negro family can be reconstructed," insisted Bayard Rustin, "only when the Negro male is permitted to be the economic and psychological head of the family," a goal of the Freedom Budget's full employment mandate.[82] CORE's James Farmer was much more critical of Moynihan but advocated a similar strategy—provide jobs for black men as the key to economic advancement and family stability.[83]

In fact, putting able-bodied men to work was the main goal of the Johnson administration's War on Poverty. Committed to a "growth liberalism" that would avoid significant redistribution and hostile to public assistance or "handout" programs, Johnson refused to propose any large-scale income maintenance programs.[84] His Committee of Economic Advisors, writing in an era of impressive economic growth, noted that "the majority of the Nation could simply tax themselves enough to provide the necessary income supplements to their less fortunate citizens" but insisted that such a policy would "leave untouched most of the roots of poverty." Americans, the administration declared, "want to *earn* the American standard of living by their own efforts and contributions."[85] At the same time, Johnson also rejected his advisors' call for federal job creation as politically unfeasible and far too expensive.[86] Instead, the Economic Opportunity Act focused on providing poor men with the skills they needed to succeed in the private labor market—to "give the desperate and downtrodden the skills and the experience that they need to lift themselves from poverty," as Johnson put it.[87]

Poor *men* were certainly the focus. Moynihan and his fellow antipoverty policymakers, along with liberal economists and policy experts outside the government, generally agreed that the "single dominant problem of poverty in the U.S." was unemployment. And, given the gender politics of the early 1960s, they "assumed," as sociologist Diana Pearce noted, "that the overwhelming majority of those who needed jobs . . . were men."[88] To Moynihan and his peers, a strong economy was one "in which men made enough money that their women can stay home and raise their family."[89] Not surprisingly, then, antipoverty planners quickly rejected proposals for day care and job creation for women.[90] From its rhetoric (failure would result in the "postponement of full responsibility and manhood") to its allocation of resources ("What we are trying especially to do," insisted a Baltimore antipoverty administrator, "is to encourage a man to stay with his family, getting him work to support them"), the War on Poverty sought to reinforce the male-breadwinner family structure.[91]

A handful of federal officials centered in the Labor Department's Women's Bureau urged policymakers to attend more directly to *women's* poverty. Created in 1920, the Bureau had from its origins the responsibility to monitor and improve the well-being of wage-earning women, but it maintained vestiges of its Progressive Era maternalist legacy. Historian Kathleen Laughlin has described the Bureau's politics and policies in the 1960s as "contradictory and inconsistent." Like many labor-oriented feminists before the 1970s, economist Mary Dublin Keyserling, who directed the Bureau from 1964 to 1968, refused to embrace equal-rights feminism or to challenge women's primary identification with motherhood. "We don't anticipate any significant increase in job-holding among younger married women," she assured a group of social workers in 1965, for "childrearing for most is a full-time occupation." She even predicted that "as living standards rise, the hard economic compulsions which now make work a necessity for so many disadvantaged young mothers will lessen."[92] At the same time, she and her staff persistently challenged the stereotype perpetuated by policymakers and popular culture that women were not serious, permanent members of the labor force. Keyserling rejected outright "the notion . . . that women . . . are merely supplementary workers," and she repeatedly denounced women's low wages, sex-typed job classifications, and the virtual absence of child care and job training for women.[93] During the 1960s, Bureau officials worked tirelessly to ensure that girls and women benefited from federal antipoverty efforts, particularly job training and placement programs.[94]

Women's voluntary organizations also addressed women's need for better wages and working conditions. In part, they merely continued their longtime lobbying to raise minimum wage rates and extend Fair Labor Standards Act protections to so-called "women's jobs." Investigations of women's poverty in the 1960s, though, motivated further advocacy. In Minneapolis, several women's groups conducted a "massive canvassing effort" into the problems of poor women, going "into poor neighborhoods" and "meeting on a woman to woman basis." The volunteers recognized that "most impoverished women have to work to provide or supplement family income." Their interviewees highlighted two primary problems: low wages and lack of affordable child care. The organizations promptly lobbied city and state government for better minimum wage laws and expanded day care facilities.[95] Attention to the needs of poor working women also led female reformers to create the National Committee on Household Employment (NCHE) in 1964. Funded largely by the Ford Foundation, the group sought to upgrade working conditions for household workers, 98 percent of whom were female.[96]

An informal women's coalition, centered in the Women's Bureau, achieved a partial victory with the establishment of the Women's Job Corps as part of the Economic Opportunity Act. In two reports prepared for War on Poverty planners, the Bureau provided a survey of the country's poor women, focusing its statistics on unemployment and low wages.[97] With the help of Congresswoman Edith Green, the Bureau convinced Congress to authorize a program to "prepare deprived girls 16 through 21 to become skilled workers, homemakers, and responsible citizens."[98] Green later recalled encountering "a lot of static from the Johnson administration" when she "suggested that the Job Corps ought to be for girls as well as boys."[99] She also fought the OEO mandate that girls represent no more than one-sixth of Job Corps participants; her amendment instead ensured young women 23 percent of Job Corps slots.[100] That the Women's Job Corps became a pet project of the Women's Bureau and its allies among middle-class women's organizations suggests a consensus that education, training, and "useful work" represented at least one answer to women's poverty.[101] The Women's Bureau's influence is evident in a Department of Labor (DOL) report on "Girls in the Neighborhood Youth Corps Program" which noted that nine of ten girls would find themselves in the labor market at some point and that their need for training "to increase their employability" was "just as acute as for boys."[102]

Nonetheless, the Women's Job Corps content and image continued to emphasize woman's primary role as wife, homemaker, and mother.[103] Women's need for training was not simply "as acute as for boys," it was "greater," the Labor Department report insisted, "since it is the girls who, because of the influence they will have on their own children's education, are most apt to make the break out of poverty a continuing thing."[104] Wom-

Figure 3. Anita Juhr, director of Portland, Oregon, Women in Community Service, interviews a prospective Job Corps enrollee. Civically active middle-class white women across the country became involved in antipoverty work during the 1960s. Manpower Administration, U.S. Department of Labor, *Manpower Magazine*, December 1972.

an's role as mother and potential transmitter of intergenerational poverty influenced the kind of training offered and how it was presented. Participants would learn much more than "job skills," an OEO brochure claimed. Girls (but not boys) would be "trained in family responsibilities," learning "how to establish a stable home atmosphere and to rear emotionally and physically healthy children."[105] In "learning how to be homemakers," female participants would develop the "self-knowledge that produces good citizens, good wives and good mothers." A *Corpsman* article assured readers that "it is in the classes which deal with home and family life . . . that a

Figure 4. Job Corps participant Ramona Romo shows off her sewing skills for Eleanor Marvin, president of the National Council of Jewish Women, one of the six organizations that composed Women in Community Service. Manpower Administration, U.S. Department of Labor, *Manpower Magazine*, December 1972.

corpswoman is usually helped the most."[106] "When you train a man, you train an individual," Lady Bird Johnson reminded a gathering of women antipoverty volunteers; "when you train a woman, you train a family."[107]

Women's Job Corps proponents also emphasized participants' primary identification with the family rather than the labor market. The middle-class volunteers of WICS saw their work with female Job Corps participants as a way to groom "the mothers of tomorrow."[108] An AFL-CIO brochure described the program's "counseling in homemaking, child care, budgeting, personal hygiene, grooming and nutrition" and assured readers that "centers will be operated on the theory that enrollees will eventually be wives and mothers, as well as members of the labor force."[109] In a speech praising the antipoverty efforts of a New Jersey NCJW Section, Keyserling worried about the "grave influence" of poor mothers "on the lives of succeeding generations." Poor mothers would likely produce children "deprived physically, educationally, and culturally," thus passing on their poverty "from generation to generation."[110] While insisting that girls needed training and jobs to support themselves and their families, these middle-class antipoverty warriors continued to emphasize women's primary responsibility as caretakers of the next generation.

Even when government training and employment programs included women, they reinforced a sex-segregated labor market which kept even wage-earning women well below the poverty line. In planning the Women's Job Corps, administration officials noted growing opportunities in "our service-oriented society," jobs that would make use of "women's innate capacities for human relationships and their homemaking and child care skills."[111] The Labor Department hoped to train girls in "skills that will be useful to them when they begin to seek permanent employment—as home economists' aides, as nurses' aides, as teachers' aides, as library aides, as clerk-typists," all jobs that paid too little to accomplish the goal of "break [ing] them out of poverty."[112] As late as 1972, a Job Corps solicitation sent to AFDC recipients in Charleston, West Virginia, offered training "in the following occupations: Secretary, Hospital Services, Food Services, Cosmetology, and Nurses Aide," while young men received training for such occupations as "Auto Mechanic, Heavy Equipment Operator, Carpentry, and Electronics." Complaining to the Department of Labor, Legal Aid attorney Gail Falk blasted administrators for "continu[ing] to perpetuate the evils of a sex-segregated job market," an offense "inexcusable at this late date."[113]

If federal antipoverty programs followed Moynihan's prescription—providing opportunities for men at the expense of women—the left wing of the antipoverty coalition failed to challenge this male-breadwinner bias. The War on Poverty's biggest critics from the left were "class-conscious liberals" committed to *empowering* poor people, an agenda ill served by Moynihan's "damage imagery."[114] A handful of radicals even insisted that the female-headed family so common in black urban neighborhoods was a healthy "adaptation" to oppressive circumstances.[115] At the same time, though, their recommendations often fell right in line with Moynihan's thinking. The Children's Bureau's Elizabeth Herzog called for "primary attention to building up the economic and social status of Negro men," for, as she and Howard University sociologist Hylan Lewis argued, "a male head of house who is not a breadwinner and provider is a hazard to the happiness of the marriage."[116] Sociologist and activist Richard Cloward, whose dedication to empowering the poor helped to lay the intellectual foundation for the welfare rights movement, nonetheless advocated creating "a stable monogamous family" by "provid[ing] men with the opportunity to be men," which "involves enabling them to perform occupationally."[117]

Beyond jobs for men, liberals and leftists also hoped to establish male economic dominance within African American households. This is what liberal journalist Charles Silberman meant when he promoted "special efforts to enhance the role of the Negro male in the family," efforts that would enable him to perform "his expected functions, responsibilities, and obligations as a husband, father, and provider."[118] Two-parent families in which the man "is not the principal earner" counted as female-headed, argued sociologist Herbert Gans, who hoped that jobs would enable the "Negro man . . . [to] assume a viable role in the family and . . . put an end to the long tradition of male marginality and inferiority."[119] Even Moynihan's fiercest critics agreed that the federal government could eliminate black disadvantage and poverty by reconstructing the black family—by turning black men into breadwinners who could take both economic and psychological control of their families.

Commitment to creating "stable," male-breadwinner families even preoccupied the President's Commission on the Status of Women (PCSW). Historian Jennifer Mittlestadt has demonstrated that participants in the 1963 PCSW, including then Women's Bureau head Esther Peterson, largely ignored the plight of poor single mothers, focusing instead on "the 'norm' for American women—economically stable two-parent families." Despite its calls for equal employment opportunity and federally funded day care, the PCSW generally "subscribed to the view that the traditional two-parent, mother-at-home model of the family was ideal."[120] Five years later, the Task

Force on Health and Welfare of the Citizens' Advisory Council on the Status of Women exhibited the same assumption in its report, *Women and Their Families in Our Rapidly Changing Society.* At least one staffer rejected the report's insistence "that the integrity of family life is essential to the soundness of the nation." This was the kind of thinking, Neal Herrick complained, "that has led the Manpower Administration to give high priority to helping men and relatively low priority to helping women."[121] But it was the position endorsed by a national panel dedicated to addressing the changing role of women in the 1960s, including even the PCSW's Consultation on the Status of Negro Women, held in April 1963. Dorothy Height, longtime president of the National Council of Negro Women (NCNW), chaired the session, which included a host of prominent African Americans and government officials, including Moynihan. Written two years before Moynihan's report, the consultation reflected Height's insistence that black women's welfare depended upon the creation of black male breadwinners. Written reports from Height and consultation staffers referred to black women as "victims of a matriarchal family life," a status which proffers "extra economic and psychological burdens" which require special "assistance" including "instruction in basic nutrition and health practices, in home management, and family living" as well as "job opportunities," Fair Labor Standards Act (FLSA) coverage for domestic workers, maternity benefits, and child care services. Yet the consultation's report coupled demands that would increase women's wage earning ability with caution about opening jobs to minority women, given "the importance of more job opportunities for Negro men."[122] Height's contention that black women's "major underlying concern" was "the status of the Negro man" permeated the consultation.[123] According to participant Caroline Ware, the group agreed that African American women's problems "stem basically from the lack of opportunity of Negro men," which "force[s] [women] into the labor market."[124]

The Women's Bureau coalition did criticize Moynihan's treatment of African American women, but their critiques represented a staunch defense of black womanhood rather than a challenge to the male-breadwinner ideal. Poor black women were caught in a terrible situation not of their own making, these defenders argued, and should not be blamed for the unfortunate breakdown of the male-breadwinner family structure in their communities. Female policymakers and activists feared that what Congresswoman Martha Griffiths called "the syrupy miasma flowing from the Moynihan report that 'Negro women have it good'," would "produce detrimental effects on their economic progress."[125] They lauded the poor black woman's "tremendous capacity to stand against every kind of adversity to provide some sense of security to her family."[126] Black women, insisted social welfare expert Elizabeth Wickenden, were "the ultimate martyrs and the true heroines."[127]

Wickenden was among only a handful of women who targeted the Moynihan Report on more explicitly feminist grounds. At the behest of the YWCA, Wickenden, a social welfare expert and advocate, prepared and circulated a response to Moynihan titled "The Negro Family: Society's Victim or Scapegoat?" She denounced Moynihan's assumption that a "fatherless" child was "handicapped in his growth and development," criticized his recommendation for more male role models in poor urban neighborhoods, and attacked the report's "patriarchal bias."[128] Women's Job Corps head Benetta Washington warned that the report could be used to deny opportunities to disadvantaged girls, which "would be tragic."[129] From the Women's Bureau, Keyserling admitted that "family breakdown is a grave cause for concern" but rejected any proposal to deny women job opportunities.[130] At the bottom of an article proposing remedial education for the poor men who failed to meet minimum draft requirements, Catherine East penned an opinion that in the 1960s was shared by only a handful of other antipoverty advocates: "When is something going to be done about the sisters?"[131]

A few voices on the margins of national debate, then, thought that "something" should be done to enable poor mothers to achieve economic self-sufficiency. The Women's Bureau spelled out this approach in a 1968 publication, "Women in Poverty—Jobs and the Need for Jobs," which focused on labor market barriers faced by women.[132] High rates of unemployment, low wages, lack of FLSA protections, deficient education and training, and lack of "day care or other supportive services," the Bureau concluded, conspired to keep women poor.[133] This was also the conclusion of a rather remarkable 1968 report from the Oregon Bureau of Labor, "They Carry the Burden Alone," which caught the attention of East and other members of the Citizens' Advisory Council on the Status of Women.[134] Its authors urged that the single mother "be given the full economic freedom of choice in the labor market"—including equal pay for equal work, equal employment opportunity, education and training, and child care—in order to fulfill her role as "head of her family and provider." These were all reforms long pressed by union women and the Women's Bureau, but rarely were they put in terms of ensuring economic independence through wage labor for mother-only families.[135]

At any rate, the largely male-dominated urban rioting of the 1960s kept African American *men* in the spotlight. In August 1964, just as the Moynihan report was going public, the Watts neighborhood of Los Angeles erupted in violence. By 1968, nearly three hundred "race riots and disturbances" had claimed more than 8,000 casualties and resulted in 50,000 arrests.[136] Whether one considered these riots to be politically motivated expressions of rebellion or merely the work of lawless criminals, the Moynihan thesis was uniquely suited to explaining them. The breakdown of the black family that social scientists described seemed to produce fatherless boys who lacked socialization, discipline, and hope for the future: in short, young men prone to violent behavior. Presidential historian (and political liberal) Theodore White blamed "broken homes and loveless breeding warrens" stemming from urban conditions that "deprive . . . Negroes of their sense of manhood" for producing the "delinquents" and "criminals" who rioted in Harlem in 1964.[137] A year later, after Watts, the conservative editors of the *Wall Street Journal* summed up the prevailing wisdom, shared by political conservatives and antipoverty liberals alike, in a headline: "Family Life Breakdown in Negro Slums Sows Seeds of Race Violence—Husbandless Homes Spawn Young Hoodlums, Impede Reforms, Sociologists Say."[138]

In 1968, a blue-ribbon panel on urban riots gave the antipoverty coalition's official imprimatur to Moynihan's argument. The government officials, labor leaders, businessmen, and civil rights activists who made up the National Advisory Commission on Civil Disorders (or Kerner Commission) had learned from the Moynihan controversy to be crystal clear about the "fundamental" cause of the problem. They began with a moral condemnation of the "white racism" that they viewed as "essentially responsible for the explosive mixture that has been accumulating in our cities since the end of World War II." As a result of that racism, black men faced "chronic unemployment," causing "persistent poverty in disadvantaged Negro areas." The inability to find any but the most menial, low-wage jobs drove men from their families, resulting in a "handicap imposed on [their] children," particularly as "mothers are forced to work to provide support" and to leave their children at the mercy of the "environmental 'jungle' of the ghetto." Summing up, the report's chapter on "Unemployment, Family Structure, and Social Disorganization" argued that "the culture of poverty that results from [male] unemployment and family breakup generates a system of ruthless, exploitative relationships within the ghetto" and produces children who are "likely participants in civil disorder." In its call for two million new jobs, both public and private—jobs that would enable black men to fulfill their proper role as providers and black mothers to care properly for their children—the Commission suggested that antipoverty liberals widely shared Moynihan's gendered analysis of black poverty and racial disadvantage.[139]

AFDC Becomes the Target

In October 1965, liberal sociologist Herbert Gans explained why antipoverty policymakers like Moynihan focused so much attention on men. While girls were "not entirely immune from [the] ill-effects" of poverty and broken families, Gans asserted, it was the boys who "more often turn to delinquency, crime, alcohol, drugs, and mental illness." Girls, according to Gans, simply "do not become a public and visible social problem."[140] Less than two years later poor girls vied with their brothers for national headlines, as journalists, pundits, and politicians responded to rising AFDC rolls by declaring a "welfare crisis." Local outbreaks of antiwelfare hysteria had occurred periodically since the 1940s, but the late 1960s welfare crisis, tied as it was to a larger urban crisis, was particularly vehement and widespread.[141] The welfare debate drew a significant number of participants, as antiwelfare conservatism gained a national stage and as the administrators who defended social welfare programs found allies within the antipoverty coalition. In the ensuing debate, in Congress and in the press, participants across the political spectrum blamed AFDC for the crisis but expressed competing visions of America's family wage system. Antiwelfare conservatives harkened back to an older ideal, a racially exclusive family wage model purchased by those whose hard work and moral behavior the free market had presumably rewarded. At the same time, the antipoverty coalition brought to this crisis the ideology they had honed over the previous several years that placed the crumbling black family at the center of America's economic and social problems. They condemned AFDC for perpetuating family breakdown and proposed a radical kind of welfare reform—a guaranteed income—designed to extend to poor African Americans the privilege of a male-breadwinner, female-homemaker family structure.

A product of journalists and politicians in the business of sensationalizing, the term "welfare crisis" described a very real phenomenon. The AFDC rolls rose precipitously in the 1960s, with the sharpest increase occurring at the end of the decade. The 3.1 million clients in 1960 rose to 4.3 million mid-decade, and climbed to nearly 8.5 million by 1970. One-fourth of the increase occurred in just two states, New York and California. Always a tiny proportion of the federal budget, the cost of AFDC and welfare-related social services nonetheless increased at a rate that fiscally conservative lawmakers viewed with alarm.[142] Occurring amidst impressive economic growth and alongside a declared War on Poverty, growing welfare caseloads and costs struck many Americans as curious, to say the least.

Complex economic and political trends underlay rising AFDC rolls. The mid-century mechanization of Southern agriculture fueled a massive out-migration of Southerners, both black and white, who sought jobs in urban areas. Shut out of most well-paid manufacturing jobs, which were beginning to leave the cities anyway, many African Americans found themselves trapped in a cycle of low-wage labor and unemployment. Beginning in the 1940s, the country's urban areas contained a growing population of poor people, many of them black, at the same time that corporate leaders began to move manufacturing to regions with lower labor costs, whether in the suburbs, the Sunbelt, or abroad.[143] Meanwhile, in the 1960s civil rights activism, government attention to poverty, and the welfare rights movement all encouraged poor women to claim their "right" to welfare and made them more likely to receive it. As poverty lawyers successfully challenged the legality of restrictive welfare policies, welfare rights advocacy and protests intimidated caseworkers and administrators. By the end of the decade, activists had significantly liberalized welfare administration. Rising AFDC rolls in the 1960s did not directly reflect a significant expansion of eligible families but the fact that by the end of the decade more eligible families were receiving benefits.[144]

Congress responded with the Public Welfare Amendments of 1967, which highlighted an emerging political showdown on AFDC. As Jennifer Mittlestadt has shown, liberal federal welfare officials responded to periodic and intensifying attacks on AFDC during the 1950s and 1960s by emphasizing "rehabilitation." With appropriate casework and incentives, they insisted, welfare mothers could become economically independent. Before the late 1960s, they were virtually alone among liberals in promoting breadwinning for AFDC recipients. In response to the welfare crisis, though, the Johnson administration asked Congress to include a work incentive in the AFDC program. Congress agreed, and beginning in 1967, recipients no longer lost welfare benefits dollar-for-dollar when they earned wages. Instead, they could keep the first $30 plus a third of additional income they earned each month without losing any benefits. Both liberal welfare administrators and antiwelfare conservatives in Congress hoped thereby to encourage poor single mothers to enter the labor market and thus lower welfare rolls and costs. At the same time, welfare administrators sought to shore up male breadwinning and keep poor husbands and wives together by mandating AFDC-UP (the Unemployed Parent program). Established in 1962 as a state option, AFDC-UP was a direct response to the commonly held and completely unsupported assumption that unemployed and low-earning fathers frequently deserted their families to enable their wives and children to qualify for welfare. The twenty-four states that had adopted AFDC-UP before 1967 hoped to prevent such opportunistic desertion, and federal policymakers wanted other states to do so, as well. The AFDC-UP program rested on the same premise as the Moynihan Report: federal policies should prop up male-breadwinner family structure.

Reacting to and feeding a growing welfare backlash that was closely linked with a contemporaneous "white backlash," conservatives in Congress proposed a number of restrictive provisions instead. From his powerful position as chairman of the Senate Finance Committee, Louisiana's Russell Long articulated an antiwelfare philosophy that, despite long roots in American politics, was now applied to the particular contours of the 1960s crisis. Throughout his long tenure in Congress, Long combined the hawkish anticommunism and staunch opposition to civil rights legislation typical of Southern Democrats of his era with a general commitment to government social welfare programs, including aid to the aged and disabled, increased Social Security and minimum wage protection, and federal aid to poor communities. Long even helped to steer many of Johnson's Great Society programs through the legislative process and was one of only four senators from the Deep South to vote for the Economic Opportunity Act. Yet his dual commitments to "fiscal responsibility" and to maintaining a racial caste system shaped his opposition to expanded income support for the "able-bodied" poor.[145]

While liberals hoped to use welfare policy to "fix" the black family, Long harkened back to an older, exclusive family wage model safely out of reach of most African Americans. Many liberals idealized stay-at-home motherhood for both middle-class and poor women, but Long's biggest beef with AFDC was that it enabled poor single nonwhite mothers to avoid wage labor. He called welfare recipients "riffraff" who leeched off the hardworking citizens who "work by the sweat of their brow to make an honest living." Long wondered aloud why poor single mothers in the welfare rights movement had time to protest but not "to pick a beer can off the street . . . in front of their own house or catch a rat."[146] His solution to the welfare crisis was to enforce low-wage employment among black mothers and to enlist social workers to help the recipient "learn to be content, and happy with his [sic] own lot in life."[147] Long was not alone; in addition to work incentives and a small amount of day care funding, Congressional majorities in 1967 introduced the first AFDC-related work requirement for single mothers, the Work Incentive Program (WIN).

To Long and his conservative allies, poor black women were simply not part of the male-breadwinner family wage system. Both their primary role as laborers and their supposedly promiscuous sexual behavior placed them well outside that ideal. When a witness challenged Long's work requirement, for example, Long responded, as he often did, by painting a picture: "that woman who just sits around the house and drinks Hi-Fi or Gypsy Gold wine all day while the children are out or in school." This archetypal woman signaled her unworthiness by her refusal to work as well as by her daytime alcohol consumption and sexual promiscuity. She "won't do anything except produce more children for the public to pay for at taxpayers' expense."[148] Here, and when he labeled protesting welfare mothers "brood mares," Long drew on the stereotype, as old as the nation itself, of the promiscuous African American woman.[149] While few others were as bold or as public with these views, many shared them; Congress voted in 1967 to freeze federal AFDC funding for children born out of wedlock. What joined the various strands of this 1960s antiwelfarism was the lingering strength of an older racial and economic order. Business concerns about federal spending met Southern concerns about preserving a racial caste system to block welfare reform that might extend to African Americans the benefits of a "traditional," male-breadwinner family.

Though liberals cried foul, dubbing Congressional restrictions "vicious," "cruel," and "an outrage to American standards of decency," they did not defend AFDC. In fact, after the Moynihan Report, welfare policies played a growing role in the antipoverty coalition's diagnosis of black poverty and disadvantage. By providing cash aid to single mother families only, antipoverty liberals argued, AFDC further undermined the black man's role as breadwinner and head of household. In his 1965 report, Moynihan referred to welfare receipt as a "*measure* of the steady disintegration of the Negro family structure," but he and other liberals also suggested that AFDC could be a *cause* of that disintegration.[150] Whitney Young blasted AFDC for "perpetuat[ing] the matriarchal family" by placing a "premium on desertion," while the Southern Christian Leadership Conference (SCLC) identified AFDC as one of twelve aspects of the ghetto's "total pattern of economic exploitation" because it "contributes to the breakdown of family life."[151] In 1971, Labor Secretary Ray Marshall even attributed the growing popularity of black nationalism to welfare policy. Given a system that provided aid "only if no able-bodied man was present," Marshall found it "not surprising that many young Negro males resorted to militancy and revolutionary rhetoric in order to protest their conditions."[152] By 1970, the antipoverty coalition had repeated this "desertion thesis" so often it had the aura of fact. The coalition wanted to reform welfare, then, in order to promote male-breadwinner family stability.

Hoping to facilitate male breadwinning, the liberal social work establishment opposed any work requirement for single mothers. Some liberal welfare administrators in HEW began during the 1960s to emphasize job training and "self-support" for AFDC recipients, but they continued to insist that poor single mothers could most benefit their children and society through full-time motherhood. In a 1966 statement, U.S. Commissioner of Welfare Ellen Winston laid out this rationale, warning proponents of "self-support" that the "question of economic independence for AFDC and other [poor single] mothers . . . must be viewed in light of the even more important value of society—that of children having the opportunity of home life and maternal care for their healthy growth and development."[153] Catherine East complained about the prevalence of this viewpoint. East, who insisted that poor single mothers would be "better served" if provided "the self-respect and confidence that comes in our society from being gainfully employed," was one of a very few who rejected the belief "still prevalent in the social work fraternity"—a belief "held with all the tenaciousness that only *belief* can inspire"—that "all children are better off when their mothers physically care for them than under any other circumstances."[154] One year after the formation of the National Organization for Women (NOW) marked what many consider the official inception of second-wave feminism, surprisingly few participants in the welfare debate ventured to propose, as did U.S. Commission on Civil Rights director William Taylor, measures "to enable [female-headed] families . . . to achieve positions of self-sufficiency and economic independence."[155] In fact, antipoverty coalition members explicitly excluded AFDC mothers from the country's pool of potential laborers. In response to conservative complaints about able-bodied loafers drawing government checks, liberal antipoverty crusaders repeatedly included AFDC mothers among the vast majority of welfare recipients whom they dubbed "unemployable."

Coalition members had good reasons to reject work requirements.

Those who were most familiar with poor women's options understood that such requirements would likely do little more than punish poor single mothers. One of the few federal agencies to investigate local welfare practices, the U.S. Commission on Civil Rights found that welfare administrators across the country routinely used work requirements to ensure low-wage employers a steady supply of desperate laborers. Local officials had long used "employable mother" rules to ensure an ample supply of agricultural labor during harvest time and to ensure the availability of private domestic laborers year round. Welfare recipients themselves knew all too well that work requirements usually meant "cleaning Mrs. A's kitchen"—in other words, the kinds of jobs that had long relegated black women especially to sub-poverty wages with no benefits or protections.[156] Certainly, Senator Long's harangues about picking up dead dogs, catching rats, and ironing his shirts provided little confidence that work requirements would improve recipients' economic situation.[157] Instead, Ruth Atkins of the National Council of Negro Women (NCNW) feared, they were more likely to further depress wages and retard unionization in already overcrowded and underpaid sectors like agriculture, food processing, and restaurant and hotel work.[158] Experience and pragmatism convinced welfare activists and their allies to oppose work requirements.

Yet ideology played a role, as well. Commitment to AFDC mothers' right to choose wage labor or full-time parenting coexisted uneasily in liberal rhetoric with sentimental appeals to the sanctity of motherhood. Nearly every antipoverty coalition witness during hearings on the 1967 welfare reforms blasted the work requirement's "thoroughly unjustified intrusion of government into the private decision-making responsibilities of a substantial number of American mothers," an intrusion the NCC's William Robinson denounced as "shamefully un-American." Yet many, like Robinson, followed up with the warning that "having over three million children in the coming generation deprived of a mother's care during many hours of the day" would "certainly" harm society, producing "a disproportionate share of the delinquents, the mentally ill, and the socially and economically unproductive citizens of the next generation."[159] Sentimental appeals from liberals like Senator Philip Hart, who warned that work requirements would interfere with a mother's "highest of all purposes, to be home with the child," and Walter Reuther, who rejected conservatives' "totalitarian philosophy" that "a growing child does not need the supervision and care of a mother and that impersonal day care centers can provide appropriate nurture and love," effectively undermined their professed commitment to a mother's right to choose.[160] Antipoverty liberals also evoked Moynihanian visions of an African American underclass in particular need of maternal affection and supervision. With "all the problems that we are having in the break up of family life," the APWA's Norman Lourie questioned the wisdom of requiring poor single mothers to work.[161] Such requirements might only deepen the problem Moynihan and others wrote about, the "dependence on the mother's income" that "deprives the position of the father." They would also "deprive [poor children] of the kind of attention . . . which is now a standard feature of middle-class upbringing."[162] Antipoverty liberals like Melvin Glasser of the UAW were "horrified at the prospect of a generation of children brought up already largely without fathers" forced by work requirements to be brought up "without mothers" as well.[163]

Reactions to changes in AFDC-UP highlight the depth of the antipoverty coalition's male-breadwinner ideology. Rather than requiring all states to implement the program, as the Johnson administration recommended, Congress voted to restrict AFDC-UP's benefits to workers with a steady and recent work history. Liberal witnesses complained that such restrictions would only further erode black family structure. AFDC-UP had been designed, after all, by liberals hoping to reduce welfare's supposed "desertion incentive" in order to "keep low-income families together and stabilize their situation until the father can find work," as the editors of the *New York Times* wrote.[164] The target was the low-earning, seasonally employed, or chronically unemployed young black father, whose tenuous attachment to the labor market disqualified him from the welfare state's first tier benefits like Unemployment Insurance. Congress thwarted this agenda by excluding exactly those men from eligibility, provoking a storm of criticism from coalition members. But when Congress explicitly limited the AFDC-UP program to families with unemployed *fathers*, the coalition remained virtually silent. Walter Reuther was the only Congressional witness who protested this provision.[165] That no other liberal or welfare rights advocate even mentioned the restriction during Congressional debate suggests just how firmly and deeply the antipoverty coalition believed in the family wage ideal. That the issue was absent from public debate suggested that black men remained at the center of liberal AFDC reform efforts. For "while mothers compose the bulk of the welfare population," opined the *New York Times* editors, "it is the deserting father, and the social and economic conditions that influence him to desert, that is the main factor causing the welfare rolls to grow."[166]

The antipoverty coalition insisted that the real answer to the AFDC problem lay in helping fathers stay with their families or form families in the first place. Just how much this vision conflicted with that of Congressional conservatives is evident in a tangled exchange between Robert Kennedy and Russell Long. Rather than discussing single mothers, Kennedy focused his remarks on the plight of "people whose frustration exploded into violence in the cities this summer," those "less than three-fifths of adult men in inner-cities" who had jobs. The solution to the AFDC problem, Kennedy insisted, lay in "an immediate impact project designed to put men to work." When Kennedy opposed work requirements for *mothers*, Long assaulted him with homespun tales about the value of work. "We must take them off welfare," Kennedy agreed, "and find them jobs and have them go to work and live their lives with their wives and with their children." Clearly, the two men were talking at cross purposes. While Long hoped to put poor single *mothers* to "work," Kennedy hoped to reverse welfare policies that "neglect the fact that the man should be head of the family." His solution to the welfare crisis was to create *male* breadwinners, for "if we had jobs available for people, men could go to work and their wives would not have to go on welfare."[167]

Welfare rights activists agreed. Sparring with Congresswoman Martha Griffiths, who argued that work requirements would *help* poor single mothers overcome poverty, Wiley insisted that "the men . . . the people who are able to be heads of households or [who] ought to be legitimate head of households be the ones that get those jobs." Male NWRO staffers also authored a call for "jobs in the ghettos for men to permit them to assume normal roles as breadwinners and heads of families."[168] But female welfare recipient activists also supplemented their demand for community-controlled child care and opportunities for job training with a call for reconstructing the male-breadwinner family. "People wonder why our men have deserted their wives and children," recipient activist Juliet Greenlaw told the 1968 Democratic Platform Committee. The answer was "very simple": "they weren't able to earn enough when they were working to support their families" and "a man can't be a man when he can't support his children." So "instead of helping families stay together, the welfare system drives them apart."[169] New York welfare rights activist Beulah Sanders pointed to the absurdity of work requirements for welfare mothers when black fathers lacked decent jobs. AFDC fathers suffering from unemployment were doubly oppressed, she insisted, because "the [Welfare] Department has run them away from their families." This was "why the women [in the welfare rights movement] are saying, give our men the jobs, let us stay home and take care of our children."[170] This commitment to enabling male breadwinning and female homemaking among poor African Americans led the antipoverty coalition—from middle-class liberals and radicals to AFDC recipients themselves—to demand a radical kind of welfare reform.

The Guaranteed Income Campaign

You can feel in your bones that within four or five years welfare and health will be nationalized in some way. (*New Republic*, 1970)[171]

In a 1965 letter to the *New York Times*, Harvard psychiatrist and former Kennedy advisor Robert Coles insisted that it was "time for this nation to guarantee every one of its families an adequate yearly income."[172] Liberal social welfare experts had been arguing for years that Congress should abolish categorical programs—Old Age Assistance, Aid to the Blind, AFDC—and instead help everyone in need, regardless of age, handicap, or marital status. Increasing attention in the 1960s to the group that we now call the "working poor" prompted liberal proposals to supplement incomes, as well. After 1966, almost every program and document the antipoverty coalition published included these two demands, and more intrepid liberals and leftists gradually began to utter the phrase that expressed their inevitable outcome: guaranteed income.[173]

The guaranteed income idea boasted an eclectic political pedigree, including conservative economist Milton Friedman on the one side and civil rights and antipoverty activists on the other.[174] Friedman advocated a small guaranteed income in the form of a "Negative Income Tax" (NIT) to replace all other social welfare programs, an idea appealed to a handful of free-market enthusiasts because of its putative efficiency, as well as the additional benefit of throwing legions of meddling social workers onto the unemployment lines. With a NIT, Friedman argued, the federal government could abolish all its antipoverty and equal opportunity programs without appearing cold-hearted, and poor Americans would have the cash they needed to participate in the capitalist marketplace. But the real energy behind the guaranteed income campaign came from the political left, first from social welfare experts who called repeatedly for noncategorical federal aid, and then from a growing list of antipoverty coalition members.

Though surprisingly absent from historical memory, the guaranteed income campaign flourished on the political left in the late 1960s. The

CCAP 1966 "Program to Abolish Poverty in the United States in Ten Years" called for a "guaranteed income" alongside full employment.[175] The same year, Martin Luther King, Jr., promised a wave of demonstrations to dramatize the need, a promise that came to fruition in 1968, when the Poor People's Campaign brought 2,600 civil rights and antipoverty activists to Washington, D.C., with a plethora of demands, including guaranteed income.[176] The National Urban League and the NAACP endorsed the concept, while liberal economist Leon Keyserling and socialist leaders Michael Harrington and Norman Hill joined Bayard Rustin to stump the country promoting the full employment and guaranteed income demands of the Freedom Budget, a program endorsed by hundreds of liberal organizations.[177] Government agencies and commissions followed suit. In 1966, the Council of Economic Advisors, the White House Conference on Civil Rights, the National Commission on Technology, Automation, and Economic Progress, and the OEO all recommended that the federal government study the guaranteed income idea.[178] By 1969, the President's Commission on Law Enforcement and Administration of Justice, the White House Conference on Food, Nutrition, and Health, the Kerner Commission, and President Nixon's Task Force on Urban Affairs all advocated some form of guaranteed income. They were joined by one thousand prominent economists and several leading American industrialists.[179] In 1968, *Time* magazine could legitimately write about a "Considerable Consensus" behind a guaranteed income.[180]

Mainstream participation in the guaranteed income campaign belies its characterization as "a radically 'un-American'" idea. In one of the few historical accounts of the campaign, Gareth Davies insists that the idea was a repudiation of the meretricious individualism that had always characterized American liberalism. In Davies's account, "shaken liberals" adopted the idea in the late 1960s as part of an "aggressive attempt . . . to win back the support and trust of former allies," namely the left wing of the civil rights movement.[181] Indeed, in Davies's telling, liberalism's declining fortunes after 1968 are largely explained by this replacement of the War on Poverty's "opportunity liberalism" with a radical "entitlement liberalism." In fact, though, only a handful of supporters—often economists concerned about the effects of automation—saw the guaranteed income as part of a larger project to decouple family income from wage labor.[182] The vast majority believed wholeheartedly in individual economic advancement through education and jobs; most agreed with the Freedom Budget's insistence that "a federally guaranteed full employment policy should be at the very heart of a guaranteed income policy."[183] But by the late 1960s many were disillusioned with the War on Poverty "opportunity" programs and disheartened by Congressional rebellion against antipoverty funding and programs.

Both pessimism and pragmatism, then, propelled liberal support for a guaranteed income. In 1969, the President's Advisory Committee on Public Welfare (or Heineman Commission) saw such a program as the only way to ensure adequate income, given that "work alone is no guarantee of escaping poverty" and that training and job creation programs had proven "expensive and slow."[184] *America*'s editors agreed. "While still holding on to the ethical idea of a family living wage," they opined, "we doubt very much that this is a practical goal for all workers in a competitive system."[185] Barring federal action to improve wage rates substantially, a guaranteed income would be the only way to bring low-wage workers and their families out of poverty. Further, antipoverty liberals saw income support as a necessary complement to, rather than a substitute for, "the other mechanisms in our fight against poverty—education, training, health, and employment."[186] "If the poor get richer," liberal *New York Times* columnist Tom Wicker hoped, "if they can afford better food and transportation and activities," then "their horizons can be broadened and their aspirations expanded," leading to a "true process of self-help and self-betterment."[187] Members of the antipoverty coalition embraced the guaranteed income concept not because they rejected American ideals like individual opportunity and the work ethic but because they saw it as a means to promote those ideals. As the editors of *Business Week* recognized, the guaranteed income evoked "the vision of the Negro integrated into the mainstream of the U.S. economy instead of languishing in a government-subsidized sub-economy of his own."[188]

Part of being in the "mainstream," as far as antipoverty coalition members were concerned, was belonging to a male-breadwinner family, and this was perhaps the most compelling reason the coalition supported a guaranteed income. Liberal economist James Tobin joined many others in offering a guaranteed income as an antidote to "the incentives currently built into welfare programs for the destruction or nonformation of families." Promoting a guaranteed income went hand-in-hand with denigrating AFDC: "a worse piece of social engineering" Tobin could not imagine.[189] By excluding the "employable and the working poor," the Heineman Commission insisted in 1969, AFDC "encourages the real or feigned break-up of poor families." Headed by Ben Heineman, president of Northwest Industries, Inc., and made up of representatives from the business world, academia, labor, and local and state government, the Commission had set out to examine the country's public assistance programs, particularly AFDC. While Johnson appointed the commission to deflect demands within his administration for a broader income policy, the group recommended a federally funded and administered "universal income supplement program" for everyone "with income needs," a guaranteed income in practice if not in name.[190]

The Commission defended its vision of a federally funded family wage even though several members expressed an alternative solution to the welfare crisis. Commission members Margaret Gordon and David Sullivan, both labor union representatives, along with longtime Democratic Party activist Anna Rosenberg Hoffman, protested that the final report should have placed more emphasis on day care to provide AFDC mothers "a reasonable freedom of choice." This was a minority report, however; the Commission's official recommendations demonstrated a strong belief in using welfare—more specifically, a guaranteed income—to preserve and recreate male-breadwinner households. The Commission dismissed fears that an income guarantee would reduce work effort, in fact, by insisting that reductions would be "concentrated among secondary family workers" and "female family heads" rather than "non-aged male family heads." As such, work reductions would prove "socially as well as individually desirable."[191]

So visible and widespread was the guaranteed income concept that in December 1966, the Chamber of Commerce of the United States held a national symposium on the subject. The Chamber itself opposed any form of guaranteed income but anticipated—feared—that the idea's increasing popularity among both "new liberals" and "some of those who can be considered liberals in the traditional sense" meant impending legislative debate.[192] To an audience of five hundred business and political leaders, Missouri Republican Thomas Curtis and journalist Henry Hazlitt denounced guaranteed income as "morally indefensible" while economists Milton Friedman, Robert Theobald, and James Tobin supported the concept.[193] Tobin—an Ivy League economist and former member of Kennedy's Council of Economic Advisors—spoke for the antipoverty coalition. As noted above, he denounced current welfare programs for destroying families and argued that a guaranteed income would reverse the growth of a "population to whom the aspirations, expectations, and norms that guide behavior elsewhere in the society mean nothing."[194] While the forum produced no consensus, its very existence suggested to many journalists "how rapidly this approach is gaining acceptance among serious-minded persons as a means of eradicating poverty."[195] If "the Chamber of Commerce of the United States had undertaken to investigate flying saucers," noted Richard Strout of the *Christian Science Monitor*, "Washington couldn't have been more surprised."[196]

If observers were surprised that the Chamber discussed a guaranteed income, they were shocked when twelve of the country's leading industrialists endorsed the concept. In November 1967, New York governor Nelson Rockefeller, a liberal Republican, invited "leading businessmen, industrial, labor, foundation, and communications executives" to the Arden House conference dedicated to developing "new and revolutionary ideas" to solve the country's welfare "problem."[197] The event, dubbed Arden House for its location, was an observance of the hundredth anniversary of New York State's Board of Social Welfare, but it was also a response to the mounting fear that "the nation stands in danger of being torn apart or permanently divided into white and non-white communities."[198] Outside the conference site, police arrested twelve welfare rights activists who were expressing outrage that such an important discussion of welfare failed to seek recipient input. Inside, America's leading business executives discussed ways to create more jobs and training opportunities and debated various forms of guaranteed income. Participants rejected the kind of "punitive approach" to welfare reform favored by Congressional conservatives, the *New York Times* reported; the "predominant attitude" was, rather, "that the real crisis in welfare was the paucity of programs for building hope and opportunity for those on the relief rolls" and that the primary solution lay in "the reorientation of public policy."[199]

More remarkable than the tone of the meeting was the subsequent report of the twelve-member steering committee. Surprisingly absent in the report were the paeans to the work ethic that characterized most business-generated welfare discussions, and the report was largely silent about broken families or "ghetto pathology." Instead it condemned the welfare system for excluding three-fourths of the nation's poor and called for improved job creation, training programs, and child care funding to help "mothers who are potentially self-supporting." In the end, though, concern about the extent of poverty and AFDC's encouragement of paternal desertion—as "many fathers, unable to find employment, abandon their families in order to have them qualify for public assistance"—prompted the committee to insist that the country adopt "a practical system of income maintenance" to "raise all thirty-million [poor] Americans to at least the poverty level."[200]

The authors of this recommendation were the chief executive officers and directors of some of the country's major corporations. All twelve had a history of civic and political engagement. Xerox founder and CEO Joseph Wilson, deeply disturbed by the 1964 riots in Xerox's hometown of Rochester, New York, had begun meeting with community activists and instituting programs to train and hire African Americans. Arjay Miller, vice chairman of Ford Motor Company, would become the founding chairman of the board for the Urban Institute, a nonprofit organization dedicated to researching public policy issues, including poverty programs. Other members were leaders in the Federation of Jewish Philanthropies, the New York State Communities Aid Association, and various foundations and federal advisory councils.[201] While not typical businessmen, the committee members' support for a guaranteed income suggests that the country's increasingly explosive urban crisis prompted many politically moderate American leaders to consider vastly expanding the federal commitment to income support.

A few antipoverty liberals were less enthusiastic than these business leaders about the guaranteed income concept. In particular, leaders associated with organized labor feared that any kind of guaranteed income would reduce pressure on Congress to create pubic service jobs and upgrade employment. Bayard Rustin, as much a labor activist as a civil rights activist, warned that any guaranteed income must be reserved "only for people who are incapacitated from working" because "in our culture, a man's judgment of himself is inevitably related to his role in the production of goods and services." A guaranteed income might wound male breadwinner pride, and liberal campaigns for it would "divert attention from the struggle for full employment."[202] The Urban Coalition, in which business and labor leaders shared control, also warned that solving all poverty through "public assistance" would "require the working poor to enter a stigmatized system."[203] The AFL-CIO leaders supported "adequate income maintenance" for "broken families" or those "in which the breadwinner has died or is incapacitated," but demanded a "massive public works program" along with expanded FLSA coverage and a higher minimum wage as the real antidote to poverty.[204] Though organized labor continued to demand expansions in the social wage, many of its leaders expressed real resistance to any kind of cash "welfare" for male breadwinners, a crack in the antipoverty consensus.

Despite labor's reservations, though, a broad coalition of American liberals lobbied for a guaranteed income by 1970, motivated in large measure by their commitment to reconstructing the black family and thereby ensuring racial equality and social order. The latter goal assumed increasing importance after 1967, as Americans feared that the country's social fabric was rupturing. "The hour is much later than many Americans . . . have realized," Walter Reuther had warned at the founding of CCAP. The "discontent of the poor has reached dangerous and explosive proportions," he advised, threatening "division, discord, and serious social unrest." It was this concern, as much as if not more than a desire for social justice, that motivated liberal antipoverty warriors.[205]

A 1970 Urban Coalition television advertisement expressed the antipoverty coalition's deep yearning for social reconciliation. The group's Advertising Council persuaded 120 famous Americans—"of all races and persuasions," from "the fields of government, industry, entertainment and the arts, athletics, civil rights, and social action"—to join the cast of the musical *Hair* in a rousing rendition of "Let the Sun Shine In." The commercial was certainly an embodiment of the breadth of the 1960s civil rights/antipoverty coalition, sporting former Mississippi sharecropper and civil rights activist Fannie Lou Hamer singing alongside Andrew Heiskell, chairman of the board of *Time.* Considered by Urban Coalition leaders to be "the most important campaign in America," the public service message, which premiered in March 1970 during the *Ed Sullivan Show,* represented an "effort to reverse the forces of divisiveness and anger in America and foster constructive attitudes toward people and the problems of the cities."[206] The guaranteed income—and its potential to reconstruct poor black families—was a tangible expression of this effort.

The antipoverty coalition called for a guaranteed income "in the name of equity and humanity, tranquility and harmony," but when the Nixon administration actually proposed one, harmony did not result.[207] The battle over welfare reform in the early 1970s did not shake liberal commitment to the family wage ideal, but it did reveal deep divisions within the antipoverty coalition. The outpouring of support for increasingly ambitious federal antipoverty and economic justice programs that characterized the late 1960s was shared by a wide variety of Americans; the specifics of a legislative proposal would pit former allies against each other and would provide antiwelfare conservatives with powerful weapons and new energy in their fight against an expanded federal social safety net.

Chapter 2
Legislating the Male-Breadwinner Family: The Family Assistance Plan

Imagine someone telling you twenty years ago that a Republican President would ask the Federal Government to guarantee a minimum annual income to every family. You would have laughed your informant out of town.

—Carl Rowan, 1970

On 8 August 1969, Americans tuned into their radios and televisions to hear President Nixon outline a plan to reform the country's welfare system. He described a country in the midst of crisis—"an urban crisis, a social crisis—and at the same time, a crisis of confidence in the capacity of government to do its job." At the center of that crisis was the "system of public welfare," a "bureaucratic monstrosity, cumbersome, unresponsive, and ineffective," a "colossal failure." Echoing a multitude of journalistic treatments of the country's welfare crisis as well as the criticisms of AFDC honed by antipoverty liberals over the previous several years, Nixon condemned the welfare system for drawing poor people into overcrowded cities, inducing fathers to abandon their families, discouraging wage labor, and being "unfair to the working poor" and middle-class taxpayers alike. Insisting that "what America needs now is not more welfare but more 'workfare'," Nixon proposed to "turn . . . around our dangerous decline into welfarism." His solution: the federal government must "build a foundation under the income of every American family with dependent children." A Republican president who had campaigned as spokesman for a "silent majority" fed up with expansive Great Society liberalism, was planning to replace AFDC with a guaranteed income for American families.[1]

Despite Nixon's repeated denials, the Family Assistance Plan (FAP) *was* a guaranteed income proposal. Through several revisions and amendments during its more than three years in and out of Congress, the FAP retained its essential structure: a basic income guarantee of $1,600 a year for a family of four which would phase out gradually as earnings increased.[2] Virtually all families with children would be eligible for the plan, "whether the family is working or not . . . united or not . . . deserving or not," as Daniel Patrick Moynihan put it.[3] The FAP included a work requirement of sorts—able-bodied adult recipients not responsible for the care of pre-school children would forfeit a portion of the family benefit if they refused to participate in available work training or job search activities. It also included a modest expansion of federal job training and child care opportunities, guaranteed fiscal relief for state governments, and offered various changes in administration. At its core, though, the FAP was a plan to drastically restructure the country's welfare system. Since its inception in 1935, federal family welfare restricted aid to families without a recognized bread-winner—that is, without an adult man present. Under the FAP, income rather than family structure would determine eligibility for welfare. According to administration estimates, the FAP would aid 65 percent of the country's poor people and virtually all its poor children, a phenomenal expansion of the nation's social safety net.[4]

The proposal provoked passionate responses across the political spectrum. Antiwelfare conservatives foresaw, quite literally, a decline of American civilization akin to the collapse of the Roman Empire. Well beyond a "giant step deeper into the quagmire of the welfare state," the FAP would mean "an end to this nation as a free Republic," "gutting traditional principles which underlie America's heritage of Liberty."[5] For the "bread and circuses" of Rome, warned *National Review* columnist Frank Meyter, "substitute a federal dole and a television set in every welfare home."[6] Welfare rights activists and their allies spoke in equally apocalyptic language. The FAP was "an act of political repression," a "brutal attack upon children," and an "affront to the dignity of humanity."[7] Clearly, both antiwelfare conservatives and welfare rights activists saw the FAP as a profound threat, though they disagreed on its nature. Mainstream liberal publications, for their part, lauded the plan as "enlightened," "singularly daring," and positively "revolutionary."[8] Daniel Patrick Moynihan, domestic advisor to President Nixon, was not alone in viewing the FAP as "the single most important piece of social legislation to be sent to the Congress in a generation," the "beginning of a new era in American social policy."[9]

Moynihan was not a disinterested observer, of course. A self-described "liberal Democrat," Moynihan brought to the Nixon administration the antipoverty coalition's analysis of racial disadvantage and the welfare crisis. While outraged conservatives liked to think of the "charming and eloquent Moynihan" as a "virtual Svengali" who "sold [Nixon] a bill of goods," Moynihan was only the most persuasive of a host of liberal policymakers who designed and sold the plan.[10] Aiming to reduce America's poverty rate, these policymakers also sought to solve a variety of social and political problems, from the dangerous frustration and social disorder they saw in the nation's African American ghettos to the apparently growing resentment and white working-class alienation that contemporaries called the "white backlash."

By 1969, many antipoverty liberals were convinced that AFDC was at least partially responsible for these problems and that a guaranteed income plan was at least a partial solution. With characteristic faith in federal power and their own abilities, armed with social science data and good intentions, they embarked on a mission in what cynical observers call social engineering. If AFDC drew poor people into overcrowded cities, the FAP would keep them where they were. If AFDC discouraged wage labor, the FAP would reward it. If AFDC turned the white working class against the federal government, the FAP would restore their faith. Above all, if AFDC destroyed male-breadwinner families, the FAP would support them, both in symbol and in practice. But antipoverty liberals, who hoped that a guaranteed income would promote social and racial reconciliation, would be sorely disappointed. On the right, antiwelfare conservatives rejected liberals' attempt to extend the family wage to the poor, particularly to African Americans. Committed to an older family wage model, which restricted the privileges of female homemaking to whites, powerful Southern Democrats twice kept the FAP bottled up in the Senate Finance Committee. They were joined in opposition by free market conservatives in business organizations and Congress, who feared that expanding the family wage would ease the imperative of wage labor for women, an increasingly important source of low-wage employees in an economy entering the throes of what economists call deindustrialization. Bitter division among liberals, radicals, and welfare rights activists also boded ill. In the vitriolic tone and militant style that had become characteristic of the political left by the late 1960s, welfare rights activists and their allies balked at the FAP potential to harm predominantly African American and urban female-headed families, while other liberals insisted that the plan was an opportunity that the country could ill afford to reject. While some AFDC families might suffer, the plan would establish the precedent of a guaranteed income and extend federal aid to two-parent households (the "working poor," in contemporary discourse) for the first time.

This rift on the left has dominated both contemporary and historical treatments of the FAP debate, blinding us to how much liberals on both sides of the issue and welfare rights activists and their allies shared. From welfare rights activists to the businessmen of the Urban Coalition, a broad coalition of antipoverty liberals and radicals insisted that the federal government ensure every American basic economic security through jobs and income policies that would promote the formation and maintenance of male-breadwinner families. While the FAP never passed Congress, the heated four-year debate it generated highlighted and reinforced deep divisions in American society about welfare, race, and family.

The Family Assistance Plan as Welfare Reform

The Family Assistance Plan "has been designed to prick the AFDC balloon and keep families together. If welfare could bust them up, maybe some more cash would stick them together." (Ira Mothner, 1970)[11]

It is not surprising that Nixon introduced his Family Assistance Plan as a response to crisis. The United States in the late 1960s abounded with talk of crisis, and the urban crisis was foremost in many Americans' minds. After World War II, the nation's industrial cities had begun a gradual decline: poor Southern migrants driven off the land flooded in while middle-class residents and well-paid manufacturing jobs poured out.[12] By the late 1960s, entrenched poverty, soaring welfare costs, mounting impatience on the part of poor black urban residents, and civil rights leaders' increasing attention to the economic foundations of racial oppression put tremendous pressure on urban mayors, who lobbied Congress for financial aid. Meanwhile, government commissions lamented the plight of those left out of the nation's most sustained economic boom. Organizations like the National Urban League and the brand new Urban Coalition devoted themselves to solving the complex problems besetting America's cities.

Welfare held a key symbolic position in the rhetoric of urban crisis, standing both for the tragedy of poverty and social disorder and for the failure of liberal policymakers to adequately address them. The Johnson administration had declared a War on Poverty, after all, only to preside over a phenomenal increase in welfare rolls and costs. Even linguistically, the "urban crisis" evoked the "welfare crisis," which became a ubiquitous story line in newsmagazines and political discourse of the late 1960s. Nixon denounced the country's welfare system as a "huge monster" that "breaks up homes . . . penalizes work . . . robs recipients of dignity . . . and grows." "Like the irrepressible creature of a B-grade movie," noted Robert Asen in an analysis of the speech's rhetoric, "the monstrous welfare system had not yet reached its full maturity," and "a larger, more powerful monster portended greater ills."[13] While Nixon proposed to address various elements of the urban crisis, he defined his Family Assistance Plan most specifically as *welfare reform*.

As a solution to the welfare crisis, though, the FAP was what one scholar has called "a seemingly illogical response."[14] Certainly the FAP made little sense to conservative critics within and outside the administration. If the problem were growing AFDC rolls and costs—as virtually all participants in the welfare debate of the late 1960s agreed—then a guaranteed income that promised to add thirteen million individuals to the welfare rolls and four billion dollars to the federal welfare bill during its first year alone seemed at best counterproductive. Administration officials sold the FAP as "a workable solution" to this "crisis in our national welfare system," as many legislators, columnists, and lobbyists legitimately wondered how vastly expanding the federal welfare system would possibly solve the fiscal or social problems associated with the welfare crisis.[15]

The FAP's pedigree helps to make sense of this mystery. Though proposed by a Republican administration, the plan was a product of the antipoverty coalition, both in inspiration and design. The Nixon administration's domestic policymaking circle boasted a number of antiwelfare conservatives, of course—those who opposed virtually any expansion of federal income maintenance programs: Harvard University political scientist Edward Banfield, Columbia University economist Martin Anderson, and economist Arthur Burns. But it also contained a group of antipoverty liberals, veterans of the Johnson administration, who convinced Nixon that the FAP would be a practical and political winner. Journalists frequently pointed to Moynihan, "the White House resident liberal," as the FAP's architect, but a number of other liberals populated Nixon's domestic policymaking circle; in approaching welfare reform, they would draw on their experience in the Johnson administration's OEO and HEW, incubators for new and increasingly expansive plans to reform the federal welfare system and institute a federally guaranteed income.[16]

Even before the inauguration, Nixon's advisors convinced the president-elect to propose national welfare standards, a longtime goal of liberal welfare policymakers and antipoverty coalition lobbyists. By requiring low-benefit states to raise welfare grants, even a relatively low federal standard would significantly increase the income of America's poorest AFDC recipients, most of whom lived in the South. Standards would also respond to the widely held "migration thesis"—the assumption that higher welfare benefits in Northern and some Western states drew the welfare poor into struggling cities. Though studies have since demonstrated that disparate welfare benefits play little role in migration, lobbyists across the political spectrum, from the Leadership Conference on Civil Rights to the Taxpayers Committee to Federalize Welfare, expounded the "migration thesis" throughout the late 1960s and early 1970s, and journalists insisted that "wretchedly inadequate" welfare grants in the South threatened to turn more generous states into "hapless dumping grounds" for poor people; higher welfare grants in the North and West surely acted as a "MAGNET FOR THE POOR."[17]

Discussions of migration and welfare receipt in the 1960s evoked images of black Southerners overrunning struggling industrial cities. During the 1960s, AFDC recipients were disproportionately African American (over 47 percent) and predominantly urban (over 72 percent), but public rhetoric exaggerated these characteristics.[18] As early as 1960, a national controversy over welfare reform in Newburgh, New York, revealed the racial subtext underlying complaints about migration. Typical of industrial cities in the 1950s and 1960s, Newburgh was simultaneously experiencing economic decline and a changing racial composition: textile mills closed, whites fled the city, and Southern African American migrants moved in. In 1961, Newburgh's City Manager, Joseph Mitchell, made national headlines with a series of welfare cutbacks aimed at black "migrants," the "dregs of humanity" who flooded into Newburgh in a "never ending pilgrimage" from the South. Widespread publicity of the Newburgh reforms—which included cuts in aid to women with out-of-wedlock children and stringent work requirements—helped cement the image of welfare recipients as African American migrants seeking a comfortable, leisured life on welfare.[19] By the late 1960s, liberals were making a similar argument in hopes of convincing Congress to establish national welfare standards. "In effect," argued economist Robert Lekachman, "the South exports its unwanted people, mostly black, to communities too humane to pay Southern scales of assistance." [20]

Nixon was less explicit about race, though he surely implied black migration when he complained of cities "where the jobless congregate in overcrowded and crime-ridden slums and load an increasingly intolerable burden on State and local treasuries."[21] In fact, the FAP's legislative language cited the migration thesis directly: "No more will poor persons be driven out of one section of the Nation by inadequate or even punitive welfare legislation and forced into crowded and hostile cities."[22] The migration argument appealed to common sense even as it ignored the long-term and complex factors underlying the migration of poor whites and African Americans out of the South in the quarter century after World War II. It also helped to solidify the picture of the welfare crisis as primarily a black problem—and as an urban and Northern one, as well.[23]

The migration thesis no doubt helped convince Nixon to support the $1.4 billion plan for national welfare standards recommended by his Task Force on Public Welfare, headed by Richard P. Nathan, a young Republican from the centrist Brookings Institute. A researcher for the Kerner Commission, the federal riot commission that recommended vastly expanded federal antipoverty and income maintenance efforts, Nathan came to the Nixon administration at the recommendation of President Johnson's HEW secretary, John Gardner, himself a proponent of more generous welfare assistance.[24] Other Task Force members included New York City welfare administrator Mitchell Ginsberg, a social worker who liberalized the city's welfare laws, and James Sundquist, a Democrat who had helped design the War on Poverty.[25] The Nathan proposal garnered enthusiastic support from Robert Finch, Nixon's HEW secretary, and "liberal in residence" Pat Moynihan, executive secretary of the administration's Urban Affairs Council.[26] Even Arthur Burns would come to support national standards but only as an alternative to the more drastic guaranteed income proposals developed by his liberal colleagues.

Whatever their practical and political benefit, national standards did not address the antipoverty coalition's fundamental concern about family structure. Worth Bateman, deputy assistant secretary for program analysis at HEW, urged the administration to attend to AFDC's supposedly harmful effects on family stability. By making AFDC more generous in some states, national standards would "intensify present inequities in the treatment of male and female headed families and provide increased financial incentives to break up intact households," especially "low income families headed by a man who works." A better answer would be to extend federal aid to two-parent families, the "working poor."[27] Bateman and OEO economist James Lyday were developing just such a proposal to present to Nixon's Urban Affairs Council. As head of a working group assigned to strengthen Nathan's plan, Bateman instead helped design a much more drastic overhaul of the country's welfare system, the FAP.[28]

In recommending the FAP to the president, the Urban Affairs Council called the "present welfare system" a "failure" because AFDC provided a "positive incentive for fathers to abandon their wives and children to the welfare rolls."[29] The Republicans who predominated in the "Working Welfare Group" assigned to write the legislation signed onto this basic premise. The group's lone Democrat, Jerome Rosow, served as assistant secretary of labor for policy development and research, the same position Moynihan had held when he wrote his infamous report about the crumbling "Negro Family." According to Moynihan, "concern with matters such as income and family structure" had "persisted" in that office, lending "surprising continuity to the analysis of the problem of dependency from the beginning to the end of the 1960s." Like Moynihan himself, Rosow served as a human link between the antipoverty coalition's interpretation of the welfare problem and the FAP.[30] Even opponents within the administration understood the terms of debate, expressing doubt that the plan would have the "beneficial effects on family structure that its proponents claim."[31] The FAP's rationale was clear: antipoverty liberals in the Nixon administration proposed to solve the welfare crisis by restructuring the welfare system to promote the formation and maintenance of male-breadwinner households.[32]

They had no way of knowing if this would work. The OEO and HEW had only recently begun demonstration projects to test the effects of a guaranteed income on the work habits and marital status of poor families. Labor Secretary George Schultz, an economist and former colleague of Milton Friedman at the University of Chicago, admitted the paucity of data in a 1969 memo. The FAP "seeks to restore to the welfare system the purpose of reducing dependency by including the male *in* rather than forcing him out," Schultz noted, yet "the prospects for success in this attempt hinge on the [largely unknown] effects of human behavior in such basic matters as working, marriage, rearing of children, and family dissolution." With little data to go on, the FAP planners and promoters could only rely on assumptions about the motives and behavior of poor people, particularly poor men, found in the voluminous literature on the psychological impact of failed breadwinning on African American men, popularized in the 1960s by civil rights activists, antipoverty liberals, and the popular press. FAP's designers and promoters understood that the "family stability problem" had roots in "complex social problems" and admitted "we do not know the exact extent to which the welfare system itself breaks up families," but insisted nonetheless that a welfare system that "provides a *prima facie* incentive—a clear financial reward—for family breakup" was both "vicious and irrational."[33]

This is the case the Nixon administration presented to Congress—that their "sensible though revolutionary plan" would keep families together and thereby reduce welfare rolls. Before a hostile Senate Finance Committee, Finch made what one senator called a "big play" about family breakup, declaring that AFDC's "preferential treatment of female-headed families has led to increased family breakup."[34] The administration even quantified AFDC's average "Family Breakup Incentive" (calculated at $2,500 for a father earning $2,000 a year) and FAP's potential "Family Togetherness Incentive" (estimated at between $500 and $700 for the same father). The FAP, Finch insisted, would mean lower welfare costs *eventually* than if AFDC were to continue driving away male breadwinners.[35] Thus did the administration present a bill to vastly expand welfare coverage as a plan to reduce welfare costs in the long run.

In order to reverse the welfare system's "perverse incentives," the FAP had to ensure that two-parent families would be better off financially than one-parent families.[36] While the two million AFDC families in low-benefit states would gain income under FAP, benefits would drop for the remaining six-and-a-half million families.[37] In part, this was a fiscal imperative. To promote family stability by helping the "working poor," the administration had to "use some dollars which might otherwise be available to raise the basic minimum standards."[38] For liberal policymakers, this seemed an easy trade-off. When welfare expert Tom Joe expressed concern that AFDC recipients might suffer under their proposal, Bateman and Lyday accused him of being a "bleeding heart trying to keep a lousy discredited AFDC system" who didn't "care about the working poor." [39] Moynihan admitted that the "short-term effect" of FAP would certainly have been to "improve the conditions of the nondependent poor [male-headed "working poor" families] relative to the dependent [single-mother AFDC families]."[40] If policymakers regarded this trade-off as unfortunate, the focus on encouraging family stability made it virtually inevitable.

FAP's liberal planners also demonstrated little commitment to moving poor single mothers into the labor force; they did not even include a work requirement in their original proposal. Moynihan later claimed that the bill's work requirement was the price for Congressional approval and denied that Nixon's increasingly frequent and severe "workfare" rhetoric referred to single mothers. Instead, he argued, it was to reassure the public

INCENTIVES UNDER AFDC BREAK UP THE FAMILY

1. FAMILIES HEADED BY UNEMPLOYED FATHERS -- NOT COVERED IN 29 JURISDICTIONS

EXAMPLE: ASSUME FAMILY OF FIVE IN STATE WHICH PAYS $2,500 UNDER AFDC
TO A FAMILY OF FOUR AND WHICH HAS NO UF PROGRAM

FAMILY INCOME IF FATHER LEAVES = $2,500 (AFDC)
FAMILY INCOME IF FATHER STAYS =   0
FAMILY BREAKUP INCENTIVE = $2,500

2. FAMILIES HEADED BY FATHERS EMPLOYED FULL-TIME-NOT COVERED BY AFDC IN ANY STATE

EXAMPLE: ASSUME FATHER EARNING $2,000, SAME FAMILY AND SAME STATE

FAMILY INCOME IF FATHER LEAVES = $2,500
FAMILY INCOME IF FATHER STAYS = 2,000
FAMILY BREAKUP INCENTIVE = $ 500

INCENTIVES UNDER FAMILY ASSISTANCE KEEP THE FAMILY TOGETHER

1. FAMILIES HEADED BY UNEMPLOYED FATHERS

EXAMPLE: ASSUME FAMILY OF FIVE IN STATE WHICH PAYS $3000 TO A FAMILY OF
FIVE AND $2500 TO A FAMILY OF FOUR

FAMILY INCOME IF FATHER STAYS = $3000 ($1900 FAP + $1100 SUPPLEMENT)
FAMILY INCOME IF FATHER LEAVES = $2500 ($1600 FAP + $900 SUPPLEMENT)
FAMILY TOGETHERNESS INCENTIVE = $ 500

2. FAMILIES HEADED BY FATHERS EMPLOYED FULL TIME

EXAMPLE: ASSUME FATHER EARNING $2000, SAME FAMILY AND SAME STATE

FAMILY INCOME IF FATHER STAYS = $3260 ($2000 WAGES + $1260 FAP)
FAMILY INCOME IF FATHER LEAVES = $2500 ($1600 FAP + $900 SUPPLEMENT)
FAMILY TOGETHERNESS INCENTIVE = $ 700

WHAT A WORKING MAN MUST EARN TO BE AS WELL OFF AS ON WELFARE

FAMILY OF FOUR – JANUARY 1970

STATE	WELFARE PAYMENT WITH NO INCOME (MONTHLY)	GROSS EARNINGS FOR NON-WELFARE FAMILY TO MATCH WELFARE INCOME [1] (MONTHLY)	(HOURLY)
CALIFORNIA	$221	$288	$1.67
CONNECTICUT	294	358	2.08
ILLINOIS	269	319	1.85
INDIANA	150	185	1.07
LOUISIANA	104	154	.90
MASSACHUSETTS	307	372	2.16
MICHIGAN	263	333	1.94
NEW YORK	313	383	2.23
NEBRASKA	200	250	1.45

[1] ASSUMES WORK-RELATED EXPENSES EQUAL TO AVERAGE CURRENT ALLOWANCE IN STATES SHOWN. (EXCLUDES DAY CARE COSTS.)

Figure 5. Charts explaining the benefits of the Nixon administration Family Assistance Plan. Policymakers hoped to convince Congress that AFDC broke up families and FAP would keep them together. Note the interest in the earnings of a "working man" compared to AFDC benefits. Senate Finance Committee, Hearings on HR 16311: Family Assistance Act of 1970, Part 1, 91st Cong., 2nd sess., 29 April 1970.

that the "able-bodied men who were to receive income supplements under the new program" would not abandon wage labor. As such, Moynihan argued, the requirement meant nothing at all: these men were already working, while AFDC mothers "were either ineligible by virtue of having preschool children, or unemployable, or anxious for such work and training as might be available."[41] Planners therefore gave little attention to the education, training, and child care that might help poor single mothers become viable breadwinners. While Nixon directed policymakers to include "day care for women with children," the FAP provisions were mere lip service. The plan's 300,000 school-age and 150,000 preschool slots, funded at less than half the HEW cost estimates, would not come close to serving even the 1.5 million children whose mothers would be subject to the plan's minimal work requirement.[42] Meanwhile, OEO director Frank Carlucci suggested how manpower services would be distributed under the plan: "we would support giving higher priority to the training and employment of men than women" to take advantage of men's "greater employment opportunities" and to avoid child care expenses.[43] As in debates over the WIN Program two years earlier, federal welfare administrators hoped to solve single mothers' poverty by attaching them to male breadwinners, not by helping them to become economic providers themselves.

The FAP family wage ideology became particularly clear during Congressional questioning about the work requirement. The bill required that all adult, able-bodied recipients accept training or work except women with preschool children and women living with an adult male. When asked why the FAP exempted married mothers, Rosow drew a picture of the "normal family" that revealed the liberal perspective on welfare. "When there are two [parents] present," he insisted, "it is more like a normal family in the sense that the emphasis is on the father . . . on upgrading and career development for him to get him into a better paying job, and to pull him out of the welfare program entirely so he becomes entirely self-supporting." In such families, "the mother role becomes one of [emotionally] supporting the family, caring for the children while he is trying to improve his income."[44] To HEW's Robert Patricelli, the very idea of a work requirement for married women was nothing short of absurd. By supposedly forcing a husband to "subject his wife to a mandatory work requirement," such a policy would "mudd[y] up the situation quite a bit."[45] When Representative Martha Griffiths insisted that the best solution to rising AFDC rolls would be to require the youngest AFDC mothers to remain in school and prepare themselves to become economic providers, Finch seemed unable to respond. The FAP rested on the "premise that most people want to be with their families, the husband wants to be with the wife and vice versa," Finch stammered, and "given two courses of action, work or nonwork, a man does want to get up in the morning and go off and do some work that is fulfilling and gives him some dignity."[46]

Like Finch, most FAP spokesmen discussed the work requirement as a male program. This may explain the ubiquitous use of male nouns and pronouns in discussions of work effort, as when Nixon condemned AFDC for "mak[ing] it more profitable for a man not to work than to work," or when he insisted that "when a man is able to work . . . that man should not be paid to loaf."[47] Perhaps this merely reflected common usage at the time, which took male pronouns and the "generic" male noun as universal; in 1971, when signing amendments to strengthen work requirements for AFDC adults, 90 percent of whom were female, Nixon lauded the "working man" who accepted any job that enabled him to "feed and clothe and shelter himself and provide for his family."[48] Vice President Spiro Agnew, too, condemned the AFDC system for "encourag[ing] idleness" among men. "If a man can make more for his family on welfare than he can make working," Agnew explained to the public in a *U.S. News and World Report* interview about the FAP, "you can bet that many men will quit work, sit back and watch soap operas on television all day." Administration rhetoric suggested, then, that the existing welfare system (AFDC) somehow discouraged *male* work effort, while the FAP would encourage it.[49]

In fact, few men had access to welfare. Arguments that the welfare system "helps men who don't work, but doesn't help those who do" fundamentally misrepresented the country's income maintenance system.[50] That system had been set up during the Great Depression and preserved a fundamentally unequal economic status quo even as it broadened social citizenship. Men with access to steady industrial jobs—and, to some extent, the women and children who were economically dependent on them—could rely on a federally administered social insurance system that protected them from the economic hazards of work-related injuries, short-term unemployment, and the indignities of aged poverty. The federal government also contributed money to state-run public assistance programs for certain categories of people: the destitute elderly, the blind, and the children of poor single mothers. These programs established at least a nominal right to assistance that welfare rights activists had successfully codified by the early 1970s. However, many individuals fell outside this system altogether, most obviously non-elderly men without steady work histories or whose work lay outside social insurance protection (predominantly domestic and agricultural labor). Some men might receive minimal "General Assistance" payments, but these were administered by local governments, typically resistant to providing aid to "able-bodied men." Accusations that "welfare" discouraged male work effort had no obvious justification, especially since to most Americans "welfare" meant AFDC. The charges expressed either genuine misunderstanding or a conviction that meager AFDC grants "indirectly and surreptitiously" supported the boyfriends of AFDC mothers.[51]

To be sure, workfare rhetoric served a useful political purpose. Nixon's victory in 1968, along with the remarkably successful third-party candidacy of Alabama governor and segregationist George Wallace, convinced opinion-makers that the New Deal Democratic coalition was falling apart. In his 1969 book *The Emerging Republican Majority*, political strategist Kevin Phillips predicted that the white working class would become a key element in an historic political realignment. Beset by a precarious economy, resentful of federal attention to minorities and the poor, and threatened by the irreverent cultural styles and militant demands of young protesters, the white working class seemed profoundly alienated from the Democratic Party. By the early 1970s, this demographic had become the focus of a multitude of conferences, commissions, sociological and anthropological studies, and a "flurry of journalistic concern."[52] According to common wisdom, these Americans had "little to show from either the New Frontier or the Great Society."[53] AFDC seemed a particular irritant to them: "You go out to a blue-collar audience and talk about this problem [welfare]," noted Ronald Reagan in 1971, "and you get standing ovations."[54] When Nixon's Labor Department studied the backlash, the *Chicago Sun-Times* summarized its findings in a headline: "Panel Tells Nixon: Welfare Irks 'Excluded and Forgotten' Workers."[55]

Nixon marketed the FAP to appeal to these "forgotten Americans," the "blue-collar man" forced to "live [in the same neighborhood] with the welfare recipient" who was "fed up" with the system.[56] Rhetorical attacks on the welfare policies of his Democratic predecessors and expressions of doubt about the federal government's capacity to "master the challenges we face" played to white working-class resentment about growing welfare rolls and skepticism about federal social programs for the poor. Nixon explicitly identified the "working poor and taxpayers" as his target audience, instructing speechwriters to avoid messages meant to appeal to welfare recipients or the "black unemployed" and later forbidding Cabinet members from discussing the FAP publicly without mentioning the work requirement.[57] Labor secretary Schultz gave speeches on the seven ways that the FAP "promoted work," while Vice President Agnew insisted incorrectly that the plan would "introduce . . . at long last a work requirement into the welfare system."[58]

Beyond its rhetoric, the FAP's very concept fit into "Nixon's broader strategy" to attract white working-class voters to a new Republican majority.[59] At the same time his staff was discussing welfare reform options, Nixon was reading Pete Hamill's *New York Magazine* article "Revolt of the White Lower Middle Class," a rather typical journalistic treatment of resentment and political volatility among this key political constituency. Nixon directed his staff to "indicate what the government can do about" the problem Hamill described. FAP supporters answered that an NIT, which would reduce the power of social workers and place cash directly in the hands of needy recipients, was "not basically a 'leftish' or liberal initiative, but rather an essentially conservative one" that worked on market principles and that would enable Nixon to eliminate the supposedly offensive War on Poverty programs. More important, the FAP would shift the rewards of the American welfare system toward families who *looked like* the typical blue-collar family. It was clear to all observers of the backlash that the "increasing discontent of the working poor" had what Finch called "ominous racial overtones," a problem the FAP could potentially solve.[60] While AFDC recipients were primarily single mothers, the "principle new group made eligible for cash assistance" was "'working poor' families headed by males employed full time."[61] Nearly 50 percent of AFDC recipients were nonwhite and 90 percent were in female-headed families. It was projected that FAP families, in contrast, would be predominantly white (62 percent), male-headed (60 percent) and working (80 percent).[62] The authors of an Urban Institute publication praised the FAP for exactly this reason: in its direction of federal aid to individuals "in the same demographic, if not financial, category as the blue-collar worker, i.e. working male heads of families," the FAP would hopefully ease antiwelfare resentment.[63] Proponents of the FAP within the administration agreed; they insisted that the FAP demonstrated the administration's support for blue-collar values by helping "the proudest poor . . . the man who is not looking for a handout, but who is trying to make ends meet by himself."[64]

This logic made little sense to FAP opponents. Arthur Burns warned Nixon that whatever the demographics of its potential recipients, the FAP was a tremendous expansion of welfare likely to "enhance the growing bitterness of the white lower middle-class" which associated welfare with benefits for "some fat welfare bitch."[65] Despite his public support, Agnew, too, predicted that the plan would "not be a political winner." Its benefits would not reach backlash voters, who earned too much to receive income supplements, and it would certainly "not attract low income groups to the Republican philosophy."[66] The editors of the *National Review* agreed: the FAP "can only damage [Nixon's] standing with the job-holding, taxpaying majority that elected him."[67] Over time, Nixon listened more and more to these anti-FAP advisors. By Labor Day 1972, as his Democratic challenger George McGovern sought to recover from his own ill-conceived guaranteed income proposal, Nixon was appealing outright to American "working-m[e]n" with antiwelfare tirades.[68]

Nixon's seemingly ambivalent and contradictory stance on welfare, work, and child care reflected both political calculation and the deep divisions within his administration. The antipoverty liberals who designed the FAP cared little about work opportunities for single mothers. The single mother was poor, in their analysis, not because she lacked a well-paying job and child care options but because she lacked a male breadwinner. The FAP's opponents in the administration, meanwhile, doubted the connection between AFDC and family breakup, questioned the wisdom of expanding federal income maintenance, and preferred less drastic welfare reforms. Congressional resistance, California governor Ronald Reagan's popular antiwelfare stance, and increasing attention to the concerns of middle-class taxpayers all fed into Nixon's increasingly "tough" rhetoric about "getting people into jobs."[69] But such rhetoric would not be enough to convince the Senate Finance Committee to support a guaranteed income.

An Older Family Wage Model: Conservative Response to the FAP

During Congressional debate over the FAP, a group of chief executive officers from Benton Harbor, Michigan, offered what Senator Russell Long called "a little common sense" from the "mainstream of . . . thinking in the United States." These businessmen claimed expertise in the issues at hand. "Second only to Detroit in our State in rates of crime, illegitimate births, unwed mothers and educational disadvantage" and "virtually bankrupt" to boot, Benton Harbor was a case study in the urban crisis, a city "destroyed by the welfare system." Members of the city's Area Resources Improvement Council (ARIC) saw Michigan's comparatively generous AFDC grants as a magnet for poor African Americans and complained that AFDC encouraged "parents to avoid marriage and its related responsibilities." If the ARIC's diagnosis of the welfare crisis superficially resembled that of the antipoverty coalition, though, its prescription was quite different. These businessmen wanted to stem the influx of poor African American migrants to Michigan with a welfare residency requirement rather than with national standards or a guaranteed income. They sought to encourage male breadwinning with strict child support enforcement measures rather than with income supplements for low-earning fathers. They hoped to convince poor women to get and stay married by excluding "illegitimate" children from welfare rather than by instituting an elaborate guaranteed income scheme that covered two-parent families. Above all, they hoped to stem soaring welfare rolls not with policies designed to create male-breadwinner families but by putting poor single mothers to work.[70]

As these voices from business suggest, antiwelfare conservatives—lawmakers, business leaders, conservative intellectuals and columnists, and many ordinary people—did not follow the FAP's logic because they did not share its designers' family wage ideology despite their commitment to the "traditional" family. Chamber of Commerce president Arch Booth urged Congress to find "ways to strengthen the family, rather than ways to facilitate its breakup," but he shared little with antipoverty liberals who sought the same goal.[71] Liberals hoped to use welfare policy to extend the "traditional family" to poor African Americans, while Booth and other conservative FAP opponents sought to enforce the boundaries that excluded them. The male-breadwinner/female-homemaker family had been a marker of race and class privilege throughout the industrial era. The New Deal welfare state and the postwar era's phenomenal economic growth favored white, two-parent families, whose male breadwinners benefited from expanded educational opportunities, a thriving labor market, a strong union movement, and the growth of both public and private welfare states. These developments provided the economic foundation for the postwar "domestic ideology" in which the family wage became a reality for a significant portion of white Americans, supplemented by married women flooding into a secondary labor market to help their families participate in a burgeoning "consumers' republic."[72] African Americans—both in the rural South and in urban areas throughout the nation—benefited much less than whites from such developments. Southern Congressmen ensured their exclusion from key social insurance programs, discrimination by employers and unions closed off skilled trades, and housing and educational segregation further blocked opportunities for economic advancement. The nation's political and economic elites had never expected African Americans to conform to the male-breadwinner family model. Conservative responses to the FAP suggest a continued commitment to this older, exclusive family wage model.

Male breadwinning was crucial to this older model, but antiwelfare conservatives and antipoverty liberals explained failed breadwinning differently. Liberals portrayed the deserting father as a victim of unemployment, low wages, blocked opportunity, and, more often than not, racial discrimination. This father, either selflessly hoping to qualify his children for welfare or simply suffering from wounded male pride, abandoned his family to the AFDC rolls. To Georgia senator Herman Talmadge, he looked much different, more like a "professional malingerer" who fathered illegitimate children with equally "irresponsible" women and left them for the taxpayers to support. For critics like Talmadge, the FAP would merely enable irresponsible men to "do a little casual labor on somebody's yard from time to time and maybe sell a little heroin or do a little burglary" and "still be in pretty good shape."[73]

Rather than reward fathers who stayed with their families, the FAP's conservative opponents wanted the government to enforce paternal support. AFDC had been hamstrung from its origins by fear that aiding children would ease the male breadwinning imperative, and by 1970, California governor Ronald Reagan was leading the charge to "strengthen family responsibility" through child support enforcement.[74] In a *Saturday Review* debate on the FAP, John Hamilton agreed that "solving the welfare problem requires solving the fatherless family problem, and solving this problem does not suggest a national family-assistance program so much as a family-planning program," one that should include "strict parental laws."[75] The editors of the blatantly antiwelfare *U.S. News and World Report* complained that "few states make much of an effort to trace missing fathers or hold them legally responsible for child support," a situation that "critics claim . . . encourages illegitimacy among those who are least equipped to bring up children."[76] One of the few provisions of the FAP that Senator Long liked was its child support provisions, which gave the federal government a variety of tools to obtain paternal income and made a federal crime of interstate travel by a deserting parent. This was the first effort, Long enthused, to "use the long arm of [the government] to reach out and grab these runaway fathers."[77]

Out-of-wedlock childbearing was proof that poor single mothers were self-imposed exiles from the family wage economy. Conservatives blamed rising welfare rolls on what the Hoover Institution's Roger Freeman called "socially unacceptable and destructive behavior" like illegitimacy rather than on blocked opportunity for poor fathers.[78] Some, like Muskogee County, Oklahoma, judge John W. Porter, Jr., urged Congress to punish "repeated illegitimacy" by "mak[ing] the mother subject to having her children taken from her," and at least one state legislature considered compulsory sterilization of welfare mothers.[79] Senator Long was notorious for making slanderous statements about welfare mothers' sexuality, and journalists frequently employed sexually suggestive language to describe growing AFDC rolls: welfare was "breed[ing] ever larger numbers of recipients" and providing the "breeding grounds of crime, delinquency, illegitimacy, prostitution and all other forms of social ills."[80] Long criticized regulations prohibiting welfare administrators from questioning AFDC applicants about their children's paternity and evoked laughter from fellow lawmakers when he quipped: "It just occurs to me that you could ask them for their best guess."[81]

Antiwelfare conservatives also excluded poor women from their sentimental notions about full-time homemaking and mothering. In a typical tale, Utah senator Wallace Bennett told his colleagues about a welfare mother he knew who spent her days drinking beer, watching television, and letting her children run wild. After getting a job and joining "the mainstream of American society," though, she began to keep a "clean and orderly" home and to discipline her children. In Bennett's tale—as in many similar ones told by FAP opponents—welfare produced "a deadening psychological effect" on the recipient and her children while wage labor represented a positive conversion experience.[82] In such stories, and in repeated appeals to the dignity of wage labor for AFDC recipients, conservative critics of the FAP, like Reconstruction Era whites who had mocked freedwomen for withdrawing from the fields to "play the lady," defined poor single mothers as workers first and foremost.

Employers who relied on low-wage female labor showed little interest in a social experiment to promote male-breadwinning households among the poor. "I find many people can't get domestic help," complained Senator Phil Landrum. "Can't domestics be taken off welfare?"[83] Meanwhile, business organizations worried about finding agricultural laborers, waitresses, and sales clerks.[84] The Southern Restaurant Association, the American Retail Federation, and many state Chambers of Commerce worried that welfare for the "working poor" would cause low-earning men to withdraw from the labor market, but they seemed even more concerned about women.[85] In a publication titled "Why Are New York's Workers Dropping Out," for example, First National City Bank cited declining labor force participation "of blacks," in particular "the younger segment of the female population."[86] Citing estimates of "'several million' domestic jobs going unfilled," the Southern States Industrial Council and others who relied on cheap female labor rejected welfare reform designed to shore up male breadwinning among the poor.[87]

The FAP was particularly threatening to Southerners dependent on underpaid African American labor. In the South the FAP's $1,600 minimum payment would have far exceeded existing AFDC grants, a serious threat to local labor markets. Richard Armstrong's June 1970 *Fortune* article, "The Looming Money Revolution Down South," could not have eased the fears of Southerner employers. According to Armstrong, the FAP could very well triple welfare rolls in the Deep South, providing cash aid to one in five Southerners. According to an "informal head count" in one Mississippi town, only two of eighteen full-time maids would be required to work under Nixon's proposal (the rest were over sixty-five, living with an adult male, or the mothers of preschool children). By improving living conditions, pressuring wages upward, and reducing black Southerners' economic dependence on whites, the FAP, Armstrong predicted, "could very well make a revolution" with both economic and political dimensions.[88] In a statement endorsed by seven Southern and eleven non-Southern branches, the Council of State Chambers of Commerce pointed to Armstrong's article to warn that the "far-reaching implications of [the FAP's] drastic dislocations of the economy could be serious for the entire country."[89]

Nixon's workfare rhetoric did little to ease the fears of conservatives, who viewed poor single mothers as "An Untapped Source of Manpower," as a Chamber of Commerce brochure put it. They rightly distrusted federal bureaucrats who had for years demonstrated a commitment to male breadwinning.[90] The FAP's opponents insisted that "bleeding heart" liberals in HEW would undermine whatever work requirements Congress might impose.[91] From *U.S. News and World Report* and *Nation's Business* to local newspapers, conservative authors and editors denounced "public officials" for promoting what New York welfare administrator Blanche Bernstein called a "new ambiance" that downplayed the work ethic.[92] It is unlikely that federal officials spent their time "thinking up regulations to demoralize and destroy the work effort in this country," as Senator Long accused.[93] But liberal administrators in HEW, the OEO, and the Department of Labor *had* traditionally emphasized male employment. There is little reason to think they would have run the FAP any differently.

Representing 3,500 trade and professional organizations and 3,000 firms—many of which relied on low-wage employees—the Chamber of Commerce of the United States launched "a massive effort to warn business and community leaders" about this "dangerous new welfare plan."[94] Even before Nixon proposed the FAP, the Chamber had designed a "Communications Campaign on the Guaranteed Income Issue," essentially a declaration of war on the welfare system that would "concentrate on the program of Aid to Families with Dependent Children." The "goal" was to "get as many as possible of the AFDC adults to work" in the private sector and convince local businesses to hire them, both with "inducements"—positive national publicity—and "through fright." The Chamber's "admonition to business should be: 'EITHER HIRE THEM OR GET READY TO PAY FOR A FEDERAL GUARANTEED INCOME PROGRAM'." This campaign suggests the alarm with which the Chamber greeted the guaranteed income concept. It also helps explain some of the "fanfare" surrounding the "business war on poverty."[95]

In contrast, the National Association of Manufacturers (NAM) actually supported the FAP until spring 1972. The NAM position helps to clarify the different visions of family and welfare reform that characterized the FAP debate. NAM's leaders focused first and foremost on work incentives and requirements—unlike the Chamber, NAM bought into Nixon's "workfare rhetoric" and felt sure that the FAP would increase work effort among poor men and women.[96] NAM also accepted the administration's "rationale" for including the working poor: AFDC "encourages the working poor to break up their families," NAM leaders insisted, while the FAP would "keep families together and . . . encourage full participation in the economic and social life of the nation."[97] As the representative of capital-intensive industries often headquartered in urban centers, the NAM was susceptible to warnings about "social decay" in America's cities, a concern evident in its attention during the second half of the 1960s to the problems of crime and "hardcore" unemployment.[98] In recommending support for the FAP, NAM's Government Operations and Expenditures Committee cited an HEW study that emphasized the importance to poor families of both the "presence of a father figure" and "the ability of the father to provide for his family and to fill adequately the role of a father."[99] To the horror of many members, the NAM's national leaders agreed, at least for a time, that the FAP "would encourage self-help . . . keep families together . . . [and become] a central factor in the eventual reduction of dependency."[100] As such, it "appear[ed] to offer the best hope of straightening out the welfare 'mess'."[101]

NAM leaders were not alone among businessmen. A number of liberal business leaders, exemplified by Benjamin Heineman and Joseph Wilson, supported expansive federal income support as a solution to poverty, racial disadvantage, and urban decay. The Committee on Economic Development (CED) study on public welfare called for an even more generous guaranteed income plan than the FAP. No problem is "more pressing," insisted these academics and businessmen, because poverty resulted in "many of our social problems."[102] C. W. Cook, chairman of General Foods Corporation and vice chairman of the CED Subcommittee on Poverty, wrote that a guaranteed income violated the "fundamental beliefs of the business system in which I have spent my entire working life and of the region of the country in which I was reared, the Southwest" and contradicted Cook's "ideals with regard to each individual's responsibilities as a citizen." Nonetheless, his study of the urban crisis—conducted through his work with the CED as well as General Foods' outreach program for disadvantaged high school students—convinced him that the "evils perpetuated by the current welfare system, the crime, the drugs, and the blight of the cities" left the nation with little choice.[103]

The Chamber, in contrast, believed two-parent poor families had little to do with the welfare crisis. Liberals had muddied the waters by addressing the poverty of the "working poor," the Chamber warned in a full-page advertisement in several leading newspapers—the first paid advertisement in the organization's history. The FAP would "hide our real welfare problem—the people on AFDC."[104] That AFDC was "*the* welfare problem" became the Chamber's mantra, eventually repeated by other conservatives including NAM. The "essence of the welfare crisis," the NAM's Arch Bolton reminded readers of *NAM Reports*, is an "explosion of the AFDC caseload with the consequent mushrooming of costs."[105] Given that fact, "no priority should be given to increasing incomes of whole families that are self-supporting and *not* on AFDC."[106] Focus on AFDC, the Chamber urged its members. "This is where the bulk of welfare is located, and it's the only group with manpower potential."[107]

The "only long-range answer to welfare" in the Chamber's view was a campaign to help the AFDC mother "become a regular breadwinner."[108] To make its case, the Chamber cynically coopted an emerging feminist rhetoric of choice and liberation. "There are those who hold that these mothers should be at home with their children," but "rather than impose such a

Figure 6. Mrs. Larry N. Hall, mother of three, learns to use a "tape-teacher" as part of a National Association of Manufacturers job training program in 1966. While federal job training overwhelmingly targeted men, business antipoverty efforts saw employment for women as the best answer to growing welfare rolls. Photo by James Hansen, Courtesy Mrs. Doris Hansen.

decision on them," the Chamber saw it as "quite in keeping with modern times and recent experience to give each of them the freedom to make that decision."[109] In an unusual twist, Chamber spokesman Seymour Wolfbein, dean of the business school at Philadelphia's Temple University, even challenged negative stereotypes about AFDC recipients: "for all we know, there may be someone on our relief rolls now who is going to find a cure for cancer or the common cold or will make the internal combustion engine run better." Wolfbein scolded liberal policymakers who wrote off AFDC mothers as unemployable. Instead, we should view them "constructively, as a manpower potential."[110] Elsewhere business leaders pointed out that 70 percent of AFDC mothers had at least an eighth grade education, making them "trainable now."[111] NAM joined the Chamber in urging lawmakers to give welfare mothers "the opportunity and encouragement to learn a marketable skill."[112]

Business organizations even discussed massive government investment in job training, job placement, and services to accomplish this goal. According to Wolfbein, the Chamber wanted "some assurance of public service employment" and would "go for free child-care because we really mean it now. We are at the fork in the road. We are either going to take this group and make them a manpower resource and part of America, or they are going to go the other way."[113] Senator Long agreed. His Finance Committee proposed an alternative to the FAP, a bill to limit welfare to mothers of preschool children and allocate $4 billion for child care and job creation. As historian Molly Michelmore noted, unlike many antiwelfare conservatives, Long "saw an expansive role for the state in the provision of job training and public works, as well as a massive new childcare infrastructure."[114] By contrast, the Chamber endorsed Oregon representative Al Ullman's timid Rehabilitation, Employment Assistance and Child Care Act of 1971 (HR 6004). Although Arch Booth described the Ullman bill as a "coordinated program of rehabilitation, job training, health and medical services, . . . job placement [and] a national program of child care," it amounted to little more than an expanded WIN Program. It would leave welfare administration with the states and require *all* mothers to participate in training or jobs programs.[115]

In fact, conservative free market ideology largely trumped any desire to help poor single mothers find and keep good jobs. Even as liberals insisted that any work requirements should be accompanied by an assurance that quality child care would be made available to welfare mothers, conservatives like New York welfare administrator Blanche Bernstein thought it not "unreasonable to put some of the responsibility for making arrangements for the care of the children on the mother."[116] A majority of women with school-age children work for wages, Senator Bennett noted. "They solved their day care problem; they don't require the construction of a big day care center with psychiatrists and trained nurses and a hospital-type atmosphere. They just go and work."[117] Despite lip service about expanded government child care and job training, then, both the Chamber and the NAM lobbied vigorously for social spending cuts. By the early 1970s both organizations began to step up their long-standing anti-spending campaigns in response to a changing economic environment. With rising inflation and growing global competition, "there is no money for new programs," the Chamber warned in 1972 as it began a "nationwide campaign" to win federal budget cuts.[118] Business leaders thus combined pronouncements favoring "investment in human beings" with more rigorous demands for "Budget Cuts: Welfare Is Ripe."[119] To antiwelfare conservatives, "*true welfare reform*" was not about creating male breadwinners among poor African Americans but about "reduc[ing] welfare costs and tak[ing] people off the welfare rolls," a program that would preserve an older, exclusive family wage model.[120]

Complaints from conservative Congressional critics and the rising tide of antiwelfare sentiment in local and state politics from New York to California prompted Nixon to rethink his welfare reform proposals. After the Senate Finance Committee killed the first FAP in late 1970, the administration offered a more punitive FAP in H.R. 1.[121] Recipients deemed employable, including mothers with children over age three, would be managed by the DOL, an agency conservatives hoped would be less "soft" on work than the social workers in HEW. The DOL would be empowered to require recipients to take jobs at less than the federal minimum wage with no regard to the job's "suitability." As a coalition of national religious organizations saw it, recipients would "virtually give up their freedom to the Labor Department," which would require mothers to work but give them no say in the adequacy of child care provisions.[122] All recipients, "employable" and "unemployable," would be subject to what liberals denounced as "onerous administrative requirements" such as mandatory biannual reapplication and a variety of behavioral conditions, including mandatory drug rehabilitation and school attendance for children. Recipients would lose "many of the constitutional rights won so recently in the courts," including the right to appeal administrative decisions.[123] Summing up the liberal assessment of this new FAP, Elizabeth Wickenden titled her analysis of the bill "H.R. 1: Welfare Policy as an Instrument of Control."[124]

H.R. 1 was much closer to conservatives' older family wage model than the original bill had been. It denied poor mothers the privilege of stay-at-home motherhood and sought to reinstitute the privatized nuclear family by declaring stepfathers financially responsible for stepchildren and strengthening paternity and child support enforcement. Mothers would be required to cooperate in identifying their children's fathers, and the federal government would gain new power to track down and punish nonsupporting parents.[125] Even the editors of the *Wall Street Journal* liked this new FAP. As an added benefit to antiwelfare conservatives, the plan would help to tear apart the antipoverty coalition in ways that in the long run undermined broad support for expanded federal income support for poor single mothers.

The Liberal Coalition Fractures

[Y]ou will never solve the problems of the poor and the blacks until you recognize that the lower middle class has got problems, too, and as long as society just looks at the poor and the black, not only will you have a schism in American society but you will have the great stresses and strains on the whole body politic. (Senator Abraham Ribicoff, 1970)[126]

The FAP had certainly taken many liberals by surprise. Unable to convince Johnson to go near a guaranteed income, few had dared to hope that Nixon would propose just such a plan. Nixon's sponsorship and the rhetoric he employed to sell the FAP to conservatives provoked suspicion on the left, while the bill's mix of progressive principles and restrictive policies required agonizing choices. The NWRO and a number of liberal and governmental organizations sponsored endless meetings throughout 1970 and 1971 as the antipoverty coalition debated how best to respond.[127] Dubbing themselves the Coalition for Adequate Welfare Reform Now, antipoverty liberals established a general consensus: they supported the bill in principle but demanded revisions to make it more generous, including higher benefits and elimination of the work requirement.[128]

To the antipoverty coalition, the "first objective" of welfare reform "must be to alleviate poverty among all our citizens."[129] This was a matter of humanitarian concern and economic justice; it also reflected a conviction that "the problems of poverty have a direct bearing upon many of our other social problems," as the CED put it in a statement supporting the FAP.[130] The FAP's basic yearly benefit of $1,600 for a family of four fell far below the already miserly federal poverty line of $4,000 in 1970 and even farther below the nearly $7,000 Lower Standard Budget that the Bureau of Labor Statistics (BLS) calculated for an urban family of four.[131] The newly covered "working poor" would benefit from any supplements, of course. But, though a "vast improvement" for the 18 percent of AFDC recipients in the South, the $1,600 would leave most AFDC recipients with lower benefits unless state legislatures decided to supplement the federal minimum, an unlikely development. With its rallying cry of "$6,500 or Fight," the NWRO led the charge for the BLS standard—a goal supported in principle by the Democratic Study Group, delegates to the White House Conference on Food, Nutrition, and Health, and the Congressional Black Caucus. Alternative guaranteed income plans from the left called for a higher basic benefit, from Congressman Fred Harris's National Basic Income and Incentive Act, which proposed to raise benefits to poverty level in gradual increments, to the NWRO's Adequate Income Act, which started benefits at $6,500.[132]

Throughout the 91st Congress, the NWRO and liberal reformers worked in uneasy partnership, denouncing the bill's shortcomings while pursuing liberalizing amendments through lobbying and negotiation. When Representatives John Byrnes and Wilbur Mills introduced H.R. 1, the coalition fractured. The left, from mainstream to radical, unanimously rejected the bill's "punitive, coercive character," but ultimately disagreed over how to respond.[133] The NWRO had opposed even the first, less restrictive FAP, though its leaders had worked quietly behind the scenes in hopes of improving the bill. Along with Nixon's increasingly punitive "workfare" rhetoric, H.R. 1 convinced welfare rights activists that the administration's "true intent" was surely to punish the poor.[134] Insisting that even liberal amendments could not eliminate the bill's dangers for poor single mothers, Wiley and the NWRO recipient leaders launched a reinvigorated "Zap FAP" campaign.[135] The YWCA, National Urban League, Child Welfare League, and a variety of other social work and religious organizations joined them, committing the Campaign for Adequate Welfare Reform Now to a "campaign to defeat H.R. 1 in the House." The LWV, AFL-CIO, UAW, Common Cause, and a variety of other civic and government groups then withdrew from the Campaign and pledged to support H.R. 1 in the House.[136] These "compromisers" hoped that Congress would eliminate the bill's worst restrictions by adopting Senator Abraham Ribicoff's numerous liberalizing amendments, and they remained committed to establishing the principle of a federally guaranteed income.[137]

Many liberals attributed the NWRO's uncompromising stance to the organization's political naiveté. But welfare mothers had good reasons to oppose H.R. 1. Approximately 90 percent of AFDC recipients stood to lose financially under the plan, while all recipients would face new restrictions and regulations. For decades, AFDC recipients had been at the mercy of local welfare administrators, who periodically purged rolls to save money and root out suspected fraud. Poverty lawyers and welfare rights activists had confronted this arbitrary power in the 1960s, and in a series of lawsuits, they finally established a recipient's right to a fair hearing and appeals process before her family's benefits could be cut or terminated. This change brought significant material benefits to thousands of welfare families and came as close as the nation had ever come to establishing a statutory right to welfare.[138] By explicitly denying recipients the right of appeal and by limiting judicial review of administrative decisions, H.R. 1 threatened to "seriously undercut" these "hard-won rights."[139] Mothers with children over three could be placed in jobs at less than minimum wage with no say as to the adequacy of child care arrangements, and they would lack the procedural means to challenge administrative decisions.

While these requirements and restrictions would affect recipients of all colors, the NWRO often framed its opposition in racial terms. This should come as no surprise; welfare policies had long been used to help maintain racial hierarchy in communities throughout the nation, particularly in the South and Southwest. While welfare provided much-needed income to some of the country's poorest Americans, who were disproportionately nonwhite, a number of official reports and testimony by the late 1960s clearly implicated welfare administrators in a system of racial control. Southern welfare officials punished African Americans who participated in civil rights activism; "suitable home" provisions targeted nonwhite women with "illegitimate" children; and "employable mother" rules cut black and Latina women off AFDC when local farmers needed cheap agricultural labor.[140] Given the NWRO's overwhelmingly nonwhite membership and the increasing salience of black identity in civil rights circles by the early 1970s, too, a racial analysis made sense. Welfare rights activists described the FAP as "anti-black," a "flagrant example of institutionalized racism."[141] Wiley, who had recently adopted an Afro hairstyle and an African dashiki, called the welfare system "one of the major instruments by which black people are kept in a position of second-class citizenship." Indeed, he ar-

Figure 7. NWRO executive director George Wiley rallies welfare rights activists in the early 1970s. Compare Wiley's hairstyle and clothing to his appearance at the 1968 Mothers' Day March in Figure 1. Courtesy Wisconsin Historical Society (WHS Image ID 10937).

gued, "one can really only understand mid-twentieth century racism if one understands the welfare system—understands how the welfare system keeps black people poor."[142] AFDC mothers and their radical and liberal allies were convinced that the FAP behavioral requirements were aimed primarily at nonwhites and that its work requirement was "designed to increase the supply of cheap [mainly nonwhite] labor for household work, for farm work, [and] for hospital work."[143] In response to Nixon's paeans to the dignity of wage labor, Wiley (a former chemistry professor who grew up decidedly middle-class) insisted that "all of us who are black have known menial stoop labor, and we know exactly what racists like President Nixon have in mind when they talk about the dignity of work, any job at any wage, be it scrubbing floors, emptying bedpans, or cleaning Miss Anne's kitchen."[144]

A racial analysis not only acknowledged the welfare system's discriminatory history; it also garnered the NWRO powerful allies. Given welfare's virtual invisibility on the national civil rights agenda, Wiley's expertise put him in a good position to influence other black leaders, and he convinced the civil rights establishment to oppose H.R. 1. Aside from attacking AFDC for breaking up black families, the major civil rights organizations had not shown any deep or sustained interest in welfare politics during the 1960s.[145] Mainstream civil rights leaders were typically committed to the male-breadwinner family model as a hallmark of respectability, and they assiduously avoided drawing attention to a politically despised program that highlighted the supposed pathology of urban black families.[146] African American organizations and leaders who wanted to respond to the FAP therefore turned to the NWRO, and Wiley in particular, for analysis and advice. While all thirteen Congressional Black Caucus (CBC) members voted in favor of the first version of the FAP in April 1970, all but one opposed H.R. 1 the following year. The shift reflects the more punitive character of the bill but also NWRO influence. After all, Caucus members hailed from urban areas outside the South, where the FAP would reduce AFDC grants and where welfare rights organizing was strongest. The NWRO staff worked hard to cultivate relationships with Caucus members, even convincing Representative John Conyers of Detroit to speak at the NWRO's 1969 convention.[147] As the FAP debate heated up, Wiley stepped up his efforts to make black lawmakers allies of organized welfare recipients. In a letter to Michigan's Charles Diggs, Wiley urged the CBC to "spearhead [the] fight" and "rally the black community" against the bill. Caucus members met with Wiley at least once and requested material and advice from him on more than one occasion. They even asked Wiley to draft the Caucus's position on H.R. 1.[148] When Caucus members and other black leaders denounced H.R. 1 as "a vicious attack on five million Black women and children," then, they were literally speaking the NWRO's language.[149]

Wiley encouraged this kind of racial analysis. He targeted the bill's differential treatment of the adult and family categories, for example, as a racially motivated distinction. H.R. 1 provided higher benefits and fewer bureaucratic hurdles for recipients in the "adult" categories—the aged, blind, and disabled—than for recipients in the "family" categories, which included both single-parent and two-parent families. This was nothing new; policymakers had traditionally been more generous to the elderly and infirm than to able-bodied adults. But able-bodied adult recipients were much more likely to be nonwhite, prompting the NWRO and its allies to denounce the distinction as "discrimination against poor, Black families."[150] And while the program's beefed-up foster care and adoptive services and its behavioral and work requirements applied to all parent recipients, Conyers warned that "poor families and Black families will be torn apart" and forced into a "twentieth century version of slavery." To Conyers, each potentially harmful provision in the bill was "aimed at a Black population."[151] Many white NWRO allies agreed with this interpretation. "Before long," complained Moynihan in mid-1971, "one was hearing middle-class ladies in lecture halls decry the 'slave labor' provision of the bill."[152]

Charges of racism prompted an understandable defensiveness from liberals who disagreed with the NWRO's uncompromising opposition. Several social welfare organizations (the National Association of Social Workers [NASW] and the American Public Welfare Association [APWA], for example), government groups (the League of Cities and the U.S. Conference of Mayors), labor organizations (the AFL-CIO and the UAW), and civic associations (Common Cause, the Center for Community Change, the American Jewish Committee, and the LWV) decided to support H.R. 1 in the House and to seek amendments to ameliorate its most punitive aspects. As predominantly middle-class, white organizations, they saw themselves as "out to hold the middle ground for reform against the extremists to the right and left of us who will join together in an unholy alliance to defeat" the FAP. Many of these groups expressed sympathy with the NWRO position: "Make no mistake about this," insisted a League official. "We *do care* about welfare mothers and their children or we wouldn't be in this fight." But, she continued, "we also have a different perspective on H.R. 1 from NWRO."[153]

Compromisers like the League's national officers complained that the NWRO's "militant posturing"—exhibited in meetings where people "literally shouted at each other"—doomed any chance for "progressive legislation."[154] When a majority of participants at an October 1971 meeting voted to support passage of H.R. 1 in the House, for example, "several NWRO delegates disrupted the meeting for about 15 minutes harassing everyone who tried to speak and accusing those who supported less than the NWRO stand of being immoral."[155] Just as the NWRO had good reasons for opposing H.R. 1, compromisers made some convincing arguments for their position. Despite the "punitive, coercive character" of the bill, reminded the *New Republic's* editors, "state governments have already started to cut back on welfare rates."[156] Recipients in high benefit states would soon see their grants reduced with or without FAP, they argued. The bill would at least provide an income floor, and the "principle of a federally guaranteed minimum income" would provide a basis for future increases.[157] Lobbying Congress for grant increases would certainly be easier than approaching lawmakers in fifty different states. And defeating the bill would deny significant income to the poorest recipients in the South.

Liberals who sought compromise resented the NWRO's criticism. Their organizations had devoted significant resources to defending welfare recipients and fighting for more generous income support. According to League president Lucy Benson, "Mr. Wiley seems to feel the need to get up at a meeting, point his finger at one of the many solid people in this coalition, and shriek, 'You don't care about poor children'."[158] As a longtime League activist from Massachusetts, a founder of the National Urban Coalition, and a member of the U.S. Commission on Civil Rights, Benson was a committed liberal, a well-educated middle-class white woman who had devoted much of her adult life to progressive reform. Little wonder she resented attacks on her motives.[159] An American Jewish Committee (AJC) leader, too, complained: "I don't like to be accused of supporting racist legislation because we disagree on its value."[160] Yet an essay by a leader of the Child Welfare League titled "In Defense of the Liberals and Their Modest Proposal, H.R. 1" hinted at some of the underlying politics involved in the liberal coalition's rupture, politics that went well beyond "disruptive tactics" and strategic decisions. "At bottom," the author insisted, "the best persons and groups to arrange such legislation *for welfare recipients* are involved in the effort," and "practical people will allow the liberal coalition to do its work." In other words, the "honorable people and honorable groups" who supported compromise were the appropriate lobbyists for the poor, far more qualified to make policy decisions than the "far left and radical groups and individuals" associated with the NWRO.[161]

Little wonder that recipient activists and their allies bristled. A key tenet of welfare rights was empowerment: recipients demanded input into the decisions and policies affecting their lives, and as poor, mostly nonwhite single mothers with extensive experience as recipients of government aid, they claimed expertise in such matters. NWRO policy ensured that middle-class "Friends" of welfare remained in a supportive role, and by the late 1960s welfare mothers began challenging the organization's largely male, predominantly white paid staff, demanding that recipients themselves control the direction of the movement.[162] "What gives us the right," asked one white, middle-class NWRO supporter, "to contend that [the bill] is 'good enough for poor people'?" In the late 1960s, many poor people were asking the same question.[163]

Those who worked closely with welfare recipients understood this. The NWRO's staunchest allies in the FAP fight were those organizations and individuals who worked alongside recipients. A number of liberals with significant experience administering the welfare program (Arthur Altmeyer and Eveline Burns, who helped design the Social Security Act in the 1930s; Alvin Schorr and Elizabeth Wickenden, who helped shepherd AFDC through the 1950s and 1960s) agreed with recipient activists that the FAP would prove more damaging than constructive.[164] But the bill's most vociferous and vocal opponents on the left were closer to the grassroots. The Child Welfare League of America, the Family Service Association of America, and the National Federation of Settlements (NFS) were all social service organizations whose members and leaders worked closely with poor families. Public social workers certainly had their own concerns about H.R. 1: by federalizing welfare administration, the bill potentially threatened their jobs and tenure. But they also identified with the needs of recipients.[165] After much debate, organizations like NASW decided they could not "go on record as at any time favoring a bill which so grossly jeopardized the lives and rights of poor people."[166] Religious organizations, too, often identified closely with recipients. Churches provided much of the NWRO's funding and encouraged their flocks to become friends and advocates of welfare recipients in their communities, and women's religious organizations in particular, from the YWCA to the NCJW, had interacted closely with AFDC recipients through their antipoverty activity since the mid-1960s. Closely connected to organized welfare recipients, these liberals were more likely than others to support the NWRO position.

The NWRO outreach to middle-class organizations paid off during the FAP debate, as several of those organizations refused to defy the wishes of recipient activists. The Women's Division of the United Methodist Church provides a useful illustration. Wiley spoke to the organization in September 1968, prompting the group to arrange a three-day meeting between the organizations' leaders. "Since that meeting," noted Mrs. Wayne Harrington, "welfare rights has become a priority concern for the Women's Division." Harrington referred to NWRO as "our consultant and 'sister organization'." The groups attended each others' conferences, and, like the NCJW's Schools for Community Action described in Chapter 1, the Women's Division invited NWRO representatives to "conference schools" in order to challenge its middle-class members' stereotypes about welfare and poverty. "The strength of our commitment to *meaningful* welfare reform and a concomitant change in national priorities has been immeasurably strengthened by our working relationship with the [NWRO]," Harrington assured Congress. "We have felt very fortunate to be able to work closely with these women and consider whatever help we've been able to give . . . small recompense for the awareness about poverty they have brought to us."[167]

Similar relationships prompted many LWV members to protest the League's decision to support H.R. 1. Writing from across the country, local Leaguers cited their "credibility" as a "trustworthy ally" to poor women as a reason to challenge or even break with national policy.[168] Of course, the League did not make its decision on the FAP lightly. The organization was a leader in welfare issues by 1971: that year it made welfare reform its primary legislative goal and appointed a Welfare Strategy Committee as well as a full-time staff member and a twelve-member lobbying corps.[169] In the process of antipoverty and welfare rights work during the previous decade, one national officer recognized, "many leagues drew in welfare recipients, poor people, and members of the NWRO."[170] As a result, Leaguers like Helen Patterson of Rochester, New York, worried that the decision to support H.R. 1 put them "in a very awkward position as well as seriously damaging our credibility with the other groups which represent the poor or work on their behalf."[171] In a letter to delegates at the organization's 1972 convention, Maya Miller, who worked closely with Nevada welfare rights activists, insisted that "Congress and the country need to hear loud and clear from the League and other liberal organizations . . . that they are standing by poor people at this time of crisis for them."[172]

As Miller's language suggests, the NWRO became, in many respects, *the* voice of poor people during the FAP debate. In part because the Nixon administration and Congressional leaders sold the FAP as a *welfare reform* measure rather than a broader antipoverty program, welfare recipients' opinions mattered on the political left. This, in fact, was one of the welfare rights movement's most significant achievements. Among activists who increasingly valued personal experience as a basis of authority, organized welfare recipients gained unprecedented credibility, not least because they claimed it. Individuals and organizations who opposed compromise on H.R. 1 frequently cited "the position of the National Welfare Rights Organization" as the deciding factor. Being "in direct conflict" with welfare rights groups was not a comfortable position for many white liberals. "We felt [the NWRO] material was most representative of the feelings of welfare recipients," argued one social worker, "who would naturally be most affected by this legislation."[173]

Of course, other constituencies would be affected by the FAP. Were the plan administered fairly, the Southern poor—both two-parent and single-parent families—stood to gain significantly. "Liberals and moderates who dismiss the Family Assistance Plan because it fails to do enough for the poor of the urban North," warned one supporter, "run the proverbial risk of throwing out the baby with the bath."[174] Indeed, the NWRO position reflected the interests of the organization's predominantly non-Southern members. From its beginnings the FAP was a plan to address an urban crisis—that is, black poverty in Northern and Western industrial cities. The plan had emerged from Nixon's Urban Affairs Council, and supporters repeatedly portrayed it as a solution to the "illness of American cities," a way to solve the "evils perpetuated by the current welfare system, the crime, the drugs, and the blight of the cities."[175] Poor Southern blacks remained on the periphery of the FAP debate, and they certainly did not form a vocal constituency.[176]

Nor did the "working poor" as a whole—a group *Time* magazine described as "intact families, headed by males."[177] Unlike AFDC mothers, this ill-defined group was not organized as such, a tremendous liability in a political system in which lobbying, Congressional testimony, and a public presence can translate to influence. The most likely spokesman for poor male workers, organized labor, remained ambivalent about the FAP. Since World War II, collective bargaining, strong economic growth, and generous veterans' benefits bought much of the pre-New Deal white working class a "middle-class lifestyle." Though that bargain was on verge of eclipse by 1970, the 1960s was not the 1930s, when the industrial union model encouraged better-off workers to link their fate to more marginalized laborers at the bottom of the economic structure. Moreover, the post-World War II assault on organized labor, which culminated in the Taft-Hartley Act of 1947, narrowed labor's power to affect social democratic change and encouraged an interest-group approach to politics among union leadership.[178] Unlikely to benefit personally from the FAP and increasingly hostile to government social programs that seemed to favor the poor and minorities at the expense of the white working class, most white union members evinced little enthusiasm for the $4 billion "welfare reform" plan.

Union leaders had their own reasons to distrust the plan. Though the AFL-CIO and the UAW attended antipoverty meetings and signed coalition statements, they were hardly leaders in the FAP campaign.[179] "Labor would join in some coalition efforts," complained Moynihan in his postmortem of the first FAP battle, "but on balance it stood apart, looking to what it perceived to be its own interests."[180] Even Walter Reuther's UAW, at the forefront of antipoverty activism during the 1960s, remained largely on the sidelines, protesting specific aspects of the bill but failing to take a leadership role. The AFL-CIO, for its part, supported the "principle embodied in FAP" and signed onto liberal demands for a more generous, less restrictive welfare system. At the same time, labor leaders recognized in the FAP significant dangers for their own constituency. Work requirements that failed to ensure "suitable work" and wage protections could undermine wage rates, especially if the requirements applied to male as well as female recipients.[181] As taxpayers, too, union members might lose. To many unionists, Nixon's plan to use federal dollars to supplement low earnings amounted to the "taxpayer support[ing] those employers who pay sub-standard wages."[182] Conservative opponents of the FAP appealed to workers' identity as taxpayers explicitly, as in an American Conservative Union pamphlet, "The Family Assistance Plan: A Guaranteed Annual Income—What It Means to YOU as a Taxpayer."[183]

When it came down to it, union leaders expressed fundamental resistance to including male breadwinner families in any kind of "welfare" program. Even as a broad coalition of liberals achieved "considerable consensus" on the need for a guaranteed income in 1969, the AFL-CIO Executive Council warned that "no one program can wipe out poverty."[184] The Council certainly supported a more generous public assistance program for those "who cannot work or cannot be expected to work," namely "mothers and children in fatherless families." But for the "working poor"—the "breadwinner who works full-time all year"—it insisted that the "road out of poverty lies in decent jobs covered by a [higher] minimum wage."[185] The AFL-CIO's Bert Seidman provided a very practical reason for keeping able-bodied men out of any welfare-type program: by making "the 'work ethic' . . . irrelevant to welfare," a more limited program could be a more generous program. Of course, Seidman assumed a cultural consensus that poor single mothers "should not be expected or even encouraged—and certainly not be required—to work," an assumption hardly sustainable given the 1967 welfare amendments, the conservative criticisms of FAP, and much of the public rhetoric surrounding welfare. Yet Seidman's argument reflected a position widely held among union leadership.[186]

Union leaders also joined welfare rights activists and their allies in religious and women's organizations in a vigorous defense of poor women's mothering. Liberals rarely protested work requirements for male recipients. Instead, across the board, their complaints targeted maternal requirements. Forcing mothers to work outside the home, they argued, "demeans this worthy full-time occupation [motherhood]."[187] Welfare rights activists articulated the most strenuous defense of poor nonwhite women's mothering.[188] "Most welfare mothers are needed full-time by their own families," the NWRO asserted, and "it's at least paradoxical, perhaps cruel, that a society which traditionally extols the virtues of motherhood is simultaneously forcing some mothers to leave their homes and children for low-wage, dead-end, outside jobs."[189] Employing a model of motherhood-as-service that reached back to maternalist reformers of the Progressive Era, the NWRO compared AFDC recipients—the "MOTHER CORPS"—to members of the Peace Corps. Welfare mothers had "been employed by your Federal, State, and Local governments to see to it that 3½ million children [are] raised to be strong, healthy, active, productive, responsible citizens of this society." The problem these citizen-mothers faced was simply "a very bad contract."[190]

Traditional women's organizations like the YWCA and the LWV echoed the NWRO position. Members of these groups fiercely defended the value of poor women's mothering. The YWCA cited H.R. 1's maternal work requirement, which "downgrades the important role and the hard work of being a mother," as a primary reason to oppose the bill.[191] Likewise, however much the League's leaders insisted that "our position on [the work requirement] *has* to be flexible for political reasons," members from around the country singled out the work requirement as "particularly appall[ing]" and a key reason to oppose compromise.[192] In letter after letter, League members asserted the value of stay-at-home motherhood and denounced society's hypocritical dismissal of poor women's mothering. Typical of dissenting locals, Nevada Leaguers insisted that national leaders "explain what is the work league ladies are willing to demand welfare mothers do while they are forced to leave their children? Is it to clean your house and do your laundry at $1.20 an hour during the day, so that they must clean their houses and do their children's laundry after work?"[193] The bill's work requirement, complained the United Methodist Church Women's Division, "reflects a widespread prejudice which implies that being a housewife is a sufficient full-time occupation only for middle class women," a position many activist liberal women rejected.[194]

If the work requirement denied the value of poor women's mothering, it also promised harassment, exploitation, and continued poverty, a crucial reason for the NWRO "highly emotional, often hyperbolic campaign" against H.R. 1 and its supposedly "shrill" complaints about "the 'slave labor' provisions of the bill."[195] As I noted in Chapter 1, decades of experience and numerous official reports demonstrated that welfare-related work programs typically "invite abuse, discriminatory treatment, and threats of reprisals against those who would assert their rights," and almost never led to "economic independence and self-sufficiency," according to the United States Commission on Civil Rights.[196] Analysts at the Center for Social Welfare Policy and Law (CSWP&L) and the Urban Coalition cited a history of widespread discrimination, racism, and collusion with employers on the part of local officials, who would be given "extensive discretion" in administering the FAP's work requirement.[197] With "virtually no standards" for suitable work, H.R. 1 could well require AFDC recipients in Mississippi to do domestic service for four dollars a day or agricultural or mill work for sixty-five cents an hour.[198] One African American single mother spoke for thousands of others when she described her experience in an OEO work training program in Gary, Indiana. "They don't give you courses with any dignity," she complained. "The courses they give you on welfare are things that Negro people have done all the time—cooking, housekeeping, washing, and things of that sort."[199] Since the bill gave mothers no input as to child care arrangements, no benefits for educational activities, and no promise of training for jobs that would pay above poverty wages, recipients' complaints about "dead-end jobs" and "slave labor" could be viewed as realistic rather than hysterical. While welfare rights activists defended black women's mothering, other antipoverty coalition members worried that maternal work requirements would only perpetuate the "culture of poverty." "In these days of rising juvenile delinquency and increasing drug addiction among the young," warned UAW president Leonard Woodcock, "parental guidance in the home is essential."[200] More than other children, AFDC children "need parental supervision and care when they are out of school," agreed the AFL-CIO Executive Council.[201]

While labor leaders hoped that mothers' presence in inner-city homes would help socialize a supposedly pathological population, other liberals like Joseph Wilson were beginning to argue that mothers' *employment* could play the same role. Like most liberals, this corporate leader insisted that "due attention . . . be paid to the mother's own judgment of where she is needed most." At the same time, Wilson characterized AFDC mothers as "a major social problem having grave consequences in terms of neglected and deprived children, who are locked into a despairing cycle of dependency and poverty." This cycle "can be broken," Wilson assured Congress, "if mothers receiving welfare are provided with the opportunity to undertake job training and to move into the labor force at decent wages that will augment the family income."²⁰² Welfare rights activists, the National Association for the Advancement of Colored People (NAACP), the Leadership Conference on Civil Rights (LCCR), and most other antipoverty liberal organizations joined Wilson in calling for better job training, job creation, and child care facilities. However, Wilson went further, expressing what would become liberal consensus by the 1980s: that in the absence of male breadwinners, welfare mothers could best teach their children the "work ethic" by participating in the labor market.²⁰³

Some welfare mothers also supported employment programs. While the NWRO's male leadership continued to demand jobs for men, recipient activists also demanded job training as an avenue toward economic independence. In an article titled "Welfare is a Women's Issue," one NWRO activist denounced H.R. 1 for "multiply[ing] the inequities of current welfare law in its treatment of women." Not only did the FAP deny women an adequate income, but it also denied them "the right to earn . . . by getting effective training for meaningful jobs and quality developmental day care."²⁰⁴ Las Vegas recipient activists continually demanded training and jobs, even as some national welfare rights leaders defended stay-at-home motherhood. As Premilla Nadasen has argued, recipient activists articulated a unique brand of feminism, one that emphasized a woman's right to self-determination and to an income—whether from the state or an employer—that enabled her to avoid dependence on male support. By 1973, when recipient leaders took full control of the NWRO, the organization adopted a full-fledged feminist identity, though one that did not always fit comfortably with other brands of second-wave feminism flourishing at the same time.²⁰⁵

A handful of self-defined feminists in NOW offered a somewhat different feminist critique of the FAP and of the liberal coalition's foundational family wage ideal. Though consistently frustrated with the lack of interest in poverty issues among NOW's leaders and members, Merrillee Dolan found a handful of allies in that organization, mostly women with experience in other economic justice campaigns—women like Dorothy Haener of the UAW and Lynn Tabb of the United Farm Workers. In Albuquerque, Dolan forged coalitions among welfare rights activists and NOW members, an experience repeated by other activists in other cities.²⁰⁶ On a national level, Dolan and her allies published reports analyzing women's poverty, exhorted members to become welfare rights supporters, and pushed their organization to take a stand against the FAP.²⁰⁷

Dolan applied an emerging feminist critique to liberal assumptions.

While most responses to the Moynihan Report had questioned its racial politics or condemned its implicit criticism of black women, Dolan retroactively blasted its defense of patriarchy. Moynihan and his fellow liberals, she wrote in 1971, worked on the "assumption . . . that women should be forced into family relationships, and this can be accomplished if they must find a man in order to obtain economic support."[208] In numerous forums, Dolan questioned the liberal conviction that "the ultimate answer to the welfare mess is to marry off adult female recipients," an ideology she saw as fundamental to the FAP.[209] Though she blasted the plan for forcing mothers into a low-wage labor market, Dolan's critique ran deeper. "Preservation of the [male-breadwinner] family is not the business of government," she insisted, but the FAP was "based on the concept of getting the female back into her role as wife and mother, dependent upon the male '*head* of household'."[210] Dolan's preferred solution to women's poverty—a generous guaranteed income with work incentives, adequate affordable child care, and full employment with vigorous antidiscrimination enforcement—aimed instead to make women "economically independent."[211] Dolan's argument made little headway at the time, either within her own organization or in the larger political debate. For the political left as a whole, the creation and maintenance of male-breadwinner families remained in the early 1970s a legitimate goal of federal welfare policy.

Given that goal, many liberals tried to steer the country's attention *away* from the plight of poor single mothers, emphasizing the FAP's potential to help two-parent "working poor" families, the bill's "most singular accomplishment."[212] Liberals who focused on the urban crisis were most likely to express the conviction that the FAP would "tend to keep families together" by allowing the father to "maintain his virility," as one state welfare administrator put it.[213] "How discouraging [fathers' exclusion from welfare] must be for these working men desperately trying to hold their families together," insisted the Urban Coalition Action Council (which had recently changed its name to Common Cause). New York Mayor John Lindsay, a liberal desperately seeking ways to cut his own city's welfare bill, called aid to "the family headed by a [working] man" the "heart" of the FAP, something worth compromising for.[214]

The NWRO accused compromisers of "desert[ing] . . . welfare mothers," but LWV president Lucy Benson insisted that her organization had a "much broader constituency" than NWRO members, "both as to our members and to the overall public interest."[215] Benson's position typified her coalition's attitude, born not simply of frustration with the NWRO's tactics but also from a conviction that the FAP could ease social disorder, antiwelfare resentment, and dangerous racial polarization. Liberal compromisers denounced organized welfare recipients for their selfishness, thereby reinforcing the rhetorical split between welfare mothers and the "working poor" and embarking, perhaps unwittingly, on discourse that would soon be used to label welfare recipients a "special interest" undeserving of government support.[216] Reflecting on the painful compromises at hand, Benson lamented, "We may have to oppose the kind of welfare reform proposals this Congress is willing to accept," which indeed occurred when liberalizing amendments failed to materialize. "But we shall certainly not do so," she continued, "without full recognition that in doing so we shall be depriving millions of working people (and about 6 million recipients) of the first opportunity they might have had to have an income above the poverty level." After years of working in and for antipoverty programs, forging relationships with recipient activists, and searching their own souls for evidence of racial and class bias, such choices seemed untenable. It was "not an easy choice for a predominantly white, middle-class group to make."[217]

The dilemma was real, and liberals were not alone in their struggle to decipher Nixon's welfare reform proposal. The FAP was a guaranteed income plan proposed by a Republican who otherwise spoke the language of antiwelfare conservatives, a plan that incorporated two contradictory family wage ideals. The antipoverty coalition sought to extend the privileges of male breadwinning and female homemaking to poor African Americans—to include this group at long last in the middle- and working-class "mainstream." Coalition members in the Nixon administration convinced the president to propose a guaranteed income with this goal in mind: If AFDC broke up families, the FAP would keep them together, largely by providing income to male breadwinners. By redistributing the benefits of the welfare system toward the two-parent "working poor," liberals hoped to encourage poor black men to stay with their wives and children *and* to "reduce the bitterness which some of the working poor feel toward those on relief."[218]

Nixon also supported the "traditional" male-breadwinner family, the "keystone of our civilization." He vetoed the Comprehensive Child Development Bill in 1971, rejecting Congressional efforts to "commit the vast moral authority of the National Government to the side of communal approaches to child rearing over against the family-centered approach."[219] But to Nixon, and to the FAP's conservative opponents, that traditional family was a privilege. Only men who valued hard work enough to find steady employment (and the women who married them) deserved to be included. This older family wage ideal excluded others—predominantly nonwhites with supposedly perverse lower-class values—and dictated a much different kind of welfare reform. As subsequent chapters will explain, these two visions clashed at a time when fewer and fewer families looked "traditional."

By 1973, conservatives' family wage model had won the FAP debate. In September 1972, Ways and Means chairman Wilbur Mills declared welfare reform "dead as a doornail."[220] Congressman Abraham Ribicoff, a liberal Democrat who struggled to secure a less punitive, more generous FAP, tutored the Senate Finance Committee: "You will never solve the problems of the poor and the blacks," he insisted, "until you recognize that the lower middle class has got problems, too," and "as long as society just looks at the poor and the black, not only will you have a schism in American society but you will have the great stresses and strains on the whole body politic."[221] In the wake of the battle over the FAP, liberals and radicals sought new strategies to combat poverty and racial inequality and new ways to sidestep the liabilities of race and family structure that helped to sink the hope for a guaranteed income. Other liberals would take their critique of AFDC—particularly their complaint that it broke up families—and join a conservative campaign to condemn federal social welfare programs for fostering a pathological ghetto subculture. The 1970s would become a key turning point in American ideas about welfare and economic justice, and family remained central to those debates.

Chapter 3

Building a New Majority: Welfare and Economic Justice in the 1970s

As we are beginning to work on the "new" issues of economic justice—on taxes, utility rates, neighborhood preservation, etc. and with "new" constituencies—the working poor, ethnic Americans, the newly awakened middle American . . .—welfare recipients and welfare as an issue are not popular. It seems safer to steer clear of welfare.

—Tim Sampson, 1974

During the 1970s, from her post at the National Social Welfare Assembly (NSWA), Elizabeth Wickenden waged a valiant campaign to keep antipoverty liberals informed about political action on welfare. Her "Washington Notes" newsletters tell a story of social services under fire and an embattled AFDC program. During the Nixon and Ford administrations, Congress and federal welfare administrators implemented many of the same restrictive features that had so offended welfare rights activists during the FAP campaign. HEW tightened eligibility requirements and limited recipients' access to fair hearings, states found numerous ways to restrict eligibility, Congress tightened work requirements, and federal administrators gave states increasing leeway to implement "workfare" programs, in which recipients "earned" their grants by performing unpaid community-service jobs.[1] At the NCSW annual forum in 1973, President Mary R. Ripley addressed welfare's growing vulnerability. "Perhaps it is hard to think of celebrating at a time when . . . the very programs and philosophy that have been our cornerstone are threatened," she noted, and "when humanitarian concerns seem to be out of style with some who hold influential positions in this, our great country."[2] Ripley captured a mood that rippled through the social welfare community, whose meetings in the mid-1970s were characterized by "gloomy reports . . . from all over the country," a belief that "the gains attained in the 1960s are eroding," and a sense that "little, if anything, can be done . . . to stop the downward, backward slide."[3]

Local welfare activists, too, found little to celebrate. The NWRO slowly petered out after 1972, and financial straits forced it to close its doors officially in 1975. Most historical accounts of the welfare rights movement end there, but grassroots welfare rights activism continued. In Georgia, Frances Freeborn Pauley, who had worked throughout the 1950s and 1960s on civil rights with the LWV and the Human Rights Council, founded the Georgia Poverty Rights Organization in the early 1970s. Pauley and her allies encouraged the development of welfare rights groups throughout the state and led a coalition that fought (unsuccessfully) to expand welfare benefits.[4] In Las Vegas, Nevada, a similar struggle met with more success. There, NWRO leader Ruby Duncan led a coalition of poor single mothers and middle-class allies to fight restrictive policies and pressure the legislature to bring food stamps, free school lunches, the Women, Infants, and Children nutrition program, and free child medical screenings to the state.[5] Meanwhile, activist Marie Ratagick organized welfare and food stamp recipients across Mississippi in 1973 and 1974, while the People's Rights Organization-Wisconsin, with support from the LWV, NOW, and tenant unions, successfully blocked state welfare cuts in 1974.[6] These stories are likely the tip of the iceberg, representing only a handful of what historian Annelise Orleck estimates are "scores of untold stories about America's antipoverty crusade of the 1960s and 1970s."[7] Still, after 1970 AFDC rolls leveled off and benefits eroded across the country.[8]

As AFDC recipients lost ground, many wage-earning Americans gained new access to federal income support during the 1970s. Congress consistently rebuffed broad measures to increase the earning power of low-wage workers, rejecting substantial minimum wage increases, national health insurance, and large-scale public service employment. But it did adopt compensatory programs to help some wage earners survive in a decade of high inflation, high unemployment, and declining job security. In 1975, Congress initiated the Earned Income Tax Credit (EITC), a kind of Negative Income Tax for poor wage earners with children, considered by many antipoverty liberals to be "the political success story" of the decade.[9] While the EITC did nothing for families without an employed adult, it did bolster the income of poor wage-earning breadwinners. "Working poor" families also benefited from an expanded Food Stamp Program and from a temporary expansion of Unemployment Insurance.[10] And even as it rejected the FAP, Congress provided additional protection for the aged, blind, and disabled. The new Supplemental Security Income (SSI) program gave these recipients the same federal funding, federal administration, and automatic cost-of-living adjustments afforded recipients of OASDI, or "Social Security." The creation of SSI left AFDC alone as a joint federal-state public assistance program. The federal government's social welfare bill continued to rise during the 1970s, then, but most of the funds went to non-poor Americans, and an increasing amount also helped low-earning breadwinners. AFDC recipients found themselves increasingly isolated and disadvantaged.

This shift was the result of political choices. Antipoverty liberals felt frustrated and exhausted in the aftermath of the disastrous and divisive battle over welfare reform by 1972, but their decision to abandon AFDC was a strategic one. In the midst of widespread political and public attention to the so-called "blue-collar backlash," AFDC seemed a liability. Its recipients flouted the male-breadwinner family system so central to the value system of working-class voters (and of liberal reformers themselves). The program's association with broken families, then, as much as its association with African Americans, erased it from the liberal agenda as the antipoverty coalition tried to construct a new progressive majority by articulating a vision of economic justice that fit comfortably with deeply held feelings about proper family and work behavior. The major liberal campaign of the 1970s, the push for federal full employment legislation, reveals how central the male-breadwinner family model remained to liberal policymaking. At the same time, feminist reaction suggests how much that model was eroding by the late 1970s and how that erosion would undermine the antipoverty liberal consensus.

An analysis of post-FAP liberal economic justice campaigns challenges the prevailing portrait of the political left in the 1970s. Most historical and popular accounts highlight liberals' embrace of a "rights-consciousness" rooted in so-called "identity politics"—a focus on organizing political constituencies based on race, gender, or sexuality rather than class or socioeconomic interests. But this emphasis misses the content of mainstream liberal politics and much grassroots organizing, as well. "Identity politics" was never the dominant tendency on the political left. Rather, civil rights and women's organizations, labor union leaders, liberal civic and religious groups, and antipoverty activists tried to "refocus their rhetoric and modify their priorities" to "build . . . the kind of acceptability needed to depolarize the American public" and build a "new majority."[11] To be sure, African Americans and women sometimes took issue with this strategy when it promised to reinforce existing racial and gender inequalities. But they faced an uphill battle.

However much many liberals and leftists struggled to articulate a new majority agenda, though, criticisms of AFDC did not disappear from political or public debate. In fact, in the 1970s, antiwelfare conservatives along with some former liberals picked up where the antipoverty coalition had left off. Many adopted the same criticism of AFDC that had animated the 1960s guaranteed income campaign: the program discouraged poor black fathers from remaining with their families and working to support them. An influential group of conservative and neoconservative intellectuals and scholars, aided by journalists attracted to sensationalistic tales of crime, violence, and promiscuity, warned the public that the nation's cities harbored a dangerous, perhaps irredeemable "underclass" of poor minorities. They insisted that AFDC had *created* minority poverty and the supposedly pathological behavior that was plaguing America's central cities. By taking antipoverty liberal critiques of AFDC to their logical conclusion, a newly energized conservative movement gained the initiative in the welfare debate and set the stage for a major federal assault on welfare.

Liberals Seek a "New Majority"

Political leaders have a special responsibility. They must take care to formulate popular grievances in ways that draw blue-collar workers and black people together, instead of driving them apart. (Fred Harris, 1971)[12]

The steady erosion of AFDC benefits and rights during the 1970s pained Elizabeth Wickenden, Mary Ripley, and other social welfare advocates, who saw themselves as defenders of poor single mothers and their children. But even as welfare restrictions fed the pessimism of social welfare advocates, so, too, did a sense of abandonment. A 1973 exchange between Wickenden and South Dakota social worker Fern Chamberlain captures their mood. Chamberlain emphasized the strength of welfare opponents: "It seems to me," she wrote, "that all voices in support of the poor are being silenced in one way or another." Wickenden in turn reported a "feeling of isolation in the absence of strong liberal leadership, either governmental or voluntary."[13] Between the demise of the FAP in 1972 and President Carter's welfare reform proposal in 1977, the American left had very little to say about welfare, particularly AFDC.

Poverty experts continued to promote NIT schemes, and a handful of social welfare-oriented organizations like the National Urban League proposed progressive income maintenance plans, but most liberal organizations turned their attention elsewhere, and few expansive welfare plans gained a hearing in Congress.[14] The NSWA had difficulty convincing liberal organizations to endorse even a very general call for guaranteed jobs and minimum income in May 1976, and AFSCME, a union representing public social workers, decided not to buy ad space in the NWRO 1973 convention program.[15] Even the LWV moved on to other issues. When an Oregon League wrote to the national office for welfare-related information in 1976, Human Resources Coordinator Nan Waterman replied that it had been "several years since we have published any information on . . . income assistance." The League "lost that battle," Waterman continued, "and the information is no longer current or even in print."[16]

Liberals did not "forget" about welfare in the 1970s. Instead, they turned away from it in their attempt to recapture the "Middle Americans" who had seemingly come unhinged from the New Deal coalition. As Chapter 2 noted, beginning in 1968, academics, journalists, activists, and political strategists discovered "The Forgotten American" and tried to figure out what made him tick. As the journalist Peter Schrag saw him, the "forgotten American" was the average American worker. "In the guise of the working class—or the American yeoman or John Smith," he was "once the hero of the civics books, the man that Andrew Jackson called 'the bone and sinew of the country'." Now, though, "he is 'the forgotten man,' perhaps the most alienated person in America." Living "between slums and suburbs," the white American working man "does all the right things, obeys the laws, goes to church and insists . . . that his kids get a better education than he had." But "the right things don't seem to be paying off." He is "still struggling while a lot of others—'them' (on welfare, in demonstrations, in the ghettos) are getting most of the attention."[17]

This "average worker," white, male, and usually blue-collared, stepped onto the national stage in the late 1960s as the lead player in an emerging political realignment. White resistance to integration had nurtured racially conservative working-class politics since the 1940s, but the Democratic New Deal coalition had since ridden economic prosperity and optimism to national power in 1960 and 1964. But as activists intensified pressure on communities outside the South to integrate housing, schools, and jobs during the 1960s, pollsters began to measure voters' "growing hostility to the gains made by the civil rights movement." By the late 1960s, too, rising taxes and consumer prices meant a "near stagnation in real wages for the average blue-collar and salaried white-collar worker" who had grown accustomed to a steadily increasing standard of living.[18] Rising crime rates, changing cultural standards, and antiwar and student protests also fed the so-called blue-collar backlash.

Just who were these resentful, put-upon Americans? "They have no generally accepted name," noted one journalist. They were called "forgotten Americans," the "little people," the "not-so-poor, the working poor, the working class, the lower middle class."[19] Yet in journalistic and official treatments, the essential characteristics remained consistent. They were "families who earn between $5,000 and $10,000 a year," about 40 percent of all Americans, headed by men with a high school education who worked "skilled and semi-skilled jobs," usually in manufacturing or "blue-collar" occupations.[20] In some accounts, these "white male family heads" were also "white ethnics," primarily Catholic descendents of Eastern and Southern European immigrants.[21]

Whatever their actual grievances, these "forgotten Americans" were as much a political and ideological construction as an identifiable constituency. George Wallace and Richard Nixon deserve much of the credit for conjuring them into being during the 1968 presidential election. The Democratic Party, the political home of working-class America since the 1930s, entered the 1968 election season riven by conflicts over U.S. policy in Vietnam and the use of federal power to overcome racial inequality. In a surprisingly successful third-party campaign, Alabama governor George Wallace targeted the Democratic Party's support for civil rights and antipoverty programs. Wallace had gained national prominence for his theatrical (and largely symbolic) "stand in the schoolhouse door" in June 1963, when he faced down federal marshals before a national television audience and refused to allow Vivian Malone and James Hood to enroll in the University of Alabama. In 1968, Wallace parlayed his notoriety into a respectable showing in the Democratic presidential primaries and onto all fifty state ballots as the American Party candidate. His appeal among Southern white voters was obvious, but he also made inroads in working-class districts in the Northeast and Midwest, downplaying explicit racist appeals and employing what one historian has called "a kind of soft-porn racism in which fear and hatred could be mobilized without mentioning race itself."[22] In a style both folksy and vicious, Wallace pronounced himself champion of "the hardworking, taxpaying, ultimate burden-bearing majority" and denounced liberal Democrats, student protesters, and federal officials and judges for promoting disruptive social and cultural change.[23] He won five Deep South states and showed "surprising strength outside his own region," ultimately winning more than 13 percent of the American electorate.[24] Republican Richard Nixon employed a more moderate version of Wallace's strategy, selling himself as a sensible and responsible advocate of "law and order," who was likely to end permissive policies toward criminals and protesters, and an opponent of a growing and "debilitating" federal welfare system.[25] Together, Wallace and Nixon took 65 percent of white votes; many observers viewed this as an outright electoral rejection of the Democratic Party and liberal policies more generally.

The "white backlash" that propelled Nixon into the White House was a golden opportunity for conservative strategists. The Democrats' association with black voters, civil rights, and the War on Poverty made resentful white voters a constituency ripe for the political picking. Conservative strategists urged Nixon to exploit racial divisiveness and promote a "positive polarization" of the electorate.[26] A young Harvard Law School graduate and Nixon campaign staffer named Kevin Phillips was perhaps the most influential. Phillips's 1969 book marshaled demographic and polling data to predict an *Emerging Republican Majority*, a political inevitability that could be hastened if Nixon took advantage of white racial resentment. Other Republicans, like *Ripon Forum* editor Howard L. Reiter and Labor Department official Jerome Rosow, promoted a more substantive approach, urging their party to address the real needs of working- and lower-middle-class voters.[27] Racial resentment may have unhinged white workers from the Democratic Party, they insisted, but "if the GOP is to win over lower-middle-class clerks in Queens, steelworkers in Youngstown, and retired police lieutenants in San Diego," it would have to offer them a positive program of tangible benefits—services that political scientist Andrew Hacker assured could "be supplied even while other measures freeze welfare payments and public housing [and] repress racial and radical protest."[28]

Democratic strategists likewise sought policies and politics to appeal to backlash voters. Richard Scammon and Ben Wattenberg's *The Real Majority*, which named the Democratic Party's "pro-black stance" as an electoral weakness and reminded liberals that the majority of the American electorate remained "unpoor, unyoung, and unblack," signaled a significant intellectual shift among liberals. Between 1968 and 1972, liberal analysts and activists devoted considerable attention to "reacting Americans."[29] The American Jewish Committee took a leading role. As early as June 1968, the AJC sponsored a National Consultation on Ethnic Americans at Fordham

University with the goal of "expand[ing] our understanding of these white groups in order to minimize their antagonism to other groups and help depolarize our cities."[30] A plethora of conferences and workshops followed, including the Philadelphia Conference on the Problems of White Ethnic America (1968), a University of Illinois-Chicago Consultation on Ethnicity (1969), a National Federation of Settlements consultation on "Working in White Ethnic Neighborhoods" (1970), and a Ford Foundation Conference on Blue-Collar Alienation (1970).[31] Organizers of these events drew on a growing body of sociological literature from research institutions like the Harvard-MIT Joint Center for Urban Studies.[32] "Discussions in university seminars and policy debates in Washington and that form the background of contemporary popular sociology," noted Peter Schrag, are "increasingly the conditions of trauma and frustration in the middle."[33]

Of course, liberal interest was not academic. Liberals sought to win back a critical constituency—what the AJC's Irving Levine called the "shock troops of anti-Negro politics"—and recharge their progressive domestic agenda.[34] In the introduction to *The White Majority: Between Poverty and Affluence*, Louise Kapp Howe articulated the stakes. The goal of all the conferences, studies, and publications was "to learn more about the people who comprise the majority of the country, how they live, what forces are compelling them to the right and what, if anything, can be done to turn them around."[35] In other words, liberal analysis of the backlash, like conservative analysis, was directed toward political advantage. And their research, commentary, and discussions were "more than simply accounts" of the backlash, as one historian has put it. Instead, the way liberals interpreted white resentment "became part of the story," shaping liberal strategy for the next decade at least.[36]

Liberal analysts almost universally blamed the backlash on their own "political blunder." They castigated liberal policymakers, politicians, intellectuals, and advocacy groups for "turn[ing] away from workers" in the 1960s and focusing "entirely on blacks or the very poor."[37] The charge has been repeated so many times that it has the aura of authority; it has become the standard interpretation of America's "right turn" after the 1960s: political commentators and scholars across the political spectrum blame the Democratic Party's emphasis on civil rights and poverty programs for alienating its white working-class base.[38] It is worth noting this narrative's historical inaccuracies. It exaggerates the meager resources devoted to antipoverty programs and overestimates the accomplishments of civil rights legislation, particularly in terms of positive economic outcomes. It also ignores the vast benefits that millions of white working- and middle-class Americans reaped from the Great Society—like Medicare and federal aid to education—and from earlier incarnations of the American welfare state, from the New Deal to several G.I. Bills. "As the American ethnic remembers his past," wrote Russell Barta in 1971, "there was no welfare state for him, [and] he was subjected to the discipline of long hours and backbreaking work."[39] Yet memories can be deceiving; whatever his real grievances, the lower-middle-class white worker had benefited significantly from the welfare state (and from white privilege) in the postwar era. Such history, however, had little place in the backlash literature.

At a June 1968 conference, Irving Levine, director of urban planning for the AJC, drew on and furthered this narrative of liberal ineptitude to present "A Strategy for White Ethnic America," setting a pattern followed by liberal strategists throughout the 1970s. The source of the "urban white backlash," Levine insisted, was "disaffection on the racial issue." "Our rightful but self-righteous transfixion on black America" in the 1960s "has developed into a 'no-win' policy, hardening the lines of polarization between white and black." In order to prevent the "very real danger of victory in America for a reactionary and repressive majority," liberals must respond to the backlash in both symbolic and tangible ways. The "progressive elements of society must convince actual or potential backlash groups that alliance and cooperation can yield constructive results for them as well as for Negroes." Liberals should therefore "refocus their rhetoric and modify their priorities": they must avoid polarizing issues like affirmative action and busing and stop "defin[ing] the major problem of America only in terms of blacks." A "targeted approach to the 'working American'" would emphasize new policies—law and order, tax reform, adequate public education, and occupational mobility that "relate to the needs of middle-class America as a whole in contrast to the needs of the so-called under-class."[40] Levine's prescription increasingly became liberal strategy.

Levine and his allies responded not only to white backlash but also to what many saw as threatening trends on the political left. The NCSW's annual forum in spring 1970 was a microcosm of the tensions plaguing liberal politics at the dawn of a new decade. In 1968, black social workers had walked out of the forum to form the Black Social Workers Association; the following year, welfare rights activists staged a "take-over"; and by 1970, Native Americans, Chicanos, and Asians were demanding representation and decision-making power. That year, NCSW leaders made various attempts to "give more opportunity than ever before to representatives of emerging groups to expound their views, criticisms, and recommendations." NCSW president Wilbur Cohen published his opening address in advance in order "to provide time for reactors representing the points of view of Black persons, Spanish speaking people, the Welfare Rights group, and Students," and the meeting featured a session on "The Colonial Mentality in American Institutions" along with special caucus meetings for the NWRO, La Raza, and black social workers. At the same time, forum participants could attend a session on "The Misunderstood Minorities" and be reminded that "preoccupation with the problems of Black and Brown minorities must not blind social welfare to the interests and influence of other increasingly vocal minorities—white ethnic groups, the middle age[d], and many middle income Americans."[41]

This struggle prompted many liberals—the labor union, civil rights, civic, and religious groups that supported antipoverty activism in the 1960s—to change both the issues they addressed and the way they talked about them. Given its constituency, organized labor was most vocal in denouncing so-called "identity politics" and promoting a majoritarian liberal agenda. In late 1969, Lane Kirkland of the AFL-CIO denounced the "new liberal politics" that rejected the white working class and followed "any hustler with a paper organization, a dashiki and a foundation grant—and access to that indispensable element, a television camera." We "must concede," Kirkland lamented, "that liberalism, as we have known it, is in a state of disarray in this country, and rent with factionalism and fratricide."[42] Some African American leaders likewise denounced "identity politics" and sought to define their goals in class rather than racial terms. Perhaps the most vociferous opponent of "identity politics" was Bayard Rustin of the A. Philip Randolph Institute. Rustin had been denouncing black nationalism since the mid-1960s, and by the early 1970s he was nearly apoplectic as he surveyed the state of the American left. An increasing number of African American leaders were rejecting liberalism and calling for blacks to become "the vanguard in the struggle for a new society." At the same time, some white leftists proposed a "New Politics" that would unite poor urban minorities with professional whites, explicitly bypassing the supposedly reactionary white working class.[43] Rustin blasted both strategies as ill-conceived and self-defeating and pointed to the New Deal and the Great Society as evidence that "the labor-liberal approach to social problems has been vindicated time and again over narrow, sectarian, 'all-black' strategies."[44] On the ten-year anniversary of the 1963 March for Jobs and Freedom, Rustin recommended a return to coalition politics focused on "traditional New Deal

liberal strategies": full employment, tax reform, adequate housing, and national health insurance. "In the coming period," he warned, "we cannot be
content to define economic programs in racial terms." To "pursue purely
'black' issues at a time when our needs increasingly converge with those of
the larger working class is to perpetuate political isolation."[45] A conservative
political environment, agreed economist Robert Lekachman, necessitated
"unifying rather than divisive issues" like "health, jobs, transportation,
[and] occupational safety."[46]

President Nixon gave the antipoverty coalition an opportunity to test
its "new majority" strategy in 1973. In his second term, Nixon moved dis-
tinctly to the right. He had routed liberal Democrat George McGovern in
the 1972 presidential election, largely because of McGovern's association
with "far-left" political positions on Vietnam, amnesty for draft resisters,
and welfare. McGovern's plan to replace welfare with a $1,000 annual "de-
mogrant" to all Americans, along with his earlier sympathy for the NWRO
guaranteed income plan, enabled his opponents to paint him as a "free-
spending, welfare-rights champion," while Nixon's rhetorical hard line on
welfare overshadowed his own guaranteed income proposal.[47] As part of his
"courtship of the labor movement," Nixon endorsed the "work ethic" and
denounced the "welfare ethic." Nixon's comfortable victory, along with the
increasing popularity of California governor Ronald Reagan and his antiwelfare histrionics, encouraged the administration to abandon many of its
relatively liberal domestic policies.[48] In his 1974 budget proposal, Nixon
took aim at the most vulnerable Great Society programs, cutting emergency
employment and housing subsidies, dissolving the OEO, restricting access
to welfare, and converting Job Corps, Model Cities, and other programs
into block grants. According to Jack Rosenthal of the *New York Times*, social program cuts "dominate[d] a list that alone occupies seven and a half
pages in the new budget."[49]

The antipoverty coalition denounced the cuts and joined forces to battle the larger threat that Nixon's budget seemed to pose. In March 1973,
representatives of at least one hundred liberal and labor organizations—
from the Amalgamated Clothing Workers of America on one end of the
alphabet to the YWCA on the other—met at Georgetown University to
form a new lobbying organization, the Coalition for Human Needs and
Budget Priorities.[50] Its coordinating committee and board of directors included representatives from unions, civic and civil rights organizations,
government, social welfare groups, religious, women's, and grassroots associations—essentially the same liberals who lobbied for a guaranteed income

in the late 1960s.[51] In that fight the antipoverty coalition had championed the needs of both welfare recipients and the "working poor." In 1973, the same group consciously broke from its image as defenders of minorities and the poor. Instead, the Coalition billed itself as "a broad cross-section of the American public—the young and the old, farmers and workers, rural and urban interests, women, homebuilders, and others" fighting for the needs of "all Americans."[52]

The Coalition insisted that Nixon's budget "seriously neglects the needs and aspirations of a *great majority* of the American people," favoring "the rich at the expense of the poor, near poor, and middle class." While Coalition members occasionally noted the needs of poor Americans specifically and protested cuts in antipoverty programs, they more often emphasized "education, health facilities and research, housing, jobs, transportation, the environment, and consumer affairs," issues around which a majority of Americans could rally.[53] In a memo to the group's steering committee, Jerry Berman laid out the rationale. Of course liberals opposed Nixon's budget "because it cuts *social programs* that assist the poor and minorities," but this put them "in a very sad position" as "a 'minority' coalition, 'defending' social programs against the President's majority against 'welfare' and 'taxes'." As such, Berman argued, "we are organized to lose." A winning strategy required "build[ing] a *majority coalition*," which meant "engag[ing] in a critique of the budget that *goes beyond Great Society program cuts* and speaks to the adverse impact of the budget on other constituencies," groups like "labor, consumers, environmentalists, veterans."[54]

As part of that strategy, the Coalition downplayed the budget's particular impact on African Americans. While civil rights leaders and organizations certainly mobilized against Nixon's budget, they too employed the new majority strategy.[55] Jesse Jackson of Operation PUSH declared: "We're asking whites to help broaden our base. . . . Nixon has manipulated people into thinking the budget cuts are a black punishment program," so in fighting against the budget, "one thing we cannot do is allow this thing to become a black issue."[56] Vernon Jordan blasted Nixon for a "policy of active hostility to the hopes, dreams, and aspirations of black Americans," but he also reminded "the silent white majority" that they, even more than blacks, had benefited from federal largesse. "The gut issues of today," he insisted, would never be addressed if they were "falsely perceived as 'black issues.'"[57] Former CORE and NWRO leader George Wiley, armed with research about how Nixon's cuts in "health, education, environmental protection and housing" would "affect the working and middle classes," reminded Congress that "although [the budget] is often billed as anti-poor and anti-black (which it certainly is), it would be more accurately billed as anti-majority."[58]

AFDC, perceived as a black program and targeted to the poor, got very little attention from the Coalition.[59] Backlash analysts agreed that welfare would "probably win hands down in any . . . unpopularity poll taken among blue-collar workers."[60] Indeed, welfare appeared as a particular irritant in nearly every treatment of the backlash.[61] Journalist Pete Hamill quoted two working-class men who suggested the connections quite vividly. "I pick up a paper and read about a million people on welfare in New York or spades rioting in some college, or some fat welfare bitch demanding . . . a credit card at Korvette's," confided ironworker Ed Cush. "You see that, and you want to go out and strangle someone." Another source complained that liberals like New York Mayor John Lindsay cared only for "the niggers." "The niggers get the schools. The niggers get the new playgrounds. The niggers get nursery schools. And they get it all without workin'." Rather than deserving such special treatment, "they take the welfare and sit on the stoop drinkin' cheap wine and throwin' the bottles on the street. They take the money outta my paycheck and they just turn it over to some lazy son of a bitch who won't work."[62] According to analysts like Peter Schrag, "the liberal wisdom about welfare [and] ghettos"—a wisdom, it is supposed, that mandated federal responsibility for ameliorating poverty and racial disadvantage—flew in the face of "the values and life of the working man," who was "taught to cherish and respect . . . hard work, order, authority, and self-reliance."[63]

But AFDC's association with African Americans was not its only liability. Liberals also avoided drawing attention to welfare because it seemed to reward what Andrew Levison called "the disorganized families of the unemployed." As such, it offended what sociologist Lee Rainwater called the "deep family orientation of the working class." Liberal backlash theorists described a white working class whose very values and lifestyle were at risk, as inflation, wage stagnation, and unemployment threatened men's precarious hold on respectability and forced their wives into the labor market. Of white families earning between $7,000 and $10,000 a year, over half had more than one wage earner by the late 1960s.[64] While married women had begun to enter the labor market in significant numbers during and after World War II, Irving Levine argued that family reliance on wives' earnings seemed a "relatively new phenomenon" in the 1970s, a "redefinition of family roles [that] clashed with many traditional values of ethnic group life and contribute[d] to a sense of disorientation and alienation."[65] As liberal theorists saw it, these "stable breadwinners, churchgoers, voters, [and] family men" had a tremendous investment in their role as provider.[66] "They way we think," one white male union member told a political scientist, "a man should be able to take care of things, so that his income doesn't have to be supplemented by his wife *having* to work."[67] These personal struggles, this loss of "pride in his importance in society" and in his family, may have made struggling white workers all the more resentful of welfare programs that seemed to reward black paternal irresponsibility and to enable black single mothers to avoid wage labor. AFDC, Rainwater insisted, did not conform to "working class logic" that prescribed a "good and faithful [male] provider" and a "sensible, responsible, and loving housewife-mother" as the ticket to respectability.[68] At least, this is how many liberal strategists saw things.[69]

These strategists hoped instead that any attention to African Americans would focus on the group that Pat Moynihan called the "silent black majority." The sociologist Charles Hamilton coined the term specifically to refer to male-breadwinner African American families.[70] As the term suggests, liberal strategists believed family structure might trump race in shaping whites' response to social programs. Media focus on a nonworking, unstable "underclass," along with residential segregation, meant that most white Americans had "very little direct contact with their stable working class black counterparts." Instead, argued Glenn Olson in a workshop on "new approaches to a hard right neighborhood," whites typically saw African Americans as violent rioters or demanding welfare recipients.[71] This misunderstanding certainly worried black leaders. The conservative African American economist Thomas Sowell tried to draw attention to "black men and women who go to work five days a week, pay their bills, try to find some happiness for themselves," and "raise their children to be decent people with better prospects than they had."[72] When the Census Bureau reported a rise in black female-headed households in 1971, the Urban League's Robert B. Hill wondered why the press never focused on "the hard-working, father-dominated families" that "constitute the great majority."[73]

In *The Real Majority*, Richard Scammon and Ben Wattenberg did just that by revealing the importance of family structure in defining this "silent black majority." Wattenberg, a former aide to Johnson and Humphrey and a supporter of hawkish Democrat Henry "Scoop" Jackson, was one of several former liberals who were becoming increasingly disaffected from the liberal wing of the Democratic Party. These emerging "neoconservatives" promoted aggressive anticommunism, rejected race-conscious social policies like busing and affirmative action, and defended bourgeois values like hard work and family stability against attacks by a youthful counterculture. Scammon and Wattenberg surveyed economic data from the 1960s and concluded that liberal reforms and economic growth had brought a slim majority of African Americans into the middle class. These stable working people—not only "the engineers and teachers" but also "the plasterers, painters, bus drivers, lathe operators, secretaries, bank tellers, and automobile assembly-line workers"—were "the kinds of people who, when they are white, are described as 'Middle Americans' or members of the silent, real, or new American majorities." The analysts urged liberals to pay more attention to these African Americans, both as a celebration of liberal success and as a strategy for further progress.[74]

The well-heeled liberals of the Urban Coalition demonstrate this shift in liberal strategy and rhetoric. As described in Chapter 1, corporate, labor, civic, and governmental interests organized the Urban Coalition in the summer of 1967 to address the inner-city poverty and disadvantage that resulted in urban riots. The Coalition continued its work into the 1970s, with thirty-four local coalitions by mid-decade, but its leaders shifted focus.[75] As a strong supporter of guaranteed income legislation in the late 1960s, the Coalition's biggest concern with welfare had been its exclusion of the "working poor."[76] By 1973, UAW president and Urban Coalition leader Leonard Woodcock urged Americans to "come together as a community, as neighbors against a common threat" around the issues of "tax reform and reordering national priorities" as well as full employment.[77] The Coalition rejected Nixon's 1974 budget proposal not only because it represented "federal abdication of responsibility regarding urban issues" but also because of its potential to harm "the middle income American," who "can expect increases in property tax, sales tax and/or state income taxes."[78]

Urban Coalition leader John Gardner took the strategy even further when he founded Common Cause in July 1970. Gardner represented the center of American politics of his time, a liberal Republican and "pinstripe radical" whose leadership of the Carnegie Corporation in the 1950s, service as Johnson's HEW secretary, and leadership in the Urban Coalition evinced a deep commitment to public activism on behalf of the poor and disadvantaged.[79] According to one *New York Times* reporter, Gardner had "the respect of liberals because of his commitment to Federal action and of conservatives because he is a Republican with a wide following in the business community."[80] By the late 1960s, Gardner sensed a "deep and pervasive feeling among all segments of the populace that 'things aren't working'."[81] Early on, Common Cause reflected its antipoverty heritage; in 1970, it called for "a drastic change in national priorities" and a "renew[ed] attack on poverty and discrimination" and lobbied for the Family Assistance Plan and an expansion in food stamps.[82] However, the organization did not define itself as a defender of poor and minority Americans. While "the problems of poverty and race must be among our first concerns," Gardner wrote in 1970, "our agenda must be an agenda for *all* Americans—for the poor, the comfortable and those in between, for old and young, for black and white, for city dweller and farmer, for men and women."[83] By 1973, Common Cause's original interest in welfare legislation and poverty programs had diminished considerably, while its emphasis on "majority" issues had expanded. In part, this reflected the group's focus on political process rather than political outcome. "We are not, for the most part, taking on issues that *directly* affect the poor and the minorities or that *directly* address themselves to the substantive problems of our society," Jack Conway noted in 1971.[84] Conway assured the NCSW in 1974 that the only way to get the needs of poor Americans met was to reform the nation's political system— political reform was the means to larger ends.[85] But Gardner's desire to "get [a] majority . . . actively and efficiently involved" and to "rally the moderates to stop the process of polarization" also contributed to his organization's declining attention to welfare and poverty programs.[86]

In a more striking shift, George Wiley led a grassroots effort in the same mold. The charismatic convener and director of the NWRO, Wiley had long envisioned an interracial movement of the poor, but his focus from 1966 to 1972 had been organizing mostly African American AFDC recipients and helping them gain a voice in national policymaking circles. In 1972 he headed in a new direction. The NWRO internal dynamics had changed, as recipient leaders—African American single mothers— challenged Wiley and the NWRO mostly male, mostly white paid staff for control of the organization. In December 1972, Wiley announced his resignation as NWRO executive director, turned control over to Johnnie Tillmon, and formed a new organization, the Movement for Economic Justice (MEJ).

Wiley's resignation from the NWRO resulted in large measure from his commitment to building a "new majority." Recipient leaders saw the NWRO as *their* organization, the only association devoted to representing the interests of AFDC mothers before powerful institutions like legislatures and welfare departments. But by the early 1970s, Wiley and several other staff members saw the need to broaden the movement's base. As Premilla Nadasen noted, staffers' commitment to organizing low-income and unemployed men "dovetailed nicely with their ultimate goal of reestablishing the traditional two-parent family."[87] In a March 1973 speech, Wiley expressed a more strategic motive. "We have a situation today where the public opinion in the majority sector is increasingly being galvanized against welfare recipients," and the "campaign rhetoric of Nixon and Rockefeller and the Reagans and many others has become increasingly strident in its attacks on welfare families as the scapegoats for many of the ills of the nation."[88] The only way to get "real reform of our welfare system" as well as other progressive domestic policies would be to "organize more broadly among poor people" and "find new allies among working and middle class people."[89] Recipient leaders generally resisted such efforts, fearing that their perspective and interests would fade if the organization incorporated other less stigmatized groups. This was why, as Wiley put it, the NWRO remained "primarily oriented toward the needs of people on welfare" and had not "seriously, and in a major way, embraced and engaged the needs of working people or even other unemployed people."[90] Wiley defined the NWRO's strategy as "minority politics," which were, by definition, "defensive politics." Wiley envisioned adopting instead "the aggressive tactics of majority politics" by helping all "the victims of economic injustice"—the over 70 percent of Americans who earned less than $15,000 a year, according to Wiley—"realize their common interest."[91]

As a clearinghouse for community organizers throughout the country, MEJ certainly recognized the growing political vulnerability of America's poor. "We thought that if we could organize the poor and minority groups, we'd have a power base from which we could make change," noted the director of Saul Alinsky's Industrial Areas Foundation in 1974. "Now we know that if you dumped all the poor people, all the blacks, Chicanos, Indians and every other poor minority group together, you wouldn't have enough power to make changes in Springfield, Illinois—much less in Washington." Like MEJ, the Industrial Areas Foundation began to send organizers to work with middle-class populations.[92]

Welfare did not fit well in the new strategy. "In recent years, we have seen the majority population grow increasingly hostile toward welfare," Wiley noted, "as well as toward blacks and other minority groups."[93] A "majority strategy," then, would necessarily downplay, if not ignore, AFDC and instead find "issues that can unite divergent groups."[94] MEJ's newsletter chronicles numerous poor people's campaigns throughout the country in the mid-1970s, from food stamp registration drives and utility rate protests to thrift-shops and food buying clubs, but AFDC is rarely mentioned.[95] The issues MEJ took on as national campaigns were those that could be portrayed as affecting "deserving" constituencies. Wiley saw Nixon's budget as a "bridge" issue, for example, as long as MEJ organizers reminded the public that "middle income people" would be "adversely affected."[96] Tax reform seemed even more promising. As inflation pushed hard-pressed families into higher tax brackets, Congress gradually redistributed the nation's tax burden, reducing corporate rates and steadily increasing regressive payroll taxes. Between 1955 and 1970, corporate income taxes dropped from 20 to 12 percent of total federal tax revenues, while payroll taxes rose from 8 to 15 percent of federal tax intake.[97] This increasingly regressive tax system, which contributed to taxpayer resentment of social spending, attracted growing attention on the left in the 1970s and even entered the Democratic Party agenda, at least nominally.[98] By 1974, liberal economists Richard Lampmann and James Tobin were touting tax reform as a "more important subject for attention" than welfare reform.[99]

Tax reform became the MEJ's first priority issue. Wiley hoped to foment a "taxpayer's revolt," one "that is shaped and directed not against welfare mothers but . . . against the real welfare recipients" like corporations and the wealthy "who are chiseling billions and billions of dollars out of the federal treasuries."[100] As part of its Tax Justice Project in spring 1973, MEJ organized more than 125 tax clinics in more than fourteen states across the country.[101] Leaders advised local organizers to ensure that "Your coalition [is] broad based. It must include as many different people and groups as possible."[102] Appearing before the House Ways and Means Committee that March, Wiley articulated his new political offensive. He had always found the Committee's antiwelfare policies "morally reprehensible but politically understandable," he noted, "since welfare families represent at most about five percent of the population, about 55% of which are black and Spanish speaking." Congressional tax policies, "just as outrageous," were less logical politically, for "the group against which you are discriminating here is over 70% of the voting population, over 80% of whom are white!"[103]

By 1974, some MEJ organizers began to recognize the dangers of this "new majority" strategy for welfare recipients. Wiley had been optimistic that "the new movement in the suburbs among the middle class on abolishing property taxes" was "just a few short steps from realizing the need for

over-all [progressive] tax reform."[104] When he visited with community organizers in Milwaukee in May 1973 he was introduced to a less progressive
possibility. Although the welfare rights movement was "neither strong nor
actively moving in Milwaukee," organizers had successfully mobilized white
homeowners around tax reform. But the organization "does not include
blacks, chicanos or Indians," and at least one local activist worried that its
demand for a three-year freeze on property taxes would "result in pressure
to lower welfare payments."[105] After Wiley's tragic death in a boating acci-
dent in August 1973, welfare rights veterans and MEJ leaders Bert DeLeeuw
and Tim Sampson expressed more significant misgivings. They feared that
AFDC recipients could become scapegoats in Wiley's organizing schema.
"Welfare is used daily to divide us, to keep a new *economic* majority of us
from getting together," Sampson recognized, and "now, as we are beginning to work on the 'new' issues of economic justice—on taxes, utility rates,
neighborhood preservation, etc." and "with 'new constituencies—the *working* poor, ethnic Americans, the newly awakened middle American," welfare
recipients and welfare "are *not* popular."[106] Bert DeLeeuw also warned organizers to ensure "that those people traditionally seen as poor are involved
in the struggle" and that "their issues receive as much attention as those of
the 'newly poor'."[107]

Despite such warnings, the "newly poor"—white, male-breadwinner
families suffering from inflation, regressive taxes, and especially unemployment in the mid-1970s—would take the starring role in the principal liberal
campaign of the decade. As campaigns for "human needs and budget priorities" and for progressive tax reform ran aground in an increasingly conservative political climate, antipoverty liberals turned their attention to the
ultimate "bridge" issue, full employment. When "a coalition of trade unionists, minority leaders, feminists and political and community activists"
developed a "Democratic Agenda" in late 1977, their purpose was to "remind President Carter and the Democratic majority in Congress of the central promise of the 1976 campaign: a job for every American who wants to
work." The group's seventeen-issue agenda called for guaranteed jobs for
all Americans willing and able to work, progressive tax reform, universal
health insurance, an array of housing and environmental programs, and an
end to sex and race discrimination. Absent from their agenda was any reference to AFDC or to welfare more generally. [108] "Most black people are not
welfare recipients or 'street dudes'," advised Andrew Levison. Instead, "the
majority of black Americans are working people, and for these close to five
million black *men*, their discontents and poverty result from being the most

oppressed sector of the working class."[109] The full employment campaign would follow liberals' "new majority" strategy in which white male-breadwinner households *and* a "silent black majority" of black male-breadwinner households took center stage as deserving recipients of federal largesse.

"Full Employment: The Key to All Goals"

Whereas welfare and other income-transfer schemes divide us—workers on one side and the poor and their intellectual and upper-middle-class supporters on the other—programs to achieve economic development and full employment at decent wages can unite us. (William Spring, Bennett Harrison, and Thomas Vietorisz, 1972)[110]

We refuse to subscribe to the 'trickle down' effects of a jobs policy that expands the opportunities for men. (Kristina Kiehl, Women's Lobby, 1977)[111]

In June 1975, more than five hundred individuals representing 150 national organizations attended the country's first annual Full Employment Conference.[112] Two years later, over one million Americans in more than three hundred towns and cities participated in a wide range of activities, from picnics and parades to teach-ins and vigils, to mark Full Employment Week and pressure Congress to pass full employment legislation.[113] Spearheading these efforts was the National Committee for Full Employment (NCFE) and its action arm, the Full Employment Action Council (FEAC), a broad-based coalition co-chaired by Murray H. Finlay, president of the Amalgamated Clothing and Textile Workers, and Coretta Scott King of the Martin Luther King, Jr., Center for Social Change. The group's membership roster includes all the major liberal players: leaders of labor unions, civil rights organizations, and women's, civic, religious, and social welfare groups. Jack Conway of Common Cause and Bert DeLeeuw of MEJ represented the recent shift among many liberals to a "new majority" strategy, while representatives from the Coalition of Labor Union Women (CLUW), the National Women's Political Caucus (NWPC), and NOW symbolized the growing influence of feminists.[114] The campaign for federal full employment legislation became a centerpiece of activism in the 1970s, replacing the antipoverty efforts and guaranteed income campaign of the 1960s as liberals' preferred solution to economic injustice and disadvantage.[115] It seemed, as Democratic Senator Henry "Scoop" Jackson called it, "the key to all goals."[116]

A full employment campaign did not necessarily preclude continued activism on behalf of progressive welfare reform. "In our enthusiasm for the work ethic," warned manpower economist Eli Ginzberg in 1976, "we must not overlook the needs of many needy families for an improved system of income maintenance."[117] But as I argued in the last section, many liberals and other progressive activists chose to practice "benign neglect" toward welfare as a way to recapture the white working class and other "middle Americans." The political shift was palpable. As Democratic lawmakers began to introduce full employment legislation in 1973, liberals increasingly defined their agenda without reference to welfare. At the opening of the Johnson Presidential Library in May 1976, Senator Hubert Humphrey "spoke passionately of federal programs to aid the poor" but declared that welfare reform was a "dead issue." His speech focused instead on the full employment bill he was co-sponsoring. Full employment, the *New Republic* editors noted, had "supplanted all other issues, including welfare, as the great cause of the year."[118]

The invisibility of AFDC on the liberal agenda would have significant consequences, as would the ways in which liberals framed the issues of unemployment and poverty during the full employment campaign. The "four-letter word" at the center of liberals' 1977 Democratic Agenda— "JOBS"—certainly promised more political success than a guaranteed income or other income maintenance plans, which lacked broad popular support. The right to a job was attractive to many welfare recipients and their advocates as well, promising a route out of poverty and the indignity imposed by a stigmatized and stigmatizing AFDC program. But the jobs focus also helped to narrow the liberal economic justice agenda and to eliminate broader claims for a "right to live" irrespective of labor market participation. It also helped to reinforce long-standing distinctions between the deserving and the undeserving poor; despite some attempts to keep the problems of minorities and poor single mothers on the public agenda, the liberal full employment campaign sought legitimacy by highlighting the particular trauma that unemployment inflicted on its most "deserving victims," white male breadwinners. Understanding the full employment campaign, then, is critical to understanding AFDC's increasing political vulnerability in the 1970s.

While full employment became central to liberal activism in the 1970s, it had a long history.[119] The various proposals that culminated in the Full Employment and Balanced Growth Act (or the Humphrey-Hawkins Bill) contained the kinds of economic planning and job guarantees that had been part of the labor-liberal agenda since the 1930s, a way to ensure workers' survival and dignity against the inevitable insecurities of a capitalist economy. Civil rights leaders also incorporated full employment as a key demand as early as the 1940s, for they had always understood "that a wider social justice agenda addressing class inequality was vital to win over working-class whites who might otherwise be persuaded by the right that advancement for African Americans would come at their expense."[120] The legislation that Congress considered in the mid-1970s followed a well-worn liberal-labor prescription: it would require Congress and the president to orient fiscal, monetary, and social policy toward the ultimate goal of a full employment economy, defined as a 3 percent unemployment rate, and to provide a public service job to any American who wanted paid employment but could not find a job in the private sector, thereby giving all American adults the "right" to remunerative employment. Congress had debated similar legislation after World War II, but powerful conservative opposition stripped that bill of any real economic planning functions or guarantees, and full employment remained a priority for activists interested in economic and social justice and a key demand in all the comprehensive reform proposals of the 1960s: the 1963 March for Jobs and Freedom, the Domestic Marshall Plan, the Freedom Budget, and the 1968 Poor People's Campaign.[121] The same antipoverty coalition that devised and supported those reforms joined in the mid-1970s to press the issue once again.

Full employment's appeal lay in its potential to unite the various, and sometimes contentious, members of the liberal-labor-civil rights coalition. Jobs had emerged by the late 1960s as a primary site of conflict between two critical Democratic constituencies, working-class whites on the one side and minorities, especially African Americans, on the other. As the historian Nancy MacLean has argued, equality movements among women, Mexican Americans, and other groups in the late 1960s and 1970s followed the example of the black freedom movement, which insisted that "genuine inclusion—full belonging as Americans—required participation in the economic mainstream—namely, access to good jobs at all levels once reserved for white men alone." The "quest for jobs and justice" that MacLean chronicles gained tremendous momentum in the decade-and-a-half after 1964, as minority groups and women used Title VII of the Civil Rights Act to "open" the American workplace and gain access to well-paid, steady jobs once denied them as a matter of course.[122] It also provoked vociferous and sometimes violent reactions, as white male union members defended traditional seniority and apprenticeship rights that had served since the 1940s to protect them from employers' arbitrary power and to preserve white, male privilege.

Liberals hoped that full employment would ensure "jobs and justice" for minorities while mitigating conflicts over affirmative action. As early as 1970, Bayard Rustin expressed this hope in a speech to building trades unionists. In "Black Rage, White Fear: The Full Employment Answer," Rustin acknowledged the economic insecurities and anxieties facing white workers and insisted that full employment was the only way to "reduce . . . black rage and white fear at the same time."[123] The liberals who dominated the full employment debate repeated this argument continually. Full employment, Coretta Scott King insisted, "could win the support of the white construction worker, currently out of work because of the housing slump, and the ghetto youth, who has never had a job," could even weaken the "entire cynical politics of racism—the exploitation of white fear of unemployment and black anger at exclusion" and "usher in a new era in the history of race relations in the U.S.A."[124] The economic insecurities plaguing America in the 1970s made a broad, universal job guarantee even more critical. While "a period of severe general unemployment is not an auspicious occasion to seek new initiatives in terms of special labor market programs for blacks," noted economist Herrington J. Bryce in 1974, it was an ideal time to pursue full employment.[125] According to an AFL-CIO official writing in 1976, the full employment campaign had already "done much to restore and reunify the black-labor-liberal coalition."[126]

Even as liberal activists and politicians touted full employment as a program for "the average worker," they constructed that average worker in very particular ways.[127] In the late 1960s, Democratic policymakers had focused job creation and training efforts on the "hard-core unemployed," particularly young black men. In the mid-1970s, economic downturn and layoffs among unionized white workers promised to broaden popular perceptions of unemployment and poverty. As the media scholar Martin Gilens has demonstrated, after the mid-1960s, print journalists and television broadcasters illustrated poverty- and welfare-related stories with images that exaggerated the proportion of African Americans among the nation's poor. But during the recessions of 1974–75 and 1982–83, as hardship reached deeper into white working- and middle-class populations, journalists briefly presented a whiter (and more sympathetic) portrait of poverty. While African Americans accounted for 70 percent of poor people and 75 percent of welfare recipients portrayed in the news during the FAP debates of 1972–

BLACK RAGE

WHITE FEAR

the full employment answer

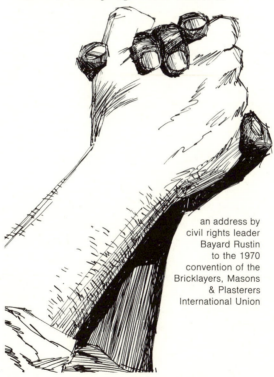

an address by
civil rights leader
Bayard Rustin
to the 1970
convention of the
Bricklayers, Masons
& Plasterers
International Union

Figure 8. Pamphlet of a speech by civil rights and labor activist Bayard Rustin in 1970. Liberals saw full employment as a way to overcome racial conflicts that arose from affirmative action, busing, and welfare, as Rustin's title and the illustration suggest. That the hands appear male may be coincidence, but liberals' "new majority" politics did emphasize male breadwinning as a bond across racial divisions. Courtesy International Union of Bricklayers and Allied Craftworkers.

1973, the following two years saw a "dramatic 'whitening' of poverty images" and a corresponding shift in tone.[128]

Liberals did not completely ignore racial or gender disadvantage. African American civil rights activists remained leaders in the liberal coalition and the Democratic Party, and the cause of racial equality retained a powerful moral hold on the liberal agenda. And by the mid-1970s, feminists had begun to influence American liberalism, making inroads on the policies and positions of male-dominated organizations and participating actively in liberal coalitions like the Coalition for Human Needs and Budget Priorities and the FEAC.[129] Indeed, full employment proponents initially touted their bill—the Equal Opportunity and Full Employment Act—as the answer to racial and gender disadvantage. "Only under conditions of genuine full employment and confidence in its continuation," the bill read, "is it easier to eliminate the bias, prejudice, discrimination, and fear that have resulted in unequal employment under unequal conditions for women, older people, younger people, [and] members of racial, ethnic, national, or religious minorities."[130]

However, in Congressional hearings, full employment proponents continually reminded legislators that women, youth, and minorities were neither the only nor the most important victims of recession and unemployment. "The people begging for jobs today are not limited to the unskilled nor to the minorities," observed Sister Regina Williams of the Milwaukee, Wisconsin, Peace and Justice Center. In fact, "many middle-class college graduates are unsuccessfully seeking employment."[131] A St. Louis, Missouri, UAW official introduced lawmakers to a model victim, James Jones, an unemployed auto worker forced to support his family with food stamps. The Congressional Black Caucus urged President Carter, a timid supporter of the bill, to issue a statement *"that Humphrey-Hawkins is for all people, not just for blacks,"* and CBC member Augustus Hawkins, a bill cosponsor, used testimony like Jones's to remind his fellow lawmakers that "there are a lot of skilled persons among the unemployed who are males and who are also white."[132]

Jones, like other white working-class victims of recession, derived his symbolic power not only from his race and occupation but from his gender and his status as a family breadwinner. In the liberal imagination, these victims avoided food stamps or welfare if they could. Like the hypothetical victims of unemployment drawn by union leader John Callahan, Jones and his peers "normally work for a living, produce and pay taxes." They were "accustomed to paying their own way and don't want to be dependent on handouts." They wanted "jobs, not Unemployment Compensation or Welfare." Welfare in these narratives appeared not as a critical safety net to which even the most "deserving" workers might have to resort, but as a symbol of degeneracy, the ultimate degradation for a man whose pride derived from his breadwinning status.[133] A similar narrative appeared in *Progressive Magazine* in early 1976. The author drew a portrait of the typical victim of the 1970s economy, a Flint, Michigan, autoworker with a "decent income, a modest house," and "unemployment compensation and union benefits" to carry him through hard times. But when long-term unemployment left him penniless, he lost the respect of his children and his wife. While once "he was the boss, the breadwinner," now he can no longer provide.[134]

Downplaying the particular plight of African Americans and other minorities had material consequences. After all, unemployment and underemployment had always fallen most heavily on nonwhite men and on women and youth. As one expert reminded Congress, Nixon's 5 percent unemployment goal had been tolerable only because "it meant two-and-a-half percent for white household heads" alongside "ten percent for nonwhites [and] thirty-three percent for nonwhite teenagers."[135] As recession set in and layoffs reached Depression-era levels, African Americans and women, who had just begun to gain a foothold in well-paid manufacturing jobs, took severe hits as seniority rules enforced a "last hired, first fired" policy and unions consistently rejected proposals to share the layoff burden more equitably.[136] In late 1977, BLS figures showed that African Americans endured a jobless rate more than twice as high as the overall level of 7.1 percent, and the black teen unemployment rate reached a whopping 40 percent.[137] A bill that promised to bring overall unemployment to 3 percent would almost certainly leave joblessness higher for more disadvantaged groups, especially if lawmakers viewed full employment as a substitute for antidiscrimination remedies like affirmative action. The 1977 BLS report, announced on the eve of Full Employment Week, briefly forced liberal attention back to black poverty and disadvantage. Jesse Jackson, Michael Myers of the NAACP, and Coretta Scott King all spoke publicly about the effect of "recession-induced unemployment" and its potential to erode "all the gains and victories" that African Americans had made in "the past fifteen years."[138]

President Carter, who won 94 percent of the black vote and the endorsement of major civil rights leaders, was ill-prepared to respond either to the general economic crisis or to the plight of urban African Americans.

At the prodding of black leaders, he directed his Labor Secretary, Ray Marshall, to conduct a "crash study of minority joblessness" and assured the CBC that minority unemployment represented "the most important domestic issue right now."[139] But Carter ignored staff recommendations to expand youth employment demonstration projects and the public service employment. He instead expressed support for "Private Sector Initiatives," which he called "the best and most cost effective approach."[140] So while assuring civil rights leaders that their issues would receive "priority attention," Carter's hostility to large-scale federal programs and his growing fiscal conservatism prevented any comprehensive urban policy and made him a cool supporter at best of the full employment bill.[141] In October 1977, OMB director James T. McIntyre, Jr., "reluctantly recommended" that the president endorse a watered-down full employment bill to "mollify . . . the Black Caucus" while "retain[ing] the support of moderates and conservatives by explaining to them that the new version is harmless."[142]

In urging Congressional action, some African American leaders offered full employment as a solution to the closely linked urban and welfare crises, the "poverty, drug addiction and crime" that plagued the nation's inner cities.[143] Though urban rioting had died down after 1968, America's cities continued their long decline, and a series of well-publicized fiscal crises kept urban problems in the news, if only sporadically. Unemployment, a critical problem in America's central cities, could hardly be removed from problems of urban deterioration and racial disadvantage. And discussion of the urban crisis invariably led to discussion of welfare. As Chapter 1 argued, both liberals and conservatives saw the supposedly damaging effects of welfare—its insatiable appetite for taxpayer dollars, its tendency to break up families and encourage socially destructive behaviors—as partially responsible for the plight of America's cities. Liberal full employment supporters drew on this antiwelfare discourse to sell jobs as a constructive solution to urban poverty. The unemployed were not only "the root cause of crime and of our urban crisis," warned Murray Finlay, but they proved "a drain on national and local budgets."[144] The "best way to balance the budget," advised Walter Fauntroy, is to provide jobs so that victims of unemployment can "become tax-payers instead of tax-eaters."[145]

The language of social disorder also kept the "pathological" black family on the political radar, and some liberals revived Moynihanian antipoverty rhetoric to discuss black family reconstruction. Norman Hill called unemployment and underemployment a "powerful force working against family stability among the poor," and he found "the increase in joblessness among the male heads of two-parent black families" to be "particularly damaging."[146] In 1975, the leader of a St. Louis, Missouri, human rights organization portrayed full employment as a way to provide "more and better paying jobs for black men" so that "they can become true breadwinners of their families," a sentiment echoed by the Reverend Buck Jones of the United Church of Christ.[147] Meanwhile, economist Leon Keyserling hoped that the bill "would . . . reduce the conditions which force so many mothers to work instead of staying home," a situation that "has grave social consequences."[148]

Conservative full employment opponents may also have pushed liberals to emphasize male breadwinners. Conservatives tried to downplay high unemployment by dismissing the plight of jobless women, whom they defined as "secondary earners," while business organizations, business publications, and Federal Reserve Board officials blamed women's presumably illegitimate (or at least less legitimate) entry into the labor market for rising unemployment rates.[149] Even if women were not responsible for the crisis, their status as "secondary" earners made their joblessness less tragic to many conservatives. Unemployment was "vastly overrated," insisted Senator Edwin (Jake) Garn, because "at least half" afflicted "someone who is not a breadwinner."[150] Congress should not get "carried away" by growing unemployment, agreed Treasury Secretary John Connelly, because "unemployment . . . for males, heads of families" remained only 3 percent.[151] In a subtler version of the same outlook, opponents of the bill's public service employment provisions, including the Chamber of Commerce and Alan Greenspan of the Council of Economic Advisors, implicitly dismissed the long-term unemployment crisis among women and minorities by insisting that economic recovery was right around the corner.[152] Calling full employment a "utopian concept," representatives from the Chamber and NAM warned that the bill would flood the labor market with individuals who had a "loose attachment to the labor force" and a "marginal propensity to work." Those individuals—women, minorities, and youth—needed training, they insisted, not a job guarantee.[153]

The focus on male breadwinning, which crossed ideological and party lines, found its way into the legislation in subtle yet profound ways. The bill's very definition of unemployment favored white, male workers, as civil rights leaders were quick to point out. Women and nonwhite men sustained significantly higher unemployment rates than white men and made up a disproportionate share of "discouraged workers." In 1975, women's unemployment rate averaged 9.3 percent, compared with men's 7.9 percent. As the economy improved in 1976, the gap actually widened, women's rate falling to 8.6 percent and men's to 7.0 percent. Further, unemployment figures did not take into account "the massive problem of underemployment for women," as economist Carolyn J. Jacobson pointed out.[154] Humphrey-Hawkins did not address these discrepancies, promising only to ensure a 3 percent *overall* unemployment rate. At the same time, the bill did nothing to address the country's deeply sex- and race-segregated labor market, either, which confined poor and working-class women to a glutted "pink-collar" job ghetto and reserved stable, well-paid work for men.

As Congress rewrote the bill, it limited the job guarantee in ways that further favored white male breadwinners. The original bill promised a public service job to any able and willing adult who could not find work in the private sector. Such open-ended spending was unlikely to win Congressional support. Congress limited the definition of "worker" to adults "actively seeking work," excluding welfare recipients, discouraged workers, and involuntary part-time workers—all disproportionately female and minority.[155] Administrators were also instructed to consider the number of employed household members and duration of unemployment when allocating public service jobs: Jobs would go first to the short-term unemployed, more likely to be white male workers suffering from recession rather than minorities and women suffering from long-term joblessness. Jobs would also be reserved for breadwinners, a category that did not include AFDC recipients, who were not considered a priority population in the bill and were not counted as officially "unemployed."[156] In any case, poor women were less likely than men to qualify for the mostly high-technology public service jobs the bill promised to create. Nonetheless, optimism prevailed among many proponents of full employment who believed that "women—especially minority women—will be liberated from systematic and pervasive discrimination on the job market" and that "if you have full employment, you cannot have discrimination."[157]

When the liberal majority proved unable to recognize gender bias, lobbyists from feminist groups were more than willing to point it out. By 1976, feminists were well-poised to become key players in the full employment campaign. Organizations like NOW, Women's Equity Action League (WEAL), and the NWPC had sophisticated lobbying outfits, while the so-called "traditional" women's organizations had gradually adopted more explicitly feminist identities. And feminists in a host of male-dominated liberal organizations, from labor unions and religious groups to the ACLU and the Ford Foundation, were successfully pressuring their colleagues to attend to issues of gender equity.[158] Feminism was in the air and gaining increasing legitimacy among the public at large and liberal circles in particular.

Full employment was a particularly good fit with the feminist agenda; it was, as a YWCA Board Member put it, "a women's issue par excellence . . . central to all our hopes and dreams."[159] Though abortion and the Equal Rights Amendment garnered media attention during the 1970s, jobs had been central to American feminism since the early twentieth century. The first real victory for second-wave feminism, predating the movement's explosion, was the Equal Pay Act of 1963, and the first official second-wave feminist organization, NOW, emerged as a response to the Equal Employment Opportunity Commission's inaction on sex-discrimination complaints.[160] During the 1970s, working women formed women's caucuses in professional associations and unions, clerical workers organized to demand "bread, not roses," and activists took advantage of federal affirmative action guidelines to train women for "non-traditional" jobs in the well-paid skilled trades. In March 1974, over three thousand female labor unionists met in Chicago to found the Coalition of Labor Union Women (CLUW), dedicated to improving the position of women within organized labor and pressuring unions, employers, and the government to ensure affirmative action policies, maternity leave and benefits, comparable worth policies, and child care facilities. Union feminists sought to address the needs of their own members as well as "millions of unorganized sisters," particularly "minority women who have traditionally been singled out for particularly blatant oppression," by improving women's access to employment and their position in the labor market.[161] Meanwhile, traditional women's organizations like the YWCA provided counseling, career planning, assertiveness training, training for nontraditional jobs, child care, and other services.[162]

Activism exploded in the 1970s as more and more married women and mothers entered the labor market. While feminism's "second wave" had various sources, including the powerful example of the black freedom struggle, increased access to higher education, and changing sexual ideas and practices, it was the contradictions faced by wage-earning women that truly lit the fires of feminist revival. The sheer number of woman workers grew tremendously in the second half of the twentieth century as their demographic profile changed. Early in the century, most female laborers had been young single women, but the average woman worker by the 1970s was married and had children in the home, a transformation that crossed racial and class barriers. As men faced stagnating wages and an unstable labor market, and as rates of divorce and single motherhood multiplied, women's wages became increasingly important to family survival. In the mid-1970s, 47 percent of working women were single, divorced, separated, or living with husbands who earned less than $7,000 annually. As Carolyn J. Jacobson informed AFL-CIO members in 1974, "clearly the notion that women work only for 'pin money' is not valid. Their employment is vital to the support of themselves and their families."[163]

The full employment campaign helped feminist poverty activists convince their colleagues to address poor women's needs. In NOW, Merrillee Dolan and her allies struggled valiantly to make the organization live up to its eloquent resolutions declaring poverty a women's issue; however, an internal report completed in 1976 detailed an overwhelming lack of interest in poverty among NOW's members, who harbored "narrow definitions of feminism" and the "erroneous . . . perception that poverty issues are not personally relevant." If the guaranteed income campaign of the 1960s had failed to attract significant feminist support, full employment seemed the perfect issue to bring feminist attention to women's poverty. Almost all of NOW's 1973 "Action Year Against Poverty" resolutions emphasized "enabl[ing] women more freedom to work outside the home," and NOW leaders saw "the answer to poverty in this country" as "not just better and fuller employment of manpower but [also of] womanpower."[164] But as early as 1975 feminists expressed concern that the full employment campaign failed to address "the needs and problems of women workers."[165] Along with the 3 percent overall rate, the bill failed to include provisions on affirmative action and comparable worth, sex segregation in the labor market, maternity leave, part-time and flex-time options, or child care. The "growing fear of unemployment by white males" was fueling "attacks on the principle of affirmative action, cries of 'reverse discrimination,' and other evidence of white male backlash," worried NOW's Lynn Darcy, making it less likely that Congress would amend the bill to address feminist concerns.[166] When major unions sponsored a "Jobs Now!" rally in 1975, CLUW asked other feminists to help draw attention to women's needs. NOW leaders urged their members to join CLUW with signs reading "Unemployment Twice as High for Women Than Men," "Women and Blacks Hit Hardest," and "NOW Fights for All Women Workers."[167]

In critiquing the full employment bill, feminists from liberal, labor union, feminist, and traditional women's organizations challenged the male-breadwinner ideology at the heart of the liberal economic agenda. Feminist critiques of full employment rested first and foremost on a fundamental insistence that all individuals had a "right to live in dignity, without deprivation and free from dependence for economic reasons on any other person."[168] This basic principle was in itself an assault on the family wage bargain, which assumed women's economic dependence on men's wages. Economic realities lent urgency to this feminist tenet. Rising rates of divorce and single motherhood meant that more families lacked a male "head of household," while stagnating wages and rising unemployment rates made more families dependent upon multiple earners. Statistics challenged the "myth that most women have a male figure contributing to her support," noted Rita Reynolds of the St. Louis, Missouri YWCA. According to the DOL, over half of woman wage earners in the mid-1970s worked because of "pressing economic need."[169] When legislators limited the job guarantee to one earner per family, they evoked the specter of Depression-era discrimination against married women workers and revealed a "feeling, hidden just below the surface today, that in times of high unemployment, equity means one job per family, and that job ought to go to the man."[170]

It was the bill's inherent male-breadwinner bias—and an understanding of how deeply the labor market was segregated by race and sex—that prompted feminists to demand what critics would come to dismiss as "special treatment." Minority activists and feminists knew that full employment was "a necessary but not sufficient condition" for equal opportunity.[171] They argued that "in order to achieve full employment and equal opportunities, special measures will be necessary for . . . disadvantaged groups," particularly women.[172] They rejected Congressional restrictions that limited the job guarantee and asked that Congress set a 3 percent unemployment target for specific groups of workers to ensure that women and minorities benefited equally. They demanded stringent antidiscrimination, affirmative action, and vocational training efforts to combat sex segregation in the labor market and relieve pressure on the glutted "pink collar ghetto" of women's service work. They insisted that child care, part-time/flex-time, and parental leave be included in the job guarantee. Some of them proposed that the government "ensure that women benefited from full employment policies" by establishing a Women's Policy Bureau as part of the bill's administration.[173] Because sexism and the family wage ideal were deeply rooted in the American labor market, feminists like Rita Reynolds of the YWCA insisted that policies "must be designed particularly for and around the gender-specific needs of women if they are to make a difference."[174] If Congress did not "do something special about [women's] problems in finding work," concurred Carol Burris of Women's Lobby, "then the bill is really designed to serve a minority population: men who are unemployed for a short period of time."[175]

The few welfare recipients who testified on full employment agreed. During the FAP campaign, the NWRO had emphasized the "income" part of its "jobs and income" demand, insisting that society value the caregiving labor of poor single mothers with an adequate guaranteed income. All along, though, welfare rights leaders also demanded access to well-paid jobs. As liberals made full employment their priority, the struggling NWRO joined the SCLC and Operation PUSH in demanding "a program for *full employment*" as "national policy," and AFDC recipients flocked to feminist antipoverty programs that trained and placed poor single mothers in nontraditional jobs.[176] Not surprisingly, the full employment campaign prompted welfare rights activists to emphasize jobs as the ticket out of poverty for poor single mothers. In a letter to Congressman Hawkins, Evelyn Sims of the Muskegon County (Michigan) Welfare Rights Organization insisted that "welfare recipients will never be able to move into the mainstream of life and live a dignified life above the level of poverty unless they are given jobs and decent pay." The welfare mothers consulted by Women's Lobby demanded jobs, and Women's Lobby in turn urged Congress to make AFDC recipients a priority group.[177] With appropriate training and job placement, Sims argued, "we would not be dependent on welfare checks but be able to work and earn our way."[178]

The full employment bill that Congress passed in 1978 did little for poor single mothers, but it did little for anyone else, either.[179] President Carter, never an enthusiastic supporter, battled recession and stagflation with fiscal austerity. Meanwhile, the conservative anti-tax movement gained steam, and liberals in the Democratic Party lacked the power and the will to approve significant new spending. The Full Employment and Balanced Growth Act of 1978 included no mandates, no guarantees, and no enforcement. But the full employment campaign illustrates the difficulties liberals faced as they struggled to ameliorate racial disadvantage while appealing broadly to white "middle Americans." It also reveals the continuing hold of the male-breadwinner ideal on the American left and the evolving feminist challenge to it. But at the same time that liberals hoped to use ostensibly universal social policies like full employment to rebuild a bigger and more inclusive New Deal coalition, a group of intellectuals and journalists were pursuing an opposite strategy, drawing on liberal critiques of AFDC and the black family to deny federal responsibility for ensuring racial equity or battling poverty. It is to this effort that I now turn.

Welfare and the "Underclass"

The disaster was that welfare, along with those who pressed its expansion, deprived the poor of New York of what was for them—as for the poor who preceded them—the best and indeed the only way to the improvement of their condition, the way that involved commitment to work and the strengthening of family ties. (Nathan Glazer, 1971)[180]

In the time since the war on poverty was launched, the moral blight of dependency has been compounded and extended to future generations by a virtual plague of family dissolution. (George Gilder, 1981)[181]

In August 1977, the editors of *Time* introduced readers to "The American Underclass: Destitute and Desperate in the Land of Plenty." The authors tried to explain why, after over a decade of antipoverty measures and expanding welfare rolls, America's inner cities harbored what many perceived as an intractable and growing poverty problem. Scholars continue to address this question, and they have detailed numerous economic and social changes that locked a growing number of urban minorities in poverty. The unemployment, low wages, and lack of opportunity that had long plagued black urban migrants only intensified in the 1970s as well-paid unskilled jobs moved to the suburbs and as wages for low-skilled work deteriorated.[182] Meanwhile, government policies, from federal highway construction and housing and urban renewal programs to corporate tax incentives, compounded the isolation of poor urban communities. Combined with persistent racial discrimination in employment, housing, and education, federal policy and economic restructuring during the second half of the twentieth century conspired to deny social mobility to a large segment of the nonwhite urban population. Whites and middle-class minorities moved out of central cities and so, too, did manufacturing jobs, leaving a declining tax base, impoverished institutions, and an increasingly isolated poor minority population. If the term "underclass" described anything new, it was a new geography of poverty.[183] In 1959, 27 percent of the nation's poor whites and 38 percent of its poor African Americans lived in central cities; by the 1980s, 43 percent of poor whites and a majority (61 percent) of poor blacks could be found there.[184]

Beginning in the early 1970s, a handful of antipoverty liberals, bucking the broader liberal "new majority" strategy, employed the term "underclass" to convince policymakers to attend to the plight of the urban poor in the face of claims that the War on Poverty had been won.[185] Touted most prominently by former Nixon aide and Hoover Institution fellow Martin Anderson and celebrated in the editorial pages of the *Wall Street Journal*, this argument had some merit; the expansion of "generous government aid in the form of cash, medical benefits, food stamps, housing, and other services" did help reduce poverty rates, particularly among the aged, and mitigated some of the worst effects of poverty like medical neglect and malnutrition.[186] In fact, it was only government transfer programs that prevented an upswing in poverty during the sluggish growth and high unemployment of the 1970s.[187] A chorus of voices in the mid-1970s also celebrated "The Rising Black Middle Class," a group that symbolized the impressive progress African Americans had made since the 1950s: marked increases in income, occupational mobility, and educational achievement.[188] But, as the head of the Black Economics Research Center warned in 1974, perhaps one-third of American blacks remained "mired in poverty," threatening to become "a permanent black underclass."[189] To counter a congratulatory sentiment that might feed federal retreat, some civil rights leaders warned that a "social underclass" remained "trapped in a cycle of poverty, ignored by state and local governments and exploited by landlords, employers, police, [and] politicians."[190] In a proposal to re-examine the 1968 Kerner Commission Report on its tenth anniversary, the NUL noted that urban rioting had been replaced by "a new kind of violence," one borne of "continued neglect and the creation of a permanent underclass of citizens whose anger is expressed in their own self-destruction."[191]

By the mid-1970s, though, the term "underclass" was acquiring a host of implications that did not bode well for liberal policy prescriptions. Many mainstream sources agreed that America's black population was splitting into "two 'nations'—one prosperous, the other impoverished," and that the latter found itself "embedded in a slum-world of fatherless families, drugs, crime, disease, privation—and resegregation."[192] The August 1977 *Time* magazine story laid out the essential features of a new genre—the journalistic underclass ethnography—which changed little in the following decade. Trapped in a "different world, a place of pock-marked streets, gutted tenements, and broken hopes," the "impoverished urban blacks" of the inner city harbored a culture just as destructive as their environment, a system of "values that are often at radical odds with those of the majority—even the majority of the poor." By producing a "highly disproportionate number of the nation's juvenile delinquents, school dropouts, drug addicts and welfare mothers," as well as "much of the adult crime, family disruption, urban decay and demand for social expenditures," this underclass was

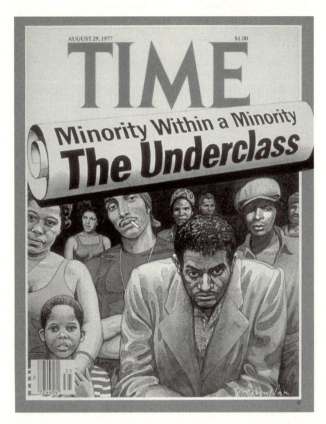

Figure 9. A 1977 *Time* magazine cover story on the "underclass." By the late 1970s, Americans across the political spectrum worried about concentrated minority poverty in the nation's cities, and scholarly and journalistic treatments of a so-called "underclass" drew on and fed concerns about AFDC's supposedly destructive effects. © 1977 Time Inc. Reprinted by permission.

distinguished not by the structural forces that limited its upward mobility but by its culture and values, especially its failure to form stable, male-breadwinner families. In the barrios of South American cities and the poor villages of West Africa, the authors noted, the poor maintained "strong traditional values," particularly family values, which prevented social disintegration and provided a buffer against the worst effects of poverty. It was "the weakness of family structure" that, above all, "makes the American underclass unique among the world's poor people." The authors profiled five individuals—two failed male breadwinners (an "ex-junkie" turned

Figure 10. Photograph from *Time* coverage of the "American Underclass." The editors' caption reads, "Three generations on welfare: discrimination's sad testament." The portrait of African American AFDC recipients and intergenerational welfare became common features of media and political discussions of poverty and income support by the 1980s. © Bob Adelman.

"panhandler" and a "wine-sipping ex-con") and three welfare mothers. All were nonwhite, and all served as the mirror image of Nixon's "silent majority," an alien population that flouted male breadwinning, hard work, and "traditional" values.[193]

A scurrilous (and false) portrait of AFDC mothers and their violent, drug-addicted sons and boyfriends took the starring role in underclass discourse. Two years before the *Time* article, in September 1975, the *New Yorker* magazine spent nearly fifty pages profiling just one member of the "underclass," Carmen Santana, a Puerto Rican AFDC recipient in Brooklyn. Journalist Susan Sheehan described Santana's personal appearance in detail: she is obese but "makes no effort to conceal her thick neck, her big breasts, her big belly, and her enormous thighs," favoring "tight-fitting" shirts and pants. The mother of four children by three different men, Santana is described as a neglectful, if not uncaring, mother, giving her children "a good cuffing" at one moment, hugging them the next, and allowing them to draw obscene graffiti on their bedroom walls. One son is addicted to heroin, and a daughter was pregnant at fourteen. Santana cheats the welfare department, hiding her occasional earnings (from factory labor and selling numbers on the street), illegally claiming her daughter and granddaughter as dependents, and failing to report the presence of her live-in boyfriend, who is employed. While her personal appearance, childrearing and housekeeping skills, and sexual history featured prominently in the story, Sheehan included nothing about the government policies and corporate decisions that shaped Santana's options.[194]

As a representative of welfare, and of the underclass more generally, Carmen Santana is a familiar figure in twentieth-century American discussions of poverty. It should come as little surprise that black and Hispanic AFDC mothers played such a key role in underclass discourse, for this kind of portrait—of a lazy, incompetent, promiscuous, and almost always nonwhite AFDC mother—has a long history. In the 1970s, both the evolving shape of urban poverty and a well-funded and intellectually sophisticated assault on government social spending gave the image broader legitimacy. Now, a host of well-respected scholars, including some former supporters of expansive antipoverty and welfare programs, gave an official and scholarly imprimatur to cultural and behavioral explanations of poverty well beyond the folksy diatribes of Senator Russell Long and his ilk. By popularizing the idea of an urban "underclass"—what Daniel Patrick Moynihan called the "twentieth century equivalent of the [nineteenth century's] 'dangerous classes'"—these antiwelfare journalists, scholars, and politicians countered liberal portraits of a deserving "new majority" with a picture of the poor with which few Americans could sympathize.[195] Underclass discourse insisted that economic hardship was *not* widely shared and was *not* visited upon the most deserving Americans, those who worked hard and lived in intact families. Poverty was the lot of people whose culture and behavior kept them at the bottom of society. Not only could government do little to help the underclass, these scholars, authors, and pundits suggested, but the "perverse incentives" of a well-meaning but wrongheaded welfare system—AFDC most of all—only encouraged and deepened their misery. Whether "passive," "hostile," or "hustler," members of the underclass were drawn, according to journalist Ken Auletta, "disproportionately from single-parent homes and from welfare-dependent families."[196]

Welfare's "perverse incentives" also became the focus of a resurgent free-market conservatism that built a powerful case against welfare in the 1970s without resorting to references to an "underclass" or speculations about either race or culture. Libertarian conservatives had been defending the free market against government interference for more than a century, insisting that the nation's prosperity and its citizens' political liberty rested first and foremost on economic freedom—that is, minimal taxation, redistribution, and regulation. During the long postwar economic boom, when Keynesian policies stimulated what seemed to be an endless expansion in productivity, wealth, corporate profits, and standards of living, such paeans to a strictly free market fell out of fashion. Business leaders, organized within the Chamber of Commerce, NAM, and a number of smaller outfits, ritually denounced federal spending, but few Americans took the threat very seriously. Though voiced by well-respected philosophers like Friedrich Hayek and Russell Kirk, these ideas rarely made their way outside local Chambers of Commerce and the fairly small circle of *National Review* subscribers, though in the 1960s they did inspire many Americans to join organizations like Young Americans for Freedom and to campaign for Barry Goldwater. As historians have amply demonstrated, American conservatism did not spring full-blown in 1980 but rather gained strength during the 1960s, even as liberalism seemed triumphant.[197]

The nation's shifting economic fortunes in the 1970s lent new weight to libertarian economic theories. By 1980, inflation was 12.5 percent, unemployment 7.5 percent, and Americans experienced the worst year for real family income since World War II.[198] Such economic difficulties, along with the disheartening conclusion to American involvement in Vietnam and the trauma of the Watergate scandal, registered in poll data, revealing a precipitous decline in public confidence in all American institutions, government most of all.[199] In this context, more Americans were inclined to believe that government social expenditures had become "the weight that . . . broke the golden egg of capitalism."[200] As international competition increased in the early 1970s, American business launched a sophisticated publicity and lobbying campaign against federal regulation and spending. "We must realize that we can alter the direction of government only by becoming a part of government in a very real sense," NAM's chairman of the board, Burt Raynes, explained in 1972. "We must become involved in the decision-making process at all levels and must be prepared to make the sacrifices in time, energy and money that such involvement requires."[201] And sacrifice they did, to the tune of billions of dollars. Beefing up their lobbying corps (NAM moved its headquarters to Washington, D.C., in 1972), coordinating campaign contributions through Political Action Committees (PACs), revitalizing existing organizations like the Business Roundtable, and funding scholarship and punditry through public policy research institutes like the Heritage Foundation, the Hoover Institution, and the American Enterprise Institute, corporate America warned policymakers and the public about the dangers of federal spending.[202] "Talk with your neighbors," NAM urged its members, and remind them that "every government program costs money . . . *their* money."[203] In a flurry of books, articles, statements, speeches, and position papers, corporate America launched all-out war on the welfare state.

By the late 1970s, crippling inflation, persistent unemployment, and sluggish productivity confounded Keyensian wisdom and encouraged a profound pessimism about the nation's economic future, making the free-market case against welfare seem increasingly plausible. Even a liberal defender of the welfare state admitted that "it is now generally assumed that large-scale, public expenditures cause inflation." All this liberal could do was to argue that "kindness and justice" demanded that we maintain a welfare system all the same.[204] On the other end of the political spectrum, some conservatives warned that America's "growing body of public parasites" was producing the inflation and the "breakdown of moral law" that could bring down an empire.[205] In his 1981 book *Wealth and Poverty*, conservative author George Gilder summed up the libertarian case against welfare (and all other forms of redistribution): "An effort to take income from the rich, thus diminishing their investment, and to give it to the poor, thus reducing their work incentives, is sure to cut American productivity, limit job opportunities, and perpetuate poverty."[206] The argument would become the basis for a new economic orthodoxy, supply-side economics, which the Reagan administration would adopt as its answer to the nation's economic and moral distress. Even before 1980, the case that welfare created an economic drag on the economy had become widely accepted. "If the U.S. economy is now stagnant, as we are told it is," intoned one journalist late in the decade, "the demoralizing, enervating effects of welfare on the poor should be considered one of the causes."[207]

To libertarians and business leaders, the most important of those "enervating effects" was welfare's work disincentive. Henry Hazlitt laid out the essential argument that dated back to the Social Darwinists of the late nineteenth century and to the Elizabethan Poor Laws before that: welfare "undermines incentives for self-support," thereby acting "to prolong and intensify the very disease [it] seek[s] . . . to cure." In other words, any protections against the vagaries of the labor market induced many, perhaps most, people to live in idleness. Antipoverty liberals had also attacked welfare's work disincentive but their solution had been to allow recipients to keep a portion of their earnings; in particular, liberals had hoped to encourage low-earning men to fulfill their role as breadwinner by supplementing their earnings with government aid. At root, they had always argued that the poor, welfare recipients included, *wanted* to work if given the opportunity, a case made repeatedly and confirmed by surveys of welfare recipients themselves. Conservatives held a much less optimistic view of humanity. Why would anyone work, particularly at the kind of low-paying, physically arduous or mind-numbingly boring jobs available to the unskilled and uneducated, unless they faced the threat of starvation?[208]

Corporate America's brief flirtation with antipoverty work, described in Chapter 1, ended abruptly in the early 1970s. Events at NAM suggest a definite hardening about welfare, probably in response to growing welfare rolls and the fear that liberals would continue to press for a guaranteed income. After briefly supporting the FAP, NAM leaders in 1972 made an about-face. Fearing that the "welfare ethic" was replacing the "work ethic" in America, the organization's board of directors denounced the NAM policy position on welfare as "too permissive." Rather than urging welfare administrators to provide recipients with "encouragement" and "motivation" to seek wage labor, the board favored explicit support for work requirements as well as "the need for tighter controls over public assistance."[209] Part of a broader campaign to slash government spending, this newly focused attack on AFDC was so designed as to reduce the bargaining power of a potentially enormous low-wage labor force, which increasingly included women.

Antipoverty liberals had always worried that AFDC relieved male breadwinners of their responsibility to work, but NAM, the Chamber of Commerce, and an increasing number of conservative intellectuals argued that its more direct effect—to relieve AFDC *mothers* of the need for wages—was just as pernicious. Corporate conservatives were less sentimental about the sanctity of motherhood (at least for poor single mothers); they demanded both strict child support enforcement to induce fathers to support their children and strict work requirements to induce mothers to do so, as well. When the First National Bank asked in a 1973 pamphlet, "Why are New York's Workers Dropping Out?" the workers it referred to were "young black women," and the answer it provided was the easy availability of welfare.[210] Reporting on a Joint Economic Committee study of AFDC recipients, the editors of *Business Week* reported that they had found the answer to "How Welfare Keeps Women from Working." AFDC, NAM insisted, "has undoubtedly lessened work incentives for many fathers *and mothers*."[211] NAM and other business organizations supported the Welfare Reform Act of 1975, one of a series of efforts to "stem the growth of the welfare rolls" by restricting eligibility and by reinforcing both male and female breadwinning through work requirements and strengthened child support enforcement.[212]

As they denounced welfare for keeping mothers out of the labor market, business lobbyists occasionally made use of the emerging underclass discourse.[213] Edward Banfield's controversial 1970 best-seller, *The Unheavenly City: The Nature and Future of Our Urban Crisis*, described the "personal problems" of a virtually intractable "lower-class culture," a style of life "learned in childhood and passed on as a collective heritage" that kept urban blacks mired in poverty. An antiwelfare conservative, Banfield drew on 1960s antipoverty liberal ideology, articulated most clearly by anthropologist Oscar Lewis, which had argued that persistent discrimination, unemployment, and material deprivation threatened to create among the African American poor a "culture of poverty" that made amelioration difficult, if not impossible.[214] Taking Lewis's argument to its logical, if distasteful, conclusion, Banfield described poor urban black men as "present-oriented," living "from moment to moment," "radically improvident," focused only on "bodily needs (especially for sex)" and working "only as he must to stay alive." This culture, Banfield argued, set clear "limits on what policymakers can accomplish" and doomed antipoverty efforts, from income supplements and job training to casework, to inevitable failure.[215]

With this kind of cultural argument, American business found the answer to an essential question, posed by NAM in 1975: "How does a 'conservative' element of the private sector make its views effective on social programs?"[216] They could blame welfare for more than inflation and low productivity, more even than enabling recipients to avoid wage labor. They could blame welfare for the persistent, intractable, socially destructive poverty and social disorder associated with the growing "underclass." "Billions of dollars spent on AFDC," the NAM argued, "have *created* problems of dependency instead of serving as a helping hand to get these people on the road to self-support and self-respect."[217] Welfare cost society financially, but it also exacted a "human" cost, because it promoted "generational dependency" with all its pathological side effects.[218] Here, the free market critique of welfare's work disincentives joined a cultural theory of poverty that blamed values, behavior, and "personal problems" for persistent economic hardship.

Unlike libertarian and business welfare critics who focused almost solely on work incentives, the authors who did the most to publicize the "underclass" concept—in widely read articles and best-selling books in the late 1970s and 1980s—placed family structure at the center of their analysis. The "culture of poverty" that Banfield described was perpetuated not only by AFDC but by its partner, the "familial anarchy among the concentrated poor of the inner city."[219] George Gilder, a liberal Republican, *Ripon Forum* editor, and one-time Nixon speechwriter, placed family and gender roles squarely at the center of his antiwelfare argument. In his 1973 book *Sexual Suicide* (an antifeminist diatribe), Gilder drew on anthropological observations and pseudo-Freudian psychology to argue that men, who lacked the primary and ongoing sexual role that childbirth provided women, were by nature "present-oriented." It was up to women to domesticate men, to civilize them by inducing them to commit to children and the future, by convincing them to become breadwinners. Without the "financial superiority" that bolstered this economic and psychological role, Gilder insisted, man would experience violence, street crime, and early death. Such consequences had already appeared in America's ghettos, exacerbated by a welfare system which "necessarily subverts the male role as provider and promotes family disintegration."[220] In widely read articles in *Harper's*, *Forbes*, and the *American Spectator* and then in his 1981 book *Wealth and Poverty*, Gilder further denounced liberal welfare policies, and AFDC in particular, for the "wreckage of broken lives and families" in the nation's ghettos. This was not the intractable culture of poverty that Banfield described; it was a "welfare culture" in which "money becomes not something earned by men through hard work but a right conferred on women by the state."[221]

Gilder's argument may sound familiar: it is essentially the same critique of AFDC that antipoverty liberals honed in the 1960s. In his description of family dysfunction among the poor, Gilder might have been quoting from a late 1960s position paper generated by the A. Philip Randolph Institute, NUL, or LWV. And like Moynihan and other liberals in the 1960s, Gilder urged "preferential treatment" for "ghetto boys" to reestablish appropriate gender relations by assuring men "financial superiority." Surprisingly, given his conservative politics, Gilder also concurred with antipoverty liberals on maternal work requirements (which he opposed) and federal child allowances (which he supported). Unlike AFDC, Gilder noted, child allowances would go to fathers and would therefore "help the man function as provider rather than threaten to usurp him."[222]

As the decade wore on, Gilder took the antipoverty liberal critique of AFDC in an increasingly conservative direction. By 1980, he had converted to supply-side economics and was advocating punitive welfare reform proposals. Because AFDC usurped the poor man's provider role, legislators should "restrict the system as much as possible, by making it unattractive and even a bit demeaning." Concern with male breadwinning had convinced antipoverty liberals to pursue expanded income support for two-parent families; it convinced Gilder to cut income support for single mothers. By ignoring the decline of low-skilled employment opportunities in the inner cities and the broader problem of wage stagnation, Gilder and the many authors and politicians who agreed with him blamed AFDC, more than any other factor, for the "wreckage of broken lives and families" that were dooming poor urban African Americans to perpetual poverty.[223]

Results of the government's large-scale NIT experiments, published in 1978, bolstered the conservative case against welfare. Designed by liberal policymakers who were confident that social science would vindicate their proposals, several large-scale demonstration projects tested the effects of various NIT programs on work effort and family stability, the two factors that preoccupied welfare reformers on the left as well as the right. The results seemed to vindicate free market arguments that income supplements would surely decrease work effort. Male breadwinners in families receiving the NIT worked an average of 6 percent fewer hours, while wives and single mothers reduced their work effort an average of 17 and 12 percent respectively.[224] These numbers did not indicate the "mass defection the prophets of doom had predicted," enthused the Denver experiment's manager. Very few adults quit their jobs entirely, and most adult men did not change their work hours at all.[225] However, conservatives insisted that even a small reduction in work effort challenged "the sanguine view of human nature adopted by those who believe that giving people money does not undermine their performance in life."[226]

A more shocking finding, one that threw many antipoverty liberals for a loop, was the NIT's apparent effect on family stability. During the first three years of the Seattle and Denver experiments, families receiving the lowest NITs proved 60 percent more likely to break up than families in the control group. Reporters called it an "astonishing *increase* in the amount of family breakup under a reform designed to have precisely the opposite effect."[227] Conservative journals delighted in reporting that the NIT increased marital breakup, and Senator Long and other antiwelfare lawmakers found the results useful in discrediting income support proposals.[228] Some liberals brushed off the findings as "the product of some statistical quirk."[229] Others pointed out that the experiments revealed a number of positive effects: many adult recipients transitioned into better-paid employment (25 percent increased their income enough to become ineligible for supplements), children's academic performance improved, and families received better nutrition and health care. "It would be unwise," concluded Andrew Cherlin, "to hold reform hostage to the rise and fall of the divorce rate."[230] But in the very terms of debate set up by antipoverty liberals—that AFDC broke up families and that a more inclusive income support system would preserve them—the NIT failed. Moynihan, still convinced that family stability represented the key to overcoming poverty and racial disadvantage, lamented that the NIT results "discredited fifteen years of social policies that I had been trying to press." Antipoverty liberals "must now be prepared to entertain the possibility that we were wrong."[231]

The NIT, some liberals now concluded, may have the same family breakup incentives as AFDC. Project leader Robert Spiegelman blamed the results on an "independence effect," arguing that increased economic security reduced wives' dependence on their husbands. John Bishop of the University of Wisconsin's Institute for Research on Poverty concurred, adding that any kind of income support reduced the morale of male family heads, which proved detrimental to family stability.[232] Both antipoverty liberals and antiwelfare conservatives believed that "husbands are more inclined to leave when their 'provider role' is undermined." The NIT experiments revealed that not only AFDC but any form of income supplement might promote family instability and threaten to swell the "underclass." Recipient marriages dissolve, argued Gilder, "not because the rules dictate it, but because the benefit levels [however administered] destroy the father's key role and authority." Whether the program is AFDC, a NIT, or some other form of income support, the poor man "has been cuckolded by the compassionate state."[233] The results of the NIT experiments, Gilder concluded, could not help but "banish all confidence in the beneficial impact of federal income supports of any sort, whether AFDC or radical reform."[234]

The NIT's supposedly "vexing social consequences" confirmed neoconservatives' growing suspicion that government programs, whatever their good intensions, only worsened social problems. This influential group of scholars and journalists defended what they viewed as traditional liberalism against the encroachments of black radicalism and the counterculture. A number of them, like Irving Kristol, Norman Podhoretz, and Nathan Glazer, were Jewish intellectuals with roots in the 1930s Marxist left. They were appalled by the antiwar insurgency within the Democratic Party, as well as by the growing trend toward détente with the Soviet Union, and they promoted a hard-line anticommunism that increasingly led them into alliances with conservative Republicans. And while most defended both the basic New Deal welfare state and the major civil rights victories of the early 1960s, they opposed busing, affirmative action, and other policies that seemed to violate the ideal of a "color-blind" society, and they increasingly displayed what one historian has called "an academic loss of faith in government."[235] Cultural issues, too, pushed neoconservatives out of the liberal camp. In the 1960s and 1970s, a younger generation of liberals and leftists rejected the bourgeois values of their parents. Liberals, it seemed to neoconservatives, were rejecting the basic tenets of the postwar liberal center: staunch anticommunism, commitment to a color-blind society, and defense of the male-breadwinner bourgeois family.[236] Even before most Americans had begun to worry that the American family was in crisis, neoconservatives like Gertrude Himmelfarb joined Moynihan in denouncing the welfare system for destroying such Victorian bourgeois values as "cleanliness, orderliness, obedience, thrift, [and especially] sexual propriety centered in the family."[237] In the late 1960s, neoconservative journals like *Commentary* and *The Public Interest* carried endless articles critiquing the "unintended consequences" of liberal social policies, and AFDC figured prominently.[238]

When historian Herbert Gutman published *The Black Family in Slavery and Freedom* in 1976, revealing that the vast majority of African Americans had lived in two-parent, nuclear families during slavery and Reconstruction, neoconservatives found another weapon against welfare. If black families were not broken before the twentieth century, then the welfare state seemed an especially logical cause of instability. "Why," Glazer asked, "in the decade after 1965, when blacks moved massively into white-collar jobs, into better-paying jobs, into colleges and universities" and "when discrimination declined in the South and North and was attacked by strong national legislation and strong administrative action, did the indices of family stability turn markedly adverse?"[239] Neoconservatives provided a simple answer: welfare policies.[240] "In New York," declared "disillusioned liberal" Irving Kristol in 1976, "we have tried to abolish poverty through a generous welfare program." And while "statistically lifted out of poverty," the city's poor had "simultaneously sunk to various depths of social pathology." Welfare had produced "a largely demoralized population, with higher rates of crime, juvenile delinquency, drug addiction, teenage pregnancy, alcoholism" and other disastrous behaviors.[241]

The indictment of AFDC became part of an underclass discourse that reached beyond scholars and political pundits to affect the way ordinary Americans understood poverty, particularly African American poverty. In the June 1976 issue of *Fortune* magazine, John Davenport mocked the "millenarianism" of the 1960s antipoverty warriors, whose goal had been "the elimination of poverty itself, the root cause, or so it was argued, of those disturbing symptoms of social pathology such as crime and broken homes," for "the indexes of social pathology have, in fact, flourished under this attack."[242] The Hoover Institution publicized Martin Anderson's claims that the welfare system had created a "poverty wall" that "sentenced" the poor "to a life of dependency on the government dole." The Heritage Foundation ensured a wide hearing for Charles Hobbs's claims that government bureaucrats intentionally fostered dependency.[243] And George Gilder's argument that welfare encouraged out-of-wedlock births featured prominently in public discussions of welfare and poverty.[244] The cocktail of fear and moral disapproval evoked by these arguments insured the underclass argument would be understood by most Americans on an emotional rather than a rational basis.

In the decade after *Time* magazine introduced the underclass, a number of journalists delved into the subject, producing lengthy articles for such well-respected magazines as the *New Yorker* and *Atlantic Monthly*. Their treatments slighted economic context and structural barriers in favor of their subjects' behavior and values. In his analysis of the drug addicts, ex-convicts, and long-term welfare mothers in a New York City supported-work program, for example, Ken Auletta, whose 1981 *New Yorker* articles were "largely responsible for making [the term underclass] part of middle-class America's working vocabulary," focused on his subjects' "matriarchal families" and "welfare mentality."[245] Nicholas Lemann emphasized the supposedly destructive behavior and distorted family patterns of Chicago's urban "underclass."[246] While these authors usually gave a nod to residential segregation, a changing job market, and other structural factors, readers came away with a picture of American poverty as rooted firmly in behavior, values, and welfare dependency.

This picture profoundly distorted reality. The Panel Study of Income Dynamics (PSID), a long-term study of five thousand families, revealed that only a small fraction of Americans experienced persistent poverty in the 1970s—only one-tenth of the families studied were poor for eight of ten years between 1968 and 1978, only 3 percent could be considered persistently poor, and nearly one-third fell into poverty in at least one year in ten.[247] Clearly a substantial portion of Americans were at risk, even those who managed to find full-time jobs. The number of full-time workers who lived in poverty increased by over 50 percent between 1978 and 1985, and by the mid-1980s, an adult with two children who worked full-time, year-round at a minimum wage job earned 23 percent less than the official poverty line.[248] Other studies, too, found no neat distinctions between the "working poor" and the "welfare poor." In a study for the DOL, the University of Michigan's Louis Ferman concluded that "the worlds of low-wage workers and welfare recipients [are so] closely intertwined" that distinctions between them were "virtually meaningless."[249] Researchers who investigated the effects of welfare receipt concurred, finding that only a small proportion of AFDC recipients could be considered "long-term users" who remained on the rolls for eight or more years, that welfare receipt had no demonstrable effect on out-of-wedlock childbirths, and that children of AFDC mothers were no more likely to become welfare recipients than children raised in similar non-welfare households.[250] The vast majority used AFDC for short periods of time, often cycling on and off welfare as family circumstances, children's needs, and job availability fluctuated. As sociologist Diana Pearce noted, AFDC served as a kind of unemployment insurance for women whose fluctuating work histories kept them out of that more formal program.[251]

These statistical studies did little to counteract the powerful public and political impact of underclass discourse. They received much less public attention than the more sensationalist accounts of intergenerational poverty. Such accounts proved comforting, characterizing the underclass as neatly segregated in the central cities and suffering from self-induced poverty, perhaps lamentable but certainly not a sign of any larger problem of postindustrial capitalism. While studies like the PSID suggested that a large portion of Americans—not only minorities living in female-headed households in the central cities—lived with the threat of poverty, underclass discourse drew very clear distinctions between the poor and the rest of the nation, erasing the problems of the "working poor" from the political agenda. NAM, the U.S. Chamber of Commerce, and other business groups had been trying to narrow the poverty debate in this way since the beginning of the War on Poverty; to counter pressure for income supplements and a guaranteed income, they minimized the plight of low-wage workers, insisting that those at the bottom of the employment ladder would work their way out of poverty. The "real welfare problem," they continually reminded anyone who would listen, was AFDC. By the late 1970s, these claims had some scholarly muscle in the form of well-funded conservative authors and scholars who narrowed the nation's poverty problem to a small group of nonwhite city dwellers who were mired in poverty not because they earned so little but because they purposely withdrew from the labor market and reproduced indiscriminately. When a 1977 blackout in New York City sparked widespread looting and violence, even an article in the left-leaning *Commonweal* worried that the cities harbored "an underclass of violent, chaotic, unattached people," largely "black and Hispanic" and "alienated, restless, [and] anarchic." Their condition, lamented journalist Thomas Powers, was likely "intractable if not ineradicable, and it has the irrepressible force of all growing things, like seedlings which can crack concrete."[252]

Even before the 1980s when the underclass concept reached its cultural apogee, conservative and neoconservative scholars and journalists had narrowed the country's poverty debate in ways that would prove devastating to poor single mothers. But the underclass concept took a great deal from the 1960s antipoverty liberal critique of AFDC. Unlike business conservatives in the 1960s, who portrayed welfare mothers as competent, well-functioning women who had the potential to support themselves and contribute productively to society, antiwelfare authors in the 1970s echoed antipoverty liberal concerns that AFDC undermined male breadwinning, discouraged family stability, and contributed to an intergenerational cycle of poverty in America's ghettos. But their critique led them to a much different conclusion. Rather than expand the welfare state, luring more and more Americans into a system of perverse incentives that would sap their will to work, promote sex and reproduction outside of marriage, and ultimately destroy the nation's economy, underclass theorists proposed a simpler solution. If welfare caused the problems, then get rid of it—or at least severely restrict access. Underclass ideology thus paved the way for the Reagan administration's welfare policies, but not before liberals had one more shot at welfare reform.

Chapter 4

Debating the Family Wage: Welfare Reform in the Carter Administration

The assumptions upon which the AFDC Program was founded are no longer valid.

—National Conference on Social Welfare, 1976

In June 1979, the U.S. Supreme Court ruled in *Califano v. Westcott* that the federal government's AFDC-Unemployed Parent program (AFDC-UP) violated the Fourteenth Amendment's equal protection clause. Begun as a temporary measure during the Kennedy administration, AFDC-UP provided federal funds to states that wished to offer cash aid to two-parent families with an unemployed breadwinner. Though the statute language included no reference to the sex of that breadwinner, liberal reformers promoted the program as a way to keep unemployed *fathers* from deserting their wives and children in order to qualify them for AFDC. By the 1970s, only twenty-two states offered the program, and by 1977 AFDC-UP's 750,000 recipients made up less than 7 percent of the nation's AFDC population.[1] Throughout the 1960s and 1970s, liberal reformers consistently urged Congress to make the program mandatory. After all, AFDC-UP epitomized liberal welfare ideology: it expanded federal welfare coverage and it seemed to promote male-breadwinner families among the poor. In fact, as Chapter 2 noted, few liberals or welfare rights activists either noticed or bothered to comment when Congress officially restricted the program to families with unemployed fathers in 1967. Over a decade later, that restriction prompted a sex discrimination lawsuit.

The force behind *Califano v. Westcott* was a relatively new player in federal welfare politics: organized feminism. NOW spearheaded the lawsuit, taking up the case of two Massachusetts families denied AFDC-UP benefits on the grounds that the unemployed parent was female. Cindy Westcott and Susan Westwood had both served as family breadwinners before losing their jobs, while their husbands remained at home as primary caregivers. Though the families qualified in all other respects, they were denied benefits solely because the unemployed breadwinners were mothers rather than fathers.[2] Eleven women's organizations signed an amicus brief in support of the plaintiffs prepared by the NOW Legal Defense and Education Fund (NOW-LDEF), the ACLU Women's Rights Project, and the Center for Law and Social Policy. They convinced five justices to support the Massachusetts district court's decision that the program's restrictions were based on the unfair stereotype "that fathers are family breadwinners and mothers are not." Justice Harry Blackmun insisted that Congress had acted "with an image of the 'traditional family' in mind" and "had simply assumed that the father would be the family breadwinner and that the mother's employment role, if any, would be 'secondary'." HEW had assumed just that. Its lawyers argued that the program "was designed to fill another goal" besides gender equity, "namely that of promoting family stability by reducing the alleged incentive for a father to desert his family." The court's majority was not impressed by HEW's defense; it ordered states which provided AFDC-UP benefits to make them available to "families left equally needy by the mother's loss of her job."[3] NOW celebrated the decision for "the recognition given to women as wage earners and breadwinners, for the denouncement of sexual stereotypes," and for the potential "dollars-and-cents benefits for economically disadvantaged families."[4]

As the *Westcott* case suggests, by the time President Jimmy Carter set out to reform America's welfare system, the political and social calculus had altered significantly since the first Nixon administration. By 1977, the family wage model that liberals had hoped to extend to poor African Americans was on its last legs. By the early 1980s, only 13 percent of all American families conformed to the male-breadwinner, female-homemaker, dependent children model.[5] American academics, journalists, politicians, and pundits pondered the potential death of the "American Family"; socially conservative activists mobilized potential constituents with attacks on feminism, gay liberation, and other supposed threats to the "traditional" family; and liberals struggled to incorporate feminist demands that they adjust public policies to new family realities. If liberals had rested earlier welfare reform campaigns on saving the traditional American family, the way to proceed no longer seemed clear.

An analysis of feminist antipoverty and welfare rights activism in the 1970s reveals a new dimension to the history of both welfare and the women's movement. The predominantly white, middle-class feminist organizations like NOW and the NWPC have been criticized repeatedly by both activists and historians for failing to address the problems of poor and minority women. Antipoverty feminists certainly struggled to convince their organizations to commit resources to poverty issues and to rethink positions that might benefit middle-class women at the expense of poor women. But their very efforts belie portraits of a class-biased movement monolithically hostile to poor women's needs; in fact, by the late 1970s, feminist organizations were forming alliances with welfare recipient activists, and both groups of women were learning from one other. Together, feminists across the class spectrum offered a vision of a new, degendered family wage, challenging the male-breadwinner bias that continued to inform liberal welfare policy prescriptions.[6] Conservative welfare policies that punished poor single women would not solve women's poverty, they argued, nor would liberal programs to shore up male breadwinning. Instead, women needed access to training, jobs, income, and support services that would enable them to support their children independent of male support.

The federal government's reaction to *Westcott* reveals an additional challenge facing liberal welfare reformers by the late 1970s. Rather than terminate the offending program (AFDC-UP), the Supreme Court insisted that states extend AFDC-UP to poor two-parent families with unemployed mothers.[7] HEW complained that such a remedy would cost the federal government $500,000,000, not to mention the additional burden on struggling state treasuries. In the midst of an economic recession, HEW suggested that the nation simply could not afford to expand the program. Liberals, then, faced a new politics of austerity; the old Keynesian economics no longer seemed to work, and a new orthodoxy emerged, one that targeted federal social spending as the culprit of the nation's declining economic fortunes. It was these inauspicious circumstances that met the Carter administration as it stepped into the quagmire of welfare reform. The battle over Carter's Program for Better Jobs and Income (PBJI) epitomized the dilemma of welfare reform in an age of austerity and amidst increasingly conflicting ideas about family and gender roles.

Family Change and Family "Crisis"

The entire history of the human race teaches us that the family unit is the best way for men and women to live their lives, the best way to raise children, and the only solid foundation upon which to build a strong nation. (Jimmy Carter, 1976)[8]

The Family Could Become a Relic by the Year 2000, Sociologists Say. (*New York Times* headline, 1977)[9]

"The family is the cornerstone of our society," intoned Lyndon Johnson in 1965. "More than any other force it shapes the attitude, the hopes, the ambitions, and the values of the child." And "when the family collapses it is the children that are usually damaged." When "that happens on a massive scale the community itself is crippled."[10] Johnson, of course, was referring to family breakdown among poor urban African Americans, but a decade later, a similar rhetoric of family crisis had reached Middle America. "White families are being fragmented progressively as well as black families," warned one expert, "and middle-class families are now approaching the social disintegration of lower-class families a decade ago."[11]

The United States, along with the rest of the industrialized world, experienced profound changes in family organization in the last four decades of the twentieth century. The end to the male-breadwinner, female-homemaker nuclear family that most Americans considered "traditional" had a profound effect on American welfare politics. It undermined the AFDC program's rationale, further fractured the liberal antipoverty consensus, and generated new challenges to the federal government's traditional antipoverty approaches. Welfare politics continued to play out on a larger social and cultural stage, one that by the late 1970s had become preoccupied with "family crisis."

By 1976, the family had become "an intellectual growth industry," as one reporter put it, the subject of "an unending flow of new journals and newsletters, conferences and workshops."[12] A host of experts and observers across the political spectrum began in the mid-1970s to warn that "the family" was in serious trouble and to investigate the causes. Scholars held conferences and published scores of articles and books on the changing family, aided by federal social science research dollars; Congressional committees held hearings, federal agencies convened expert panels; and nongovernmental groups, from Christian parish ministers to the NCSW, sponsored meetings to discuss the so-called crisis of the American family.[13] Congress even hoped to stem the "national drift toward the disintegration of the family unit" by establishing "National Family Week" in 1977. Television and print journalists dutifully reported the family's precarious state in alternately alarming and reassuring treatments, from "The American Family in Decline" and "Saving the Family" to "The American Family: Bent—But Not Broken."[14] When presidential candidate Jimmy Carter called the family "the primary source of our nation's moral and social strength," warned of its "erosion and weakening," and promised to "reverse the trend[s]" that had "destroyed the American family" in 1976, he was well within the mainstream of American opinion.[15] In fact, by the end of his term, more than half of Americans polled felt that family life had deteriorated in the previous decade.[16]

The concern was not unfounded. While American history has been punctuated by periodic warnings of family collapse, the changes in the last four decades of the twentieth century added up to something demographers considered "truly revolutionary."[17] The marriage age rose, fertility rates fell, and increasing numbers of adults lived alone or cohabited without taking marriage vows, but rising rates of divorce and nonmarital births caused the most alarm. Between 1960 and the early 1980s, the American divorce rate tripled, and the proportion of nonmarital births rose steadily, from 5 percent of births in 1960 to more than 30 percent by the last decade of the century.[18] In the last decades of the twentieth century, then, a complex (and not yet fully understood) combination of economic, social, and cultural changes seemed to have resulted in both the "increasing separation of sexual intercourse, marriage, and childbearing," and the multiplication of children raised in single-parent, usually single-mother, households. In 1960, 88 percent of American children lived with two parents; by the mid-1980s, more than one-fourth lived in single-parent homes.[19]

A profound transformation *within* the family—the proliferation of the "working wife"—also provoked concern. Prior to the mid-twentieth century, most white female wage earners had been young single girls and women contributing to their parental families. Beginning in the 1940s rising consumption standards and a burgeoning service sector drew more and more married white women into the labor market. Though confined to a narrow range of "women's jobs" and disadvantaged in terms of pay, benefits, and advancement, married women flooded into the labor market in unprecedented numbers, a trend that accelerated as inflation and male unemployment increased in the 1970s. The year 1975 marked the first time that a majority of mothers of children aged six to eighteen (54 percent) worked for wages, the "first time in history that the *typical* school-age child has a mother who works outside the home," noted the Carnegie Council on Children.[20] Mothers of younger children entered the labor market at an even faster rate: by 1975, 39 percent of women with pre-school children worked for wages, more than three times the 1948 figure.[21]

Widespread inclusion of "working mothers" in lists of the "devastating societal changes" that were "shaking the foundations of the traditional family structure" suggests just how deeply American understandings of proper family life rested on male breadwinning and female homemaking.[22] Certainly, the widespread entry of mothers into the paid labor market posed new challenges, given the country's reluctance to provide the kinds of social supports that helped parents in many other industrialized countries to balance work and family life. But popular accounts of family change in the 1970s and 1980s cavalierly blamed working mothers and changing family structure for a whole host of social problems, from alcoholism, drug use, and criminal activity to teen pregnancy and a more general "alienation and torpor" among American youth.[23] Respected public officials, like Matthew P. Boylan of the Justice Department, blamed growing rates of street crime on "the disintegrating family structure," while highly touted experts like developmental psychologist Urie Bronfenbrenner worried that both single-parent households and working mothers put American children at risk.[24] If such trends continued, warned Harvard psychiatrist and conservative columnist Armand M. Nicholi II, the nation would see a marked increase in mental illness, assassinations and other violent crimes, and "bizarre experimenting and widespread perversion."[25]

The anxiety surrounding changing family norms fed a burgeoning "pro-family" movement, a key element in American conservatism's increasing political power after 1970. Feminist proliferation alarmed many Americans who believed the "traditional family" offered an ideological and economic haven in a heartless new world. Fear and confusion accompanying the erosion of the male-breadwinner family system thereby fueled the development of a "New Right" focused on "sexual, reproductive, and family issues."[26] A group of politically savvy conservative organizers like Paul Weyrich, Richard Viguerie, Howard Phillips, Phyllis Schlafly, Connaught Marshner, and Tim and Beverly LeHaye began in the mid-1970s to build a powerful new movement with funding from conservative philanthropists and donations solicited through well-targeted direct mail. Weyrich's Free Congress Foundation, funded by Colorado beer magnate Joseph Coors, became one of the first conservative think tanks to target family-related issues, but others soon followed.[27] Thus armed, "pro-family" conservatives set out to convince devout Catholics and newly politicized evangelical Protestants that the "secular humanists" who ran the federal government and their allies in the feminist movement were out to destroy the traditional family.[28] The message resonated with many women as well as men, particularly women who had the most at stake if the family wage bargain collapsed.[29]

Mobilizing female opposition to the ERA, Republican activist Phyllis Schlafly warned that feminism would erode the male breadwinning imperative and threaten a woman's right "to be a housewife."[30]

Women, of course, had never had such a "right." Despite nineteenth-century unionists' call for a "family wage," high enough to support a non-working wife and children, private employers and government labor laws had never answered with any guarantee. Even at the height of the "traditional family" in the 1950s, only two-thirds of white families, and a much smaller proportion of black families, could get by on one income.[31] That number declined after 1973, as real wages stagnated and employment, particularly at the lower end, became less secure.[32] In 1963, for example, 60 percent of men in their early twenties earned enough to keep a family of three above the poverty line; by 1984, only 48 percent did. Stephanie Coontz points out that "modern two-parent families have avoided poverty only to the extent that they, too, have broken with traditional family arrangements" by sending wives into the labor force.[33] If married women struggled economically, single mothers were even worse off. In reality, society provided no financial compensation for women's labor in the home, as AFDC mothers well knew, as did women who divorced before their twentieth anniversary and found themselves ineligible for social insurance benefits. In fact, a growing number of divorced women were beginning to experience what one feminist economist called the "economic risks of being a housewife."[34]

Such economic analysis was sorely lacking in most family crisis discussions during the 1970s and 1980s. Most popular explanations of family change echoed pro-family conservatives who blamed family changes on the women's movement and the cultural trends it wrought. When conservative critics blamed family breakdown on Americans' "preoccupation with self-fulfillment," they really meant American *women*'s preoccupation with self-fulfillment. The "traditional family" they celebrated rested, after all, on a woman's dependence, on her willingness to place others' needs above her own, and on her ability to perpetuate such non-market virtues as selflessness and compassion. Women's liberation, complained Armand Nicholi, "appears eager to deny the responsibility of being a wife and mother." It was therefore the "sexual revolution and the women's movement," agreed Dr. Lee Salk of the American Psychological Association, that was causing family crisis.[35]

Pro-family commentators viewed women's employment, like welfare, as particularly harmful because it provided women a measure of self-sufficiency that made them less dependent upon marriage. "Young wives who are contributing to the family income," noted one popular article on family change, "are asserting a new independence in marriage, which causes friction in many instances," and "more women in the workforce means that more women are economically in a position to undertake living alone."[36] This assessment was remarkably similar to late 1960s concerns that welfare payments displaced fathers but it was now applied to white, middle-class America. "What has changed for the worse," insisted even a liberal *New York Times* columnist, "is not the family's income but the younger woman's attitude."[37] Of course the feminist movement and changing cultural standards *did* challenge the main pillars of the "traditional" family: the confinement of sex and childrearing within heterosexual marriage and the assumption of women's dependence. But these changes began well before second-wave feminism, and they cannot be divorced from the transformation of America's economy in the last decades of the twentieth century.

Controversy surrounding the White House Conference on Families (WHCF) starkly illustrates the politics of family crisis in the late 1970s.[38] Political liberals expressed concern about the family, but they had begun to exhibit some tolerance of multiple family forms. The liberal commitment to the male-breadwinner family, a powerful force in the welfare debate in the late 1960s and early 1970s, had never been absolute. Since World War II, working-class women in unions had been demanding pay equity and a greater "social wage" to help them combine parenting and wage labor, and in the 1970s feminists across the class spectrum demanded employment opportunities and tolerance for diverse family forms. In 1965 the Moynihan Report had generated only a handful of criticisms for condemning female-headed families as "pathological," but many liberals admitted by the mid-1970s that "no longer is the independent nuclear family the idealized American type," as the members of a joint HEW-NCSW Commission on Families and Public Policies put it.[39] Only a handful of radicals, including some radical feminists and some gay liberation activists, celebrated the demise of the male-breadwinner family as an unmitigated good. A majority of liberals, like Senator Walter F. Mondale, continued to worry that family change was causing rising crime rates, rising out-of-wedlock births, and a host of other social problems, but they spoke in less judgmental ways than pro-family conservatives about family structure.[40]

The White House Conference on Families became a battleground that pitted pro-family conservatives, who defined the family as "the marriage of one man and woman together for a lifetime with their biological or adopted children" against a moderate-to-liberal majority that promoted tolerance, diversity, and antidiscrimination. White House planners fell into the latter category, refusing to define "the family" and urging attention to "differences in structure and lifestyle."[41] Their willingness to recognize a variety of family forms was evident in their choice for the conference title; early on, planners replaced the singular "Family" with the plural "Families."[42] The Coalition for the WHCF, composed of over fifty moderate and liberal organizations including the American Red Cross, NASW, NCC, U.S. Catholic Conference, Synagogue Council of America, Parent-Teacher Association, and NUL, likewise urged participants to recognize the growing diversity of family styles and structures.[43] Even Carter, who held fairly traditional ideas about family, insisted that the Conference would "recognize the pluralism of family life in America."[44]

To Alabama governor Fob James and his wife, Bobbie, this kind of pluralism threatened to grant legitimacy to homosexual unions and single-parent families and thereby failed to conform to "traditional Judeo-Christian values concerning the family." James refused to call a state conference to elect delegates to one of the three regional WHCF meetings, and some pro-family activists organized their own competing conferences.[45] Other pro-family conservatives sought to influence the WHCF from within. About 150 groups formed the "National Pro-Family Coalition," led by Connaught (Connie) Marshner, who edited the Free Congress Foundation's *Family Protection Report*.[46] To activists like Jo Ann Gasper of Virginia, editor of a newsletter called *The Right Woman*, "it seem[ed] obvious" that the WHCF was "structured to redefine and dramatically change the family."[47]

The New Right promoted an explicitly hierarchical, companionate male-breadwinner family model more closely aligned with postwar middle-class ideals than with any biblical injunction.[48] Pro-family conservatives were therefore just as concerned with internal family dynamics as with the family's outward structure. Single-parent families violated traditional family norms, but so too did working wives, who challenged their husbands' economic dominance and rejected their own childrearing duties. New Right organizations like the National Christian Action Council condemned feminists who tried to "force" mothers "out of the home and onto the battlefield" and attacked public schools and textbooks that "denigrate, diminish, or deny the historically understood role differences between the sexes." Their list of "enemies of the family" included television and film producers, feminist and gay rights lobbyists, and, of course, "social engineers" in the federal government. Conspicuously absent from their list were corporate leaders and their political allies who helped eviscerate the economic foundation of the male-breadwinner family.[49]

In defending the male-breadwinner family form, pro-family conservatives thus took up where 1960s antipoverty liberals had left off, but their policy recommendations differed significantly. The antipoverty coalition had promoted expanded federal income support to shore up the breadwinning capacities of poor men. The New Right instead exhibited a deep anti-statism reinforced by its financial and ideological ties to a resurgent corporate-led laissez-faire conservatism. STOP ERA, the Pro-Family Coalition, and other New Right groups opposed any expansion of welfare state protection and any efforts to eliminate sex discrimination in the labor market or to upgrade women's pay through comparable worth measures. Like antipoverty liberals, pro-family conservatives targeted AFDC, demanding an end to government support for unmarried mothers. While this seems to contradict their argument that children (and society) flourished only when mothers devoted themselves full time to childrearing, theirs was the same exclusionary family wage system favored by other antiwelfare conservatives. They assumed that without interference by liberal government planners and regulators, the economy would reward those who practiced sexual restraint and marital fidelity with male breadwinner wages.[50] They argued that federal payments to poor single mothers, who had clearly violated the rules, would only encourage irresponsible and even sinful behavior, undermining marriage and "mak[ing] parents less responsible for their children."[51] As the left-leaning *Dollars & Sense* magazine saw it, the New Right's agenda "aimed at preventing women from leaving marriage" as well as "punishing those families who do not fit the traditional mold," including single mothers.[52]

Some former liberals joined pro-family conservatives in promulgating ideological rather than economic arguments for family change. The political flip-flop these neoconservatives made was a sign that liberalism itself was in turmoil. As explained in Chapter 3, a number of foreign and domestic policies had pushed some former liberals in a generally conservative direction. These emerging neoconservatives found that they had more in common with traditionalist conservatives than with their former liberal allies, whose cultural pluralism seemed a "nihilistic assault on the social fabric that rendered vulnerable the fragile institutions of liberal democratic society."[53] Neoconservatives began in the 1970s to defend "traditional family values and structures" as essential to social order and to attack feminists as the main culprits in a dangerous collapse of the male-breadwinner household.[54] Some neoconservatives even argued, as Selma Frailberg did in her 1977 book *Every Child's Birthright: In Defense of Mothering*, that the federal government should increase income support for poor single mothers in order to allow them to care for their own children. Most, though, rejected such federal interventions, warning that government social engineering brought "unintended consequences," like AFDC's supposed family breakup effect. Neoconservatives generally rejected federal social programs, and defended the free operation of the market.[55]

Disagreement over family structure also divided antipoverty liberals in the 1970s, as conflicts over the leadership of the WHCF illustrates. Dissention within the moderate-liberal coalition surfaced early, when the administration appointed HEW assistant secretary Patricia Fleming as WHCF executive secretary. An African American divorced mother of three teenage sons, Fleming caused discomfort among some liberals within and outside the administration. According to John Donohue of the liberal Catholic journal *America*, "some people at the White House were troubled by the symbolism of a divorced person as executive secretary."[56] Other observers claimed that several Catholic leaders pressured HEW secretary Joseph Califano to replace Fleming with a white married man, preferably a Roman Catholic.[57] When Califano sought to diffuse the situation by proposing a co-secretary, Fleming resigned in protest, and Califano replaced her with John Carr, former director of the Full Employment Action Council who was "white, male, married, and Catholic."[58]

At least one liberal organization, the NCJW, criticized the administration's handling of the Fleming affair. A leader in the antipoverty coalition, the NCJW, like the LWV and other traditional women's groups, had supported liberal efforts in the 1960s to shore up male breadwinning among poor black men but at the same time launched a job training program for poor young minority women. Early on, then, these women's organizations had demonstrated a more flexible understanding of family than some of their liberal allies, a flexibility that only deepened as growing numbers of women headed families in the 1970s. The administration's treatment of Fleming, declared the NCJW, ignored the increase in female-headed households, promoted a narrow and outdated picture of the American family, and demonstrated "a total lack of understanding of the purpose of this conference," which, according to the NCJW, was to address these very changes.[59] The League made a similar point in a letter to the White House, praising the administration's "special emphasis on family and family life" but reminding Califano that "the definition of the family now includes single-parent families—most of which are female-headed."[60]

This kind of tolerance sparked protest from pro-family conservatives. Connie Marshner spearheaded efforts to elect pro-family delegates in the states, hoping to steer the three regional conferences in a conservative direction. However, even where such campaigns succeeded only one-third of each state's delegation consisted of elected members; the rest were appointed by governors and special committees, who tended to balance the elected delegates with liberal and moderate representatives more likely to favor federal child care, abortion rights, and the ERA. "I don't feel the delegation represents traditional families and traditional values," complained Carol Lyon of Connecticut's Conservative Union.[61] Marshner and her allies led walk-outs at all three meetings, complaining that pro-family positions were not receiving a fair hearing.[62] The liberal coalition had its share of dissention, as well. The National Conference of Catholic Bishops and the U.S. Catholic Conference withdrew from the Coalition for the WHCF when some of the group's members issued a voting guide advising opposition to a Catholic-sponsored anti-abortion recommendation, and a majority of delegates at the Minneapolis meeting approved a statement defining the family as "two or more persons related by blood, heterosexual marriage, adoption, or extended families."[63] Opposition to abortion and homosexuality were not confined to pro-family conservatives; the family was a minefield for liberals, as well.

Many antipoverty liberals tried to avoid contentious issues like abortion, homosexuality, and single-parent families and instead use the national family debate to bolster support for ensuring jobs and income. What families and children most need, they insisted, was economic security, "made possible by a job and a living wage" for parents.[64] Califano advised presidential candidate Jimmy Carter that the biggest threat facing American families was unemployment and income insecurity, and liberals outside the administration added specific policy recommendations.[65] Norman Lourie of the NCSW proposed full employment and generous income support as the answer to family crisis, while the NUL blamed widespread family instability on economic decline and once again demanded a Domestic Marshall Plan.[66] The National Academy of Sciences, the AFL-CIO, and the National Commission on Families and Public Policies ignored family structure and pressed for full employment and expanded antipoverty efforts, while the National Research Council's Advisory Committee on Child Development and the Carnegie Council on Children both identified economic security as the family's primary need.[67] The Carnegie Council, a $2.5 million project funded by the Carnegie Corporation, targeted poverty as the biggest threat to American children and issued a series of "heavily economic recommendations" including job creation and a generous guaranteed annual income.[68]

But liberals could hardly avoid the issues of divorce, out-of-wedlock births, and single-parent families. Traditionalist conservatives and some of their neoconservative allies argued that the male-breadwinner family was critical to maintaining social order, serving to "control the unruly affections of a sinful human race whose passions would otherwise lead them into moral and social anarchy."[69] Female-headed households, they insisted, produced damaged children, mired in "deep moral confusion," who only perpetuated the cycle of poverty and despair, while single men were "disposed to criminality, drugs and violence," destined for "a Hobbesian life—solitary poor, nasty, brutish, and short."[70] By the 1980s, researchers were spending millions of dollars to measure the presumed negative effects of growing up in a single-mother family despite evidence that much of the risk was a result of economic insecurity and a lack of social supports. Social science and psychology thereby added weight to the moralistic assertion that "only families based on male breadwinning and female childrearing can shape preference formation in a way that preserves both economic self-reliance and interpersonal obligation."[71] Though they spoke in a language of tolerance and nondiscrimination, many liberals continued to be haunted by their commitment to the male-breadwinner family as a solution to social disorder and racial disadvantage.

At the same time, feminists became outspoken proponents of government efforts to address new family realities, calling for "parental furloughs with guaranteed restoration of seniority, flextime work schedules, . . . child care facilities" and a host of other adjustments that would respond to single parenting and maternal employment.[72] Feminists were thus at the forefront of a broader liberal effort to adjust the nation's economic and social structure to the demise of the family wage. With only one in five households containing a working father supporting a nonworking mother and children, insisted the editors of the *New York Times* in 1980, government "must deal with what is, not with what it wishes."[73]

Welfare Becomes a Women's Issue

As a society, we persist in the stereotype of the American family as one male breadwinner, a homemaker wife, 2.5 children, and a life of economic affluence. But the stereotype no longer matches the lives around us. . . . It cannot continue to be the basis for public policy. (Wider Opportunities for Women, 1981)[74]

Throughout American history, female-headed families faced a greater risk of poverty than male-headed families, but the difference took on new shape in the second half of the twentieth century. The postwar political economy provided many men—especially white men—with good jobs, union protection, and an impressive array of social welfare benefits: employer-provided pension and health insurance packages, Unemployment Insurance, and generous veterans' benefits. In 1980, a National Advisory Council on Economic Opportunity concluded that the main "winners" of the nation's fight against poverty had been "male—and mainly white."[75] Women continued to be disadvantaged in the labor market and in the welfare state's most generous social insurance programs.[76] As a result, as two Urban Institute researchers concluded in 1975, America's poverty population "is coming increasingly to be dominated by female-headed families."[77]

In the mid-1970s, as journalists and politicians fretted about family crisis, this "feminization of poverty" attracted the attention of a wide array of female activists: women in organized labor, feminist organizations, traditional women's organizations, and welfare recipient activists and their advocates. Though some did not self-identify as "feminist," all were committed to women's economic security and self-determination. But organized feminists did not come easily to the welfare debate. The major organizations counted few poor women as either leaders or members, and their priorities—determined by a generally well-educated, white constituency—sometimes seemed less than relevant to the most disadvantaged women. In 1976, Margaret Mason produced a scathing critique of NOW's class bias and ignorance of poverty-related issues. Though the organization's founders pledged to address "the plight of women who now live in poverty," Mason found a "substantial gap between NOW's commitments and actions on poverty."[78] Merrillee Dolan, who headed NOW's Women and Poverty Task Force in the late 1960s and early 1970s, confirmed Mason's assessment, recalling blocked resolutions, unattended and cancelled workshops, and unsuccessful calls to action.[79] A 1975 NOW issues survey points to the crux of the problem. Members ranked "employment/economic security" as their top priority issue, a vote that echoed poor and working-class women's major concerns, but a majority chose "compliance with present anti-discrimination and equal pay laws" as their preferred strategy. These laws had the full support of working-class women, but they had proven more helpful to well-educated women in the professions than to the majority of women in female-dominated service jobs, and they did little to help women combine childrearing with wage labor. They also proved ineffective for the most economically vulnerable women, who were either unemployed or employed in temporary, seasonal, and casual jobs. Meanwhile, only 13 percent of NOW members chose full employment as an important strategy; even fewer, 9 percent, supported a guaranteed annual income.[80] Compared to the in-depth education and lobbying efforts mounted by traditional women's organizations like the LWV and the NCJW in the late 1960s, action by major feminist organizations seemed timid at best.

Organizations like NOW and the NWPC had never fully joined the 1960s antipoverty coalition. As new organizations with broad agendas, their absence is not entirely surprising, but ideological differences also kept them apart. While traditional women's organizations and welfare rights activists continued to defend the value of women's caregiving labor and demand policies that would turn poor men into viable breadwinners, liberal feminists promoted wage labor as the solution to women's poverty and to their economic dependence on men or on the state. As Merrillee Dolan's reaction to the FAP suggests, many liberal and radical feminists rejected public policies that promised to solve women's economic plight by providing income and jobs for men.

During the 1970s, a handful of antipoverty feminists pushed their organizations to take a stronger stand on antipoverty programs and welfare rights. In Nevada, Maya Miller, an academic from a wealthy oil family, began working on poverty and race issues with the LWV in the mid-1960s as a way to "connect with the civil rights movement" in overwhelmingly Caucasian Carson City. It was Miller who helped push the national League to make welfare rights a priority, and by the early 1970s, she was spending significant amounts of time, money, and energy helping Nevada welfare mothers battle benefit cuts and demand resources. Meanwhile, in New Mexico, Merrillee Dolan organized a poor women's "speak out," an opportunity to convince NOW's Board of Directors, which was meeting in Albuquerque, that poverty should receive higher priority.[81] In a number of other local settings, NOW began to reach out to welfare rights activists, protest welfare cuts, and publicize welfare as a "women's issue," as NWRO leader Johnnie Tillmon urged middle-class feminists to recognize.[82]

Antipoverty feminists often had past experience with poverty and/or a history of relationships with poor women. Dolan had grown up on the edge of poverty herself, largely the result of her parents' early divorce and her mother's subsequent marriage to an alcoholic. Working her way through school as a retail clerk in North Carolina and a nurse's aide in Waco, Texas, alongside adult women who struggled to support families, Dolan was attuned to women's economic disadvantage even before she immersed herself in Albuquerque's radical activist community as a young adult. In the late 1960s, she made friends and allies among Chicano "Brown Berets" and welfare rights activists as well as participants in the city's growing feminist movement.[83] Tish Sommers had a long history of leftist, antiracist, and antipoverty work, and had been deeply involved in a YWCA-sponsored School for Community Action on welfare in the late 1960s.[84] Lynn Tabb of California cut her teeth as an organizer for the United Farm Workers of America, while Dorothy Haener of the UAW had been active in Detroit's antipoverty and welfare rights movements. A founder of NOW, Haener took her turn as head of that group's Women and Poverty Task Force in 1973 and pressured the organization to mount "a multi-faceted venture aimed at improving women's economic lot." By the mid-1970s, feminist organizations had established task forces and lobbying packages on poverty and welfare, and it had become almost second nature to refer to poverty and welfare as feminist issues. In 1975, Mary Jo Binder and Catherine Day Jermany, a one-time California AFDC recipient and welfare rights activist, convinced NOW to hire a full-time staff member devoted to poverty issues.[85] That staffer, Margaret Mason, spent the next several years convincing the organization's largely middle-class members that "feminists' attention to poverty is not a divergence from women's problems" but was instead "an essential focus on one of the basest manifestations of sexism and racism" in the United States.[86] That year, Maya Miller relocated to Washington, D.C., where she helped found Women's Lobby and took charge of its Women, Work and Welfare Project.[87] In 1977, African American AFDC mothers Beulah Sanders and Frankie Jeter convinced the National Commission on the Observance of International Women's Year to adopt a resolution declaring welfare a women's issue and calling for more generous welfare programs, and Lupe Anguiano, who had grown up as a migrant farm laborer and lived and worked with AFDC recipients in San Antonio, convinced the NWPC to prioritize welfare reform—"*an issue which deeply affects women.*"[88]

The founding of the National Council on Women, Work, and Welfare (NCWWW) in 1976 symbolized the growing interconnections between welfare rights and feminist activism and demonstrates welfare recipients' crucial role in the feminist antipoverty network. In 1973, when welfare mothers took control of the NWRO from the predominantly male, middle-class staff, the group's feminism became more explicit, and in the first issue of *Ms.* magazine, Johnnie Tillmon declared welfare a women's issue.[89] In 1975, AFDC recipient Theresa Funiciello founded New York's Downtown Welfare Advocacy Center (DWAC), a second-generation welfare rights organization. DWAC advertised in *Ms.* magazine, networked with a variety of feminist groups, and scored a publicity coup in 1981 when a host of feminist luminaries, from Gloria Steinem, Bella Abzug, and Robin Morgan to television star Mary Tyler Moore, joined welfare mothers at a press conference that "marked a recognition by feminists that the issue of welfare is of vital concern to all women in our society."[90] And in 1976 and 1977, antipoverty feminists created the NCWWW, opened a Washington, D.C., office, and began meeting with "public interest groups, Administration officials, Congressional staff members, and poor and low-income women" to devise and lobby for new approaches to women's poverty. The NCWWW also served as a network for recipient activists from around the country, and it gathered both quantitative and qualitative data to demonstrate women's economic disadvantage.[91]

Feminist attention to poverty did not always translate into support for more generous welfare policies, however. Coalition between poor welfare mothers and the larger feminist movement proved problematic as activists sought to respond to women's disadvantage in ways that resonated with their own experiences. As both groups responded to the "feminization of poverty," their class perspectives informed their policy preferences and strategies. These differences emerged forcefully around the issue of child support enforcement legislation. Feminist researchers argued that women frequently ended up the clear losers in divorce, particularly as states instituted no-fault divorce laws in the 1960s and 1970s. Often left to raise children on meager AFDC grants or low wages (women continued to earn sixty cents to a man's dollar), even formerly middle-class divorced mothers often experienced downward mobility and, in some cases, severe economic hardship.[92] The negative economic consequences of divorce helped antipoverty feminists convince their peers to consider poverty an important issue since even *they* might be at risk of becoming poor someday. "Affluent women supported by men and working class women have not always understood their commonality with women on welfare," Women's Lobby instructed the Congressional Women's Caucus in 1977. "But that is an understanding gap fast being closed as the divorce rate climbs."[93]

Many feminists responded by demanding rigorous child support enforcement, which allied them with antiwelfare conservatives seeking to cut welfare costs and reprivatize the cost of childrearing.[94] Child support advocates insisted that "prosperous men," abetted by sexist family courts, "forced . . . children onto the welfare rolls" and stuck "taxpayers" with the bill.[95] In other words, as two officials from HEW's Office of Child Support Enforcement put it, "the problem of welfare in the United States is a problem of the nonsupport of children by their absent parents."[96] Researchers at the Rand Corporation admitted that there was little data to back up claims like those of a HEW official that "many welfare cases were formerly middle-class families," but they did note that 18 percent of AFDC mothers were college educated.[97] Feminists tended to focus on the plight of formerly middle-class divorced mothers and insisted that absent fathers were simply unwilling to pay. "Much of the upsurge in Welfare is not taking place in the ghettos," reported NOW, "but rather in the suburbs where the husband is able but unwilling to pay."[98] As a result, Betty Spalding, who headed NOW's Marriage and Divorce Task Force, testified in favor of federal child support enforcement legislation throughout the 1970s.

Social welfare lobbyists like the NCSW, traditional women's organizations like the LWV, and antipoverty feminists contested this view. They insisted that many AFDC fathers lacked "steady employment" and could therefore contribute little to their children's support.[99] They added that child support was a particularly ineffective solution for African American poverty: two of three poor black single mothers had been poor prior to divorce or separation.[100] These advocates therefore denounced proposed enforcement legislation as "futile, a waste of administrative effort and funds, and an unconstitutional harassment of many families."[101] This last point caused significant controversy within NOW when antipoverty feminists protested the organization's support for child support legislation.[102] Legislative sponsors were almost always conservative lawmakers with "abysmal" records on women's issues who typically viewed the policy as a way to reduce welfare rolls, privatize family support, and enforce male breadwinning, even among the most disadvantaged men. The bill that NOW's Betty Spalding supported required that AFDC applicants identify their children's fathers, cooperate in locating them, and assign any resulting support payments to the welfare department.[103] Adele Blong of the Center for Social Welfare Policy and Law (CSWP&L) warned that many welfare mothers "have good reason to avoid pursuing" the absent father, including "fear of violence." NOW's Women and Poverty Task Force members urged the organization's leaders to reconsider their support. While not opposed to child support enforcement per se, they insisted that NOW had a "moral obligation to oppose" policies "punitive to welfare mothers" and announced their commitment to fighting "any action by NOW . . . which may destroy or damage the already fragile and tenuous rights of poor women to ready access to dignified public assistance."[104] Their message finally got through in 1976 when NOW's board of directors passed a resolution opposing mandatory participation in child support enforcement.[105]

Class conflicts continued to affect organized feminism, but by the late 1970s a feminist antipoverty network was taking shape. The major feminist organizations were publishing papers, passing resolutions, and lobbying Congress alongside social welfare and poverty rights groups on a variety of policies affecting poor women, including extending FLSA coverage to household and agricultural workers (some of America's poorest working women), expanding women's access to job training, and increasing federal income support. They were also forging alliances. Groups like the LWV and NCJW were adopting more explicitly feminist positions, and both groups were seeking ways to incorporate welfare recipient voices into their positions. In 1978, for example, the Center for Community Change's Income Policy Project, an "informal group of mostly Washington-based organizations," decided to discuss "Women and Welfare," no doubt at the urging of feminist participants. The "lively discussion" prompted Margaret Mason and Nancy Duff Campbell (both of the CSWP&L's Women's Rights Project) to bring "women's organizations" together to create "a forum for the planning of advocacy on behalf of poor women's issues." Their meetings brought representatives from a variety of women's organizations, including the LWV, NCJW, NOW, and WEAL Education and Legal Defense Fund, together with federal officials, Congressional staffers, and speakers from feminist welfare and job training groups like Wider Opportunities for Women (WOW), Women Working in Construction, and the NCWWW. The coalition addressed gender inequities in Social Security and suggested using using federal manpower policies to address "the employment problems of poor women."[106]

This network's emphasis on economic independence through employment marked a significant break from the liberal past. Though still opposed to coercive work requirements for welfare mothers, activists in traditional women's, feminist, and welfare rights organizations began to argue that "the answer to poverty" was "not just better and fuller employment of manpower, but [also of] womanpower."[107] During the 1970s feminists pressured unions and employers to commit to affirmative action policies in the skilled trades, which had for years offered men with little education a route out of poverty. Those jobs, insisted the labor feminists who formed the Coalition of Labor Union Women (CLUW) in 1975, were "the only way you're going to move women out of poverty," and activists set out to train and place women in the "sweaty, smelly, non-Ph.D. jobs" that would allow them to support themselves and their children.[108] By 1979, the clearinghouse Women's Work Force Network counted over eighty women's training and employment groups.[109] Wider Opportunities for Women, which created the network, began in the mid-1960s as an employment service for homemakers whose children had grown, and in the 1970s developed a series of job training and job placement programs for a variety of "disadvantaged" women, from welfare mothers to ex-convicts. Most such programs were small-scale, and all faced formidable barriers, but for the women they helped—who made up a mere 2 percent of the skilled trades by 1980—it was well worth the effort, bringing a new sense of confidence along with economic security.[110] A Boston-based initiative to train minority *women* as drafters and machinists took the name "The Breadwinner Program," starkly revealing how much feminist antipoverty efforts differed from earlier liberal ones.[111]

The shift is evident not only in these new, explicitly feminist projects but also in traditional women's organizations. Groups like the LWV and the NCJW had been welfare rights allies in the late 1960s and staunch supporters of poor women's right to stay-at-home motherhood. By the late 1970s, they were placing greater emphasis on jobs. While still opposed to maternal work requirements, the NCJW insisted in 1978 that "women should be allowed to work so that they can escape dependency on public assistance."[112] The League, too, dropped its support for male-targeted job training and now insisted that welfare *mothers* were much better employment candidates than poor men. The League cited studies that "poor male-headed families live more often on farms or in other non-metropolitan areas, where jobs and training are in short supply" while "poor female household heads are generally younger, better educated and healthier than their male counterparts," and denounced "federal jobs programs" for thus far concentrating on "training and placing men."[113]

At the same time, both feminist and traditional women's organizations joined welfare rights activists in asserting the value of women's unpaid domestic labor and seeking policies to reward it. Some advocates, like Nancy Seifer of the AJC National Project on Ethnic America, saw "proposals to attach monetary values to housewifery" as a way to "help slow the disintegration of the American family" by enabling women to stay out of the workforce, but to most feminist proponents, it was a potential source of economic security for women.[114] "Homemaking is work," insisted NOW's Karen DeCrow in her 1977 Women's State of the Union address, "and the fact that it is not salaried must not keep us from moving towards benefits enjoyed by other workers—social security, pensions, unemployment benefits, and disability and health insurance."[115] Others demanded the salary, as well. Black Women for Wages for Housework (BWWH) found inspiration in European socialist feminists' "wages for housework" campaigns as well as among America's "black welfare mothers" who had "demand[ed] money for the work of raising Black children and being the support and comfort of Black men in the ghettos of America." As this organization saw it, welfare rights activists in the late 1960s and early 1970s had "won the first wage for housework" by bolstering women's legal right to welfare and had helped to "establish . . . once and for all that Every Mother is a Working Mother."[116] The welfare rights movement's campaign to reinterpret AFDC as "working wage . . . to adults who care for children" gradually made its way into feminist antipoverty demands.[117]

But wages for housework was not a convincing demand in the political and economic context of the 1970s. During the Progressive Era, when President Teddy Roosevelt announced the first "Mother's Day," upper-crust white Protestants had feared race suicide, and most female wage earners were young single women, a "mothers' pension" movement proved viable. At the same time, organized labor's demand for a family wage, as Dorothy Sue Cobble noted, "did recognize, if only implicitly, the necessity and value of domestic labor."[118] But even in the early twentieth century and the postwar era, when cultural support for women's domestic role was strongest, that role remained largely unpaid. And by the 1980s, the ideological and economic scaffold of the family wage system had eroded. Most American women could expect to spend at least part of their adult lives in the labor force, and the onward march toward gender equality privileged labor market participation rather than caregiving labor.

The demand for jobs rather than welfare thus fit the tenor of the times and meshed more neatly with liberal feminist ideology, but it sometimes generated tension. When feminists demanded jobs for welfare mothers to allow them to play a "rewarding and productive role in our society," they implicitly suggested that caring for children was *not* rewarding and productive.[119] The generally nuanced position adopted by most national feminist leaders—one that saw employment as a positive alternative to welfare but that continued to defend poor women's choices—was not always echoed at the grassroots. Theresa Funiciello spent months convincing New York NOW to include a welfare recipient speaker in its Urban Women conference. When the group finally agreed but requested that the speaker be white (in order to avoid perpetuating racial stereotypes, they said) and relate personal experiences rather than address political issues, Funiciello (who was white but far from apolitical) decided to appear herself and "do a little consciousness raising" about women's poverty. She complained that one of the group's leaders "told me that NOW's position on welfare was jobs." Funiciello retorted that many AFDC mothers, like many middle-class mothers, preferred to be "full-time mothers," particularly when "any realistic job option for welfare mothers for decades to come would mean low pay and no substantial upgrading of our living circumstances." While defending "individual *choices*," Funiciello reminded her primarily middle-class audience that poor women's chance of escaping poverty through wage labor remained slim and took issue with the tendency among feminists to promote work as *the* alternative to welfare.[120] DWAC leaders expressed similar concerns when they withdrew from a New York welfare coalition in the late 1970s. The coalition, like New York's NOW, promoted jobs as a way to reduce welfare rolls. But DWAC's leaders observed that "a job outside the home is not what many mothers would choose," particularly when adequate childcare remained scarce and expensive. More importantly, "when welfare folks first make their shout the shout for JOBS," DWAC warned, "WORKFARE is what we get." DWAC feared that recipients would end up "with no ability to choose" and "WILL STILL END UP BEING POOR." The group's leaders insisted that the "first and most important fight" for welfare rights "is the fight for a *guaranteed livable income* for all poor people."[121] DWAC continued to demand good jobs for welfare mothers even as it sued New York State to raise welfare grants to the state's standard of need.[122]

Despite reservations, many welfare mothers were also concluding that jobs were the preferred solution to their poverty. As AFDC benefits declined and the political chances for generous income support faded, New York City welfare recipients demanded "decent jobs for decent pay," Boston antipoverty organizations launched a "Campaign for Jobs at Eastern Airline," and AFDC mothers in Chicago formed an organization called "Women, Work & Welfare." That group's Eve Dembaugh advised the President's Commission for a National Agenda for the Eighties. Her testimony mocked the naiveté of those who saw jobs as an easy answer to welfare, and she stressed that income support was a tool that could help poor women earn wages. With few skills and little education, "my future as a worker holds little more promise for me than my life now as an A[F]DC recipient," Dembaugh pointed out, and welfare rules caused her "panic at the thought of total loss of income" if a job situation turned sour. Dembaugh described the survival strategy practiced by so many poor single mothers and urged policymakers to "allow me to pass on and off welfare or on and off WIN quickly and frequently, if necessary, because that's probably how my life is going to be as a low-income worker." She was asking not for social support for her caregiving labor but rather for "the security to go to work."[123]

The welfare mothers with whom Lupe Anguiano worked in San Antonio, Texas, also hoped to make the transition from welfare to employment. The daughter of Mexican American migrant laborers, Anguiano had worked as a Catholic nun, an organizer for the United Farm Workers of America, and an HEW staffer during the 1960s. As director of a National Council of Catholic Bishops project, Anguiano moved into a San Antonio housing project in the 1970s and initiated meetings among the women who lived there, many of whom were on the AFDC rolls. "The women," she told Congress, "saw employment as the only viable alternative to assist them and their families become self-sufficient." Anguiano started a "Let's Get Off Welfare" campaign to find jobs and training for AFDC recipients. She cajoled local employers to hire welfare mothers, organized carpools, arranged child care, and even convinced the local Kiwanis Club to pledge scholarships to help thirty-eight AFDC mothers attend San Antonio Junior College. Another three hundred participants completed a nurse's aide training program and secured jobs, and though their families were generally no better off financially than they had been on AFDC, Anguiano cited their efforts as a testament to poor women's desire for self-sufficiency. To the poor single mothers she knew, "*the welfare system is beyond repair,*" and "*the only solution they found was to find a way to get out of welfare.*" In a 1980 interview with Harry Reasoner for the television program *Sixty Minutes*, Anguiano had few kind words for AFDC. "When [a poor woman] comes into the welfare office, that's her undoing," she insisted, because nobody says "we'll help you find a job, we'll help you become self-supporting." Instead, she gets "caught in this web" of welfare. When Reasoner asked her if the welfare system could be reformed, Anguiano noted that she had been trying for several years to reform it—to convince federal policymakers to emphasize job training rather than cash support. While her project did attract a small amount of federal funding, she remained skeptical. "I guess I've lost hope," she concluded, "and I'm going the other way"—the way of getting women *off* of welfare.[124]

Anguiano found a number of allies in the wider feminist movement. A member of the Board of Directors of Women's Lobby and chair of the NWPC's Welfare Reform Task Force, Anguiano offered a solution to welfare that resonated with liberal feminists.[125] When the Women's Bureau, a federal agency within the Department of Labor, decided to investigate the causes of women's poverty in 1977, it turned to Anguiano. Like Anguiano, the Bureau's new director, Alexis Herman, an African American, had begun her career in the Catholic social welfare establishment as a social worker for Catholic Charities.[126] As she took leadership in 1977, the Women's Bureau was "becom[ing] increasingly concerned about the difficulties experienced by women who live at or below the poverty level," particularly "when they attempt to enter the labor market and become economically self-sufficient."[127] The Bureau's Low Income Women Project brought twelve hundred poor women—Caucasian, Indian, Spanish-speaking, African American, married, single, working, and on welfare—together with service providers and community leaders in fifty-two meetings and thirteen regional consultations. The Bureau wanted the "'real experts,' low-income women," to identify the major barriers they faced in finding and keeping jobs.[128] Anguiano helped to coordinate the project, and NOW, Women's Lobby, and various welfare rights groups provided local coordination and support.

The barriers that low-income women identified added up to a critique of a labor market and a welfare state still designed to promote the male-breadwinner family. When they met together, low-income women, whatever their region, race, or marital or employment status, identified a host of policies that blocked their quest to "leave a life of poverty behind" and "take [their] place in America's economic mainstream."[129] They complained that federal training and jobs programs, including WIN, channeled women into "low paying dead end jobs in traditional women's occupations" like "clerical and service fields" which paid too little to bring a family out of poverty. In just one example, women from an Appalachian coal community had been offered training as nurse's aides, a poorly paid "surplus occupation" in their region, while lucrative jobs as "mine machinery mechanics" went begging. A number of studies supported the women's complaints, demonstrating that federal jobs programs did a much better job serving men, who received a disproportionate number of training and job opportunities and commanded much higher salaries than female participants.[130] Federal job administrators, participants complained, tended to "see women as 'temporarily without husbands'" rather than as "a permanent part of the workforce." They also ignored women's need for adequate and affordable child care, a significant barrier to women's employment, particularly for mothers "who must work overtime, at night, on weekends, or on swing shifts," requirements characteristic of the low-wage service positions for which poor women were most often considered. A 1977 Labor Department study of the WIN program demonstrated conclusively that "the chances of a low-income—and especially black—family headed by a woman permanently moving out of poverty are much less than they are for a family with a male head . . . not because welfare mothers refuse to work" but because "they are not able to command a high enough salary."[131]

The Low Income Women Project's very mission—to investigate barriers to employment—assured that participants would emphasize jobs. But in other forums, too, poor women demanded employment opportunities as their preferred route out of poverty. In the late 1970s, the National Congress of Neighborhood Women, a Brooklyn, New York-based group that grew out of the Low Income Women Project, surveyed poor women, who listed employment, day care, and training/education as their primary needs. The Congress's "Women in Poverty Leadership Trainings" evoked similar responses.[132] Lobbying New York officials for more job training and child care resources, as well as the opportunity to run their own education and job placement programs "that fit women's unique needs," the group advised that if city officials "really want to reform the welfare system" they would "have to put their money where their mouths are and fund more skills training and education programs in our neighborhood."[133] The welfare recipients who attended the NCWWW "Sex and Poverty" conference in late 1977 agreed. The "major goal" of AFDC mothers, the organization reported, was "escaping from the welfare system and finding economic independence," which required career counseling, education, training, jobs, and child care.[134]

In some ways, the arguments made by feminists and welfare activists in the late 1970s differed little from those made by late 1960s welfare rights leaders. Poor women and their allies continued to insist on adequate, dignified income assistance; they also retained an emphasis on choice, arguing that poor single mothers should be given access to training, well-paid jobs, and child care if they chose to work, but defending their right to withdraw from the labor market to care for their children full-time. Only the emphasis differed. The NWRO and its allies in social welfare and traditional wom-

Why work if you can live better on welfare?

Figure 11. As more and more women entered the labor market, some observers criticized AFDC, which in theory enabled single mothers to care for their children full-time, as an anachronism and unfair to working women. This cartoon, featured in a 1973 issue of *Business Week*, contrasts the purchases of the thin "working mother" with those of the overweight "welfare mother." Courtesy Roy Doty.

en's organizations had celebrated poor women's mothering labor and placed a demand for income and a "right to live" at the forefront of their campaign for welfare rights in the late 1960s. In the late 1970s, most participants in the feminist antipoverty network continued to assert the value of women's childrearing labor, to oppose coercive work requirements, and to insist on poor women's right to choose wage labor or full-time motherhood. But the diffusion of liberal feminist ideology, liberal demands for full employment, and a political climate increasingly hostile to welfare—along with the continuing flood of mothers into the labor market—prompted a shift in emphasis. Now, employment took center stage. Recipient activists and the leaders of feminist and traditional women's organizations had given up hope that women could achieve economic independence via public assistance, and many poor women had begun to reject welfare as a respectable option.[135]

In the new feminist vision of welfare reform, then, calls for education, training, jobs, and child care had displaced the cry for "welfare rights" as the central demand. The shift is evident in the very structure of the arguments as well as in the specificity of demands. General calls for more adequate income support replaced the more detailed guaranteed income plans of the late 1960s. At the same time, in place of earlier, vague demands for good jobs and child care, the women's antipoverty network in the late 1970s spelled out for lawmakers exactly what poor women would need to achieve self-sufficiency through wage labor. That list included access to nontraditional jobs (and its broader implication, occupational desegregation), a fair share of federal job training and public works positions, adequate and affordable child care, access to affordable health care, and transitional income support. The Ad Hoc Coalition for Women, the Women's Bureau, individual feminist and women's organizations, and low-income women themselves advised the Carter administration to place employment opportunities for poor single mothers at the center of its welfare reform plan.[136]

Of course, as most feminists realized, moving women "from cash assistance to economic independence" meant "confronting a wall of socially acceptable white male institutions that keep women 'in their place'," as the NCWWW put it.[137] These institutions included media that promoted gender stereotypes, educational institutions that socialized women to dependence, and a deeply sex-segregated labor market and welfare state that continued to regard women as "secondary earners" at best. They also included liberal policymakers, like those in the Carter administration, who for a variety of reasons seemed unable and unwilling to commit, ideologically or practically, to ensuring real economic independence for poor women.

The Program for Better Jobs and Income

This administration understands that we are a diverse and pluralistic nation; that there is no single, ideal model for family; and that government must not try to impose one. (Walter Mondale, 1977)[138]

Members of the antipoverty coalition greeted Jimmy Carter's 1976 election with cautious optimism. Many had not supported Carter in the Democratic primaries, for his politics never fell neatly into a New Deal-Great Society liberal mold. Yet his victory promised a return to Democratic rule after eight years of Republican executive leadership. Despite his fiscal conservatism and ideological ambiguity, Carter had been the only Southern governor to support the FAP, he made the "family" a central campaign theme, and he chose two Great Society policymakers, Stuart Eizenstat and Joseph Califano, as his domestic policy chief and his HEW secretary respectively. These appointments seemed to promise a return to power for the antipoverty coalition after several years in the political wilderness. Califano announced at an early staff meeting: "We've got to pick up where we were in 1968. . . . We've lost a lot of time."[139] Liberals outside the government dared to hope, as well. Leaders of the NCSW were "excited," viewing Carter's election as "an opportunity to make significant progress towards improving the quality of life for . . . the poor, the socially, politically and economically disadvantaged."[140] With overwhelming Democratic majorities in both houses of Congress and Hubert Humphrey's protégé Walter Mondale as vice president, some liberals anticipated that Carter would "make up for the long period of Republican neglect by enacting ambitious social welfare programs."[141]

What those programs would look like was a matter of some controversy. In 1976 when the NCSW joined with HEW, the Social Security Administration, and Social and Rehabilitative Services to make welfare reform recommendations, participants were unable to agree on several fundamental issues and offered only "basic principles for an income security system."[142] A leader in the guaranteed income campaign, the LWV warned its members to avoid membership in any formal coalitions and pledged only to participate in a "sharing of the minds."[143] When the Center for Community Change called a meeting of its Income Policy Project in October 1976, the attendees—representatives from the AFL-CIO, LWV, Common Cause, and a handful of other interested liberal organizations—"could not agree on a single approach" and determined not to adopt a position until the new administration announced its own welfare reform plan.[144]

They had good reason to believe that it would. Carter had promised during his campaign to undertake a "comprehensive reform" of the welfare system. Although AFDC rolls had stabilized and Carter did not face the kind of welfare crisis that had motivated Nixon, a number of factors prompted the new president to tackle what Califano famously called "the Middle East of domestic politics."[145] The decade's economic troubles were hitting state and local governments hard, and older industrial cities faced declining jobs, population, and tax revenues as they "lumbered through financial crises of a magnitude not seen since the Great Depression."[146] State and local governments lobbied vigorously for welfare reform, hoping to pressure the federal government to take on a larger share of costs.[147] And although media hysteria about soaring welfare rolls had certainly died down by the mid-1970s, as AFDC caseloads leveled off, stories about welfare fraud and inefficiency appeared more and more frequently in the popular press.[148] The federal government was spending increasing sums on social services, food stamps, Medicaid, and other welfare programs aimed at both the poor and the non-poor.[149] Such "trends point to larger and larger social-welfare outlays," warned the *U.S. News and World Report*, "unless Carter steps in."[150] The opportunity to solve such problems and to simplify a complex and inefficient system, which Califano denounced as an "administrative jungle," particularly appealed to Carter, a tireless advocate of "good government" with a serious "technocratic impulse."[151]

However much Carter harped on the welfare system's inefficiencies, his emphasis on the technical could not obscure the moral and ideological issues that had always motivated welfare reformers. Welfare rights activists and most liberal organizations continued to press for more adequate AFDC grants, whose real value had declined during the 1970s. But simple grant increases would do little to solve the more fundamental problems liberals saw in the system. The president believed that the welfare system was "corrupting people," that it was "anti-work, anti-family [and] inequitable in its treatment of the poor."[152] In a Father's Day interview in 1977, Carter denounced welfare laws for "benefit[ing] handsomely the divided family" and called AFDC "a divisive force that the Government artificially imposes on the family system."[153] Elsewhere, he promised to "provide strong incentives to keep families together rather than tear them apart" by "ending rules which prohibit assistance when the father of a family remains within the household" and by providing jobs to "offer . . . the dignity of useful work to family heads." Like Nixon, Carter billed this more inclusive approach to welfare as a way to "dramatically reduce reliance on welfare payments" by encouraging the poor to form stable, male-breadwinner families.[154] Carter's communications assistant captured this goal in his suggestions for a program title: "A Workable Plan for Jobs and Family Life," the "Jobs Security and Family Stability Plan," or the "Family Security and Jobs Program."[155] But while Carter's policymakers agreed that their proposal should be "pro-family and pro-work," they disagreed about the best way to achieve those goals.

Califano and his staff in HEW saw a Negative Income Tax, or NIT, as the most efficient and equitable device for relieving poverty. All the poor, regardless of family structure or work status, would receive cash benefits. A NIT would therefore reverse AFDC's supposed incentive for poor fathers to abandon their families (this was, of course, before the NIT experiments revealed potential increases in separation and divorce), and a more inclusive welfare system might also become "more acceptable to the public."[156] While the NIT would have fulfilled Carter's desire for a simple, unified income maintenance system, officials outside HEW virulently opposed the idea. Domestic policy staffers Jack Watson and Jim Parnham warned Carter that a NIT meant adding "several million heretofore ineligible families" to the welfare rolls, a result sure to have "very serious social and political implications."[157]

The NIT's liberal opponents viewed the plan as a mere extension of "welfare," which was already a target of popular and political antipathy. The AFL-CIO rejected any attempt to include able-bodied adults in the welfare system. When the president proposed to eliminate extended Unemployment Insurance and provide similar benefits under his welfare reform package, for example, the AFL-CIO Executive Council insisted that the "working poor should not be forced to rely on welfare programs." Instead, organized labor wanted Congress to extend "less divisive and less stigmatizing" income support programs—Unemployment Insurance, food stamps, and the EITC—to help the working poor "*without labeling them as welfare recipients*," as Watson and Parnham put it.[158] The president was sympathetic to such appeals. During his campaign, Carter had promised to address the problems of poor "people who are able to work . . . outside the so-called welfare system itself," and he forwarded Watson and Parnham's memo to other top advisors with the message "this concerns me also" penned at the top.[159]

Labor Department staffers agreed. Arnold Packer, an economist who served as Assistant Secretary for Policy Evaluation and Research and led the Labor Department's welfare reform team, pressed the administration to offer guaranteed employment rather than cash benefits. Guaranteed employment was, of course, a longtime liberal demand that Congress was concurrently discussing as it debated the Humphrey-Hawkins Bill. But advocates for some of the most vulnerable victims of poverty—single mothers and their children—did not see jobs as the appropriate focus for *welfare reform*. While "decent jobs are ultimately the best route out of welfare dependency," argued Marian Wright Edelman of the Children's Defense Fund

(CDF), job training and creation should "be dealt with separately" from income maintenance.[160] Jobs were not "an appropriate mechanism for large-scale income transfers to the poor," agreed the NASW, because "too many of the poor cannot work" but needed "adequate benefits" nonetheless.[161]

Other policymakers proposed a "multiple-track" approach to overcome this dilemma. By dividing the poor into categories based on their ability to work, this system would protect the most vulnerable victims of poverty—the aged, blind, disabled, and single mothers of young children—who would be placed in a "residual [welfare] program." Because society generally agreed that these adults were "unemployable," policymakers could ensure them adequate benefit levels without worrying about work incentives. Tom Joe, longtime welfare expert and member of Carter's "informal cabinet," pushed the administration to consider this approach. Divide the poor into three categories, he argued, and apply three different remedies: cash benefits for the unemployable, an expanded EITC for the working poor, and public service jobs for the unemployed.[162] A multiple-track system would not fulfill HEW's desire to treat all the poor equally, nor would it produce a simple, unified system. But it would address HEW's concerns about unemployable recipients while meeting DOL determination to "keep working-age adults away from the welfare system."[163]

Already locked in "heated debate" about the structure of welfare reform, staffers encountered an additional obstacle. Carter stunned staffers and outside interest groups alike when he insisted they design a welfare plan at "no higher initial cost than the present system's." As governor of Georgia, Carter had become a fan of "zero-cost" budgeting, a management technique aimed at keeping costs down by forcing policymakers to justify each expenditure. Califano insisted that Carter's zero-cost directive for welfare reform was merely this, a technique to ensure efficiency and thoughtful planning, though at times the president appeared almost messianic about the cost constraint. When Califano pointed out the myriad problems with the three zero-cost proposals he presented at an April briefing, Carter was incredulous. "As far as I'm concerned," he replied, "what you've just told me is that our welfare system can't get any better. . . . Why not say to hell with it!"[164] Convinced that a more efficient system could cover more recipients with the same dollars, Carter was also pressured by his Office of Management and Budget (OMB) staff—a decidedly conservative group—to keep costs down.[165] But policymakers found that the cost constraint imposed impossible trade-offs, and Carter's tightfistedness contributed to a "sense of disappointment and frustration among Congressional and other proponents of reform," noted Elizabeth Wickenden. To most antipoverty liberals, "the indispensable element in any true welfare reform is more money."[166] While the president eventually agreed to add $2.8 billion (the CBO estimated the real figure to be more like $14 billion), Carter continued to respond angrily to requests for additional funds. To Carter, as to fellow Democrat and Senate majority leader Robert Byrd, welfare reform meant "more careful spending rather than more costly programs."[167]

In the end, the Program for Better Jobs and Income (PBJI), which the administration introduced in August 1977, promised a system at least as complicated and cumbersome as the one Carter sought to replace. Disagreements had taken their toll; instead of introducing his proposal in May, as promised, Carter could only issue a list of guiding principles for welfare reform while his policymakers hammered out a compromise. Finally, in August, Carter appeared on national television to introduce the PBJI, which had been explained to him in a sixty-two page, single-spaced memo accompanied by an additional seventy-five pages of tables and charts. Like the FAP, the PBJI would have replaced AFDC and other federal public assistance with a federally guaranteed income for all poor households, including two-parent "working poor" families. The aged, blind, and disabled and single mothers with young children would receive $4,200 (yearly, for a family of four) on an HEW-administered "Income Support Tier," while families with an employable adult would be offered $2,300 (yearly, for a family of four), administered by the DOL. Employable recipients would also be subject to a mandatory eight-week annual job search and, if they failed to get a job in the private sector, would be offered temporary public service employment. The proposal included funding for 1.4 million jobs.

As longtime welfare administrator Alvin Schorr pointed out, "sweeping changes without additional spending"—or even with minimal additional spending—"produces winners and losers," and the PBJI's biggest losers were current AFDC recipients.[168] The PBJI would cover about thirty-two million people, only slightly higher than the thirty million receiving AFDC, SSI, food stamps, and General Assistance in the mid-1970s, but would have "substantially redistribute[d]" those benefits. The "biggest share of . . . betteroffness" would be among "two-parent families" of the "working poor," who, according to Califano, "deserve higher benefits." Fewer than half of the country's 15 million AFDC recipients, those who lived in twelve states with very low benefits, would receive a small grant increase. One million more would become ineligible, while the rest would lose benefits, an average of $400 per recipient per year, due to a number of eligibility and administrative changes. "The total amount of worseoffness" in the PBJI, Califano concluded, would be "concentrated among AFDC recipients."[169]

Discussions within the administration suggest that Carter and some of his staffers considered AFDC recipients a "special interest group," less deserving than adults in two-parent families. Justifying the PBJI's harmful impact on AFDC recipients, Califano noted that the current system sometimes rewarded some recipients "at the expense of others who are more deserving," while Carter reminded Congress that reform would "inevitably require reduction of special benefits for some who receive favored treatment now."[170] The administration certainly treated SSI recipients—the aged, blind, and disabled poor—as more deserving than single-mother families. "Reluctant to disadvantage *any* SSI beneficiary," policymakers convinced Carter to "grandfather" the 100,000–200,000 SSI recipients who might see reduced benefits because of new eligibility and administrative restrictions. They also decided to ensure that these recipients' benefits would not decline in real value by indexing them to the inflation rate, a change to which even the fiscally conservative OMB staff assented.[171] But policymakers did *not* recommend grandfathering the 8.7 million AFDC recipients whose benefits would decrease, claiming this course of action would prove "quite costly" and produce "substantial administrative difficulties."[172] Carter and his policymakers thus reinforced the historic distinction between the "deserving poor"—aged, blind, and disabled adults legitimately exempted from the labor market—and the "undeserving poor," increasingly including poor single mothers and their children.

In fact, AFDC recipients were being "sacrificed," as a welfare rights activist put it, for the promotion of male-breadwinner families.[173] As Carter's policymakers saw it, the "principal inequity in the present system" was exclusion of the "intact families" of the working poor. In response, they, like the FAP's designers, intentionally created a system "in which the benefits for most working poor families would be better . . . than AFDC benefits," a situation many welfare experts across the political spectrum considered "desirable."[174] Though two-parent families would earn lower benefits than families on the "Income Support Tier," their newly won grants would most often supplement earnings, and they would be eligible for one of the PBJI's 1.4 million public service jobs. While two-parent families would gain new benefits from the PBJI, then, a majority of poor single mothers on AFDC would lose under the new system. DOL's Arnold Packer justified the differential treatment of single-mother and two-parent families, waxing nostalgic about the "traditional American family structure with two parents and children in which the family head goes out to work and makes enough of a living to keep the family together." The "thrust of any [welfare] program," Packer insisted, "ought to be to support this as the predominant situation for Americans," and the administration should arrange the plan's incentives "so that individuals prefer the two-parent arrangement." Jobs, job training, and income subsidies to "working poor families"—in particular, "providing the male head of the family with the opportunity to work"—would ensure that two-parent families were always better off financially than poor single mothers.[175]

So while Carter had promised to cut the welfare rolls by "doubling the number of single-parent family heads who support themselves through earnings from work," both cost constraint and a lingering family wage ideal significantly reduced opportunities for single mothers to "work" their way out of poverty under the PBJI.[176] Packer lobbied for guaranteed jobs at $3.00-$4.00 an hour, well above the minimum wage, but Carter's Council of Economic Advisors convinced the president that jobs should "*not* be on entitlement basis" and should be kept at minimum wage; they feared that better-paid jobs would prove "attractive" to low-wage private sector workers, and the administration assured Congress that the PBJI was "carefully designed to avoid disruptive effects to the regular economy."[177] Organized labor objected strenuously, fearing that a bargain-basement work program would "undercut hard-won wage standards." The American Federation of State, County, and Municipal Employees (AFSCME) was particularly concerned that welfare recipients would be forced into "dead-end employment" and that they would displace "trained, full-time public workers" whom the union represented.[178] Tom Joe, too, feared that "the jobs will become 'welfare jobs' rather than real opportunities for people trapped in the welfare system."[179]

This limited opportunity would be reserved primarily for male breadwinners. Almost all single mothers were relegated to the PBJI "Income Support Tier," where recipients were considered "unemployable" and thus ineligible for jobs or job training. Congressional conservatives pressed Carter to include mothers of school-age children or even younger in the "employable track" but policymakers had compelling reasons not to do so. Many Carter staffers remembered the battle over the FAP and feared that any maternal work requirement would become "an additional rallying point for liberals who oppose the program."[180] They also knew Congressional liberals, who made up a decisive plurality of the House Welfare Reform Subcommittee, would be "very resistant to work requirements" for mothers "without what they consider to be adequate provision of day care."[181] In response to "strong political pressure to set the age at an extremely low level (3–6 years)," staffers calculated the costs of including all mothers in the program's "employable" tier: at least $6.7 billion for 900,000 additional public service jobs and another $1.6 billion to create 1.8 million child care slots.[182] This was money that Carter was simply unwilling to spend. "Providing day care to a woman with three children so that she can take a full-time job at the minimum wage," concluded the Domestic Policy Staff, "is simply not a cost-effective proposition."[183] The administration eventually placed mothers whose youngest child had reached fifteen (about 10 percent of AFDC mothers) on the "employable" track and required mothers of six- to fourteen-year-olds to work part-time if such jobs were available. Against the advice of the DOL, OMB, and DPS, Carter agreed to spend $700 million to add 300,000 part-time, nine-month public service jobs to add legitimacy to this last requirement.[184] But these mothers, and any who volunteered to enter the "employable track," would receive little help with child care. The vast majority of public service jobs were reserved for "principal earners" in two-parent families—almost always men.

Not that the administration didn't "recognize the changes in work patterns that have occurred over the past quarter century"—that is, women's increasing presence in the labor market—as Senator Russell Long accused.[185] Policymakers certainly knew that poor single mothers and wives in poor two-parent families already participated in the labor market, and they wanted this labor to continue. In lobbying for a child care deduction (the only recognition of child care needs in the PBJI), Califano urged the administration to "encourage single parents of younger children and secondary earners in two-parent families to work."[186] But according to the DPS, offering these women public service jobs would merely threaten the country's "secondary part-time and seasonal labor force."[187] Far from being ignorant about women's position in the labor market, policymakers were reluctant to improve that position by providing job opportunities or access to child care. Instead, they accepted a sex-segregated, two-tier labor market in which women served as "secondary" workers.

But when domestic policy staffers worried that including mothers in the "employable" track would become a "rallying point for liberals who oppose the program," they drastically underestimated the impact of feminist ideology and activism on the political left by 1977. They should have known better. Carter considered feminists an important constituency during his presidential bid and subsequently appointed a "relatively large number" of avowed feminists to executive staff positions in his administration. Midge Costanza, Jan Peterson, and Sarah Weddington in the Office of Public Liaison, Mary King in ACTION (the federal agency that oversaw volunteer programs), and a number of others brought to the White House feminist ideals that went well beyond Carter's formal commitment to equal rights.[188] They saw social welfare programs as essential to combating the feminization of poverty and enabling women to achieve substantive equality. As historian Susan M. Hartmann noted, feminists inside and outside the administration "expressed their concern for disadvantaged women . . . from the beginning" of Carter's tenure.[189] In two famous cases, Carter fired feminists for criticizing policies that hurt disadvantaged women: Midge Costanza for urging him to reconsider his position on the Hyde Amendment, which prohibited Medicaid funding for abortions, and Bella Abzug for publicly criticizing his budgetary priorities. Economics, Carter scolded Abzug, was not a "women's issue."[190]

The administration acknowledged women's particular interest in welfare reform, a recognition of the emerging feminist antipoverty network. In response to Carter's directive to gather "wide input," Califano initiated what one expert called a "nationwide 'buzz session,'" soliciting comments from more than 350 individuals and groups, including "recipient representatives, ethnic groups, women's groups, etc.," he directed his staff to "meet personally with relevant organizations," and he held several public hearings on the proposal. "It is my firm intent," the secretary assured Carter in February 1977, "that at the conclusion of this study, no group, public or private, and no constituency will accurately be able to say that they were not fully consulted."[191] Califano initially resisted including welfare rights activists in the formal Welfare Reform Consulting Group, insisting that "the typical welfare mother who beats and screams across the table . . . lose[s] more votes than [she] gets," but he eventually included three, including former AFDC recipient and head of NOW's Women in Poverty Task Force, Catherine Day Jermany. The administration also held a working session on "Women's Perspectives on Issues of Welfare Reform," during which HEW and DOL officials met with representatives from the welfare rights movement, NOW, WEAL, NWPC, LWV, NCJW, and women's religious organizations.[192] These groups stayed in close contact with staffers as the PBJI was being drafted: the LWV, NOW, and Women's Lobby had full-time lobbyists working on welfare reform.[193] Policymakers, then, were well acquainted with the feminist critique of welfare and the growing criticism of public policies that rested on the male-breadwinner ideal.

In fact, the emerging feminist network provided the only critique of the PBJI that articulated a comprehensive alternative framework for reform. Most liberal organizations that commented on the bill demonstrated "lukewarm support" and criticized particulars—benefit levels were too low, jobs were too few, eligibility restrictions were harmful. AFDC recipients voiced similar complaints. Grassroots welfare rights groups testified, and organizations like the NCWWW sponsored meetings to gather recipient opinion. The CSWP&L, the Food Research and Action Center (FRAC), and the Movement for Economic Justice (MEJ) sponsored six grassroots conferences across the country in late 1977 where recipients met with representatives from various liberal organizations, unions, and church groups.[194] Recipients most frequently criticized the PBJI's low benefit levels. With a basic grant at only 65 percent of the federal poverty line, the Income Support Tier would relegate families "to subpoverty existence," and reduce grants in all but twelve states.[195] Faith Evans, a welfare rights veteran who now headed the United Church of Christ's Commission for Racial Justice, rallied recipients at an October 1977 conference in Washington, D.C., against what he facetiously called the "Jobs and Income Program," or JIP. "We, the poor and minorities of this nation," he declared, "really went whole hog for the Jimmy Carter line" and hoped the new president would finally provide "a way out of poverty and degradation."[196] Recipients testifying before Congress also felt that this hope had been dashed. The PBJI, noted Pennsylvania recipient activist Louise Brookins, "proposes to redistribute a limited amount of assistance dollars from the poorest of the poor to the not so poor." Indeed, the Congressional Budget Office estimated that 45 percent of the program's benefits would go to households with incomes above the poverty line.[197] Some recipients, like a handful at a Utah welfare rights meeting attended by LWV representative Ruth Petajan, even expressed "scorn for giving any help to the 'working poor'." Petajan reported that most attendees, recipients included, were more reasonable and wanted to "discuss the Carter proposal . . . in hopes of finding ways to make it function better," but the tension was real. It echoed the fight that split the antipoverty coalition during the FAP debates.[198]

Missing from the PBJI debate was the emphasis on racial discrimination that had played such an important role during FAP deliberations. Many of the provisions that the NWRO and its allies had denounced as racist five years earlier were repeated in the PBJI, particularly higher benefit levels for the aged, blind, and disabled than for poor families. Now, the NUL condemned the PBJI for "discriminat[ing] against the poor" rather than against blacks, and Parren Mitchell of the CBC accused Carter of "benign neglect of poor families," not African Americans.[199] Meanwhile, women's organizations took the benefit discrepancies in a new direction. Recipients in the family category were not only more likely to be non-white—they were also more likely to be female. Women's organizations therefore denounced the bill for its "philosophy of 'women and children last,'" an argument virtually absent from the FAP debates.[200] Congress-woman Pat Schroeder summed up the shift from race to gender when she instructed her fellow lawmakers that welfare was a women's issue because "the fastest growing poverty group in America . . . is not black, and it's not brown." Instead, it "happens to be female."[201]

As in the FAP debates, too, some welfare rights advocates continued to insist that the federal government support the caregiving work of poor single mothers. Despite the PBJI's fairly anemic maternal work require-ment, BWWH condemned the administration for "forc[ing] welfare moth-ers with children" to take jobs outside the home, thus denying that AFDC recipients "are already working and entitled to a wage for that work." Poor women "don't want more jobs and token training programs," the group insisted, but needed instead "more money to work less." Black women's history of oppression and continued disadvantage led BWWH to demand economic security divorced from an exploitative labor market.[202] Faith Evans also denounced the plan for "ignor[ing] the value of child rearing in the home by forcing mothers of children seven years or over into demean-ing work," and Petajan reported that a few participants at the Utah meeting insisted that "women have a right to stay home and take care of their chil-dren" and to be given a decent level of support to do so.[203] Miami Arch-bishop Edward A. McCarthy agreed, arguing that "children should be cared for by their mothers" full-time.[204]

But most liberals now emphasized employment rather than full-time motherhood as the desired option for poor single mothers. Carol Payne gave two reasons that the LWV might "reconsider our opposition to the work requirement." Firstly, "the whole structure" of the PBJI seemed to be "predicated on requiring 'employables' to work and providing increased job opportunities." Second, "many welfare recipients who opposed work requirements in FAP are now demanding jobs."[205] Even the CDF, which continued to demand adequate income support, had begun to see "jobs and job training" as the "best route out of welfare dependency" for poor single mothers.[206] Policymakers recognized the shift. Moynihan noted that a decade earlier "an emphasis on jobs would have looked like slave labor," but by 1977 "the women's movement and welfare groups had changed their whole attitude toward welfare." The biggest complaint about the PBJI from welfare rights and women's groups, noted a DOL official, "was that the jobs might not pay enough or there might not be sufficient training and so forth," but "there was a clear indication from the welfare groups themselves that providing work was an important objective."[207] Invited to speak on welfare at the NWPC's 1977 convention, a DOL official tapped into the new mood with a talk titled "Welfare Reform Proposal—How It Will Assist Women Heads of Families Become Self-Supporting."[208]

Accordingly, most recipients who weighed in on the bill applauded the PBJI's jobs focus. During hearings in Miami, Florida, AFDC recipient and mother of four Carolyn Jones told lawmakers that jobs were "something that we have long needed," while a Legal Services attorney reported that "welfare recipients would prefer to work at meaningful, productive jobs rather than collecting public assistance benefits."[209] Recipient opinion generally echoed the position taken by feminist organizations, which "expressed strong support for the heavy emphasis" that the PBJI "places on job opportunities and the whole notion of self-support opportunities for poor people."[210] The "promise of work," insisted Women's Lobby, was "the most attractive part [of the bill] to the welfare women" the group had consulted. Indeed, by the late 1970s, most welfare and poverty rights efforts demanded not "Jobs or Income Now," the NWRO's cry in the early 1970s, but, rather "Jobs and Justice for All," or "mercy and mobility, justice and jobs."[211] When members of New York's DWAC picketed the city's welfare office (in Robin Hood costumes) they demanded not a guaranteed income but "decent jobs for decent pay."[212]

Because they had begun to see employment as women's only route out of poverty, many recipients joined feminist lobbyists in trying to change, rather than defeat, the PBJI. Initially the Welfare Group of the Ad Hoc Coalition for Women's Appointments was "pleasantly surprised . . . to find that the proposals are more positive toward women than we had anticipated" and was particularly impressed with the PBJI's 300,000 part-time jobs for mothers (though other women's groups noted how paltry the number seemed compared to the 3 million adults on AFDC).[213] "Despite [the bill's] many drawbacks," welfare recipients at an NCWWW conference "agreed that it is more constructive to support the bill while trying to change it" rather than "work[ing] to defeat the measure entirely," particularly because the PBJI was "a jobs-based plan." As Las Vegas welfare rights leader Ruby Duncan put it, "let's create rather than destroy."[214]

This optimism disappeared once the bill was finalized. As early as February 1977, the League of Women Voters expressed concern that a two-track system would "confine women with child care responsibilities to a dead-end 'unemployable' category," a prescient warning.[215] The eventual bill validated that prediction. Defined as "unemployable," the vast majority of single mothers would not have access to public service employment. Labeled "unemployable" and placed on the "Income Support Tier," single mothers were unlikely to volunteer for the "employable track" with its lower benefit levels, lack of a job guarantee, and nonexistent child care assistance. The program thereby "unfairly discriminat[ed] against female involvement in the labor force."[216] Single mothers, the National Women's Agenda declared, "would be served last, if at all, by the jobs program."[217] The two-track system, concluded the NCWWW, "is more than deficient and inadequate, it is destructive" because it "merely keeps women poor" and "denies them access to employment and education for at least seven, possibly fourteen years."[218] As the feminist antipoverty network saw it, the administration had "decided that it is cheaper to keep women at home than to provide job opportunities."[219]

Feminists' foremost concern was with poor single mothers, but they also denounced the PBJI's "principal wage earner" provision. In two-parent families on the "employable track," only the one adult who had earned the most in the previous year would be eligible for a public service job. Some organizations, like the LWV, argued that each family should decide for itself which adult got the job, but most feminists denounced the very idea of a "principal wage earner."[220] Many families by the late 1970s required two incomes to stay above poverty, particularly if the jobs paid minimum wage, as the PBJI's public service jobs would. Even liberal organizations that had championed the male-breadwinner family a decade earlier realized that times had changed. The NUL, for example, rejected the PBJI's "anachronistic view of the American family . . . based on the assumption that the man's role is to go out and work while the woman should stay home and take care of the children."[221] Feminist critics went one step further. By allocating only one job per family, reserving it for the "principal wage earner," and providing no child care for two-parent households, they argued, the PBJI would not only prove ineffective in fighting family poverty; it would also perpetuate women's economic dependence on men.

Feminists clearly recognized the lingering family wage ideal in the

PBJI. They had only to look to Andrew Hacker's memo, in which he "drew an idyllic picture of the 'traditional American family' as a male breadwinner supporting mother and children" and "suggested that 'incentives should be arranged . . . to encourage women who are single parents to remarry'." Hacker's very premise reflected what WEAL lobbyist Leslie Gladstone called the administration's "perception gap."[222] Some liberal allies suffered from the same ailment. John Bishop of the Institute for Poverty Research praised the "primary breadwinner" provision because it would avoid "drawing wives in two-parent families into the labor market" and thereby minimize the welfare system's "destabilizing independence effects"—a wife's ability to leave a marriage or avoid marriage altogether that an independent income might afford. Bishop even proposed adding income supplements to the husband's paychecks, covertly if possible, to enable him to "retain the image of a successful breadwinner."[223] Helen Parolla of the YWCA pointed to Senator Moynihan's comments, published in the *Congressional Record*, that "the single most important element of a successful urban policy should be the level of *male* employment."[224] Moynihan was saying nothing new—he had been making the same argument since 1965. But times had changed.

Carter's policymakers "have simply not understood," complained feminist Jo Freeman, "that the principal economic unit is no longer, if it ever was, a two-adult family with only one primary wage earner."[225] Others saw sinister intent rather than innocent misunderstanding. The NCWWW analysts argued that the PBJI "actually penalizes a woman for not living with a man." According to their calculations, a single mother with two small children could double her family income by marrying.[226] As many feminists saw it, the only way to ensure economic independence for women, whether married or single, was to stop seeing "economic dependency on men as the ultimate fallback position" and to recognize "the fact that all adults have a responsibility for the support of themselves and their children, regardless of their individual living situation."[227] Carter's own Advisory Committee for Women concluded that the individual, not the family, should be the "economic basis for determining benefits."[228] "Only in this way," insisted NOW, "will women be freed."[229]

Ultimately, welfare recipients and their feminist allies demanded much more than the Carter administration and Congress were willing to provide—real resources to enable poor single mothers to escape poverty through employment. Taking a page from WOW and other job training initiatives, they demanded access to nontraditional jobs and insisted on "specific language prohibiting sex discrimination" to ensure single mothers "full participation in training and job programs *regardless of the opinion of some local officials that they belong in the home."* One welfare recipient, who attributed her poor health to her efforts to combine parenting five children with full-time work as a nurse's aide, insisted that welfare mothers needed "more nontraditional jobs," by which she meant "good paying jobs."[230] Another, Kathy Alana, advised, "we want the type of job that will keep us off welfare, not put us right back on it."[231] Dr. Aida T. Levitan, director of Latin Affairs in Dade County, Florida, spelled out what a truly effective welfare reform package might look like—a program of "part-time work, part-time study, and partial welfare assistance" to help poor mothers train for and obtain the kinds of jobs that would support their children.[232] Congresswoman Pat Schroeder, testifying on the PBJI, suggested the breadth of feminist responses to women's poverty. Women need nontraditional jobs, stringent affirmative action measures, child care, parental leave, alternative work schedules—all "innovative things [that] just have not been looked at, because we still have the concept that every worker in America is a male supporting a family."[233]

But some lawmakers continued to hear what they wanted to hear. After participating in thirty public hearings on welfare reform, Congressman Joseph LeFante, a New Jersey Democrat, had never heard one person who "asked for welfare." Instead, "they are asking for jobs, for work." But LeFante could not have been listening very closely to single mothers, who demanded education, training, jobs and child care. Instead, he fondly recalled the "men [who] have appeared and said they wanted to be king of the castle." Rather than "hanging around the house all day," these hopeful breadwinners, LeFante approvingly noted, "want to come home at night and have their wife and family waiting for them at the door, as all working men do." To LeFante, this was "getting back to old fashioned living," and he was "glad to hear it."[234]

The PBJI never made it to the floor of either the House or the Senate.[235] By 1979, the administration hesitated to propose even a much less costly welfare reform plan. By then, California voters had passed Proposition 13, which capped property taxes and required a two-thirds legislative majority for any tax hikes. Soon, a tax revolt—one much different from the calls for progressive tax reform issued by the left—was spreading across the nation.[236] The day Proposition 13 passed, a leading Senate Democrat stopped Califano in the Capitol hallway and implored, "you've got to bury that damn welfare bill."[237] He needn't have worried. By then, Carter was fully committed to battling crippling inflation rates with budgetary restraint.[238] Though staffers warned him against becoming identified "with a new, liberal spending intiative," Carter agreed to propose a second, more modest welfare reform package at the behest of Eizenstat, Califano, Marshall, and others who argued that it would be "one of the very few Presidential issues for liberals and civil rights groups," our "*badly* estranged friends."[239] That proposal stalled in the Senate. As the historian James Patterson has concluded, the PBJI's failure "represented a dying gasp of enthusiasm for guaranteed income plans in the United States."[240] Surely, the changing public and political mood had much to do with that death. But just as surely, a transformation in family economics and new dynamics within the liberal coalition, such as the growing influence of feminism, weakened the rationale for a welfare system dedicated to recreating a rapidly disappearing "traditional family."

Chapter 5

Relinquishing Responsibility for Poor Families: Reagan's Family Wage for the Wealthy

The old policy of excluding mothers of young children from registration in employment programs should be reconsidered in light of women's liberation and their strong role in the labor force.

—Preston Kayanagh, Chicago businessman, 1980

In 1981, President Ronald Reagan regaled a corporate audience with a tale from his welfare-reforming days as governor of California. "After we undertook our welfare reforms" in the early 1970s, Reagan had received a letter from a former AFDC recipient who thanked him for cutting the state's welfare rolls. "She wrote that she had become so dependent on the welfare check that she even turned down offers of marriage," Reagan recounted; "she just could not give up that security blanket that [welfare] represented." Reagan's cuts allowed her to break free from welfare dependence. The woman's conversion narrative ended with employment; she moved to Alaska to be with relatives, found a "good job" and a "great deal of self-respect," and realized, finally, that a job "sure beats daytime television."[1]

Reagan did not mention whether the woman had escaped poverty, nor did he reveal her marital status. This morality tale reveals the fundamental priorities of Reagan's welfare politics. Antiwelfare conservatives like Reagan certainly denounced AFDC and "welfare" more generally for contributing to family breakdown and its supposed consequences, from gang violence and drug use to declining SAT scores and teen pregnancies. Drawing on the antipoverty coalition's 1960s critique, antiwelfare conservatives in the 1980s blamed poverty itself on an overly generous welfare system that destroyed self-reliant, two-parent, heterosexual families. However, for Reagan, family structure among the poor was more a rhetorical weapon than a policy focus. He did not relate that his reforms in California had succeeded in pushing his thankful letter-writer into marriage, whether to a stable male provider or to a poor man with whom she could share breadwinning duties. Instead, they had pushed her out from under her "welfare security blanket" and into the labor market.[2] The "traditional family" that antiwelfare conservatives like those in the Reagan administration celebrated, then, was race- and class-specific. Though the 1980 Republican Party Platform promised "legislation protecting and defending the traditional American family against the ongoing erosion of its base in our society," that promise did not include social policies that might improve the economic security of poor families, even the "traditional," male-breadwinner kind that the 1960s antipoverty coalition had hoped to promote. Reagan provided a handful of tax breaks to help middle-class mothers, whether they worked for wages or cared for children full-time, but restricted access to public assistance for poor mothers, leaving them at the mercy of a sex-segregated and increasingly precarious low-wage labor market.[3]

Contrary to many historical accounts, members of an increasingly fragmented antipoverty coalition did not take Reagan's attack on the welfare state lying down. Democratic lawmakers, advocacy organizations, and grassroots activists condemned the administration's economic and social policies as class warfare. The Reagan Revolution's social spending cuts and regressive tax policies, they declared, denied social responsibility for Americans' economic well-being and proved harmful to white workers and urban black youth alike. But liberals offered only a timid defense of AFDC, a program they had been attacking since the 1960s. Those who bothered to speak for AFDC recipients attempted to redefine welfare and welfare mothers. Reagan's early reforms, which denied that wage-earning AFDC mothers were "truly needy," pushed liberals to broaden their conception of the "working poor" by acknowledging the low-wage, temporary, and casual labor of poor, single, and nonwhite mothers. By the 1980s, the demise of the family wage ideal—as a realistic option for American families, as a policy goal, and as a dominant cultural construction—profoundly altered welfare politics. No longer did antipoverty liberals, or even many welfare recipient activists themselves, demand its revival. Employment remained as the sole answer to the poverty of poor single mothers.

At the same time, the supposed pathology of urban black families remained at the center of American welfare debates. This focus, along with liberals' about-face on maternal employment, fed a "new consensus" on welfare by the late 1980s. In an atmosphere of fiscal and political constraints, poverty "experts" across the political spectrum demanded government policies that enforced both paternal breadwinning (through child support enforcement) and maternal breadwinning (through mandatory wage labor). Antipoverty liberals' concern about the family structure of the poor was no longer coupled to demands for expanded federal income support; instead, it had become a powerful weapon in the antiwelfare campaign which many liberals joined. The "new consensus" of the mid-1980s increasingly resembled the old antiwelfare conservatism, an ideology that frankly excluded nonwhites and the poor from the privileges of male breadwinning and female homemaking.

Welfare Reform in the First Reagan Administration

The arc of Ronald Reagan's political ascendance left little doubt that as president he would mount an assault on the nation's welfare system. An arch foe of the guaranteed income, Reagan had publicly denounced Nixon's Family Assistance Plan and had made criticism of AFDC a "central theme" in his 1970 California gubernatorial campaign.[4] He called welfare a "costly and tragic failure" that was "destroying people, our most precious resource, by creating a permanent and growing poverty class."[5] As part of a nationwide "crackdown" on welfare, described in Chapter 2, Reagan and the state legislature tightened eligibility for public assistance and won a federal waiver to require work in exchange for AFDC grants (such "workfare" programs were at that time against HEW policy).[6] In March 1971, as more than 250,000 American military personnel remained bogged down in a guerrilla war in Vietnam, as antiwar protesters and police clashed violently on campuses and in the streets, and as unemployment rates among minority urban youth climbed to staggering levels, Reagan declared welfare "America's No. 1 Problem."[7]

In part, the Reagan administration's attack on welfare was simply part of a larger battle against federal social spending with both ideological and practical motives. A New Deal Democrat until the 1950s, Reagan experienced a profound political conversion in the postwar years. By 1964 he was a registered Republican and was gaining national notoriety running Barry Goldwater's presidential campaign in California. He had become a free market evangelist, opposing federal interference in corporate regulation or social spending.[8] Free market conservatives had long insisted that American political freedom depended first and foremost upon economic freedom and denounced any form of encroaching "statism" as a sure route to communist totalitarianism. As the economy soured during the 1970s, neoconservative analysts honed a more practical criticism of federal spending. They insisted that by taxing and redistributing private wealth, the federal government fueled rampant inflation, soaring budget deficits, and general economic ruin. Once on the fringes of American political and economic debate, this neo-laissez-faire economics had moved decidedly to the center by the late 1970s.

The Reagan administration insisted that "the tremendous increase in social programs over the past decade has put the federal budget out of whack and contributed to inflation."[9] In the administration's "Principles for Responsible Welfare Reform," Robert Carleson and Kevin Hopkins charged that "redistribution of income has dramatically reduced incentives to work, produce, save and invest," creating "high marginal tax rates, large budget deficits, and low productivity" which "have greatly slowed economic growth and accelerated inflation." Restricting the welfare system would thus prove "economically salutary" for a nation unsettled by recent economic dislocations.[10] The resulting spending limitations, contained in the Omnibus Budget Reconciliation Act of 1981 (OBRA), cut AFDC rolls by 400,000 individuals, reduced benefits for hundreds of thousands more, and cut federal AFDC costs by $1 billion, or 12 percent, in fiscal year 1982. By the end of Reagan's first term, federal spending on food stamps and AFDC was 13 percent less than it would have been without OBRA's cuts, and other means-tested programs entailed similar losses.[11]

A purely economic perspective fails to account for the disproportionate share of Reagan's budget cuts shouldered by AFDC and other federal programs for the poor—70 percent, according to one analyst.[12] AFDC costs made up a mere 1 percent of the federal budget; even including food stamps and SSI, "welfare" spending represented only 4 percent of federal spending, compared to nearly 20 percent for OASDI or "Social Security."[13] The programs that the administration explicitly exempted from cuts were not those aimed at the "truly needy," as Reagan's spokespeople claimed; Social Security retirement benefits, Medicare, and veterans' benefits went overwhelmingly to the nonpoor, and they escaped the chopping block because of their political popularity. In fact, Reagan's brief foray in limiting OASDI—a reform urged by the Business Roundtable and other likeminded conservatives, including Reagan's own OMB director, David Stockman—proved politically disastrous. His proposal to reduce Social Security payments of early retirees provoked an outcry from the well-organized old age lobby and failed to garner support even among Congressional Republicans.[14] Programs for the poor, from low-income housing subsidies to food stamps to Medicaid to AFDC, were much easier targets.

AFDC's declining reputation made it a particularly easy target. By 1978, tales of welfare fraud, long a staple of antiwelfare conservatives and enterprising journalists, proliferated in national news venues, serving as a powerful symbol to a public increasingly skeptical about the federal government's ability to operate fairly and efficiently. Popular newsmagazines and newspapers introduced readers to a series of flagrant welfare abusers, all African American or Latina and each one more outrageous than the next: Maria Rodriguez, who received welfare for herself and her five children despite her husband's success as the "kingpin of a prosperous ring of drug pushers"; the Reverend Roland Gray and his wife, who collected tremendous sums in AFDC, food stamp, and Medicaid benefits even as they cruised Chicago's South Side in stylish suits, fur coats, and one of four luxury cars; and a series of "welfare queens" like Chicago's Linda Taylor, all amassing excessive wealth by engaging in flagrant welfare abuse.[15] These tales invariably turned out to be either false or greatly exaggerated, and official reports documented very little intentional fraud in public assistance programs. But the stories confirmed what many Americans had long suspected—that the welfare system was a mess, a haven for enterprising crooks as well as lazy ne'er-do-wells, and that "a significant proportion of tax funds spent on welfare is consumed by fraud, waste, and abuse."[16]

Far from defending AFDC against such charges, the Carter administration merely fed the fire. Its plan to "turn [around] the public mood of cynicism" about federal social programs was not to *defend* those programs or to insist that the vast majority of recipients had a legitimate claim to the nation's common resources.[17] Instead, the administration pledged to launch a "war on waste and fraud" in welfare.[18] Under the watchful eye of Califano—Lyndon Johnson's domestic policy advisor during the heyday of the Great Society—HEW initiated "Project Integrity" and "Project Match," antifraud measures coordinated by the Offices of Inspector General, a team of over one thousand auditors, investigators, and managers added to the federal payroll to help "root out fraud and abuse."[19] Staffers urged the president himself to leap "squarely out in front on this volatile issue" with a major public speech, and despite personal reservations, Carter agreed, addressing the HEW Conference on Fraud, Abuse, and Error in Social Programs in December 1978.[20] By declaring "war on waste and fraud in government programs," Carter predicted that his administration could help "to restore and rebuild the trust that must exist in any democracy between a free people and their government."[21] Califano defended the move by insisting that "the heart of President Carter is no less compassionate than that of Lyndon Johnson" but merely "beats in a different time," a time when "liberals and progressives . . . must match their compassion and generosity with competence and efficiency." Califano expressed the dilemma that proponents of a welfare state for America's poorest citizens confronted as the nation reached the end of what had seemed to be an eternal economic boom, announcing "there is a new breed of liberal in town" who would be "deeply committed to social programs—and equally committed to sound management."[22]

But a war on waste and fraud was hardly a convincing defense of federal income support; it merely fed political attacks on welfare. With his penchant for the telling anecdote, Reagan found tales of welfare fraud a useful answer to critics of his social spending cuts. He seemed to regard the invocation of a "woman in Chicago that's getting checks under 127 different names" and another in Pasadena "charged with collecting $300,000 in a welfare scheme" as the definitive answer to claims that his AFDC restrictions may have harmed poor families.[23] But he went further, painting even nonfraudulent AFDC recipients as undeserving and restricting access in multiple ways. OBRA ended state policies granting AFDC benefits to pregnant women, prohibited states from providing AFDC benefits to children between eighteen and twenty-one who were full-time students, required monthly income reporting and retrospective budgeting, counted receipt of "in-kind" benefits like low-income energy assistance and housing subsidies as income (reducing recipients' cash grants), and included the income of all household members when calculating AFDC benefits, whether or not those who shared housing with the AFDC family were either legally required to or actually contributing to recipient children's upkeep.[24] An administration Fact Sheet insisted that the aim was to "refocus AFDC on its original goal: to serve as a safety net for dependent children in families where the resources for self-support do not exist."[25] In other words, the cuts would enable policymakers to redirect AFDC aid from "those who don't really need help" to those the administration called the "truly needy."[26]

A majority of OBRA's AFDC cuts targeted mothers with earnings, which temporarily reversed over a decade of bipartisan support for work incentives. The "well-meaning policy" of offering work incentives, Robert Carleson insisted, "*has not* worked but has had the opposite effect, bringing millions of working Americans into a state of dependency." Carleson argued that non-AFDC mothers were likely to quit work, get on welfare, then begin working again in order to benefit from the thirty-and-a-third rule, though there was no evidence to suggest anything of the sort. He also denounced work incentives for diverting "limited funds" to "families with incomes well above the national average," though in fact employed AFDC mothers rarely had earnings much higher than the federal poverty line.[27] To restrict aid to the "truly needy," OBRA standardized AFDC's work expense deduction at $75 per month, lower than the average deduction claimed by working recipients. It also allowed only $50 per month for each child's care, well below actual cost. Though AFDC recipients typically earned wages well below the poverty line and worked seasonally and temporarily, OBRA limited work incentives to four months.[28] Before OBRA, AFDC mothers with earned income were able to raise their families out of poverty in twenty-nine states; afterwards, these families fell once again into poverty. Yet the Reagan administration continued to insist that these families were *not* "truly needy."[29] Replacing the carrot of work incentives with the stick of workfare, OBRA also allowed states to replace WIN—a combination of job search requirements and training with social services—with workfare, which required recipients to "work off" their welfare grants by performing community service jobs.[30] By 1986, twenty-four states had implemented some form of workfare in at least some counties.[31]

With OBRA, the Reagan administration and majorities in Congress declared firmly that single mothers would no longer be treated differently from other poor able-bodied adults. According to David Stockman, welfare should go only to "the aged, blind, and disabled—whose eligibility can be ascertained by reference to physical characteristics."[32] Reagan's policymakers thus announced that poor single mothers would no longer be exempt from labor market participation. Like other antiwelfare conservatives, Reagan had been making this argument since the 1960s. "By what right does a welfare worker say that just because a woman has children no one should expect her ever again to be self-supporting?" he demanded in a 1971 interview.[33] Carleson and Hopkins placed a mother's private financial responsibility for her children at the center of the administration's "Principles for Responsible Welfare Reform." Parents of children "should support them—whether they are a mother or father, married or not," they insisted.[34]

In fact, drawing on earlier liberal critiques of AFDC, the administration insisted that welfare harmed the poor; restricting it would only improve the lives of the nation's most disadvantaged. George Gilder, "widely regarded as providing a philosophical foundation for the Reagan administration's domestic policy," defended the administration from charges of unfairness and coldheartedness by insisting that welfare and other antipoverty programs had "halted in its tracks an ongoing improvement in the lives of the poor and left a wreckage of broken families and broken communities which it will take decades to retrieve."[35] Reagan picked up on such language, assuring audiences that the programs he was targeting, the "well-intentioned . . . social experiments" initiated by elite liberal policymakers, had themselves "created a new kind of bondage for millions of Americans," trapping them into dependency and promoting a range of disorderly and self-destructive behaviors.[36] Family breakup and single motherhood emerged as the most reviled of these welfare-induced pathologies.

In this vein, some advisors urged Reagan to make family breakdown the center of his welfare critique. In July 1982, OMB general counsel Mike Horowitz proposed that a focus on the family could help Reagan counter criticism from Democrats and liberal advocacy groups that his tax and budget cuts disproportionately affected the nation's most vulnerable citizens. In particular, Horowitz was interested in addressing the concerns of middle-class "women voters" who seemed to perceive the administration as "uncaring, perhaps cruel." Horowitz blamed AFDC for the family breakdown at the heart of the feminization of poverty. "The breakdown of the family was not a lamentable but unavoidable trend in American society," he insisted. The availability of AFDC along with "changes in prevailing moral values, inflation and the decline of private sector productivity—our issues—were behind the tragedy of what the 70's did to (and the extent to which it created) single, poor women."[37]

In 1984, political scientist Charles Murray made exactly that argument in his groundbreaking case against the liberal welfare state, *Losing Ground: American Social Policy, 1950–1980*. Funded and aggressively marketed by the conservative Manhattan Institute, *Losing Ground* was soon hailed as "the 'social Bible' of the Reagan Administration."[38] In a series of "thought experiments" and in pages of tables, graphs, and data sets, Murray sought to add social scientific legitimacy to the case that antiwelfare conservatives had long argued and that neoconservatives had taken up in the 1970s: that the expansion of AFDC and other income support programs in the 1960s and 1970s had "changed the rules," making it "profitable for the poor to behave in the short term in ways that were destructive in the long term." According to to Murray, AFDC, food stamps, Medicaid, and other means-tested programs in the 1960s and 1970s prompted poor young men (especially poor young *black* men, a racial disparity that Murray did not explain) to reject low-wage jobs and poor young women (again, especially poor young black women) to produce illegitimate children. In 1960, Murray's "unremarkable" hypothetical young couple, Harold and the pregnant Phyllis, would have been best off economically if they had married and Harold had taken low-wage work. Ten years later, according to Murray, liberal policymakers and a powerful welfare rights movement had drastically altered Harold and Phyllis's calculations by eliminating AFDC's "man-in-the-house rule" (meaning a couple could live together without marrying while the woman still collected welfare) and various other restrictions. Now, they would be better off financially if they remained unmarried and Harold participated only casually in the labor market. By 1970, then, "the old-fashioned solution of getting married and living off their earned income had become markedly inferior," Murray argued, "to staying unmarried and collecting welfare."[39]

Liberal analysts identified a number of problems with Murray's argument. The decline in black male labor force participation and the increase in female-headed households among African Americans accelerated during the 1970s, even as the value of AFDC benefits *declined*, casting doubt on Murray's causal argument. At the same time, the case of Harold and Phyllis used an atypical state system and ignored benefits like food stamps that were available to poor two-parent, working families to exaggerate the disincentives for work and marriage. Liberal scholars pronounced Murray's treatise "seriously flawed—distorted as description, incomplete as explanation, and lethal as prescription."[40] But, as historian Alice O'Connor has noted, the liberals who dominated the "poverty knowledge industry" by the early 1980s offered little more than an "empirical rebuttal." Even as they pointed out the flaws in Murray's analysis they failed to offer alternative explanations for the dismal conditions among inner-city minorities or "a coherent political agenda for achieving a more equitable welfare state." Murray's prescription to scrap all federal assistance to working-age adults was liberal sacrilege, but poverty analysts, whose research remained focused on the behavioral patterns of the poor, had little positive defense of the welfare system, and welfare's destabilizing effect on poor black families had been at the center of the liberal campaign for a more universal and generous income support policy a decade-and-a-half earlier.[41] The irony of the unintended consequences of these earlier views seems to have been largely lost on them.

Unlike George Gilder and Charles Murray, often referred to as the philosophical architects of the Reagan domestic policy revolution,[42] the president's actual welfare advisors, Martin Anderson and Robert Carleson, expressed little interest in family breakup or illegitimacy rates. Anderson's scathing 1978 critique of the nation's public assistance system, *Welfare*, had virtually nothing to say about family structure. Nor did Carleson's long and detailed justifications of the administration's social spending cuts. The problem, he and Hopkins insisted, was not broken families but families "in which the ethic of work has been replaced by an ethic of dependence." Welfare's primary incentive problem was its tendency to "substantially reduce . . . a person's incentive to work," to produce children with no work ethic, and thereby to create "an intergenerational welfare cycle."[43]

Family became a priority issue for the Reagan administration only when pollsters began to identify a "gender gap" among American voters.[44] According to *Public Opinion* magazine, no clear ideological or partisan differences had separated men and women before the late 1970s. By 1982, though, Democratic candidates were doing "five to fifteen points better among women than men," and *New York Times* political correspondent Adam Clymer was predicting that "this so-called gender gap may influence American life in the 1980s as much as the civil rights revolution did in the 1960s."[45] Reagan's advisors regarded the gender gap as "one of the most severe challenges facing the Administration in the next two years." With female voters "emerging as considerably more liberal and Democratic than men," Republican strategist Lee Atwater warned that "if the sexes continue to realign, the Republicans will be once again locked into a minority status." "Clearly," Atwater concluded, "we will have to take some action."[46] Reagan appointed an assistant for public liaison, Elizabeth Hanford Dole, to head a Coordinating Council on Women, which he charged with analyzing "the changing role of women in the United States" and suggesting "appropriate action for government."

The Coordinating Council on Women recognized that the administration's budget cuts "adversely affect[ed] the growing number of single parent families (90% of which are headed by a female) which rely heavily on federal aid."[47] A number of other advisors also saw his social welfare cuts as critical to Republicans' woman problem. They recognized that "lower socioeconomic status women are more critical [of the president] than higher socioeconomic status women," particularly those who were single, separated, and divorced and between twenty-five and fifty-four years of age, prime childrearing years. Ronald H. Hinckley of the White House Office of Planning and Evaluation concluded the obvious: these women's economic vulnerability meant that they "frequently must look beyond their own resources to keep themselves and their families going."[48] Advisors also understood that these same social program cuts alienated the middle-class members of "feminist women's groups," which included not only explicitly feminist organizations like NOW and the NWPC but longtime advocates of more generous welfare policies like the League of Women Voters.[49] Polls that documented the gender gap found that women "favored candidates perceived to be more peace-oriented in foreign affairs" but also more "caring on social programs and the economy."[50]

But Reagan was not prepared to court such voters by reversing his antiwelfare policies. He ignored Women's Bureau director Lenora Cole-Alexander's suggestion that the president court women voters by "lessen [ing] or resolv[ing] the impact of budget cuts on women and their families" and funding child care and training for jobs that were "higher paying and will provide self-sufficiency."[51] Nor did the administration follow Ronald Hinkley's proposal to provide tax relief for the working poor, a way to "benefit a sizable majority of single female-headed households without exclusively doing so."[52] The administration had little hope of luring into the Republican Party either poor single mothers or the feminists who sometimes spoke on their behalf. And poor single mothers commanded much less political capital than New Right voters, who supported welfare cuts. Reagan had little to offer low-income women and their allies, as a 1982 administration document titled "The Feminization of Poverty—Press Guidance" reveals. The document suggested that spokespersons answer questions about women's poverty by touting the administration's success in reducing estate taxes, improving married women's access to Individual Retirement Accounts, and increasing the child care tax credit, programs with little relevance to women living below the poverty line.[53]

If "women on welfare or otherwise supported by the Federal government" were a "very poor prospect for the Administration . . . minority women who are moving into the middle class" and both married and single "upscale actives" were more likely targets for a Republican campaign to attract woman voters. "Send speakers to organized women's groups such as organizations of women in business, real estate agents, etc.," public relations experts urged.[54] To the Reaganites most committed to the "traditional" family (at least for the nonpoor), an appeal to upwardly mobile career women represented a distasteful but necessary sacrifice. Lee Atwater compared the imperative to cater to working women to the ideological and political sacrifices forced on the segregationist South in the 1960s. "It always hurts to give up something you like," he lamented about courting women who rejected the "traditional" family, and "who knows what the GOP will have to give up in response to the women's movement." But the time had come for the party and the administration to begin "exploring the dimensions of what Elizabeth Dole recently described as the 'Quiet Revolution,' the enormous surge of women into the workplace in the last ten years."[55] To "close the gender gap," Reagan strategists advised, the president must communicate "recognition of the changing role of women as breadwinners as well as homemakers" and demonstrate "sympathy" for working women.[56] By 1984, the Republican National Committee was spending $200,000 on a series of workshops aimed at America's working women. The topics—not only politics but also "managing money, managing time, managing the family, [and] Jazzercise"—suggest a middle- to upper-class target audience.[57]

For Reagan and other free market conservatives, responding to the concerns of *middle-class* career women seemed relatively unproblematic. Here was a feminism that the Reagan administration could embrace, for as the editors of the *National Review* noted in 1981, "the feminist movement has made legitimate and irreversible gains in those areas where it is in harmony with the individualism in American culture" like breaking down the kind of overt sex discrimination that had prevented large numbers of women from entering the professions and rising in the corporate hierarchy. Absent outright legal barriers, conservatives argued, women were now free to compete on the basis of merit and personal preference.[58]

The Coordinating Council on Women therefore emphasized Reagan's efforts to further *"legal equity"* and "the removal of artificial barriers that prevent women from making choices." The administration's self-described "solid record of achievement" in this area rested in the work of a Task Force on Legal Equity, charged with finding and eliminating explicitly gender-biased language in federal laws and regulations, and its "50 States Project," which did the same at the state level.[59] Some Republican women complained that the administration had "retreat[ed] from aggressive enforcement of our civil rights laws affecting equal pay and equal opportunity for women," but Reagan staffers hoped that symbolic efforts like the creation of the Task Force on Legal Equity and the Coordinating Council on Women would demonstrate to business and professional women that Reagan cared about protecting them from overt discrimination.[60]

Yet the administration went beyond public relations in its effort to "show working women that Republican policies are . . . beneficial to them."[61] Reagan claimed credit for a number of policies aimed at addressing working women's concerns. In some cases, he merely signed onto Congressional initiatives like the Flexible and Compressed Work Schedules Act of 1982, a response to feminist demands that the labor market adapt to the needs of working parents.[62] The administration also took credit for reducing the so-called "marriage penalty," an anachronism in the tax system that meant higher tax bills for dual-earner couples, and Reagan's 1981 tax reform plan provided a useful vehicle for the administration to address another critical issue for working women. Six of ten women with children under age eighteen were in the labor market in 1984, and child care needs had become acute.[63] Ideologically opposed to explicit federal intervention in child care, the administration increased child care funding via tax credits.[64] Historian Sonya Michel has noted, "federal expenditures for childcare for middle- and upper-income families increased markedly," as the total value of tax dollars lost through child care exemptions more than tripled to almost one billion dollars between 1980 and 1986.[65] The administration touted these policies, along with the work of its Private Sector Initiative Office to encourage development of private child care centers, as part of its effort to "make it resoundingly and decisively clear that we accept the new role of women, especially working women."[66]

At the same time, the administration significantly reduced child care funding available to the poor. Since 1962 Congress had appropriated funds to pay for some welfare recipients' child care needs and stepped up the effort under the Social Services Block Grant (Title XX of the Social Security Act) in 1974.[67] OBRA went in the opposite direction. It not only limited AFDC recipients' child care deductions, it also reduced child care funding in federal jobs programs. Perhaps more importantly, OBRA significantly reduced funding for Title XX, the source of most low-income child care assistance, and removed the law's child care earmark.[68] One scholar has described the "impact of Reagan-era cutbacks on the funding and regulation of public childcare" as "devastating," reducing already inadequate funding by over 14 percent between 1980 and 1986. Policymakers well understood that low-income families benefited little from the kind of indirect tax credits that increasingly accounted for federal child care expenditures.[69] In 1982, millions of low-income mothers had access to a mere 467,000 government-subsidized child care slots.[70] The shift toward the middle class was clear. According to one analyst, in 1972 some 80 percent of federal child care spending went to low-income families. By the end of Reagan's second term, it had fallen to 50 percent.[71]

Reagan's position on women's unpaid domestic role betrayed a similar class bias. Even as it courted professional women, the administration still hoped to retain the support of the "Schlafly constituency," "Christian women's groups," and "non-working women over fifty."[72] Reagan's endorsement of a Constitutional amendment banning abortion might have helped mobilize the small but powerful cadre of New Right women, but his advisors worried that the gender gap strategy, which benefited working women, might alienate some of the president's most avid conservative supporters. The administration co-opted a feminist language of choice to appeal to both of these groups at the same time. "All women share at least one objective," according to a 1983 White House Office of Policy Information Issue Update, "the opportunity to choose their own destinies and attain individual self-fulfillment as fully participating citizens."[73] So for women who "wish to enter the job market or advance in their careers, the President has sought to remove barriers and disincentives to employment," while "for women who wish to concentrate on their roles as wives, mothers and homemakers" the administration "implemented economic policies which will allow them to more easily do so."[74] To this end, Reagan promised (before Phyllis Schlafly's Eagle Forum) "to end the blatant discrimination against the traditional homemaker which exists in the Individual Retirement Accounts and other provisions of the income tax law."[75] Reagan's first major tax plan increased the amount that a family could allocate to the so-called "Homemaker IRA" established in 1976, and reduced the estate tax, which it touted as a boon to homemakers, whose wage-earning husbands could now pass on more wealth to their economically vulnerable wives.[76] Homemakers would also benefit from social security reforms which "ended the inequitable treatment of elderly divorced or disabled women, who before lost benefits if they married again."[77] None of these reforms extended help to poor women, and each rewarded (albeit minimally) the homemaking labor of married (or once married) women only.

Reagan even claimed that his policies would promote the economic growth necessary to enable women to fulfill their role in the home once again. Officials expressed concern, even sympathy, for wives "forced out of their homes into the job market by the eroding value of single family incomes." They offered Reagan's tax and spending cuts as the path to a "noninflationary economy" that would provide "the only feasible way of providing a choice between a job away from home or full-time work at raising families."[78] Faith Whittlesey, a White House public affairs aide, made the same point. "We respect the choice to work in the home and the choice to work outside the home," she told a gathering of Republican women, "and we don't think inflation or [a] stagnant economy should eliminate choice itself."[79] "Federal spending," Republican strategist Richard Viguerie declared, "eats into the family's income, forcing mothers to go to work to pay for food, clothing, shelter, and other family basics."[80]

Reagan's Working Group on the Family went further. Chaired by Undersecretary of Education Gary L. Bauer, an evangelical Christian with strong ties to the religious right, the group pointed to Europe, where because of "state-funded day care, child allowances, national health systems, school feeding programs, and other welfare programs," government "grew and taxed, pinching pocketbooks and forcing mothers into the workplace." The United States faced a similar threat, as the Working Group saw it. "Millions of mothers entered the workforce, full or part-time, out of financial need during a period of bad economic policy in Washington." Ideally, as Reagan "lighten[ed] the heavy hand of government," the group hoped that fewer mothers would resort to wage labor, never mind that the administration's broader policies contributed to a long-term erosion of wages such that even an exceptionally low-inflation economy would leave most families in need of more than one income.[81] Rhetorically, while peddling short-term nostrums that benefited mostly working women, the Reagan administration continued to trumpet an older, exclusive family wage ideal.

Many liberals had battled that older family wage model since the mid-1960s, but by the 1980s the antipoverty coalition was both fragmented and much less sure of itself. As countless scholars have noted, a whole series of events and trends contributed to liberalism's sense of crisis by the late 1970s: the economic dislocations that undermined faith in Keynesian economics and sparked a tax revolt; cultural transformations—especially those involving gender and sexuality—that many Americans associated with the political left; a demographic shift that concentrated more affluent and politically conservative families in the nation's suburban rings and undermined the economic and political power of older industrial cities; and a highly effective political mobilization by which corporate America produced its own cadre of ideologically oriented scholars and policymakers. The erosion of the family wage proved critically important, as well. The male-breadwinner family ideal continued to shape liberal social welfare campaigns during the 1970s, even as feminists proposed a different model of economic justice. With the Reagan administration's assault on all welfare subventions, the liberal antipoverty coalition found itself in an uncomfortable position, defending a program (AFDC) that it had spent the last fifteen years criticizing.

In the process, some liberals began to redefine the very purpose of AFDC to better acknowledge the erosion of the family wage.

A Fragmented Response

No single group will be more adversely affected by the budget cuts than the AFDC family. While organizing efforts have begun around Reagan's budget cut plans, there has not been a coordinated attempt to attack the proposed cuts AS A WHOLE. Most of these organizing efforts have focused on the traditionally "safe" victims, i.e., the "deserving poor" (the elderly) or on specific cuts in "safe" programs, like Social Security, Legal Services, or Food Stamps. This ignores the largest population on fixed incomes—the AFDC population, two-thirds of whom are children under the age of ten. (Theresa Funiciello, Downtown Welfare Advocacy Center, 1982)[82]

On 19 September 1981, more than a quarter of a million protesters marched up Constitution Avenue in Washington, D.C., following a route familiar to members of the antipoverty coalition, who had made the same trek in the 1960s in support of civil rights legislation. Now, in 1981, the national leadership of the AFL-CIO had called its allies together for "Solidarity Day," the "first time in history" that the labor federation had sponsored a mass demonstration of any kind.[83] More than two hundred organizations answered the call, launching what the *Washington Post* estimated was "the biggest political protest in Washington during the past twenty years."[84] At the front of the marchers, civil rights leaders Bayard Rustin, Coretta Scott King, and the heads of the NUL and the NAACP walked alongside the AFL-CIO's Lane Kirkland and NOW president Eleanor Smeal. Behind them marched what the *New York Times* called a "potpourri of protesters": union members, women, African Americans, Hispanics, the elderly and disabled. With black activists, organized labor, and feminists at its core, the coalition's demands for economic justice might have sparked a new and more egalitarian guaranteed income campaign based not on an old family wage model but rooted instead in an expansive vision of citizenship—a "right to live" guaranteed by a federal government determined to ensure the "welfare" of all.[85]

That no such movement emerged is due in part to the forces arrayed against it. Opponents of federal regulation and social spending had gained increasing influence, and inflation, "bracket creep," and regressive taxation sparked a popular tax revolt that lent populist energy to the anti-spending

Figure 12. A diverse crowd of labor unionists, civil rights and feminist activists, and liberal advocates march to protest Reagan's economic policies in September 1981. Courtesy George Meany Memorial Archives (YN1542–85–34A).

crusade.[86] Reagan owed his election to the nation's economic affliction and
Jimmy Carter's failure to solve it, and the scope of the 1980 Republican victory which gave the GOP the presidency, control of the Senate, and thirty-
three additional seats in the House lent credibility to the administration's
claimed "mandate" for a new approach. And after a deep recession in 1982,
the deregulation and tax and domestic spending cuts that made up the administration's "supply-side revolution" seemed to do the trick, slaying the
inflation beast and initiating economic growth. Of course the same policies
triggered a mounting deficit and growing economic inequality, but their
benefits reached broadly into the professional suburban middle class, a
growing population with high voter turnout and disproportionate influence. Liberals, both contemporary critics and historians argue, responded
with timidity and uncertainty. The welfare state they had built depended
upon a strong economy that was able to distribute the nation's ever-
growing prosperity. Economic crisis in the 1970s shook that foundation,
and Reagan's success put liberals on the defensive. Democratic lawmakers
were cowed by the 1980 election, and Congressional Democrats mounted
only "feeble opposition" to OBRA.[87] The editors of the *New York Times*
wondered "Where are the Democrats?" while leaders of the NUL complained that "there was no strong public outcry" against OBRA and "no
real coalition developed to speak for the poor."[88]

Such lamentations were premature, as the crowds at Solidarity Day
suggest. Even before that massive demonstration, the AFL-CIO, the NUL,
the NAACP, the LWV, the NWPC, the UAW, the U.S. Conference of Mayors, and the U.S. Catholic Conference organized a Budget Coalition, which
spoke for 157 organizations opposed to the administration's tax and spending cuts.[89] Other coalitions like the Jobs with Peace Campaign and the Food
Research and Action Center's (FRAC) Fair Budget Action Campaign organized to defend federal social spending, while citizens of ten cities passed
Jobs with Peace referenda demanding a "nationwide effort to transfer
money from wasteful military programs to pressing domestic needs."[90]
Meanwhile, organizations like the Children's Defense Fund (CDF) and the
NUL published scathing critiques of OBRA, and NUL's Vernon Jordan repeatedly denounced the turn to a "meaner America, an America unwilling
to build a better society for all."[91] Locally, welfare rights groups like Philadelphia Citizens in Action, Mississippi's Coalition for Mothers and Babies,
and the Downtown Welfare Advocacy Center (DWAC) continued to find
occasional allies in local unions and civil rights, women's, and civic organizations as they protested AFDC cuts and fought for expanded benefits and

services for the poor.[92] By 1982, liberal advocacy was making a difference. Congressional Democrats had found their voices and offered more robust opposition to Reagan's second round of spending cuts, while the administration pondered how to respond to the "fairness issue"—the increasing perception among Americans that the president cared little about the poor and elderly.[93]

What was missing on the political left was a coherent and effective justification for federal income support for the poor. While members of the antipoverty coalition could agree to *oppose* massive cuts in welfare and social services, they did not seem to share a compelling vision of social citizenship, at least when it came to poor single mothers and their children. As Frances Fox Piven and Richard Cloward saw it, the major problem was "absence of an intellectual framework" that would give liberal defense of the welfare state "coherence and legitimacy." The antipoverty coalition had become fragmented and "for the most part narrowly defensive, lacking a positive agenda beyond the preservation of the status quo."[94]

Solidarity Day exemplifies one kind of liberal response, which employed populist language to denounce the administration as an enemy of "the people." Populism had long ago belonged to the left, and Reagan offered an ideal target for liberals who sought to re-appropriate it. But because anti-Reagan liberal populism sought the widest possible constituency, it precluded sustained attention to welfare cuts. Strategist Steve Max, for example, insisted that the key to forging "a new populism" lay in addressing "what [Reagan is doing] to his own base in the white middle class," not simply to the poor working classes that often had to rely on welfare aid.[95] Many liberals and leftists accused Reagan of waging a "war on the poor" but generally avoided mentioning AFDC or other "welfare" programs, which had absorbed the most significant cuts.[96] The liberal *New Republic* left welfare out of its call for "basic redistribution—food, health care, education, and so on," and Philip Green, a columnist for the left-leaning *Nation*, continued to offer full employment as the one and only sure answer to poverty.[97] Solidarity Day speakers emphasized Reagan's "abandonment of social responsibility" for a broad range of Americans but said little about welfare or poor single mothers in particular. In the AFL-CIO's transcripts of the event, only Sam Church of the United Mine Workers mentioned AFDC, while Vernon Jordan was alone in mentioning "welfare" more generally. Occasional appeals to America's "social responsibility to the old, to the sick, to the poor, and to all who are disadvantaged"—a call issued by American Federation of State, County, and Municipal Employees (AFS-

CME) president Jerry Wurf—were largely drowned out by proclamations in defense of "the working men and women of this country" and attacks on cuts in education grants, Social Security, Unemployment Insurance, and other programs with greater popular support than AFDC.[98]

Solidarity Day also reveals how this populist language could implicitly undermine the very "social responsibility" that its organizers claimed to defend. Many on the left saw Reagan's policies as an attack on American workers; given organized labor's predominant role in organizing Solidarity Day, it should come as little surprise that virtually without exception, speakers pronounced themselves representatives and defenders of Americans who "work for our living." Yet when Jesse Jackson of Operation PUSH declared, "I am somebody. I want to work," and when Tony Bonilla of United Latin American Citizens insisted, "We do not want handouts, we want jobs and job training for our unemployed," they denied the value of poor women's unpaid caregiving labor and helped to sharpen the artificial distinction between deserving American workers and undeserving welfare recipients.[99] The LWV did the same when it warned that cuts in child care and other services would push "more women into a permanent underclass of poverty and public assistance."[100] Some opponents of Reagan's spending cuts drew even more explicit distinctions by appropriating the language of antiwelfare conservatives. Walter Fauntroy of the Congressional Black Caucus (CBC) denounced cuts in job training and child care for preventing AFDC mothers from becoming "productive citizens on the tax rolls of the country rather than tax eaters on the welfare program."[101]

Some welfare rights activists articulated a different kind of populism, one that sought to break down what they saw as insidious and inaccurate distinctions between "workers" and "welfare recipients." At the forefront of this effort was New York's Downtown Welfare Advocacy Center (DWAC), which had blossomed from a small scale welfare rights effort providing legal help and advocacy in New York City's poor neighborhoods to an organization of six thousand members and eleven full-time staff members by 1980. With church and foundation funding, DWAC became a major player in New York's welfare politics, garnering enough allies in 1980 to win a 15 percent increase in state AFDC benefits.[102] In 1978, DWAC created the Redistribute America Movement (RAM), an effort to spread its message beyond AFDC recipients to other low-income New Yorkers.[103] But like NWRO leaders a decade before, the groups worried that the interests of poor single mothers might disappear in a broader movement. In 1982, when DWAC cosponsored a spring protest against Reagan's budget cuts (with the

UAW local, the Women's International League for Peace and Freedom, and several others), Theresa Funiciello worried about how to "broaden participation without diminishing focus on the needs of poor people" and AFDC recipients in particular. "No single group of people will be more adversely affected by the budget cuts than the AFDC family," Funiciello warned, but "most of the organizing efforts" thus far had "focused on the traditionally 'safe' victims: i.e., the 'deserving poor' (the elderly) or on specific cuts in 'safe' programs, like Social Security, Legal Services, or Food Stamps."[104]

In response, DWAC and RAM fashioned a clever and welfare-friendly populism that contrasted miserly income support programs with vast government subsidies to the well-off. In 1981, as Democrats in Congress capitulated to the administration's tax and spending cuts, RAM picketed the site of a new Hyatt Hotel in downtown Manhattan, denouncing the $50 million tax abatement the city offered developer Donald Trump. Chanting "Trump stole our taxes, we repeat/So he's the real welfare cheat!" demonstrators aimed to "inform *all* New Yorkers that the biggest welfare recipients aren't the women and kids with low incomes and heatless apartments." Instead, "far more welfare goes to corporations and the wealthy in the form of tax abatements and other tax breaks." RAM held similar demonstrations later that year at Saratoga Springs, where Richard Cloward addressed a crowd protesting "welfare for the rich" in the form of tax deductions to owners of race horses, and on a bus tour that took journalists, labor leaders, politicians, and religious leaders past "outrageous instances of corporate subsidy" in Manhattan and then through poor neighborhoods in the Lower East Side and Brooklyn. In each instance, organizers created symbolic displays, from a Santa Claus throwing jelly beans to the crowd (using Reagan's favorite candy to symbolize "trickle-down economics"), to Ron and Nancy Reagan stand-ins presenting corporate leaders with a giant "welfare check," to a baby doll frozen in ice (to represent the administration's cuts in programs for poor children). And in each instance, protesters repeated chants that proclaimed "Reaganomics," "corporate subsidies," "tax incentives," and "Aid to Dependent Corporations" as the nation's *real* welfare problem.[105]

However, RAM's version of populism did not in itself present a positive and convincing vision for AFDC; that would be left to the NUL, which characterized AFDC mothers as wage earners—both actual and aspiring—whose very efforts at self-support would be undermined by OBRA. In early 1982, the NUL brought over three hundred witnesses to sixteen hearings across the country to discuss the impact of AFDC cuts on poor women and

BUDGET CUTS:
STOP THE REAL WELFARE CHEATS.....
stop welfare for the rich!

← IN 1980 THE VANDERBILTS, WHITNEYS, PHIPPSES, HUNTS, duPONTS, MELONS, AND A FEW OTHERS RECEIVED OVER $18 MILLION IN "WELFARE" BENEFITS FOR THEIR HORSE TAX SHELTERS IN SARATOGA SPRINGS ALONE. EVERY TAX DOLLAR THE RICH DIDN'T PAY, WE THE TAX PAYERS HAD TO PAY FOR THEM.

IN 1980 FAMILIES IN NEED RECEIVED $2.08 PER PERSON PER DAY, FOOD STAMPS & SLUM RENT ALLOTMENTS & MEDICAID. 87% OF THESE FAMILIES ARE CHILDREN & THEIR MOTHERS. →

The first foals by 1978 triple crown winner, Affirmed, were born this spring. One, a colt, shadows its grazing mother.

IF YOU ARE CONCERNED ABOUT WELFARE, FOOD STAMPS, SOCIAL SECURITY, CHILD NUTRITION, CETA, FORCED WORK PROGRAMS, UNEMPLOYMENT, HOUSING, COMMUNITY DEVELOPMENT, PUBLIC TRANSPORTATION, DISABILITY, BLOCK GRANTS.....YOU WILL BE AFFECTED BY REAGAN'S BUDGET CUTS....

come to a community meeting wed. JULY 29, 1981
cafe lena's 7pm and FIND OUT
WHAT YOU CAN DO

Redistribute America Movement

RAM IS A STATEWIDE POOR PEOPLE'S ORGANIZATION SPONSORED BY THE DOWNTOWN WELFARE ADVOCATE CENTER. FOR MORE INFORMATION CALL 587-0393 or 587-3758 10:00 am - 12:00 noon.

Figure 13. A populist critique of Reaganomics from New York's Downtown Welfare Advocacy Center and its affiliate, Redistribute America Movement. DWAC and RAM contrasted government subsidies to the wealthy with meager income support for the poor and sought to mobilize a broad cross-section of Americans to oppose Reagan's budget proposals. Courtesy Social Welfare History Archives, University of Minnesota.

their children. Other antipoverty organizations signed on to help, including social welfare groups like NASW, the American Public Welfare Association (APWA), the CDF, and the Child Welfare League; religious groups like the National Council of Churches of Christ (NCC) and the National Conference of Catholic Churches; and AFSCME and the AFL-CIO.[106] The official report on the hearings, "'Don't Just Stand There and Kill Us' (A People's Report on AFDC)," suggests how much had changed since the antipoverty coalition defended full-time mothering for AFDC mothers in the late 1960s. The report's authors echoed those earlier arguments when they insisted that AFDC "does not support employable adults" because only 1 percent of recipients were adult men, but the bulk of the report emphasized the impact of Reagan's AFDC cuts on "working poor" recipients. "Time after time," it announced, "witnesses told of how they were struggling to raise families and get off welfare by working at low paying jobs." But with OBRA's changes—which sharply limited recipients' ability to earn wages and remain on the welfare rolls—"they had lost their AFDC grants, pushing them further back into poverty and killing their dreams."[107]

The nature of OBRA's AFDC cuts, then, pushed liberal advocates into broadening older definitions of the "working poor," which in the FAP and full employment campaigns had typically described two-parent families with male breadwinners. As women flooded into the labor market and feminists identified employment as the key to women's economic security, antipoverty liberals found that they could more easily defend aid to the working poor like the Earned Income Tax Credit (EITC) than AFDC. Some liberal strategists suggested abandoning AFDC altogether. "The past consensus that a woman without a husband should remain at home to care for her children" had eroded, intoned Sheldon Danziger of the Institute for Research on Poverty, and liberal advocates and lawmakers should focus their efforts on defending public employment, the EITC, and other programs for the working poor.[108] But others tried to write AFDC into this category. Since most of OBRA's AFDC changes targeted recipients with earnings, liberals could label the cuts an "attack on the working poor," a group that AFSCME now defined as "female heads of household who work full-time and who receive a reduced, supplemental AFDC payment."[109] OBRA's impact on these most "deserving" AFDC recipients became the central theme among liberals who bothered to defend AFDC in the early 1980s. From the CBC to the AFL-CIO and AFSCME, from the LWV to the U.S. Commission on Civil Rights, liberal witnesses before Congressional committees denounced the administration for punishing "countless numbers of working poor mothers who under the most adverse conditions are trying to work their way off of the welfare rolls."[110]

Liberal and left-leaning journals as well as more mainstream publications echoed this theme. *Newsweek* and the *New York Times* featured stories about employed welfare mothers destined to lose AFDC benefits due to OBRA's reforms, women like Mrs. Jessie Mae Hurst of Harlem, a single mother of two sons who worked full-time as a Wall Street typist and relied on supplemental AFDC payments and food stamps to get by. "They're penalizing the very people who want to do for themselves," Hurst complained, "who don't want to depend on the government to do it for them."[111] While conservatives were constructing a picture of a welfare "underclass," unwilling and unable to work for a living, some liberals were insisting that "most welfare recipients are not members of a permanent class of idle misfits and cheats" but were instead "adults who must depend on welfare to supplement seasonal low-wage jobs."[112]

Liberals thus defended AFDC by redefining its purpose. Rather than a program that enabled poor single mothers to devote their time to childrearing, as Progressive reformers viewed it, or a miserly, ill-conceived destroyer of families, as the antipoverty coalition had argued in the 1960s, AFDC became an income supplement program—a crucial safety net for women struggling to survive and attain economic self-sufficiency in an insecure low-wage labor market. Of course, that is how AFDC had functioned for many, perhaps most, recipients virtually from its origins. But it took OBRA's outright attack on the program's work incentives to bring this perspective to the center of liberal welfare ideology.

A study of OBRA's potential effect on poor families in ten states, conducted by the Center for the Study of Social Policy and the Congressional Budget Office, attacked OBRA in precisely these terms. Reagan's reforms violated "the basic notion that those who work should be better off than those who do not," the study concluded.[113] The reforms would therefore fail not only to reduce poverty but also to limit welfare rolls. After all, if a woman found that struggling in a low-wage job would leave her family just as poor as AFDC, and without Medicaid to boot, she might just not bother. OBRA's work disincentives, one Reagan critic concluded, would thereby "deny upward mobility to millions on welfare and . . . force many of the working poor into welfare dependency."[114] The Reagan administration challenged the report's "philosophical base," arguing that AFDC should be a last resort for families unable to survive without it, not an "income supplement program" as liberals had begun to argue.[115] But the potential work disincentives even worried some conservatives. While the administration denounced the study as "biased," its author, Tom Joe, had a "reputation among social scientists as being one of the most reliable sources of nonpartisan information on welfare matters," making it difficult for OBRA's authors to deny the findings.[116] An economist at the American Enterprise Institute labeled OBRA's work incentive cuts "philosophically perverse," while *Business Week* found that business leaders across the nation were "disturbed by the work disincentive created for women" under OBRA. Even the NAM and the Business Roundtable, no fans of welfare, criticized the administration's reduction of AFDC's work incentives.[117]

Liberal advocacy groups, including women's organizations, agreed. Marian Wright Edelman of the CDF was one of very few liberals who continued to argue that the "choice to stay home to care for young children" remained "a legitimate one," yet even she concluded that the solution to the poverty of single mothers "lies in increased training and increasing job provisions."[118] The dominant feminist voices in the discussion went further. Speaking for twenty-three women's organizations, Nancy Duff Campbell of the Center for Law and Social Policy's Women's Rights Project did not offer even a limited defense of poor women's mothering. Instead, she joined other liberals in arguing that OBRA's cuts hurt recipient efforts toward "becom[ing] self-sufficient."[119] Wider Opportunities for Women (WOW) worried that AFDC cuts would "foreclose . . . avenues of escape from poverty and will force many of the 'working poor' back into total dependency."[120] WOW's two organizational responses to Reagan's budget cuts—the Women's Campaign for Jobs and Economic Justice and the Working for Women Workers Budget Campaign—focused exclusively on spending cuts affecting wage-earning women.[121] And while opposing workfare, which "would require work with no pay, or benefits," a coalition of more than three dozen women's and public interest groups was "*most* concerned about the reduction of funds for social service programs" like child care and job training, services that would help women "eventually achieve economic self-sufficiency."[122]

Middle-class feminists like the Business and Professional Women's Foundation, which demanded "public policies that start with the assumption that women need and want to be able to support themselves and their families," and NYU law professor Sylvia Law, who recommended a sex discrimination suit against federal jobs programs and a renewed child care campaign, made the same argument.[123] So, too, did welfare mothers. Testifying before Congress, Boston AFDC mother and welfare rights activist

Figure 14. Hundreds of women march on New York City Hall to protest the city's decision to eliminate funding for an employment program run by the National Congress of Neighborhood Women in 1980. The child's sign suggests the profound shift in thinking about poverty and gender since the 1960s. Courtesy Sophia Smith Collection, Smith College, and Janie Eisenberg.

Mary Ann Mortorana described the plight of Cheryl Lanford, a fellow recipient forced to quit her job because of cuts in Title XX child care funding. "I do not want to be on welfare," Lanford insisted, "but the Reagan Administration's policy has forced me into it, in spite of all the trouble I went through to remain independent." Sandy Helling of New York City's Welfare Grant Coalition concurred. "Besides increased suffering," she told a Congressional committee, "we have witnessed the hopes of numerous welfare recipients to get off public assistance shattered by the AFDC and CETA cuts that eliminated employment possibilities for the poor."[124] The Reagan administration "is really telling women to quit their jobs," concluded Lillie Benjamin of RAM. OBRA's welfare reforms "eliminate . . . the few opportunities for women to support their families and get off welfare."[125]

Despite a shared commitment to employment as preferable to welfare, recipient activists and feminist advocates shared little ground with conservative ideologues who denied federal responsibility for the welfare of poor women and their children. "Mr. President," announced Joyce Miller, "we at the Coalition of Labor Union Women work for our living," but "we don't need fewer social programs." Instead, "we need programs that will nurture our children while we are at work and elder care that will help our sick and aged parents," along with stringent equal pay enforcement and other government-sponsored reforms to ensure working women a chance for economic self-sufficiency.[126] Feminists organized against the administration's lax enforcement of antidiscrimination regulations and affirmative action as well as the spending cuts that hit women hardest. An impressively broad collection of women's organizations—religious, feminist, professional, working-class, and labor—endorsed a scathing critique of Reagan's budget policies prepared by the Coalition on Women and the Budget. Spearheaded by Nancy Duff Campbell, Cindy Marano of WOW, and Pat Reuss of Women's Equity Action League (WEAL), among others, the 1983 report, titled *Inequality of Sacrifice*, spelled out the importance of state support for women's well-being.[127] Feminist opposition to AFDC cuts was part of a broader resistance to the erosion of an array of government programs aimed at enabling women to achieve economic independence through wage labor.

Though many liberals and feminists opposed AFDC cuts, few had anything positive to say about the program. When the NAACP, the NUL, the Center for Community Change, the AAUW, the LWV, the Center for Social Welfare Policy and Law (CSWP&L), and a range of other advocates met in a January 1984 National Consultation on Economic Justice for Women

Who Are Poor, their major conclusion about AFDC was that it "has been extremely damaging to women and children," built on "false assumptions about women, children and society," and "built on a patriarchal system."[128] Many recipient activists also turned against the system. The National Congress of Neighborhood Women blasted the very premises of welfare. The "principal lesson" the organization gleaned from New York's five public hearings on the "Feminization of Poverty" in 1984 was "the frustration and disillusionment of poor female recipients of 'help' from state-funded programs and their demand for an approach to their problems that helps them help themselves." That fall, the group brought together sixty-nine poor women and professionals in a Dialogue on Community Development and Female Poverty in which "the grassroots women took a strong stand for self-sufficiency and self-help approaches to development" and "rejected dependency-inducing, fragmented and inadequate service programs." AFDC and other welfare and social service programs, poor women complained, "demean the recipients and divide neighborhoods" because "those who work for a living feel devalued [because they] don't get a 'free ride'," while "those getting the 'free ride' want to become self-sufficient and can't."[129]

"Self-sufficiency" became a new byword for many welfare recipient activists. The 1960s antipoverty coalition had criticized AFDC for providing too much self-sufficiency to poor mothers, enabling them to raise children outside of stable, heterosexual marriages, but by the 1980s feminist academics and some welfare recipient activists had begun to argue that the system's biggest flaw lay in making women *dependent*. Antiwelfare conservatives had long complained about recipients' supposed psychological dependency on cash aid, but feminist advocates and welfare recipient activists complained instead about their practical dependence on a system that failed to encourage and reward women's self-support efforts. "We need to look at the way the welfare system interfered with women's attempts toward self-sufficiency," the National Congress of Neighborhood Women insisted, by denying benefits to women with earned income and by failing to provide constructive job training, public service employment, and adequate and affordable child care options.[130] Christians Overcoming Underclass Repression Together (COURT), a coalition of low-income women in Chicago, issued a similar complaint, though it did not see federal or state policy changes as the solution. COURT pledged to work to increase welfare grants but saw its "major goal" as becoming "more supportive of each other as we job hunt, by sharing such things as child care and job counseling."[131]

As COURT's statement suggests, resentment of the welfare bureaucracy and frustration with the absurdities of AFDC regulations pushed some welfare activists to emphasize community self-help solutions to poverty. The National Congress of Neighborhood Women looked to the work of Robert Woodson, one of a rising cohort of African American conservative theorists. In 1981, Woodson founded the National Center for Neighborhood Enterprise, which drew funding from conservative foundations committed to replacing government welfare protections with "self-help, market-oriented strategies" for "economic empowerment." Ronnie Feit cited Woodson's advocacy of local community development as an alternative to "ineffective maintenance programs that produce dependency" among the poor. "Like neighborhood women in New York State," Feit noted, Woodson "is fed up with old approaches," and his self-help emphasis has "some of our strongest women leaders, long-time Democrats . . . wondering whether their only hope lies in the Republican Party, which is at least talking about helping people help themselves."[132]

This was a far cry from the NWRO's demands for "Jobs or Income Now." In fact, the larger vision of a guaranteed income, one that included the right of poor single mothers to remain outside the paid labor market, had largely disappeared by 1980. Liberals had never been wholehearted supporters, and the goal no longer seemed politically possible or socially desirable. In meetings with liberal advocates, Funiciello recalled "argu[ing ad] infinitum that we already had jobs, we simply weren't paid for them." But "we might as well have been speaking in tongues."[133] Funiciello was among a handful of feminists, welfare recipient activists, and religious officials who continued to assert the basic premise of the 1960s welfare rights movement—that the federal government was responsible for ensuring all Americans a basic "right to live," irrespective of labor force participation. During congressional hearings on Reagan's budget cuts, religious leaders almost alone dared utter what had a decade before been a widespread liberal demand, a guaranteed income.[134] The Association of Community Organizations for Reform Now (ACORN), which grew out of the NWRO and the Movement for Economic Justice (MEJ), also called for both a guaranteed job at a living wage and a guaranteed income in its 1980 People's Platform, while Women for Economic Justice, a coalition of community development activists, called for the federal government to "guarantee to individuals access to an adequate standard of living" in the form of public service employment, a guaranteed annual income, and various social service programs in its 1983 Feminist Economic Agenda.[135] But no longer did a broad liberal coalition pursue a guaranteed income.

Further, liberals' single-minded emphasis on the plight of *working* AFDC recipients under OBRA left them with little positive defense of AFDC's basic benefits, which faced additional cuts in 1982, when the administration proposed to reduce benefits for as many as 900,000 more AFDC families.[136] In Congressional hearings, some liberal witnesses, including the NUL, the American Jewish Committee (AJC), the Full Employment Action Council (FEAC), Democratic Representative Patricia Schroeder, and WEAL, ignored the proposed AFDC reforms altogether and focused solely on Reagan's proposals to restrict Unemployment Insurance. Some Democrats, like North Carolina Governor James B. Hunt, Jr., who represented the National Governors Association, opposed "further cuts" in income security programs but also offered "support" for the "need to tighten rules." Bert Seidman, speaking for the AFL-CIO, stuck to the previous year's argument, warning that AFDC cuts would "decrease even more drastically the financial incentive that once existed for families to work their way off of welfare," even though the proposed cuts had little to do with work incentives.[137]

The best that most liberals could do in 1982 was to denounce AFDC cuts as a "war on children," as one Congressional Democrat put it.[138] The CDF brought a number of religious, social welfare, and women's organizations together to conduct "Child Watch," an effort to "monitor what is happening to children in many communities" as a result of Reagan's social spending cuts, and House Democrats organized hearings to examine the "impact of the Administration's budget cuts on children."[139] In hearings in St. Louis, that city's Junior League and National Council of Jewish Women (NCJW), longtime advocates for welfare mothers, confined their comments to child care cuts and made no mention of AFDC. Other liberals, like Adele Blong of the Center on Social Welfare Policy and Law, who represented four poverty/welfare rights groups, and Kenyon Burke of the NCC, reminded lawmakers that "it is primarily children that are hurt by cuts in AFDC."[140] The image of "innocent children [looking] towards us with tear stained eyes, and wet diapers, pleading for help" may have helped to convince some Democratic lawmakers to oppose further cuts in AFDC, but it did little to construct a positive defense of the program or to challenge conservative arguments that welfare proved harmful to poor children in the long run.[141]

A "New Consensus" on Welfare

[There is] a surprising degree of consensus [about welfare] among ideological opposites . . . Both sides agree that more efforts must be directed at the small but significant minority of the poor who stay on welfare rolls for long periods of time. There's enthusiasm in both camps for greater work requirements for welfare recipients and a crackdown on absent fathers of families on welfare. (Julie Kosterlitz, 1986)[142]

In 1987, twenty-two years after articulating the 1960s antipoverty coalition consensus on racial disadvantage, poverty, and public policy, Pat Moynihan, now a senator from New York and chair of the Senate Finance Committee's Subcommittee on Social Security and Family Policy, proposed a new approach to these contentious issues. AFDC should be abolished, Moynihan argued, and replaced with two new programs. One, a national child support program, would ensure that absent fathers provide for their children, a virtual work requirement for welfare fathers. The other, a combination of job training and social services, would enable poor single mothers to support their children through paid employment.[143] In the 1960s, Moynihan proposed federal job creation and expanded income support as a way to fight poverty and racial disadvantage by fostering male breadwinning among the poor. Twenty years later, his vision of federal responsibility had narrowed considerably: he offered poor fathers only coercion and poor mothers the same work programs that had done little to help poor single mothers climb out of poverty for the past two decades. By the 1980s, as political scientist Wendy Sarvasy noted, Moynihan "assumes the traditional model of the male breadwinner family cannot be saved."[144]

Moynihan's proposal was the product of what many observers dubbed a "new consensus" on welfare that emerged in the second half of the 1980s, a consensus that can be traced in the official analyses and policy recommendations of conservative think tanks like the American Enterprise Institute, public welfare organizations like the APWA, and moderate-to-liberal groups like the Ford Foundation, as well as in the books and testimony of individual scholars and advocates between 1985 and 1989.[145] In his 1987 report *The New Consensus on Family and Welfare*, conservative author Michael Novak celebrated what he saw as an end to the intense ideological battles that had characterized welfare politics for the past fifteen years. Americans from a "broad spectrum of philosophies" had finally begun to agree on the problem, causes, and solution to America's ever-present welfare crisis.[146] Liberals, like two attorneys for the Center for Law and Social Policy who recognized a "general agreement" on a new direction for welfare policy, agreed. Brookings Institution fellow Robert Reischauer was not alone, then, in concluding that "liberals and conservatives are closer together than they have been in several decades."[147]

But the "new consensus" looked an awful lot like the old antiwelfare conservatism. Antiwelfare conservatives, state and local welfare administrators, and Southern Democrats and business lobbyists in the 1960s had generally viewed poor, especially nonwhite, women as wage laborers first and foremost; their maternal role was irrelevant if they were married, deplorable if not. This class- and race-specific family wage ideal makes sense of seemingly contradictory conservative principles in the way it logically combined a defense of the "traditional," male-breadwinner family for middle-income white families with support for stringent work requirements for poor single mothers. Thus the Reverend Jerry Falwell could insist that children had a right "to live in an economic system that makes it possible for husbands to support their wives as full-time mothers in the home and that enables families to survive on one income instead of two" but still oppose federal income supplements for poor families, and the Reagan administration could insist that welfare mothers with young children find paid employment while asserting that "home care for youngsters is vastly preferable to institutional arrangements."[148]

What was new about the "new consensus" was liberal support for contracting public assistance and pushing mothers into the low-wage labor market.[149] Because liberals had given up on their commitment to extend the male-breadwinner family to poor African Americans, they also discarded their defense of poor women's caregiving role. The Ford Foundation Project on Social Welfare and the American Future, which included labor and civil rights leaders, academics, and businessmen, called AFDC "an anachronism" given the "revolution that has occurred in female labor-force participation since AFDC was enacted a half century ago." The group advised that the welfare system be "fundamentally overhauled to become a work readiness and support program, rather than a limitless income-maintenance program."[150] The liberal academics and policymakers on New York governor Mario Cuomo's Task Force on Poverty and Welfare agreed. "In an age where most mothers work at least part of the time, it no longer seems appropriate to base public assistance on the expectation that poor mothers should not work at all." Instead, "many Americans from all sides of the political spectrum want to see welfare transformed into a short-term support program that helps those who can to achieve self-sufficiency through work."[151] AFDC, insisted Moynihan, "will not be supported" in a world where mothers are poor because they are unsupported by their divorced husbands or because they are unwed. After all, "a program that was designed to pay mothers to stay at home with their children cannot succeed when we now observe most mothers going out to work."[152] As Wendy Sarvasy noted, "both sides" in the current welfare debate "presume that it is no longer justifiable to support a program that allows [AFDC] recipients the option of full-time motherhood."[153]

Sarvasy was one of a mere handful of feminists and recipient activists who rejected the new focus on wage labor as the only alternative for poor single mothers. In a "feminist recasting" of the welfare debate, she called for a "revaluing of nurturing and caretaking work," reminiscent of the "feminist potential of the mothers' pension concept." She hoped to redefine AFDC as "caretakers' pensions," which would "provide social support, both financial and moral, for performing the important roles of taking care of children, sick parents, or perhaps a friend with AIDS." In this way, the welfare system could help the nation "reformulate our entire notion of citizenship."[154] Margaret Prescod of Black Women for Wages for Housework (BWWH) made the same argument before Congress.[155] But a majority of antipoverty feminists rejected this position as both highly impractical and ideologically problematic. "To argue that the state should support women to stay home (rather than to combine work and parenting) concedes ground to the dominant conservative gender politics," warned feminist sociologist Johanna Brenner. Besides, "poor and working women themselves would prefer to combine work and parenting."[156] Brenner saw the Family Support Act of 1988, which increased education and job training for AFDC mothers, as a victory for the "women's policy network" that had "made women's impoverishment a political issue and shaped proposed solutions."[157]

Liberal "new consensus" proponents took comfort in feminist support for work-focused welfare reform and pointed to feminist and recipient activism, which had begun in the 1970s to develop programs to help poor single mothers "move from economic dependency [on AFDC] to skilled and productive self-sufficiency."[158] Despite an increasingly inhospitable political and economic environment, feminist organizations in the 1980s continued to offer programs to train women for the kind of unionized blue-collar jobs that paid significantly more than pink-collar service or second-tier manufacturing jobs. WOW sponsored a five-year demonstration project to provide comprehensive training and support services to poor minority single mothers in Washington, D.C., during the 1980s and brought together twenty-five partners "representing women's organizations, civil rights groups, social welfare agencies, and unions" into a National Coalition on Women, Work, and Welfare Reform (not to be confused with the National Council on Women, Work, and Welfare, formed in 1976) to demand a national program. In its 1987 publication "Changing Welfare: An Investment in Women and Children in Poverty," the coalition proposed broader income maintenance, but its major emphasis was on services—from education and training to child care, health care, and transportation that would support women's employment.[159] Other liberals followed suit, promoting "self-sufficiency" for welfare mothers. The Rockefeller Foundation, whose president considered the growth of households headed by minority women "the most conspicuous and urgent single poverty problem in the country," initiated a $1.7 million program to train minority women for jobs.[160] The "individual citizens" whom APWA urged to "assume the responsibility of achieving independence on behalf of themselves and their families" now included mothers as well as fathers.[161] This was a significant change in emphasis since the 1960s when job training had been focused primarily on men, the failed or struggling *fathers* of AFDC children.

At the same time, feminists and some liberals continued to oppose workfare and to defend a decent minimum standard of public assistance. AFDC and other income support measures should be "streamlined and strengthened" and refocused on "encourag[ing] . . . women to seek better employment," but "in no way" should such programs "be reduced or eliminated," instructed WEAL.[162] Many liberal advocacy groups continued to lobby for a national minimum AFDC standard, as an effort to fight poverty rather than a step toward a guaranteed income. More often, liberals demanded government efforts to ensure that "no one who works full time should be poor."[163] Job training and a higher minimum wage, child care, an expanded EITC, and broadened health insurance coverage, they argued, would ensure that poor men *and* women could support children. Single mothers, insisted Michael Harrington in his 1984 book *The New American Poverty*, do not need "sermons on the glories of work" but "programs making it possible . . . to go out into the labor market . . . and guarantees that when they *do* work it will raise . . . their income."[164] After all, "the federal government," WOW's Avril Madison reminded a Congressional committee in 1984, "is still the primary protector and promoter of women's economic self-sufficiency in the marketplace."[165]

Even as the economy provided fewer stable, living wage jobs for those without a college education, however, liberal calls for helping the working poor grew increasingly timid. The optimism of the 1960s seemed distant, as did the expansive vision of government economic planning for full employment. "Clearly the scope for new government spending is limited," members of the Ford Foundation's Project on Social Welfare averred, so current revenue must be "spent more wisely" in order to expand EITC, Medicaid, and child welfare programs.[166] Governor Cuomo's Task Force proposed a high-employment economy, quality educational system, public sector work program, affordable child care, and expanded access to health care, all paid for by "balanc[ing] new initiatives with the fiscal constraints imposed by the federal budget deficit."[167]

Fiscal timidity aside, liberal new consensus proponents undercut their own demand for bold federal programs by focusing on dependency rather than poverty. The Office of the Assistant Secretary for Planning and Evaluation in the Department of Health and Human Services (HHS, which replaced HEW when Congress established a separate Department of Education) supported a project on dependency in the early 1980s, and various task forces and reports on welfare that emerged mid-decade highlighted the issue of "dependence."[168] The liberals who made up the American Horizons Foundation's Project on the Welfare of Families, a group co-chaired by former HEW secretary Arthur Flemming, hoped to "break the complex web of dependency" and turn AFDC mothers "from passive recipients of aid to active contributors to our economic output."[169] The Ford Foundation's Project on Social Welfare, which included civil rights leaders Eleanor Holmes Norton and Vernon Jordan, dismissed the very idea of "guarantee-[ing] everyone a minimum, poverty-line income." Such a system would fail to solve "the problem of persistent poverty and long-term welfare dependency." Into "underclass" neighborhoods, the Project's report insisted, "today's welfare system injects a message of passive maintenance and dependency," a message that improved benefits would only reinforce. Instead, "the welfare system should be overhauled to emphasize work instead of long-term dependency," to include new education and training efforts, and to provide only "time-limited" income support (followed, if necessary, by a public-sector job).[170] Not surprisingly, family structure played a key role in this ascendant discourse of dependency. According to liberal poverty "experts," women *chose* poverty and dependency by bearing children out of wedlock and heading families without male support—the same argument antiwelfare conservatives had been making since the 1960s. As David Ellwood saw it, single mothers needed "both help and pressure" to achieve "real economic independence through their own effort."[171] Ellwood and his colleague Mary Jo Bane, both well-respected liberal policy experts centered at Harvard University's John F. Kennedy School of Government, published a number of papers targeting welfare dependence as a key problem and "household formation decisions" as a primary cause. Ellwood and Bane's research thus "help[ed] to confirm popular suspicions, and conservative allegations, that poverty was less an economic problem than a sign of disturbing new demographic and behavioral trends."[172]

This focus on a dependent "underclass" undermined liberal proposals to "make work pay." Of course, conservatives took the lead in denouncing the supposedly pathological behaviors of the "underclass." In a widely read book-length polemic, political scientist Lawrence Mead called work "the strongest and clearest social obligation" for all able-bodied family heads as well as "other adult members of families that are needy."[173] According to this line of reasoning, rejection of marriage and breadwinning fostered the "high incidence of dropping out from school, of failure to prepare themselves for future employment, of begetting children out of wedlock, of crime, of drug abuse, and of other visible disorders" of the underclass, in the words of Michael Novak. To conservatives like Novak, these disorders—not poverty—were the real problem that government should address. The "working poor," those who are "taking care of themselves," simply "do not really present a public policy problem," he argued, while the "behaviorally dependent" would "scarcely be helped by income supplement alone." Even if they remained poor, Novak agreed, "both absent fathers and AFDC mothers would benefit by having full-time work year round," for "their pride and dignity would be helped, even if their financial situation were little better than with welfare alone."[174]

Liberals, too, targeted behavioral "disorders" rather than poverty and invoked the language of "obligation" and "individual responsibility."[175] Governor Cuomo's Task Force recognized the need for more jobs, quality job training, and higher wages but insisted that the "most important" element of a "new approach" to welfare was the recognition of recipients' "obligation to work or prepare themselves to work."[176] In Congressional hearings on welfare reform, liberal and antipoverty groups like the CSWP&L, the United Church of Christ's Office for Church in Society, FRAC, and the Child Welfare League, along with organized labor, opposed mandatory "workfare" programs, but a number of liberal-leaning new consensus reports recommended either work requirements or time limits on welfare receipt.[177] "Increasingly," noted Blanche Bernstein in 1988, "even liberal spokesmen are saying those who can work should work."[178] They joined conservatives in arguing that working mothers would serve as good role models for their children, thus helping to break the "intergenerational cycle of dependency" that perpetuated poverty and social chaos in the nation's central cities. A single mother's earnings "are likely to be modest," insisted Bernstein, but she would prove "a much better model for children than the mother who is a long-term dependent on welfare."[179] "Gainful employment," insisted Eleanor Holmes Norton, would "augment self-esteem by exposing women to the values and discipline associated with work, allowing them to pass on to their children more than their own disadvantages."[180] "Children do not benefit in the long run from having the single parent at home full time," APWA's panel on welfare reform pronounced, "if they do not also learn about self sufficiency and the options available to them in the larger community."[181]

Behind the concern about dependency and intergenerational poverty rested the real target of new consensus welfare reform: the "small but significant minority of the poor who stay on the welfare rolls for long periods of time."[182] As always, the discussion about welfare reform took place within a larger context, and the late 1980s witnessed tremendous public attention to the problems of a seemingly growing and intractable urban poor population. HHS's Office of the Assistant Secretary for Planning and Evaluation called. for research on the "neighborhood effects" of underclass behaviors such as "teen pregnancy, school dropout, welfare dependency, drug use, and crime," a call answered by the Urban Institute, the Institute for Research on Poverty, and other centers of poverty expertise. Perhaps the most "ambitious" project, the Social Science Research Council's Program for Research on the Urban Underclass, a five-year, $6 million fellowship and research program, focused almost exclusively on "social isolation," "disorganization," and "family 'dysfunction'," in other words on behavioral pathologies rather than the historical patterns of discrimination, long-term structural changes, or political and policy decisions that drastically altered the life chances of America's low-wage labor force, those trapped in high-poverty central cities most of all.[183]

The same focus characterized journalistic treatments of urban poverty in the late 1980s. Perhaps most important was Bill Moyers's 1986 *CBS Reports* documentary, "The Vanishing Family—Crisis in Black America." Moyers, a liberal who had served in the Johnson administration, explored Newark, New Jersey's "underclass" by interviewing men like Timothy McSneed, a twenty-six-year-old father of six children (by four different mothers) who demonstrated no remorse about leaving the support of his children to the welfare system, and his current girlfriend, Alice Sondra Jackson, who speculated that she would not have had her second or third child "if I didn't think welfare was there." The hour-long program paid no attention to the larger social and economic context of inner-city Newark, focusing instead on the personal decisions and "values" of a handful of residents. These individual portraits merely confirmed antiwelfare conservative charges—and liberal suspicions—that "the social structure erected by the state can be counterproductive." The lesson, concluded a *Newsweek* reporter, was that "it's no longer only racism or an unsympathetic government that is destroying black America." Instead, "the problem now lies in the black community itself, and in its failure to pass on moral values to the next generation."[184] Columnist Robert Samuelson articulated a second conclusion: "More welfare is not the answer," he wrote, "it's part of the mess."[185] Liberals joined conservatives in lauding Moyers's documentary for its "unflinching" and "gripping" look at the underclass, and a House Subcommittee studying black teenage pregnancy reviewed the show as part of its investigation. Moyers's show became an important reference point for pundits and policymakers who advocated stricter welfare regulations.[186] "No one who has watched Bill Moyers' 'CBS Reports' on the black family's decline," journalist Mickey Kaus insisted in an article introduced into the *Congressional Record*, "or read Leon Dash's series on black teenage pregnancy in the *Washington Post*, or Nicholas Lemann's recent *Atlantic* article on 'The Origins of the Underclass,' or Ken Auletta's book on the same subject, can doubt that there is a culture of poverty out there that has taken on a life of its own."[187]

As Kaus noted, the "underclass" also attracted renewed attention from black organizations in the mid-1980s. Black leaders had never abandoned the issue of urban poverty; throughout the 1970s, civil rights organizations pushed presidents and lawmakers to invest resources and energy into improving conditions in inner-city communities, which had suffered decades of job loss, declining tax revenues, and disinvestment. These groups had also joined in a larger liberal campaign to downplay the specific problems of minorities and garner support for "universal" programs like full employment, but by the mid-1980s, popular attention to the underclass prompted renewed attention to urban minority poverty. In 1983, the Joint Center for Political Studies, an African American think tank, published a "frank statement of the problems of the black family and a call for solutions," which was endorsed by a wide range of black organizations, including the NUL, the NAACP, the National Council of Negro Women, and the Urban Coalition.[188] Over the next few years, several African American organizations approached the family problem with the language of self-help. When the NAACP and the NUL invited two hundred participants to attend a Black

Family Summit at Fisk University in May 1984, the *New York Times* chose
to headline the story "Blacks See Blacks Saving the Family." Indeed, the
NUL's John L. Jacob noted that "some of our problems may be self-
inflicted," solvable with "self-discipline and strengthened community
values."[189]

In a June 1985 *New York Times* article titled "Restoring the Traditional
Black Family," former chair of the Equal Employment Opportunities Commission Eleanor Holmes Norton lauded African Americans' growing attention to the "self-perpetuating culture of the ghetto." Until recently, she
wrote, "many blacks have had an almost visceral reaction to mention of
black family problems," and "discussion of problems in the black family
has been an issue in search of leadership." Now that "nearly half of all black
children are being raised in poverty," Norton insisted that "further delay"
in finding "workable solutions" had become "unthinkable." Norton acknowledged the structural roots of family changes among urban African
Americans, particularly "the appearance of permanent joblessness and the
devaluation of working-class black men" in post-World War II cities. But,
she argued, "the process has advanced so far that renewal of the black family goes beyond the indispensable economic ingredients." To overturn the
"predatory ghetto subculture," in which unemployed and unemployable
black men rejected marriage and engaged in "antisocial" behaviors, Norton
advocated intensive government programs to "change . . . lifestyles as
well as impart . . . skills and education" with the aim of promoting "self-
sufficiency" among ghetto fathers and mothers—including a welfare system
"built around education or work." Beyond that, "nothing can substitute
for or have a greater impact than the full-scale involvement of the black
community." From "churches, Girl Scout troops and settlement houses to
civil rights organizations, Boys' Clubs and athletic teams," Norton issued a
summons to black America to embark on "the work of family reinforce-
ment."[190]

Black leaders' attention to black family structure—and their self-help
rhetoric—provided comfort to "new consensus" proponents. After all, if
"the scholars, leaders, and rank-and-file members of black and other
minority-group organizations are speaking frankly about behavioral dependency," as Novak put it, then one of the biggest obstacles to welfare state
retrenchment—the moral authority of the civil rights community and the
fear of being labeled racist—had finally been overcome.[191] Self-help fit
nicely with Reagan's neo-laissez-faire ideology, and the administration was
quick to capitalize on the idea; a 1988 White House Workshop on Self-Help

Efforts and Welfare Reform brought eighteen "self-help leaders" to Washington, including Lupe Anguiano, who by then headed a group called National Women's Employment and Education, Inc.[192] The administration's "welfare reform idea exchange" collected information on four hundred self-help programs among the poor in hopes of "mak[ing] community-based solutions to reducing dependency and poverty more visible" and publicizing the lesson that "low income people and communities can devise approaches to make progress with little or no reliance on government aid."[193] Government retrenchment was not exactly what African American organizations had in mind, of course. But the language of "self-help" suited and helped to legitimize free market conservatism.

At the same time, the sociologist and self-described "social democrat" William Julius Wilson resurrected the 1960s antipoverty coalition's analysis by highlighting the economic plight of poor black fathers. Wilson called Moynihan's 1965 report "prophetic" and blamed family breakdown in the central cities not on AFDC but on "a long-term decline in the proportion of black men . . . who are in a position to support a family." Only a broad program of universal social policies, from full employment to comprehensive manpower programs, could "strengthen low-income black families" by creating more marriageable black men. Wilson pointed to the structural forces that prevented black men from becoming stable breadwinners, as middle-class African Americans and good jobs moved out of American ghettos, leaving an increasingly isolated poor population with few stabilizing institutions or legitimate economic opportunities. And like the 1960s antipoverty coalition, he attributed the poverty of women and children to black male economic disadvantage, "reinforc[ing] the notion that 'dependency' was the poverty problem for women while joblessness was primarily a problem for men."[194]

As Wilson's analysis suggests, concern about the pathological black family remained at the rhetorical center of welfare politics. Conservative authors sounded off in moral tones, condemning "self-damaging social behaviors" like out-of-wedlock births and asserting that single-parent households were "empirically associated with unusual social, medical, and moral hazards." Like 1960s antipoverty liberals, new consensus conservatives saw "marriage and work" as the "keys to climbing out of poverty." Two-parent families, Novak insisted, "present fewer problems for public policy," so "wise social policy will treasure this model of family life."[195] Conservatives in the 1980s, like those in the 1960s, saw welfare cuts and coercive requirements as a way to punish single-parent families and thereby encourage marriage and breadwinning. Liberal new consensus proponents, like anti-poverty liberals in the 1960s, offered federal programs like job creation and a higher minimum wage to "make work pay." Yet they too insisted that "the welfare system does not reflect and reinforce our commonly held values and expectations." If the nation hoped to "change the environment and the attitudes, hopes, and expectations of the ghetto poor," David Ellwood insisted, "replacing the welfare system seems the obvious and important place to start."[196]

Against all evidence, both conservatives and liberals insisted that government income support—whether in the form of AFDC or a broader public assistance program—discouraged the creation and maintenance of two-parent families among the "underclass." In a 1985 report for the White House Office of Policy Development, Leslie Lenkowski of the neoconservative Smith Richardson Foundation cited the Negative Income Tax (NIT) experiments as "persuasive evidence" that "whatever the rules of eligibility, public assistance really seems to serve as a kind of alimony for low-income women, enabling them to head their own households and raise their children alone." But even Lenkowski recognized that the data was far from clear. "AFDC *may be responsible*," he noted, "for encouraging the formation of these high-risk [female-headed] families."[197] Novak, too, admitted a lack of "sufficient evidence that welfare causes" family breakups and out-of-wedlock births.[198] Even President Reagan's own General Accounting Office concluded, after over a decade of serious scholarly attention to the relationship between public assistance and family structure, that "research does not support the view that welfare encourages two-parent family breakup" or nonmarital births.[199] Yet some liberals joined conservatives in arguing just that. In his 1988 book *Poor Support*, David Ellwood claimed that income support, whether to single- or two-parent families, would "inevitably increase the incentives to form single-parent families" by "encourag[ing] unmarried women to have children and then become dependent on welfare for a long time" even though Ellwood's own careful research found that welfare had had virtually no effect on family structure among the poor.[200]

In the end, supporters of the "new consensus" of the late 1980s employed family breakdown as a rhetorical weapon to condemn AFDC rather than as a springboard to new plans to combat economic inequality and disadvantage. Reagan's White House Working Group on the Family forthrightly condemned the "anti-family agenda" and "abrasive experiments" of American liberals—welfare in particular—for destroying the American family. "Welfare contributes to the failure to form the family in the first place," the group insisted, and creates instead "a mother dependent upon public charity." The "easy availability of welfare in all its forms" had thus "become a powerful force for the destruction of family life through perpetuation of the welfare culture." While Reagan's speechwriters had Gary Bauer invoking "the well-being of families," the administration cared much more about the "formation and maintenance of *economically self-reliant families*"—families that did not rely on public assistance—than about either recreating male-breadwinner households among the poor or ensuring that two-parent families could escape poverty. After all, the administration measured the success of any welfare plan by "how many of its recipients become independent of welfare," not by reductions in poverty or changes in family structure.[201]

The language of family deterioration permeated the administration's welfare reform rhetoric in 1986 and 1987 as the president called for "real welfare reform . . . that will lead to lasting emancipation from welfare dependency."[202] The administration insisted that "in the welfare culture, the breakdown of the family, the most basic support system, has reached crisis proportions" and blamed that welfare-induced family breakdown for "female and child poverty, child abandonment, horrible crimes and deteriorating schools."[203] Citing George Gilder in its report, *Up from Dependency*, Reagan's Low Income Opportunity Working Group denounced welfare for "weaken[ing] families," or, more specifically, for "replac[ing] the breadwinner" and "enabl[ing] young mothers to raise children without fathers."[204] "It is fitting that the word 'family' figures prominently in the title of this legislation," Reagan announced upon signing the Family Support Act of 1988, "for this bill restores the family to its rightful place in our welfare system." For too long, he continued, "the Federal Government—with the best of intentions—has usurped responsibilities that appropriately lie with parents," and in doing so "has separated welfare recipients from the mainstream of American society."[205]

But the Family Support Act (FSA) offered nothing to encourage the formation or maintenance of two-parent families. It reinforced paternal financial responsibility with new child support enforcement measures (and new obligations that mothers cooperate) but did nothing to improve poor fathers' earnings. The bill's major provisions were aimed at moving single mothers into the labor market and off the welfare rolls. It replaced WIN with the Job Opportunities and Basic Skills (JOBS) program "to provide employment, education, training, and work-related assistance to welfare recipients," reflecting the near-universal view that poor single mothers should support their children by working for wages.[206] No less an expert than the president of the Manpower Development Research Corporation—the leader in conducting welfare-to-work experiments—warned that "research suggests that employment programs alone are unlikely to lead to major reductions in poverty or the welfare rolls." And the bill contained a "complex balance of mandatory and voluntary elements," including mandatory participation for women with children three and older (or one and older at state discretion) and allowances for state "workfare" programs.[207] Nonetheless, conservatives and liberals alike hailed it as the answer to welfare "dependency" once and for all.

That many liberals viewed the FSA as a victory suggests how much had changed, and how much had not changed, since the 1960s. Then, a broad and committed coalition of liberals identified the black, female-headed family as a problem and as a target for reconstruction. But that antipoverty coalition laid the blame on low wages and lack of opportunities for African American fathers, a problem that stemmed from both racial discrimination and disadvantage and from the very structure of the American economy. If their analysis relied on an increasingly outdated male-breadwinner, female-homemaker family model, it nonetheless implicated a whole range of economic and political decisions, both past and present, in impoverishing African Americans, and it acknowledged a broad social responsibility to alleviate the economic conditions that contributed to changing family patterns in the nation's central cities.

Two decades later, the calculus was reversed. Liberals acknowledged the validity of mothers' breadwinning role while rejecting grand federal efforts to combat poverty and racial disadvantage. Condemnation of the "pathological" black family remained at the center of welfare politics, but it now served a much different purpose. Liberals supported the emphasis on workfare by pointing to feminist critiques of AFDC and demands for jobs, but the policy results of the "new consensus" resembled a much older antiwelfare conservatism. The family wage would remain a privilege available to a rapidly shrinking proportion of American families. Poor, working-class, and growing numbers of middle-class mothers and fathers were left to fend for themselves in an economy characterized by deepening inequality.

Conclusion: Beyond the Family Wage

The termination of AFDC in 1996, sixty-one years after its creation, was rightly described as marking the end of an era. The Personal Responsibility and Work Opportunity Reconciliation Act (PRWORA) not only ended a relatively small, perpetually besieged entitlement program. It also marked the conclusion of a political-economic order that stretched from the New Deal of the 1930s through the Great Society of the 1960s and came to an end in the 1980s and 1990s.

The social basis of that now defunct order was the male-breadwinner household. This family form encapsulated and prescribed a particular set of relationships between home and work, between individual wealth and social welfare, and between private enterprise and public regulation. It was materially sustained by a "family wage" nourished by private sector employment policies, collective bargaining, and public sector social welfare provision. It was culturally sustained by prevailing gender roles and marital norms which reinforced expectations about women's economic dependence and men's duty to provide economically for a wife and children. This model of the male-breadwinner nuclear household as both the bulwark and the beneficiary of American growth and prosperity framed the major political and economic conflicts of the mid-twentieth century, from Franklin Roosevelt to Ronald Reagan; it set the stakes and parameters of social and economic struggle. From the furthest reaches of a social democratic vision to the fiercest commitment to "free enterprise," discussions about the nation's political-economic order occurred within the boundaries of the male-breadwinner family ideal. That ideal defined both the expansive possibilities and the inherent limits of the New Deal/Great Society order; it animated proposals to construct a more egalitarian economic structure as well as policies that reinforced class and race inequality.

AFDC engendered vehement political controversy because it represented the "other"—the negative image—against which the prosperous, self-supporting nuclear household was defined: the impoverished single mother visibly dependent on state support. The program represented the possibilities and the perils of the New Deal order. In the eyes of its design-ers, AFDC shored up the family wage ideal by replacing the wages of a lost male breadwinner and enabling a solo mother to provide round-the-clock care for her children. To its detractors, AFDC undermined the nuclear fam-ily system by replacing the wages of a male provider with a government check. Private support gave way to public provision, male breadwinning gave way to paternal irresponsibility, and wifely dependence gave way to some measure of female autonomy. AFDC, then, represented both a bridge and a barrier between the celebrated American "middle class," the locus of the New Deal order's hopes, and the pitied and deplored "underclass," its deepest fear. And as the ranks of the "welfare poor" grew alongside the ranks of the middle class in the postwar era, AFDC came to represent the contradictions and tensions in the family wage model itself—contradictions and tensions that came to the fore in the 1960s.

The War on Poverty, and the welfare battles that followed, became a war over the embattled family wage. On the one side, an antipoverty coali-tion envisioned an inclusive family wage that would enable Americans of all races and classes to achieve the male-breadwinner ideal. Liberals in the Democratic Party, academia, and a broad range of civic, religious, and civil rights organizations joined welfare rights activists and political radicals to demand a variety of public policies to this end: massive job creation and public service employment programs; more generous income support, par-ticularly for two-parent families; a negative income tax, family allowance, or other form of guaranteed income; and effective and enforceable full em-ployment policies. They insisted that if all men had access to remunerative employment, if all families had access to sufficient income, then Americans would form stable, male-breadwinner households and the nation would thereby end poverty, racial disadvantage, and various social disorders, from unwed motherhood to juvenile delinquency.

On the other side, antiwelfare conservatives pursued policies that would continue to exclude large numbers of Americans from the family wage system. Southern lawmakers, corporate and businesses lobbyists, con-servative academics and pundits, and an increasingly conservative Republi-can Party resisted efforts to expand the social safety net and denied public responsibility for family well-being. They viewed the male-breadwinner family structure as a privilege reserved for white men able to earn enough in the private labor market and women respectable enough to marry them. They argued against minimum wage increases, union organizing rights, public employment programs, and other policies designed to shore up men's wages. They denounced guaranteed income proposals and lobbied instead for restrictive welfare policies at both the state and federal levels. Work requirements and workfare programs, stringent paternal child support enforcement, and various other restrictive policies were designed to reduce welfare rolls and costs and to force poor single mothers to rely on nongovernmental means of support, especially wage labor. Antiwelfare conservatives aimed to ensure that only wealthy and middle-class Americans could achieve what they saw as a privatized male-breadwinner ideal.

AFDC fell victim to that protracted struggle, one in which race played a starring role. Liberals critiqued the program as part of their effort to achieve broader, more universal policies; AFDC destroyed families (primarily black families), they argued, by supporting single mothers, while a guaranteed income or full employment policies would keep them together by shoring up the earnings of male breadwinners. Conservatives harnessed liberal criticisms to their own ends. Mobilizing long-standing stereotypes of black women as lazy, promiscuous, and maternally neglectful and black men as lazy, sexually predatory, and paternally irresponsible, they succeeded in making AFDC the poster child for misguided, even malevolent, government social engineering. The attack on AFDC—from liberals and conservatives who jointly prized the male-breadwinner household—helped to defeat the broader Great Society agenda that aimed to expand federal responsibility for eradicating poverty and racial inequality.

While "welfare as we knew it," symbolized by AFDC, went down to defeat in the 1980s and 1990s, poverty and economic inequality emerged the unheralded victors. From World War II through the 1960s, poverty and economic inequality declined substantially. A mildly redistributive federal government harnessed some of the profits of sustained economic growth to provide generous social insurance and veterans' benefits as well as a variety of public assistance programs for the poor. In the 1980s, the contraction of government income support combined with declining real wages among low-income workers to reverse these trends. As of 2007, 12.5 percent of the American population, or 37.3 million people, lived below the federal poverty line. At $17,170 annually for a family of three, the poverty line is itself an outdated and inadequate measure of real economic hardship. The poverty rate remains significantly higher for African Americans (24.5%), Hispanics (21.5%), and children under eighteen (18% or 13.3 million children), the highest child poverty rate among thirteen Western European countries and Canada.[1]

More than a quarter of American families headed by single mothers

(28.3%) are officially poor.[2] Since 1996, these families can no longer rely on AFDC which, despite its limitations, provided much-needed support, however paltry. Critics' claims to the contrary, AFDC did not encourage nonmarital childbearing, teen pregnancy, or family breakup, nor did it erode recipients' work ethic or create intergenerational poverty or "dependency." Rather, it enabled poor mothers to escape relationships with violent partners, pay the rent when they lost a low-wage job, provide care for sick and disabled children, and sometimes earn a college degree and escape poverty once and for all.[3] The end of AFDC—particularly in an age of deepening economic inequality—left these families without a crucial safety net.

The 1996 bill replaced AFDC with Temporary Aid to Needy Families (TANF), a much more restrictive program that has left solo mothers and their children more economically vulnerable than before. TANF is a block grant, so states receive a fixed amount of federal funds no matter how many families are in need. Congress limited TANF receipt to two years consecutively and five years over a lifetime, and many states have imposed even shorter time limits. Adults, including mothers of newborn infants, must participate full-time in work-related activities, while administrators keep rolls low with a variety of diversion tactics, like requiring applicants to ask family members for financial help or fill out a certain number of job applications, and sanctions, such as cutting aid if a recipient misses an appointment or fills out paperwork incorrectly. Not surprisingly, caseloads, which had already begun to drop as the economy revived in the mid-1990s, dropped drastically, plummeting from 4.5 million families in 1996 to 2.1 million by 2002. Republicans and Democrats alike celebrated the bill's success in reducing welfare rolls, but most women who move "from welfare to work" find themselves in unstable, low-wage dead-end jobs that fail to lift their families out of poverty.[4]

Their plight, and the termination of AFDC that worsened it, is part of a broader transformation: the downfall of the economic and political order of which welfare was a part. The persistence of poverty and the growth of economic inequality since the 1970s attest to the ultimate demise of the "family wage" model, in reality if not in rhetoric. Cultural transformations—challenges to postwar gender roles from feminists and gay liberationists, loosening strictures on sexual expression and behavior, rising divorce rates—played a role. More fundamental, though, are changes that undermined the material basis of the male-breadwinner household. The loss of well-paid manufacturing jobs, the explosion of the low-wage service sector, the decline of organized labor, wage stagnation and contraction, and an increasingly regressive tax structure mean that few American families can achieve economic security with only one adult worker.[5] Those long excluded from the family wage model—especially nonwhite families, single mothers, and those trapped in communities of concentrated poverty—suffer most acutely from the end of the postwar economic boom and the erosion of federal redistributive policies.

Politically, the bond between work and family represented by the family wage model effectively broke during the 1970s. Liberal critics of AFDC in the 1960s had, for better and worse, called attention to that bond. They hoped to use federal policy, including expanded income support, to ensure the material base for the formation of male-breadwinner households. But those who discussed "the family" in the 1980s and 1990s, predominantly fundamentalist Christian conservatives and their political allies who lamented the decline of the "traditional" family, did so primarily in moral rather than economic terms. Even discussions of poor families rarely acknowledged economic context. When Daniel Patrick Moynihan worried in 1965 that black family breakdown had become a self-generating cultural pattern, he nonetheless recommended economic policies like job creation and broadened income support as essential solutions. When he revisited his report in 1991, he discussed single motherhood and welfare "dependency" as entirely divorced from structural economic constraints like unemployment and underemployment, a plummeting minimum wage, the erosion of private benefit packages, and the plight of high-poverty areas lacking jobs and basic services. Instead, he approvingly cited conservative author Lawrence Mead: "The inequalities that stem from the workplace are now trivial in comparison to those stemming from family structure."[6]

The main political beneficiaries of this break between issues of family and issues of the economy have thus far been on the right. But in recent years Democratic appeals to "working families" have begun to draw renewed attention to poverty, if not economic inequality. Senator John Edwards made poverty, which he called "the great moral issue of our time," a focus of his campaign for the 2008 Democratic presidential nomination, and Senators Hillary Clinton and Barack Obama joined him in offering proposals for expanded federal antipoverty measures: raising the minimum wage and indexing it to inflation, raising and expanding the Earned Income Tax Credit, and creating transitional or short-term federal job and job training programs.[7] Democratic candidates have also proposed substantial investments in high-poverty communities in both rural and urban America and increased federal aid to enable more Americans to earn college degrees.[8]

These proposals assert a renewed public responsibility for ameliorating poverty, and they would certainly provide much-needed financial help to millions of American families, including those headed by single mothers. So, too, would the continued spread of "living wage" campaigns, an encouraging sign of grassroots activism on the part of and on behalf of low-income Americans. By 2006 coalitions of poverty rights activists, organized labor, and civic and religious organizations had won living wage ordinances, which require companies with municipal contracts to pay higher than federal and state minimum wage rates, in 134 cities across the country. Spirited organizing campaigns among low-wage service workers, like Janitors for Justice and Hotel Workers Rising, have also called attention to the struggles of the "working poor" and have won significant victories.[9] These efforts not only provide tangible benefits for low-wage workers but also frame low wages, unaffordable and inaccessible health care, and poor working conditions—rather than nonmarital childbearing and single motherhood—as the nation's most pressing "moral-values" issues.[10]

Is this activism a step toward building a new kind of antipoverty politics, one no longer predicated on the "family wage" but built instead on a new model of the relationship between home and work, public and private responsibility? Some observers are hopeful. The end of AFDC has a silver lining, they argue; it has shifted the terms of debate and offered the potential for coalitions among poor single mothers who participate in TANF and in the labor market and other low-wage workers and their progressive allies—coalitions like the living wage campaigns. Once despised as pathological "welfare mothers," poor single mothers have now visibly joined the ranks of the "working poor." Arguments that their poverty resulted from their own bad behavior or their "dependence" on welfare are suddenly less convincing. "Having forced poor mothers into the labor market," Nancy MacLean argues, "conservatives are now hard-pressed to explain why, if the 'free enterprise' system is the cure-all they assured Americans it was, one in four adults working full-time year-round is still poor."[11]

But campaigns to improve the wages and conditions of low-wage workers are only half the battle. While supporters discuss these efforts as a way to help "working families," the campaigns often do not address parents' struggles outside the workplace. American workers—single mothers in particular—are unlikely to achieve real economic security until society provides greater support for parenting.[12] In the 1970s, welfare rights activists and antipoverty feminists proposed a new, degendered family wage: policies to improve work opportunities and wages for women as well as men, programs like universal child care, flexible work hours, and paid leave to enable adults to combine wage labor and parenting, along with a more generous AFDC or other income support for adults whose dependents require a full-time caregiver. More recently, single mothers in the TANF program and some feminist scholars have echoed these demands that we revise labor market and welfare state to recognize and reward labor in both the private and public spheres.[13] These policies are largely absent from today's political discussion.[14] If we are serious about fighting poverty and offering economic opportunity for all Americans, we must attend to these efforts, both past and present, to forge a new relationship between family and economy.

The long battle over AFDC offers this enduring lesson. Activists, organizations, and political leaders who are truly committed to fighting poverty and ensuring economic justice must reject an outdated family wage model that privileges male breadwinning, disadvantages women, and demonizes single mothers. But we must also reject a politics that treats all able-bodied adults only as wage earners. We must forge a new model of the relationship between private enterprise and public responsibility, individual wealth and social welfare, home and work, family and economy. In other words, we must articulate an agenda for economic justice that links family well-being to labor market conditions but that also asserts broad, social responsibility for supporting parents of all races and classes in the essential job of raising the next generation.

Notes

Introduction

1. The Social Security Act provided matching funds to states that wanted to establish an ADC program and allowed states to set specific eligibility requirements, but poverty lawyers and welfare rights activists in the 1960s and 1970s made temporary headway establishing rights to welfare aid.

2. For an overview of the politics and provisions of PRWORA, see R. Kent Weaver, *Ending Welfare as We Know It* (Washington, D.C.: Brookings Institution Press, 2000), chap. 9.

3. While the War on Poverty's planners and boosters explicitly distanced their programs from "welfare"—promising a "hand up rather than a hand out"—contemporary critics tend to conflate the War on Poverty (and the Great Society more generally) with "welfare."

4. Sections 101 and 401 of H.R. 3734: Personal Responsibility and Work Opportunity Reconciliation Act of 1996, as passed by both houses of Congress. For Bush's welfare reform proposals, see Robin Toner and Robert Pear, "Bush's Plan on Welfare Law Increases Work Requirement," *NYT*, 26 February 2002, 23 and Richard W. Stevenson, "Bush Urges Congress to Extend Welfare Law, with Changes," *NYT*, 15 January 2003, 18.

5. Office of Policy Planning and Research, U.S. Department of Labor, *The Negro Family: The Case for National Action* (Washington, D.C.: Government Printing Office, March 1965), 5, in Lee Rainwater and William L. Yancey, *The Moynihan Report and the Politics of Controversy* (Cambridge, Mass.: MIT Press, 1967), 51.

6. Mrs. L. M. Joyce Greene to Mrs. Bruce Benson, 10 August 1971, Series 4, Box 579, Folder "WR Action letters, 1971–72," LWV Papers.

7. Stephanie Coontz, *The Way We Never Were: American Families and the Nostalgia Trap* (New York: Basic Books, 1992), 30; Dennis Deslippe, *"Rights, Not Roses": Unions and the Rise of Working-Class Feminism, 1945–80* (Urbana: University of Illinois Press, 2000), 15–21; Dorothy Sue Cobble, *The Other Women's Movement: Workplace Justice and Social Rights in Modern America* (Princeton, N.J.: Princeton University Press, 2004); Susan M. Hartmann, "Women's Employment and the Domestic Ideal in the Early Cold War Years," in *Not June Cleaver: Women and Gender in Postwar America, 1945–1960*, ed. Joanne Meyerowitz (Philadelphia: Temple University Press, 1994), 84–100.

8. Barbara Reskin and Irene Padevic, *Women and Men at Work* (Thousand Oaks, Calif.: Pine Forge Press, 1994), 150; McKinley L. Blackburn, David E. Bloom, and Richard B. Freeman, "The Declining Economic Position of Less Skilled Men,"

in *A Future of Lousy Jobs? The Changing Structure of U.S. Wages*, ed. Gary Burtless (Washington, D.C.: Brookings Institution Press, 1990); Henry Farber, "Job Loss in the United States, 1981–2001," NBER Working Paper W9707 (Cambridge, Mass.: National Bureau of Economic Research, 2003); Jacob S. Hacker, "Privatizing Risk Without Privatizing the Welfare State: The Hidden Politics of Social Policy Retrenchment in the United States," *American Political Science Review* 98, 2 (2004), 243–60; Lillian Rubin, *Worlds of Pain: Life in the Working-Class Family* (New York: Basic Books, 1976); Bennett Harrison and Barry Bluestone, *The Great U-Turn: Corporate Restructuring and the Polarizing of America* (New York: Basic Books, 1988); Frank Levy, *Dollars and Dreams: The Changing American Income Distribution* (New York: Russell Sage, 1987); Sheldon Danziger and Peter Gottschalk, *America Unequal* (Cambridge, Mass.: Harvard University Press, 1995).

9. Sanford F. Schram, *After Welfare: The Culture of Postindustrial Social Policy* (New York: New York University Press, 2000), 1.

10. While concerns about family structure are much less prominent in debates about these other programs, the overwhelming emphasis on "dependency" among erstwhile breadwinners that characterized AFDC's politics is very evident. To some extent, each program garnered its own particular allies, opponents, and arguments, but the powerful campaign against AFDC in the 1970s and 1980s became, in effect, a broader case against federal social welfare for non-aged adults.

11. Thomas F. Jackson, "The State, the Movement, and the Urban Poor: The War on Poverty and Political Mobilization in the 1960s," in *The "Underclass" Debate: Views from History*, ed. Michael B. Katz (Princeton, N.J.: Princeton University Press, 1993), 403–39; Charles Noble, *Welfare as We Knew It: A Political History of the American Welfare State* (New York: Oxford University Press, 1997), chap. 5; Jennifer Mittlestadt, *From Welfare to Workfare: The Unintended Consequences of Liberal Reform, 1945–1965* (Chapel Hill: University of North Carolina Press, 2005), 11; Michael B. Katz, *In the Shadow of the Poorhouse: A Social History of Welfare in America*, 10th anniversary ed., rev. and updated (New York: Basic Books, 1996), 262–69; James T. Patterson, *America's Struggle Against Poverty, 1900–1994* (Cambridge, Mass.: Harvard University Press, 1994), chaps. 6–9; Frances Fox Piven and Richard A. Cloward, *Regulating the Poor: The Functions of Public Welfare*, updated ed. (New York: Vintage, 1993), chap. 9; Ira Katznelson, "Was the Great Society a Lost Opportunity?" in *The Rise and Fall of the New Deal Order, 1930–1980*, ed. Steve Fraser and Gary Gerstle (Princeton, N.J.: Princeton University Press, 1989), 185–211; Lawrence M. Friedman, "The Social and Political Context of the War on Poverty: An Overview," in *A Decade of Federal Antipoverty Programs: Achievements, Failures, and Lessons*, ed. Robert Haveman (New York: Academic Press, 1977), 21–47. For the opposite argument (that 1960s liberals embraced far-left radical politics and policies, see Steven F. Hayward, *The Age of Reagan: The Fall of the Old Liberal Order, 1964–1980* (Roseville, Calif.: Prima, 2001), 55–56 and Gareth Davies, *From Opportunity to Entitlement: The Transformation and Decline of Great Society Liberalism* (Lawrence: University Press of Kansas, 1996).

12. William G. Mayer, *The Changing American Mind: How and Why American Public Opinion Changed Between 1960 and 1988* (Ann Arbor: University of Michigan Press, 1992), 323–26; David Frum, *How We Got Here—the 70's: The Decade That*

Brought You Modern Life (For Better or Worse) (New York: Basic Books, 2000); David Steigerwald, *The Sixties and the End of Modern America* (New York: St. Martin's, 1995), 262; Hayward, *The Age of Reagan*, xxx.

13. Piven and Cloward, *Regulating the Poor.*

14. On race, see Michael K. Brown, *Race, Money, and the American Welfare State* (Ithaca, N.Y.: Cornell University Press, 1999); Robert C. Lieberman, *Shifting the Color Line: Race and the American Welfare State* (Cambridge, Mass.: Harvard University Press, 1998); Jill Quadagno, *The Color of Welfare: How Racism Undermined the War on Poverty* (New York: Oxford University Press, 1994); Mary Poole, "Securing Race and Enshrining Dependence: The Social Security Act of 1935" (Ph.D. diss., Rutgers University, 2000); Kenneth J. Neubeck and Noel A. Cazenave, *Welfare Racism: Playing the Race Card Against America's Poor* (New York: Routledge, 2001). On gender, see Linda Gordon, *Pitied But Not Entitled: Single Mothers and the History of Welfare, 1890–1935* (Cambridge, Mass.: Harvard University Press, 1994); S. J. Kleinberg, *Widows and Orphans First: The Family Economy and Social Welfare Policy, 1880–1939* (Urbana: University of Illinois Press, 2006); Linda Gordon, ed., *Women, the State, and Welfare* (Madison: University of Wisconsin Press, 1990); Nancy Fraser, *Unruly Practices: Power, Discourse, and Gender in Contemporary Social Theory* (Minneapolis: University of Minnesota Press, 1989); Miriam Cohen and Michael Hanagan, "The Politics of Gender and the Making of the Welfare State, 1900–1940: A Comparative Perspective," *Journal of Social History* 24, 3 (1991): 469–84.

15. Theda Skocpol, *Protecting Soldiers and Mothers: The Political Origins of Social Policy in the United States* (Cambridge, Mass.: Belknap Press of Harvard University Press, 1992); Weir, Orloff, and Skocpol, *The Politics of Social Policy in the United States.*

16. Eileen Boris and S. J. Kleinberg, "Mothers and Other Workers: (Re)Conceiving Labor, Maternalism, and the State," *Journal of Women's History* 15, 3 (2003): 91.

17. Jeanne Boydston, *Home and Work: Housework, Wages, and the Ideology of Labor in the Early Republic* (New York: Oxford University Press, 1990); Kathryn Kish Sklar, *Catharine Beecher: A Study in American Domesticity* (New Haven, Conn.: Yale University Press, 1973); Christine Stansell, *City of Women: Sex and Class in New York, 1789–1860* (Urbana: University of Illinois Press, 1982). For the origins of race and class distinctions in the domestic ideology, see Kathleen M. Brown, *Good Wives, Nasty Wenches, and Anxious Patriarchs: Gender, Race, and Power in Colonial Virginia* (Chapel Hill: University of North Carolina Press, 1996).

18. Lawrence B. Glickman, *A Living Wage: American Workers and the Making of Consumer Society* (Ithaca, N.Y.: Cornell University Press, 1997).

19. Alice Kessler-Harris, *A Woman's Wage: Historical Meanings and Social Consequences* (Lexington: University Press of Kentucky, 1990), 39.

20. Kleinberg, *Widows and Orphans First*, 70; Vicki L. Ruiz, *From Out of the Shadows: Mexican Women in Twentieth-Century America* (New York: Oxford University Press, 1998); Jacquelyn Jones, *Labor of Love, Labor of Sorrow: Black Women, Work, and the Family, From Slavery to the Present* (New York: Vintage, 1985); Tera

Hunter, *To 'Joy My Freedom: Southern Black Women's Lives and Labors After the Civil War* (Cambridge, Mass.: Harvard University Press, 1997).

21. Mimi Abramovitz called this the "family ethic." I refer to it as the "family wage ideal" or the "male-breadwinner ideal." Abramovitz, *Regulating the Lives of Women: Social Welfare Policy from Colonial Times to the Present* (Boston: South End Press, 1988), 13. See also Gordon, *Pitied But Not Entitled*; Kessler-Harris, *In Pursuit of Equity: Women, Men, and the Quest for Economic Equity in 20th-Century America* (New York: Oxford University Press, 2001); Beatrix Hoffman, *The Wages of Sickness: The Politics of Health Insurance in Progressive America* (New York: Oxford University Press, 2001), 121–22, 129, 131–32, 135–36; John Fabian Witt, *The Accidental Republic: Crippled Workingmen, Destitute Widows, and the Remaking of American Law* (Cambridge, Mass.: Harvard University Press, 2004), 126–51; Gwendolyn Mink, *The Wages of Motherhood: Inequality in the Welfare State, 1917–1942* (Ithaca, N.Y.: Cornell University Press, 1995), 42, 45–47, 125, 129, 155, 172; Sonya Michel, "The Limits of Maternalism: Policies Toward American Wage-Earning Mothers During the Progressive Era," in *Mothers of a New World: Maternalist Politics and the Origins of Welfare States*, ed. Seth Koven and Sonya Michel (New York: Routledge, 1993), 277–320; Diane Sainsbury, *Gender, Equality, and Welfare States* (Cambridge: Cambridge University Press, 1996).

22. Skocpol, *Protecting Soldiers and Mothers*; Ann Shola Orloff, "The Political Origins of America's Belated Welfare State," in Weir, Orloff, and Skopcol, *Politics of Social Policy in the United States*, 37–80, and "Gender in Early U.S. Social Policy," *Journal of Policy History* 3, 3 (1991): 249–81; Kathryn Kish Sklar, "The Historical Foundations of Women's Power in the Creation of the American Welfare State, 1830–1930," in Koven and Michel, *Mothers of a New World*, 43–93.

23. Linda Gordon, "Black and White Visions of Welfare: Women's Welfare Activism, 1890–1945," *Journal of American History* (September 1991): 559–90; Eileen Boris, "The Power of Motherhood: Black and White Activist Women Redefine the 'Political'," in Koven and Michel, *Mothers of a New World*, 213–45.

24. New York State Commission on Relief for Widowed Mothers, 1914, quoted in Kleinberg, *Widows and Orphans First*, 9.

25. The most comprehensive treatment is Mink, *Wages of Motherhood*.

26. Joanne Goodwin, "An American Experiment in Paid Motherhood: The Implementation of Mothers' Pensions in Early Twentieth-Century Chicago," *Gender and History* 4, 3 (Autumn 1992): 337; Joanne Goodwin, *Gender and the Politics of Welfare Reform: Mothers' Pensions in Chicago, 1911–1929* (Chicago: University of Chicago Press, 1997); Christopher Howard, "Sowing the Seeds of 'Welfare': The Transformation of Mothers' Pensions, 1900–1940," *Journal of Policy History* 4, 2 (1992), 196, 200–201; Winifred Bell, *Aid to Dependent Children* (New York: Columbia University Press, 1965), 9–10. Prescilla Ferguson Clement shows the longer history of these restrictive policies in "Nineteenth-Century Welfare Policy, Programs, and Poor Women: Philadelphia as a Case Study," *Feminist Studies* 18, 1 (Spring 1992): 35–59.

27. Kleinberg, *Widows and Orphans*, 10.

28. Jerry Cates, *Insuring Inequality: Administrative Leadership in Social Security, 1935–1954* (Ann Arbor: University of Michigan Press, 1983).

29. Alice Kessler-Harris, "Designing Women and Old Fools: Writing Gender into Social Security Law," in *Women's America: Refocusing the Past*, 6th ed., ed. Linda K. Kerber and Jane Sherron De Hart (New York: Oxford University Press, 2004), 435–47 ("gendered imagination" 444); Blanche D. Coll, *Safety Net: Welfare and Social Security, 1929–1979* (New Brunswick, N.J.: Rutgers University Press, 1995), 103; Arthur J. Altmeyer, *The Formative Years of Social Security* (Madison: University of Wisconsin Press, 1966), 16.

30. On how the "two tiers" of the welfare system mapped and then reinforced gender, race, and class inequalities, see Nancy Fraser and Linda Gordon, "Dependency Demystified: Inscriptions of Power in a Keyword of the Welfare State," *Social Politics* 1 (1994): 4–31; Michael K. Brown, "Race in the American Welfare State: The Ambiguities of 'Universalistic' Social Policy Since the New Deal," in *Without Justice for All*, ed. Adolph Reed (Boulder, Colo.: Westview Press, 1999), 93–122; Mink, *Wages of Motherhood*; Quadagno, *Color of Welfare*; Nancy Ellen Rose, *Put to Work: Relief Programs of the Great Depression* (New York: Monthly Review Press, 1994), and "Gender, Race, and the Welfare State: Government Work Programs from the 1930s to the Present," *Feminist Studies* 19 (1993): 319–42; Poole, "Securing Race and Enshrining Dependence"; Lieberman, *Shifting the Color Line*; Gordon, *Pitied But Not Entitled*.

31. Mittlestadt, *From Welfare to Workfare*; Coll, *Safety Net*; Ellen Reese, *Backlash Against Welfare Mothers Past and Present* (Berkeley: University of California Press, 2005), Part II; Bell, *Aid to Dependent Children*; Lisa Levenstein, "From Innocent Children to Unwanted Migrants and Unwed Moms: Two Chapters in the Public Discourse on Welfare in the United States, 1960–1961," *Journal of Women's History* 11, 4 (Winter 2000): 10–13.

32. Kessler-Harris, *In Pursuit of Equity*, 135. The creation of Aid to the Permanently and Totally Disabled in 1950 had a similar effect. Until then, about 25% of the AFDC caseload had an incapacitated breadwinner, but APTD removed those two-parent families from the rolls. Coll, *Safety Net*, 173.

33. Quoted in Bell, *Aid to Dependent Children*, 34–35.

34. Edwin Amenta and Theda Skocpol, "Redefining the New Deal: World War II and the Development of Social Provision in the United States," in *The Politics of Social Policy in the United States*, ed. Margaret Weir, Ann Shola Orloff, and Theda Skocpol (Princeton, N.J.: Princeton University Press, 1988), 81–122; Katznelson, "Was the Great Society a Lost Opportunity?"; Brown, *Race, Money*, chap. 3.

35. Ira Katznelson, *When Affirmative Action Was White: An Untold Story of Racial Inequality in Twentieth-Century America* (New York: Norton, 2005), chaps. 2–5; Michael J. Bennett, *When Dreams Came True: The GI Bill and the Making of Modern America* (Washington, D.C.: Brassey's, 1996); Beth Stevens, "Blurring the Boundaries: How the Federal Government Has Influenced Welfare Benefits in the Private Sector," in Weir, Orloff, and Skocpol, *Politics of Social Policy*, 123–48; Jennifer Klein, *For All These Rights: Business, Labor, and the Shaping of America's Public-Private Welfare State* (Princeton, N.J.: Princeton University Press, 2003), 13, 38, 111.

36. Thomas J. Sugrue, *The Origins of the Urban Crisis: Race and Inequality in Postwar Detroit* (Princeton, N.J.: Princeton University Press, 1996); Katz, *Price of Citizenship*, chap. 2; Katz, *The "Underclass" Debate*; Katznelson, *When Affirmative*

Action Was White, and "Was the Great Society a Lost Opportunity?"; Brown, *Race, Money*, chap. 5; Gary Gerstle, "Race and the Myth of the Liberal Consensus," *Journal of American History* (September 1995): 579–86.

37. Levenstein, "From Innocent Children to Unwed Mothers," 20–21. African Americans made up only 3% of mothers' pension recipients in 1931, 15% of ADC recipients in the late 1930s, and 31% in 1948. Howard, "Sowing the Seeds," 214–15.

38. Ladd-Taylor, *Mother-Work*, 200.

39. Mary Jo Bane and David T. Ellwood, *Welfare Realities: From Rhetoric to Reform* (Cambridge, Mass.: Harvard University Press, 1994), chap. 3; Diana M. Pearce, "Toil and Trouble: Women Workers and Unemployment Compensation," in *Women and Poverty*, ed. Barbara C. Gelpi, Nancy C. M. Harstock, Clare C. Novak, and Myra H. Strober (Chicago: University of Chicago Press, 1986), 141–61.

40. R. Kent Weaver, *Ending Welfare as We Know It* (Washington, D.C.: Brookings Institution Press, 2000); Sanford F. Schram, *After Welfare: The Culture of Postindustrial Social Policy* (New York: New York University Press, 2000); Michael Meeropol, *Surrender: How the Clinton Administration Completed the Reagan Revolution* (Ann Arbor: University of Michigan Press, 1998).

41. Jonus Pontusson, *Inequality and Prosperity: Social Europe versus Liberal America* (Ithaca, N.Y.: Cornell University Press, 2005), 181–82.

42. Jacob S. Hacker, "Privatizing Risk Without Privatizing the Welfare State: The Hidden Politics of Social Policy Retrenchment in the United States," *American Political Science Review* 98, 2 (2004): 243–60; Peter Taylor-Goody, ed., *Welfare States Under Pressure* (London: Sage, 2001); Jill Quadagno and Debra Street, "Ideology and Public Policy: Antistatism in American Welfare State Transformation," *Journal of Policy History* 17, 1 (2005): 52–71; Nancy J. Hirschmann and Ulrike Liebert, "Introduction: Engendering Welfare, Degendering Care: Theoretical and Comparative Perspectives on the United States and Europe," in *Women and Welfare: Theory and Practice in the United States and Europe*, ed. Nancy J. Hirschmann and Ulrike Liebert (New Brunswick, N.J.: Rutgers University Press, 2001), 1–22; Martin Rhodes, "Globalization and West European Welfare States: A Critical Review of Recent Debates," *Journal of European Social Policy* 6 (1996): 305–27; Gosta Esping-Anderson, *Social Foundations of Post-Industrial Economies* (New York: Oxford University Press, 1999); Katz, *Price of Citizenship*, 18; Richard Clayton and Jonus Pontusson, "Welfare State Retrenchment Revisited: Entitlement Cuts, Public Sector Restructuring, and Inegalitarian Trends in Advanced Capitalist Societies," *World Politics* 51 (1998): 67–98; Frances Fox Piven, "Welfare Policy and American Politics," in *Work, Welfare, and Politics: Confronting Poverty in the Wake of Welfare Reform*, ed. Piven, Joan Acker, Margaret Hallock, and Sandra Morgan (Eugene: University of Oregon Press, 2002), 19–33.

43. Stephen Pimpare, *The New Victorians: Poverty, Politics, and Propaganda in Two Gilded Ages* (New York: New York University Press, 2004), 111–13; Katz, *The Price of Citizenship*; Reese, *Backlash Against Welfare Mothers*, chaps. 8–9; Jamie Peck, *Workfare States* (New York: Guilford Press, 2001). These interpretations follow the logic of Piven and Cloward's influential analysis in *Regulating the Poor*. For scholarship that highlights conservative mobilization in the 1970s and 1980s, see David Brian Robertson, "Introduction: Loss of Confidence and Policy Change in

the 1970s," *Journal of Policy History* 10, 1 (1998): 1–18; Thomas Byrne Edsall, *The New Politics of Inequality* (New York: Norton, 1984); Thomas Ferguson and Joel Rogers, *Right Turn: The Decline of the Democrats and the Future of American Politics* (New York: Hill and Wang, 1986).

44. Diane Sainsbury, *Gender, Equality, and Welfare States* (Cambridge: Cambridge University Press, 1996), chap. 9; Marcia K. Meyers and Janet C. Gornick with Katerin E. Ross, "Gendering Welfare State Variation: Income Transfers, Employment Supports, and Family Poverty," in Hirschmann and Liebert, *Women and Welfare*, 215–43.

45. Noble, *Welfare as We Knew It*, 151.

46. Michael Katz, "Introduction: The Urban 'Underclass' as a Metaphor of Social Transformation," in *The "Underclass" Debate*, 13. See also Katz, *The Price of Citizenship*, 7; Reese, *Backlash Against Welfare Mothers*; Martin Gilens, *Why Americans Hate Welfare: Race, Media, and the Politics of Antipoverty Policy* (Chicago: University of Chicago Press, 1999); Kenneth J. Neubeck and Noel A. Cazenave, *Welfare Racism: Playing the Race Card Against America's Poor* (New York: Routledge, 2001).

47. Moynihan, "Beyond Welfare," Statement before Senate Subcommittee on Social Security and Family Policy, 23 January 1987, quoted in Michael Novak, *The New Consensus on Family and Welfare: A Community of Self-Reliance*, (New York: American Enterprise Institute, 1987), 52.

48. Ann Orloff, "Ending the Entitlements of Poor Single Mothers: Changing Social Policies, Women's Employment, and Caregiving in the Contemporary United States," in Hirschmann and Liebert, *Women and Welfare*, 134; Joyce Marie Mushaben, "Challenging the Maternalist Presumption: The Gender Politics of Welfare Reform in Germany and the United States," in *Women and Welfare*, 193; Nancy Fraser, "After the Family Wage: Gender Equity and the Welfare State," *Political Theory* 22, 4 (1994): 591–618.

49. Jane Lewis and Gertrude Arstrom, "Equality, Difference, and State Welfare: Labor Market and Family Policies in Sweden," *Feminist Studies* 18, 1 (Spring 1992): 59–87; Gro Hagemann, "Citizenship and Social Order: Gender Politics in Twentieth-Century Norway and Sweden," *Women's History Review* 11, 3 (2002): 417–29; Sheila B. Kamerman and Alfred J. Kahn, "Social Policy and Children in the United States and Europe," in *The Vulnerable*, ed. John L. Palmer and Elizabeth Sawhill (Washington, D.C.: Urban Institute, 1988), 351–80; *Income Transfers for Families with Children: An Eight Country Study* (Philadelphia: Temple University Press, 1983).

50. Thomas Byrne Edsall with Mary D. Edsall, *Chain Reaction: The Impact of Race, Rights, and Taxes on American Politics* (New York: Norton, 1991), for example, relies heavily on growing public antipathy to welfare. Detailed studies of public opinion suggest that most Americans are fairly ambivalent about public assistance programs. Faye Lomax Cook and Edith J. Barrett, *Support for the American Welfare State: The Views of Congress and the Public* (New York: Columbia University Press, 1992); Weaver, *Ending Welfare*, chap. 7; Noble, *Welfare as We Knew It*, 12; Joya Misra, Stephanie Moller, and Marina Karides, "Envisioning Dependency: Changing Media Depictions of Welfare in the Twentieth Century," *Social Problems* 50, 4 (2003): 482–504.

51. Premilla Nadasen, *Welfare Warriors: The Welfare Rights Movement in the United States* (New York: Routledge, 2005); Felicia Kornbluh, *The Battle for Welfare Rights: Politics and Poverty in Modern America* (Philadelphia: University of Pennsylvania Press, 2007); Annelise Orleck, *Storming Caesars Palace: How Black Mothers Fought Their Own War on Poverty* (Boston: Beacon Press, 2005); Anne M. Valk, "'Mother Power': The Movement for Welfare Rights in Washington, D.C., 1966–1972," *Journal of Women's History* 11, 4 (Winter 2000): 34–58; Frances Fox Piven and Richard A. Cloward, *Poor People's Movements: Why They Succeed, How They Fail* (New York: Pantheon, 1977), chap. 5; Nick Kotz and Mary Lynn Kotz, *A Passion for Equality: George A. Wiley and the Movement* (New York: Norton, 1977); Guida West, *The National Welfare Rights Movement: The Social Protest of Poor Women* (New York: Praeger, 1981).

52. After 1966, Hayward argues, "liberals . . . beat a hasty retreat; it would be twenty years before the subject of black family stability could be discussed again." Hayward, *Age of Reagan*, 94. See also Michael B. Katz, *The Undeserving Poor: From the War on Poverty to the War on Welfare* (New York: Pantheon, 1990), 24, 125, 138–39; Edsall and Edsall, *Chain Reaction*, 15.

53. Tentative Program, 58th Annual Meeting, Chamber of Commerce of the United States, April 26–28, Washington, D.C., Series I, Box 27, Folder "Welfare," Chamber of Commerce Records, Hagley Museum and Library, Wilmington, Delaware (hereafter Chamber of Commerce Records).

54. Katz, *Undeserving Poor*, 138–39, 125. See also Edsall and Edsall, *Chain Reaction*, 52, 121–22.

55. Todd Gitlin, *The Twilight of Common Dreams: Why America Is Wracked by Culture Wars* (New York: Holt, 1995); Steigerwald, *The Sixties*, 22; Robert Huckfeldt and Carol Weitzel Kohfeld, *Race and the Decline of Class in American Politics* (Urbana: University of Illinois Press, 1989); Jim Sleeper, *The Closest of Strangers: Liberalism and the Politics of Race in New York* (New York: Norton, 1990); William H. Chafe, *Unfinished Journey: America Since World War II* (New York: Oxford University Press, 1999), 461, 468; Bruce J. Schulman, *The Seventies: A Great Shift in American Culture, Society, and Politics* (New York: Free Press, 2001), chap. 2; Hugh Davis Graham, "Legacies of the 1960s: The American 'Rights Revolution' in an Era of Divided Governance," *Journal of Policy History* 10, 3 (1998): 267–88; J. David Hoeveler, Jr., *The Postmodernist Turn: American Thought and Culture in the 1970s* (New York: Twayne, 1996), chap. 9; David Farber, *The Age of Great Dreams: America in the 1960s* (New York: Hill and Wang, 1994), 265–56; David Burner, *Making Peace with the 60s* (Princeton, N.J.: Princeton University Press, 1996), 224, 218; William C. Berman, *America's Right Turn: From Nixon to Bush* (Baltimore: Johns Hopkins University Press, 1994). Some scholars also insist that liberals rejected "opportunity" in favor of "entitlement." See, e.g., Davies, *From Opportunity to Entitlement*; Alonzo L. Hamby, *Liberalism and Its Challengers: FDR to Reagan* (New York: Oxford University Press, 1985), 347–48; Hayward, *Age of Reagan*, 55.

56. Nadasen dismisses feminist interest in poverty and welfare in the early 1970s as "temporary and superficial." Nadasen, *Welfare Warriors*, 220. Guida West calls feminist involvement "negligible." West, *The National Welfare Rights Movement*, 234. See also Martha Davis, "Welfare Rights and Women's Rights in the

1960s," *Journal of Policy History* 8, 1 (1996): 144–65. Mimi Abramovitz acknowledged feminists' increasing interest in welfare and poverty in *Under Attack, Fighting Back: Women and Welfare in the United States* (New York: Monthly Review Press, 1996), 130–37.

57. Cobble, *The Other Women's Movement*, 116–19, 168.

58. On AFDC as a virtual "unemployment insurance" program for poor single mothers, see Robert Spalter-Roth, Beverly Burr, Heidi Hartmann, and Lois Shaw, *Welfare That Works: The Working Lives of AFDC Recipients: A Report to the Ford Foundation* (Washington, D.C.: Institute for Women's Policy Research, 1995).

Chapter 1. Reconstructing the Black Family: The Liberal Antipoverty Coalition in the 1960s

Epigraph: Eleanor Holmes Norton, "The Black Family: An Appraisal," reprinted in *Black Woman's Voice*, April 1980, Box 368, Folder "NCNW, 1970–80, n.d.," NCJW Washington, D.C. Office Records.

1. Walter P. Reuther, "The Elimination of Poverty in the United States—A Citizens' Crusade," 26 May 1965, Series I, Box 57, Folder 17, UAW Research Department Papers, Walter P. Reuther Library, Wayne State University, Detroit, Michigan, 2, 6; "CCAP: Second Annual Meeting," April 1966, Box 3, Folder 1, George Wiley Papers, Wisconsin Historical Society, Madison, Wisconsin (hereafter Wiley Papers).

2. "CCAP: Second Annual Meeting." See membership lists in Box 3, Folder 1, Wiley Papers.

3. Michael Harrington, *The Other America: Poverty in the United States* (New York: Macmillan, 1962).

4. Michael B. Katz, *In the Shadow of the Poorhouse: A Social History of Welfare in America*, 10th anniversary ed., rev. and updated (New York: Basic Books, 1996), 263.

5. Constitution of CCAP, RG21–001, Legislative Office, Box 41, Folder 4, George Meany Memorial Archive, Silver Spring, Maryland (hereafter Meany Archive).

6. "A Program to Abolish Poverty in the United States in 10 Years," n.d., Box 1, Folder "Annual Meeting-CCAP, April 13–14, 1966," Citizens Crusade Against Poverty Records, Walter P. Reuther Library, Wayne State University, Detroit, Michigan (hereafter CCAP Records), 2–3.

7. Walter Reuther to William F. Schnitzler, 17 April 1964, RG21–001, Legislative Office, Box 41, Folder 4, Meany Archive, 3.

8. Don Bonafede, "A Middleman in the Anti-Poverty War," *Herald Tribune*, n.d. (reprint), Box 3, Folder 2, Wiley Papers; "Crusade Training Program for Poor Moves Ahead" (CCAP Bulletin), September 1966, Box 1, Folder "CCAP Background," CCAP Records, 1; "The 'New Look' in UAW," *UAW Agenda for Action*, June 1968, Box 3, Folder 2, UAW Women's Department: Lillian Hatcher Papers, Walter P. Reuther Library, Wayne State University, Detroit, Michigan (hereafter Hatcher Papers).

9. Crusade Against Poverty, Statement of Policy and Program, 13 October 1964, RG21–001, Legislative Office, Box 41, Folder 3, Meany Archive, 1, 9; Constitution of CCAP, RG21–001, Legislative Office, Box 41, Folder 4, Meany Archive.

10. UAW Press Release, 26 May 1965, Box 8, Folder 31, UAW Women's Department: Dorothy Haener Papers, Walter P. Reuther Library, Wayne State University, Detroit, Michigan (hereafter Haener Papers).

11. Davies, *From Opportunity to Entitlement*, 3, 129, 136–37, 220, 242. Steven Hayward makes the same point about "liberal guilt among whites" and the shift to an "entitlement mentality." Steven F. Hayward, *The Age of Reagan: The Fall of the Old Liberal Order, 1964–1980* (Roseville, Calif.: Prima, 2001), 91–92, 146–47.

12. "Continuing Crusade," Industrial Union Department (AFL-CIO) *Agenda*, May 1966, Box 23, Folder 4, Haener Papers, 15.

13. "Sargent Shriver to House Subcommittee on War on Poverty," 12 April 1965, reprinted in *The Great Society Reader: The Failure of American Liberalism*, ed. Marvin E. Gettleman and David Mermelstein (New York: Random House, 1967), 207.

14. James Reston, "The Problem of Pessimism in the Poverty Program," *NYT*, 19 February 1965, 20.

15. H.R. Committee on Education and Labor, Hearings on the Economic Opportunity Act Amendments of 1967, 90th Cong., 2nd sess., 14 July 1967, 1953–54.

16. "Sargent Shriver to House Subcommittee," 205; Julius F. Rothman, "A Look at the War on Poverty," reprinted in *American Federationist*, November 1967, Box 8, Folder 31, Haener Papers.

17. Dona Cooper Hamilton and Charles V. Hamilton, *The Dual Agenda: The African-American Struggle for Civil and Economic Equality* (New York: Columbia University Press, 1997), 126, 123.

18. Most Kennedy-Johnson policymakers and historians deny that the War on Poverty *originated* as a response to African American demands. Davies, *From Opportunity to Entitlement*, 47, 61–67.

19. Whitney M. Young, Jr., *To Be Equal* (New York: McGraw-Hill, 1964), 26–67, 31, 239.

20. MacLean, *Freedom Is Not Enough: The Opening of the American Workplace* (Cambridge, Mass.: Harvard University Press, 2006), 105.

21. Walter P. Reuther, "The Elimination of Poverty in the United States—A Citizens' Crusade," 26 May 1965, Series I, Box 57, Folder 17, UAW Research Department Papers, 2, 6.

22. "Waging War on Poverty" (AFL-CIO Executive Council Statement), *American Federationist*, April 1964 (reprint), RG98–002, Vertical File, Box 46, Folder 14, Meany Archive, 1.

23. David Sullivan, "Labor's Role in the War on Poverty," *American Federationist*, April 1966, 10; Rothman, "A Look at the War on Poverty"; Carroll M. Hutton to Local Union Presidents and Education Committee Chairmen, 10 March 1965, Series I, Box 57, Folder 17, UAW Research Department Papers; UAW Citizenship-Education, "The Outsiders," n.d., Box 15, Folder 11, Haener Papers; "Labor's Role in the War on Poverty . . . An AFL-CIO Guide," RG98–002, Vertical File, Box 46, Folder 14, Meany Archive; George Meany to Presidents of National and Interna-

tional Unions, 16 July 1965, RG1-038, Office of the President, Box 48, Folder 15, Meany Archive.

24. "Remarks by the Honorable Jerome P. Cavanagh Before Labor Conference to Mobilize Against Poverty," and Roberta McBride and Mike Marasco to Dorothy Haener, 30 April 1965, both in Box 23, Folder 4, Haener Papers; Maryann Mahaffey to members of Detroit Task Force on Hunger and Malnutrition, 12 June 1972, Box 15, Folder 1, Haener Papers; City of Detroit Task Force on Hunger and Malnutrition, Interim Report, 16 March 1971, Box 14, Folder 20, Haener Papers.

25. Rothman, "A Look at the War on Poverty," 8. For evidence and examples of labor participation in antipoverty programs, see, for example, "Report of AFL-CIO Activities in the Poverty Program," 7 July 1965, RG1–038, Office of the President, Box 48, Folder 15, Meany Archive. There is little evidence that union members, as a group, were as enthusiastic about federal antipoverty efforts as their leaders were. Michael Brown, among others, has argued that support for broad social welfare programs was largely "confined to the leadership of the labor movement." Brown, *Race, Money, and the American Welfare State*, 277–78.

26. Joseph E. Allen, John Johnson, and Harold Fleming to Andrew Heiskell and A. Philip Randolph, "Report of the Urban Coalition Task Force on Communications and Public Support," 3 January 1968, Box 535, Folder 2, UAW President's Office: Walter P. Reuther Records, Walter P. Reuther Library, Wayne State University, Detroit, Michigan (hereafter Reuther Records), 2; John B. Babcock to Chief Editors, 14 November 1967, Box 535, Folder 1, Reuther Records, 1–2, 4.

27. Joan Doolittle, "Rochester Revisited," *Issues in Industrial Society* 1 (1969), RG98–002, Vertical Files, Box 14, Folder 2, Meany Archive, 45–47.

28. National Association of Manufacturers, "The Answer is Jobs," n.d. (1968), Accession 1411, Series I, Box 241, Folder "Urban Affairs Division, General, 1968 #200-A" and Statement of the NAM on Economic Opportunity Programs, 11 August 1967, Series IV, Box 120, Folder "Poverty," both in National Association of Manufacturers Papers, Hagley Museum and Library, Wilmington, Delaware (hereafter NAM Papers).

29. NAM, "The Answer Is Jobs."

30. See various "Action Reports" and the pamphlet "The Quiet Revolution," Series I, Box 241, Folder "Urban Affairs Division," NAM Papers.

31. "Report of Attendance at a Meeting of the Urban Coalition—Emergency Convocation," 24 August 1967, Series I, Box 80, Folder "Economics-Fact-Finding Council Material-Urban Coalition," NCJW National Office Records; "Statement of Principles, Goals, and Commitments: Emergency Convocation: The Urban Coalition," n.d., Box 532, Folder 4, Reuther Records, 1; Urban Coalition Action Council, "A Minimum Standard of Decency Beneath Which No American Shall Live," Box 533, Folder 6, Reuther Records.

32. Articles of Incorporation of The Urban Coalition, 8 April 1968, Box 10, Folder 13, Center for Community Change Records, Reuther Library, 1–2.

33. "The Urban Coalition and Urban America Merge," *National Urban Coalition Report*, March 1970, Box 33, Folder 6, Reuther Records, 1.

34. "From the Locals," *National Urban Coalition Report*, March 1970, President's Office, Box 533, Folder 6, Reuther Records, 7–8.

35. For NWRO membership statistics and racial and gender breakdown, see Guida West, *The National Welfare Rights Movement: The Social Protest of Poor Women* (New York: Praeger, 1981), 44–50.

36. Preston R. Wilcox to Interested Observers, n.d.; Faith A. Seidenberg to Michael Harrington, 19 April 1966; and Michael Harrington, "Truth and Tactics," *Herald-Tribune,* 17 April 1966 (reprint), all in Box 3, Folder 2, Wiley Papers.

37. "By or For the Poor?" *New Republic,* 30 April 1966, 5–6;

38. "The Poor Are Human," *Nation,* 2 May 1966, 508.

39. George Wiley to Richard Boone, 4 April 1966, Box 3, Folder 1, Wiley Papers, 1.

40. George Wiley, "Proposal for the Establishment of an Anti-Poverty Action Center," 7 April 1966, Box 5, Folder 13; George Wiley to Sidney Emerman, 12 May 1966, Box 10, Folder 8, Wiley Papers.

41. Nick Kotz and Mary Lynn Kotz, *A Passion for Equality: George A. Wiley and the Movement* (New York: Norton, 1977), 184–91.

42. Wiley's papers are full of requests for membership, opinions, and advice.

43. Mildred Jeffrey to Walter Reuther, 10 September 1969, Box 510, Folder 16, Reuther Records, 1.

44. "The Urban Crisis and New Challenges to Women: An Address by Mary Dublin Keyserling to Presidents of New Jersey Women's Clubs and Organizations," Trenton, 2 October 1967, Box 4, Folder 120, Mary Dublin Keyserling Papers, Arthur and Elizabeth Schlesinger Library, Radcliffe Institute for Advanced Study, Cambridge, Massachussetts (hereafter Keyserling Papers), 6.

45. "Helping People Help Themselves—The Attack on Poverty: An Address by Mary Dublin Keyserling," Maryland, Virginia, and District of Columbia Home Economics Workshop, University of Maryland, 29 October 1965, Box 4, Folder 111, Keyserling Papers, 13.

46. Keyserling, "The Urban Crisis and New Challenges to Women," 1.

47. H.R. Committee on Education and Labor, Hearing on H.R. 8311, The Economic Opportunity Act Amendments of 1967, 90th Cong., 1st sess., 14 July 1967, 1991–94.

48. Keyserling, "The Urban Crisis and New Challenges to Women," 4–5.

49. H.R. Committee on Education and Labor, Hearing on the Economic Opportunity Amendments of 1971, 92nd Cong., 1st sess., 12 May 1971, 1722; Mrs. Joanne Kissinger to Honorable John Meyers, "Excerpts from League Responses to First Time Action on Welfare Reform," Series 4, Box 598, Folder "Welfare Reform: Time for Action Letters—8 February 1971—Misc.," League of WomenVoters Papers, Library of Congress, Washington, D.C. (hereafter LWV Papers); Mrs. Erwin C. Hannum, "A Summary of League Position, Strategy and Action on Welfare: January–October 1971," Series 4, Box 582, Folder "Welfare Reform: Basic Documents, 1971–72," LWV Papers, 1–2.

50. Ms. Mary A. Hallaren, Executive Director's Report, Women in Community Service, Inc., Twelfth Annual Meeting, 2–4 May 1977, Box 257, Folder "WICS Annual Meetings 1977, part II," NCJW Washington, D.C., Office Records, 3.

51. Documents in Box 9, Folder 22, Catherine East Papers, Schlesinger Library (hereafter East Papers); Citizens' Advisory Council on the Status of Women, Task

Force on Health and Welfare, Special Meeting on Volunteer Services, 31 July 1967, Box 50, Folder 986, Esther Peterson Papers, Schlesinger Library (hereafter Peterson Papers), 7–9.

52. Hearings on H.R. 8311, 14 August 1967, 1954, 1956, 1992–93.

53. Christopher Norwood, "The War on Poverty: Substitute for an Integrated Society," *Commonweal*, 15 November 1968, 258.

54. Conference Proceedings, Second Annual Conference on Women in the War on Poverty, May 1968, Box 11, Folder 4, Hatcher Papers, 3.

55. Report: NCJW School for Community Action #3: Women on the Move, n.d., Box 11, Folder 3, Hatcher Papers, 2.

56. "Women Support the War on Poverty," *NYT*, 13 November 1967, 55.

57. H.R., Hearings on H.R. 8311, 13 July 1967, 1763.

58. Susie Berg Waldman, *The Immovable Middle Class: 1964–1965 School for Community Action*, June 1964, Series I, Box 128, Folder "Public Affairs Schools II—1964," NCJW National Office Records, 1 (Introduction), 2 (Section II Lecture).

59. Mrs. Leonard H. Weiner to Section President, 29 August 1969, Series II, Box 17, Folder "Community Action School 'Poverty Issue' 1969 (No. 5)," NCJW National Office Records, 2; NCJW Press Release, 31 October 1969, Series II, Box 19, Folder "Economics: Anti-Poverty Council Material," NCJW National Office Records, 1.

60. NCJW, "Early Report on Women on the Move," n.d., Series II, Box 17, Folder "Community Action School, No. 3," NCJW National Office Records, 1.

61. "Report: NCJW School for Community Action #3: Women on the Move," n.d., Box 11, Folder 3, Hatcher Papers, 2.

62. Citizens' Advisory Council on the Status of Women, Task Force on Health and Welfare, Special Meeting on Volunteer Services, 31 July 1967, Box 50, Folder 986, Peterson Papers, 14.

63. NCJW News Release, 31 October 1969, Series II, Box 17, Folder "Community Action School 'Poverty Issue' 1969 (No. 5)," NCJW National Office Records, 2.

64. "The Pearl Lerner Willen Institute," October 1969; "NCJW School for Community Action V," 6 October 1969; Arthur Hillman to Discussion Leaders, n.d., all in Box 47, Folder "Poverty Institute, April 1970," National Federation of Settlements and Neighborhood Centers Records, Social Welfare History Archives, University of Minnesota, Minneapolis (hereafter NFS Records).

65. Catherine Gelles (UAW Women's Auxiliaries), Press Release, 26 May 1967, and OEO Press Release, 8 May 1967, both in Box 11, Folder 1, Hatcher Papers.

66. Text of Remarks of the President to Participants in the Conference on Women in the War on Poverty, 8 May 1967, Box 11, Folder 1, Hatcher Papers, 1.

67. Sargent Shriver to Conference on Women in the War on Poverty, 8 May 1967, Box 11, Folder 1, Hatcher Papers, 3–4.

68. Charles E. Silberman, "Is Education Enough?" Address, 16th Annual Conference, Council on Foundations, 19 May 1965, Box 3, Folder 3, Wiley Papers, 4–5.

69. Lee Rainwater and William L. Yancey, *The Moynihan Report and the Politics of Controversy* (Cambridge, Mass.: MIT Press, 1967), 126.

70. Daryl Michael Scott, *Contempt and Pity: Social Policy and the Image of the Damaged Black Psyche, 1880–1996* (Chapel Hill: University of North Carolina Press,

1997), 161–82; Nicholas Lemann, *The Promised Land: The Great Black Migration and How it Changed America* (New York: Vintage, 1991), 177; Michael Katz, *The Undeserving Poor: From the War on Poverty to the War on Welfare* (New York: Pantheon Books, 1989), 24; William Julius Wilson, *The Truly Disadvantaged: The Inner City, the Underclass, and Public Policy* (Chicago: University of Chicago Press, 1987), 21.

71. Daniel P. Moynihan, "The President and the Negro: The Moment Lost," *Commentary*, February 1967, 31–45; Daryl Michael Scott, "The Politics of Pathology: The Ideological Origins of the Moynihan Controversy," *Journal of Policy History* 8, 1 (1996), 100–101; Lemann, *Promised Land*, 177.

72. Rainwater and Yancey, *Moynihan Report*, 248.

73. Moynihan, *The Negro Family*, March 1965, reprinted in Rainwater and Yancey, *The Moynihan Report*.

74. Rainwater and Yancey, *The Moynihan Report*, 7.

75. Scott, *Contempt and Pity*, 5, 75, 80; Alice O'Connor, *Poverty Knowledge: Social Science, Social Policy, and the Poor in Twentieth-Century United States History* (Princeton, N.J.: Princeton University Press, 2001), 195–209.

76. James Farmer, "The Controversial Moynihan Report," 18 December 1965, in Rainwater and Yancey, *The Moynihan Report*, 410.

77. Moynihan, *The Negro Family*, 47.

78. James Farmer, "The Controversial Moynihan Report," 410.

79. "An Address by Dr. Martin Luther King, Jr.," Abbott House, Westchester County, New York, 29 October 1965, reprinted in Rainwater and Yancey, *The Moynihan Report*, 403, 406–7.

80. Ibid., 413–14.

81. "A Man Around the House," *Ebony* (n.d.) (reprint), Box 5, Folder 8, Wiley Papers.

82. Bayard Rustin, "Why Don't Negroes," in Rainwater and Yancey, *The Moynihan Report*, 418.

83. Farmer, "The Controversial Moynihan Report," 410. While Moynihan did not include his policy proposals in his Report, he advocated jobs for black men in a number of other venues. See, for example, "Employment, Income, and the Ordeal of the Negro Family," *Daedalus* 94, 4 (Fall 1965): 745–70.

84. As Michael Katz points out, administration policymakers well understood the structural barriers that kept black Americans poor but advocated a service strategy nonetheless. Katz, *Undeserving Poor*, chap 3.

85. Quoted in Lawrence Lynn, Jr., "A Decade of Policy Developments in the Income Maintenance System," in *A Decade of Federal Antipoverty Programs: Achievements, Failures, and Lessons*, ed. Robert H. Haveman (New York: Academic Press, 1977), 99.

86. Katznelson, "Was the Great Society a Lost Opportunity?"; Davies, *From Opportunity to Entitlement*, chap. 1; Noble, *Welfare as We Knew It*, chap. 5; Mittlestadt, *From Welfare to Workfare*, 11.

87. Lyndon Baines Johnson, Speech at Detroit Democratic Fundraising Dinner, 26 June 1964, in *Great Society Reader*, 21.

88. Michael Harrington, Paul Jacobs, and Frank Mankiewicz quoted in Daniel Patrick Moynihan, *Maximum Feasible Misunderstanding: Community Action in the*

War on Poverty (New York: The Free Press, 1969), 84; Diana Pearce, "Welfare Is Not *for* Women: Why the War on Poverty Cannot Conquer the Feminization of Poverty," in *Women, the State, and Welfare*, ed. Linda Gordon (Madison: University of Wisconsin Press, 1990), 271.

89. Quoted in Kathleen A. Laughlin, *Women's Work and Public Policy: A History of the Women's Bureau, U.S. Department of Labor, 1945–1970* (Boston: Northeastern University Press, 2000), 83.

90. Moynihan, *Maximum Feasible Misunderstanding*, 85, 99.

91. Pearce, "Welfare is Not *for* Women," 271–72; Congress, Senate, Committee on Labor and Public Welfare, *Examination of the War on Poverty*, Part 7, 90th Cong., 1st sess., 8 June 1967, 2361; Jill Quadagno and Catherine Forbes, "The Welfare State and the Cultural Reproduction of Gender: Making Good Girls and Boys in the Job Corps," *Social Problems* 42, 2 (1995): 171–90; Eileen Boris, "Contested Rights: The Great Society Between Home and Work" in *The Great Society and the High Tide of Liberalism*, ed. Sidney M. Milkis and Jerome M. Mileur (Amherst: University of Massachusetts Press, 2005), 115–44; Ellen Reese, *Backlash Against Welfare Mothers: Past and Present* (Berkeley: University of California Press, 2005), 109–13.

92. "Facing the Facts About Women's Lives Today: An Address by Mary Dublin Keyserling," Midwest Regional Pilot Conference on New Approaches to Counseling Girls in the 1960s, Chicago, 26 February 1965, Box 4, Folder 110, Keyserling Papers, 8, 9.

93. "The Nation's Working Mothers and the Need for Day Care: Address by Mary Dublin Keyserling," National Conference on Day-Care Services, Washington, D.C., 14 May 1965, Box 4, Folder 110, Keyserling Papers, 1; "Women in Poverty: An Address by Mary Dublin Keyserling," NCJW Essex County Section, 9 March 1966, Milburn, N.J., Box 4, Folder 114, Keyserling Papers, 4, 6, 8–11.

94. Laughlin, *Women's Work and Public Policy*, 115–19; Esther Peterson to Dr. Esther Westervelt, 19 April 1968, Box 26, Folder 488, Peterson Papers; Notes for Mrs. Peterson on Manpower Programs—and Women, July 1968, Box 62, Folder 1191, Peterson Papers.

95. Keyserling, "The Urban Crisis and New Challenges to Women," 5.

96. Prospectus of the National Committee on Household Employment, n.d., Box 15, Folder 18, Haener Papers.

97. Women's Bureau, "Who Are the Disadvantaged Girls 16–21 Years Old?" and "Women in Poverty," July 1964, Box 199, Folder "Women's Bureau 1965," NCJW Washington, D.C. Office Records.

98. Notes for Keynote Address, Women on the Move: A Community Forum Concerning Household Employment, 16 November 1966, Series I, Box 99, Folder "Labor: NCHE, 1964," NCJW National Office Records, 2; Office of Equal Opportunity, Job Corps Centers for Women, n.d., Box 13, Folder 4, East Papers, 1.

99. Quoted in Quadagno and Forbes, "The Welfare State and the Cultural Reproduction of Gender," 175.

100. Laughlin, *Women's Work and Public Policy*, 117.

101. Jeanne L. Noble to Participants in National Conference on the Proposed Job Corps for Women, 23 August 1964, Box 13, Folder 4, East Papers, 2.

102. Department of Labor, Manpower Administration, Bureau of Work Pro-

grams, "Girls in the Neighborhood Youth Corps Program," February 1967, Box 15, Folder 6, Hatcher Papers, 1, 3.

103. Quadagno and Forbes, "The Welfare State and the Cultural Reproduction of Gender."

104. DOL, "Girls in the Neighborhood Youth Corps Program," 1, 3.

105. OEO, "Job Corps Facts," n.d., Box 23, Folder 4, Haener Papers, 3.

106. "Women's Program Growing, Changing," *The Corpsman*, 20 April 1967, Box 18, Folder 10, Hatcher Papers, 2; "Job Corps Education Is Not Just Training for Jobs," *Corspman*, 20 April 1967, Box 18, Folder 10, Hatcher Papers, 5.

107. Quoted in Benetta B. Washington, Ph.D., to Conference of Women in the War on Poverty, 8 May 1967, Box 11, Folder 1, Hatcher Papers, 4.

108. Working Paper: WICS, Inc., Memorandum for Mr. Shriver, 21 October 1965, Series I, Box 29, Folder "NCJW Board Meeting 11/65," NCJW National Office Records, 2.

109. "Labor's Role in the War on Poverty . . . An AFL-CIO Guide," RG98–002, Vertical File, Box 46, Folder 14, Meany Archive, 8.

110. "Women in Poverty, An Address by Mary Dublin Keyserling" NCJW, Essex County Section, 9 March 1966, Milburn, New Jersey, Box 4, Folder 114, Keyserling Papers, 5.

111. The President's Task Force on the War Against Poverty, "Working Paper: The Women's Job Corps—An Attack on Persistent Poverty," July 1964, Box 13, Folder 4, East Papers, 6.

112. DOL, "Girls in the Neighborhood Youth Corps Program."

113. Gail Falk [Staff Attorney, Legal Aid Society of Charleston, West Virginia] to Sir [Department of Labor], 11 January 1972, Box 13, Folder 4, East Papers, 1–2.

114. The term "class-conscious liberals" is from Daryl Michael Scott, who uses it to distinguish between "racial liberals" who emphasized cultural pathology and structuralists (the "class-conscious liberals") who emphasized instead the social causes of poverty. He notes that these positions largely coexisted until the 1960s and then began to diverge. Scott, "The Politics of Pathology," 81–105.

115. Frank Riessman, "In Defense of the Negro Family" in Rainwater and Yancey, *Moynihan Report*, 475.

116. Elizabeth Herzog, "Is There a 'Breakdown' of the Negro Family?" in Rainwater and Yancy, *The Moynihan Report*, 353; Hylan Lewis, "Agenda Paper No. V: The Family: Resources for Change—Planning Session for the White House Conference 'To Fulfill These Rights'," ibid., 335.

117. Quoted ibid., 235.

118. Charles Silberman, *Crisis in Black and White* (New York: Random House, 1964), 118.

119. Herbert J. Gans, "The Negro Family: Reflections on the Moynihan Report," *Commonweal*, 15 October 1965, reprinted in Rainwater and Yancey, *The Moynihan Report.*, 447, 452–53.

120. Mittlestadt, *From Welfare to Workfare*, 139–41.

121. Neal Herrick, "Note for Esther Peterson Re: Task Force on Health and Welfare Report," 25 April 1968," and Citizens' Advisory Council on the Status of

Women, Task Force on Health and Welfare, *Women and Their Families in Our Rapidly Changing Society*, April 1968, both in Box 50, Folder 987, Peterson Papers.

122. Women in Minority Groups—Confidential Preliminary Draft, 14 March 1963, Box 46, Folder 912, Peterson Papers, 4, 7–8; Dorothy Height, *The Negro Woman*, 1–2.

123. Quoted in Mittlestadt, *From Welfare to Workfare*, 143.

124. Caroline Ware, "Report to Commission on Consultation on Minority Groups," 23 April 1963, Box 46, Folder 912, Peterson Papers, 1–2.

125. Martha W. Griffiths to Honorable W. Willard Wirtz, 24 August 1967, Box 10, Folder 48, East Papers, 4.

126. Task Force on the Disadvantaged Family, "To Fulfill the Rights of Negro Women in Disadvantaged Families. A Statement for the White House Conference 'To Fulfill These Rights'," 1–2 June, 1966, Box 11, Folder 4, East Papers, 6. See also Pauli Murray to Editors, *Newsweek* Magazine, 4 September 1965, Box 10, Folder 47, East Papers, 2.

127. Elizabeth Wickenden, "The Negro Family: Society's Victim or Scapegoat?" Box 11, Folder 5, East Papers, 3.

128. Ibid.

129. Susan Filson, "Aid Plans Seen Slighting Role of Negro Women," *Washington Post*, 7 November 1967 (reprint), Box 11, Folder 5, East Papers.

130. Mary Dublin Keyserling, "The Negro Woman at Work—Gains and Problems," presented to the Conference on The Negro Woman in the USA: New Roles in Family and Community Life, Washington, D.C., 11 November 1965, Box 4, Folder 111, Keyserling Papers, 6–8.

131. Article reprint, 20 October 1967, in Box 11, Folder 5, East Papers. "I know of no woman, white or Negro, concerned with the status of women," East insisted, "who does not consider [Moynihan] an anti-feminist." Alan Reitman to Catherine East, 1 November 1967 and Catherine East to Bob (?), 10 December 1967, both in Box 10, Folder 48, East Papers.

132. Women's Bureau, "Economic Security and Welfare: Background Paper—Economic Status of Negro Women," 26 May 1966, Box 199, Folder "White House Conference, 'To Fulfill These Rights,' 1966—Miscellany," NCJW Washington, D.C., Office Records.

133. Women's Bureau, "Women in Poverty—Jobs and the Need for Jobs," April 1968, Box 153, Folder "Conference on Women in the War on Poverty, 1968," NCJW Washington, D.C., Office Records.

134. Catherine East to Dr. Eric J. Weiss, 27 November 1968, Box 11, Folder 3, East Papers.

135. Norman O. Wilson and Eric J. Weiss, "'They Carry the Burden Alone . . .': The Socio-Economic Living Pattern of Oregon Women with Dependents, A Research Report," Oregon Bureau of Labor, 1968, Box 11, Folder 2, East Papers, 98, 101, 106–8.

136. Rhoda Lois Blumberg, *Civil Rights: The 1960s Freedom Struggle*, rev. ed. (Boston: Twayne, 1991), 167.

137. Scott, *Contempt and Pity*, 147.

138. Rainwater and Yancey, *The Moynihan Report*, 139–40.

139. *Report of the National Advisory Committee on Civil Disorders* (New York: New York Times, 1968), 1, 14, 258, 262, 417.

140. Gans, "The Negro Family," 448.

141. On state-level welfare "backlashes" in the 1950s, see Reese, *Backlash Against Welfare Mothers*, chaps. 3–6.

142. Mittlestadt, *From Welfare to Workfare*, 163.

143. Arnold Hirsch, *Making the Second Ghetto: Race and Housing in Chicago, 1940–1960* (New York: Cambridge University Press, 1983); Thomas J. Sugrue, *The Origins of the Urban Crisis: Race and Inequality in Postwar Detroit* (Princeton, N.J.: Princeton University Press, 1996).

144. Frances Fox Piven and Richard A. Cloward, *Regulating the Poor: The Functions of Public Welfare*, updated ed. (New York: Vintage, 1993), chap. 6; Brown, *Race, Money*, 368.

145. For a detailed analysis of Long's political ideology, see Michael Sterling Martin, "Senator Russell B. Long of Louisiana: A Political Biography, 1948–1986" (Ph.D. diss., University of Arkansas, 2003).

146. Sen. Finance Committee, Hearings on H.R. 12080, 21 September 1967, 1652.

147. Ibid., 22–24 August 1967, 405.

148. Ibid., 21 September 1967, 1648.

149. Annelise Orleck, *Storming Caesars Palace: How Black Mothers Fought Their Own War on Poverty* (Boston, 2005), 83. For a useful discussion of the development of this stereotype, see Deborah Gray White, *Ar'n't I a Woman? Female Slaves in the Plantation South* (New York: Norton, 1985), 27–61.

150. Moynihan, *The Negro Family*, 60.

151. Whitney Young, *To Be Equal*, 175; Sen. Finance Committee, Hearings on H.R. 12080, 29 August 1967, 780; "A Proposal by the Southern Christian Leadership Conference for the Development of a Nonviolent Action Movement for the Greater Chicago Area," in Clayborne Carson et al., *The Eyes on the Prize: Civil Rights Reader* (New York: Penguin, 1991), 296.

152. Ray Marshall, "Black and White Blue-Collar Workers and Unions," in *Blue-Collar Workers: A Symposium on Middle America*, ed. Sar A. Levitan (New York: McGraw-Hill, 1971), 184.

153. Ellen Winston, "Mothers Working or Preparing for Employment," 20 May 1966, Box 11, Folder 5, East Papers.

154. Catherine East to Toni (?), 20 June 1967, Box 10, Folder 48, East Papers, 1.

155. "Statement of William L. Taylor, Staff Director of the United States Commission on Civil Rights, in Connection with Title II of H.R. 12080 (90th Congress)," n.d., Series 5, Box C43, Folder "U.S. Commission on Civil Rights, 1966–68," National Association for the Advancement of Colored People Papers, Library of Congress (hereafter NAACP Papers), 1–2. For a rare dissent from this viewpoint, see Antonia Chayes to the Honorable Maurine Neuberger, 22 May 1967, Box 10, Folder 48, East Papers, 1–2.

156. Joint Economic Committee, Subcommittee on Fiscal Policy, Hearings on Income Maintenance, 90th Cong., 2nd sess., 12 June 1968, 79.

157. Sen. Finance Committee, Hearings on HR 12080, Part 1, 22 August 1967, 262–63.

158. Ibid., Part 2, 19 September 1967, 1503–4.

159. Ibid., 22 September 1967, 1729.

160. Hart quoted in Sylvia Law, "Women, Work, and Patriarchy," 1263; Reuther in Sen. Finance Committee, Hearings on H.R. 12080, 21 September 1967, 1688.

161. Sen. Finance Committee, Hearings on H.R. 12080, 11 September 1967, 1001–1002.

162. Moynihan, *The Negro Family*, 71.

163. Sen. Finance Committee, Hearings on H.R. 12080, 21 September 1967, 1648.

164. "A Vote for Children," *NYT*, 22 June 1965, 34.

165. Sen. Finance Committee, Hearings on H.R. 12080, 21 September 1967, 1685.

166. "Flat Grants in Welfare," *NYT*, 17 July 1968, 42.

167. Sen. Finance Committee, Hearings on H.R. 12080, 29 August 1967, 780, 787–88.

168. Quoted in Premilla Nadasen, *Welfare Warriors: The Welfare Rights Movement in the United States* (New York: Routledge, 2005) 143.

169. Quoted in Felicia Kornbluh, "A Right to Welfare? Poor Women, Professionals, and Poverty Programs, 1935–1975" (Ph.D. diss., Princeton University, 2000), 126.

170. Joint Economic Committee, Hearings on Income Maintenance, 12 June 1968, 66–69, 77–78.

171. "The Smith Experiment," *New Republic*, 21 February 1970, 8.

172. Robert Coles, "The Poor Don't Want to Be Middle-Class," *NYT*, 19 December 1965, VI, 58.

173. "A Proposal to Establish a National Citizens Committee for a Guaranteed Income," n.d., and "Minutes, Organizing Meeting for a National Citizens Committee on Guaranteed Income, 8 May 1968," both in Box 189, Folder 12, Reuther Records.

174. Davies, *From Opportunity to Entitlement*; Gilbert Steiner, *The State of Welfare* (Washington, D.C.: Brookings Institution, 1971), 6–9; Kornbluh, "A Right to Welfare?" chaps. 1 and 2.

175. A Program to Abolish Poverty in the United States in 10 Years, n.d., Box 1, Folder "Annual Meeting-CCAP April 13–14, 1966," CCAP Records, 2–3.

176. "The Rights Movement Broadens," *Providence Evening Bulletin*, 17 August 1966, Box 27, Folder 7, Wiley Papers; Robert B. Semple, Jr., "2 More Score U.S. Help for Poor," *NYT*, 7 December 1966, 32; "Dr. King to Press Antiwar Stand," *NYT*, 24 March 1967, 2. For Poor People's Campaign, see Robert T. Chase, "Class Resurrection: The Poor People's Campaign of 1968 and Resurrection City," *Essays in History* 40 (1998), http://etext.virginia.edu/journals.

177. Thomas A. Johnson, "State's NAACP Opposes the War and New Charter," *NYT*, 23 October 1967, 35; John Leo, "Urban League Urges Guaranteed Annual Income to Replace Welfare System," *NYT*, 23 January 1969, 15; Ernest Garvey, "A Substitute for Welfare," *Commonweal*, 12 July 1968, 462; Bayard Rustin to Mrs. Mar-

tin S. Barol, 20 January 1968, Box 19, Folder 11, Bayard Rustin Papers, Library of Congress (hereafter Rustin Papers), 1.

178. Robert Theobald, "The Guaranteed Income: What and Why" in Chamber of Commerce of the United States, *Proceedings of the National Symposium on Guaranteed Income*, 9 December 1966, Series 4, Box 77, NAM Papers, 35–44.

179. Fred P. Graham, "Crime Panel Asks Sweeping Reform in 18-Month Study," *NYT*, 19 February 1967, 69; Leroy F. Aarons, "Welfare Rights Unit Scores," *Washington Post*, 7 December 1967, D13; *Report of the National Advisory Committee on Civil Disorders* (New York: New York Times, 1968), 462; *Poverty amid Plenty*, 12 November 1969 (Washington, D.C.: Government Printing Office, 1970), 60–61; John Herbers, "Nixon Panel Asks Revenue Sharing," *NYT*, 15 January 1969, 30; Albert L. Kraus, "Income for the Poor," *NYT*, 5 June 1968, 61; "Businessmen Weigh Welfare Mess," *Business Week*, 18 May 1968, 102.

180. "Welfare and Illfare: The Alternatives to Poverty," *Time*, 13 December 1968, 25.

181. Davies, *From Opportunity to Entitlement*, 3, 129.

182. The Ad Hoc Committee on the Triple Revolution held this view. Gettleman and Mermelstein, *Great Society Reader*, 178; Davies, *From Opportunity to Entitlement*, 47–48.

183. *A Freedom Budget for All Americans* (New York: A. Philip Randolph Institute, 1966), viii, 32.

184. *Poverty amid Plenty*, 8.

185. "OEO and the Working Poor," *America*, 5 April 1969, 391.

186. *Poverty amid Plenty*, 8.

187. Tom Wicker, "Should the Poor Get Richer?—III," *NYT*, 22 December 1966, 32.

188. "A Freedom Budget for the Poor," *Business Week*, 4 May 1968, 70.

189. James Tobin, "Income Guarantees and Incentives," *Agenda*, January 1967, RG98–002, Vertical File, Box 20, Folder 4, Meany Archive, 25.

190. *Poverty amid Plenty*, 5, 7, 47.

191. Ibid., ii, 5, 8, 25–27, 47, 59, 81–82.

192. Chamber of Commerce of the United States, "The Concept of Poverty," Series I, Box 27, Chamber Records, 11–13; Chamber of Commerce of the United States, "Proceedings of the National Symposium on Guaranteed Income," 9 December 1966, Series IV, Box 77, NAM Papers, 1; "Chamber Symposium Airs Pros and Cons: Does Everyone Have a Right to Guaranteed Income?" *Washington Report*, 16 December 1966, Series 1,Box 27, NAM Papers, 1.

193. "Guaranteed Income Topic Sparks Sharp Controversy," *Spokane (Washington) Spokesman-Review*, 10 December 1966 (reprint), Series IV, Box 77, NAM Papers; Chamber of Commerce, "Proceedings," 56.

194. Ibid., 45–46.

195. "Income Subsidies Gain Acceptance," *Ft. Worth Star Telegram*, 19 December 1966 (reprint), Series IV, Box 77, NAM Papers.

196. Richard L. Strout, "Negative Income Tax Argued," *Christian Science Monitor*, 12 December 1966, ibid.

197. Richard L. Madden, "Governor Plans Welfare Parley," *NYT*, 13 May 1967,

35; "Report from the Steering Committee of the Arden House Conference on Public Welfare" in Joint Economic Committee, Hearings on Income Maintenance, Volume 2 (1968), 449–50.

198. "Report from the Steering Committee," 449, 468.

199. "Welfare Industrialists," *NYT*, 6 November 1967, 46.

200. "Report from the Steering Committee," 453, 455–58, 460, 462–63, 469.

201. Ibid., 446–47.

202. Bayard Rustin, "The Lessons of the Long Hot Summer" (New York: A. Philip Randolph Institute, 1967), Box 140, Folder "A. Philip Randolph Institute, 1967," NCJW Washington, D.C. Office Records, 4; Bayard Rustin, "On to a Guaranteed Income," *New York Tribune*, 5 September 1965 (reprint), RG1–038, Office of the President, Box 31, Folder 22, Meany Archive.

203. Urban Coalition, Draft Position Paper on Welfare and Poverty, 11 December 1968, Box 532, Folder 9, Reuther Papers, 3.

204. Statement by AFL-CIO Executive Council on Waging War Against Poverty, 21 February 1964, RG1–038, Office of the President, Box 48, Folder 14, 5; News from the AFL-CIO, 7 July 1965, RG98–002, Vertical File, Box 46, Folder 15, Meany Archive.

205. Walter P. Reuther, CCAP Press Release, 17 April 1966, Series IV, Box A43, Folder "CCAP, 66–67," NAACP Papers, 3.

206. "Coalition Television Message Premiered," *National Urban Coalition Report*, March 1970, President's Office, Box 533, Folder 6, Reuther Papers, 3–4; John W. Gardner to George Meany, 11 November 1969, RG1–038, Office of the President, Box 54, Folder 11, Meany Archive.

207. Tobin, "Income Guarantees and Incentives," 25.

Chapter 2. Legislating the Male-Breadwinner Family: The Family Assistance Plan

Epigraph: Quoted in Sen. Finance Committee, Hearing on H.R. 16311: Family Assistance Act of 1970, 91st Cong., 2nd sess., 26 August 1970, 1602.

1. "Transcript of Nixon's Address to Nation Outlining Proposals for Welfare Reform," *NYT*, 9 August 1969, 10.

2. A family of four was the standard method of describing the basic yearly benefit, $500 per adult and $300 per child. The second version of FAP, contained in H.R. 1, raised the basic benefit to $2,400 by "cashing out" food stamps, so the value of the benefit remained virtually identical. Families could keep the first $720 of earnings each year plus 50% of additional earnings without having benefits reduced. This provision, the "earnings disregard," promised to provide an incentive for adult recipients to earn wages—the "carrot" to the "stick" of the work requirement.

3. Quoted in Arch N. Booth, "Open Letter About the Welfare Bill," 8 May 1970, Series 4, Box 77, NAM Papers, 2.

4. In contrast, the administration noted that AFDC covered only 17% of the

nation's poor people and 35% of poor children. Sen. Finance Committee, Hearing on H.R. 16311, 29 April 1970, 198.

5. Henry Hazlitt, "Welfarism Out of Control," *National Review*, 9 September 1969, 903; Lester Maddox to Russell Long, Sen. Finance Committee, Hearing on H.R. 16311, 28 April 1970, 2133; Hamilton A. Long to Russell Long, Hearing on H.R. 16311,1 May 1970, 2284.

6. Frank S. Meyter, "Tory Men and Whig Measures," *National Review*, 7 October 1969, 1013.

7. George Wiley Memo, 12 April 1972, Series 4, Box 581, Folder "Welfare Reform Analysis—NWRO 71–72"; LWV Detroit to Lucy Benson, 24 February 1972, Series 4, Box 598, Folder "Welfare Reform: State and Local—Michigan-Wisconsin, 71–72," both in LWV Papers.

8. "New Weapon Against Poverty," *NYT*, 16 November 1969, Section IV, p. 12; "Welfare: Time for Reform," *Saturday Review*, 23 May 1970, 19.

9. Daniel P. Moynihan, "The Step We Must Take," *Saturday Review*, 23 May 1970, 22.

10. "FAP: Is It Back?" *National Review*, 4 February 1972, 87.

11. Ira Mothner, "Will Money Ruin the Poor?" *Look*, 2 June 1970, 58.

12. Thomas Sugrue, *The Origins of the Urban Crisis: Race and Inequality in Postwar Detroit* (Princeton, N.J.: Princeton University Press, 1996); Arnold R. Hirsch, *Making the Second Ghetto: Race and Housing in Chicago, 1940–1960* (Cambridge: Cambridge University Press, 1983).

13. Robert Asen, "Nixon's Welfare Reform: Enacting Historical Contradictions of Poverty Discourses," *Rhetoric and Public Affairs* 4, 2 (2001): 271.

14. Jill Quadagno, *The Color of Welfare: How Racism Undermined the War on Poverty* (New York: Oxford University Press, 1994), 121.

15. Sen. Finance Committee, Hearing on H.R. 16311, 29 April 1970, 161.

16. "Workfare Belabored," *Time*, 5 October 1970, 18; "The Smith Experiment," *New Republic*, 21 February 1970, 8. The Johnson administration had been "teeming with economist-planners drawing up various negative income tax schemes and trying to sell them to their superiors." Vincent J. Burke and Vee Burke, *Nixon's Good Deed: Welfare Reform* (New York: Columbia University Press, 1974), 18–19, 56, 58, 133.

17. James T. Patterson, *America's Struggle Against Poverty, 1900–1994* (Cambridge, Mass.: Harvard University Press, 1994), 173; Leadership Conference on Civil Rights, "A Legislative and Enforcement Program for the 91st Congress and the Administration, 1969–70," Series 6, Box A24, Folder "Govt-Fed-91st Congress 1969–72," NAACP Papers; "The Taxpayers Committee to Federalize Welfare," *NYT*, 29 March 1969, 72; "Federalizing Welfare," *NYT*, 12 February 1969, 38; "Booming Relief in Prosperous Times," *U.S. News and World Report*, May 1968, 83.

18. Statistics from HEW study, cited in "Behind Rising Alarm over Welfare Costs," *U.S. News and World Report*, 30 November 1970, 32.

19. Lisa Levenstein, "From Innocent Children to Unwanted Migrants and Unwed Moms: Two Chapters in the Public Discourse on Welfare in the United States, 1960–1961," *Journal of Women's History* 2, 4 (Winter 2000): 16–24.

20. Robert Lekachman, "Welfare Reform and Revenue Sharing," *Dun's Review*, October 1970, 9.

21. Quoted in "The Welfare Mess Needs Total Reform," *Life*, 31 July 1970, 28.

22. Quoted in Christopher Leman, *The Collapse of Welfare Reform: Political Institutions, Policy, and the Poor in Canada and the United States* (Cambridge, Mass.: MIT Press, 1980), 211.

23. Michael K. Brown, "Race in the American Welfare State: The Ambiguities of 'Universalistic' Social Policy Since the New Deal," in *Without Justice for All: The New Liberalism and Our Retreat from Racial Equality*, ed. Adolph Reed, Jr. (Boulder, Colo.: Westview Press, 1999): 93–122.

24. Asen, "Nixon's Welfare Reform," 265.

25. Moynihan, *Politics of a Guaranteed Income*, 71–72.

26. Ira Mothner, "The Odd Alliance: Moynihan and 'The Robber Barons'," *Look*, 7 April 1970, 19; "Doubts About Guaranteed Income Grow as Senate Takes Up Bill," *Washington Report*, 4 May 1970, Series 1, Box 27, Chamber of Commerce Records.

27. Burke and Burke, *Nixon's Good Deed*, 53.

28. The plan was originally titled "Family Security System," a name the administration jettisoned because it sounded "too New Dealish." Molly Michelmore, "American Conservatism and the Politics of Welfare Reform," paper delivered at Social Science History Association Annual Meeting, Seattle, November 2005, 13.

29. Moynihan, *Politics of a Guaranteed Income*, 161.

30. Ibid., 194.

31. Ibid., 181.

32. Jill Quadagno, "Race, Class, and Gender in the U.S. Welfare State: Nixon's Failed Family Assistance Plan," *American Sociological Review* 55 (February 1990): 11–28.

33. Sen. Finance Committee, Hearing on H.R. 16311, 29 April 1970, 167.

34. Ibid., 268; Moynihan, *Politics of a Guaranteed Income*, 230.

35. Sen. Finance Committee, Hearing on H.R. 16311, 29 April 1970, 193–95, 197.

36. Ibid., 198.

37. Moynihan, *Politics of a Guaranteed Income*, 407. The original FAP fulfilled Nixon's pledge to ensure no current recipient would be worse off by requiring the lowest-benefit states to supplement the FAP basic benefit for single-mother families, making them better off in most states than "working poor," two-parent family recipients. Congressional critics pointed out that the plan retained AFDC's supposed "desertion incentive," and the administration dropped the mandatory supplements.

38. Sen. Finance Committee, Hearing on H.R. 16311, 29 April 1970, 198.

39. Quoted in Burke and Burke, *Nixon's Good Deed*, 58.

40. Moynihan, *Politics of a Guaranteed Income*, 335. As Alice O'Connor points out, the distinction between the working and the dependent or welfare poor "was loaded with unspoken reference to race and gender: the typical 'working poor' family was two-parent, male-headed, and white." O'Connor, "The False Dawn of Poor-Law Reform: Nixon, Carter, and the Quest for a Guaranteed Income," *Journal of Policy History* 10, 1 (1998), 109.

41. Moynihan, *Politics of a Guaranteed Income*, 172, 218–20, 362, 529.

42. Burke and Burke, *Nixon's Good Deed*, 90; Sen. Finance Committee, Hearing on H.R. 16311, 29 April 1970, 241–42; Quadagno, "Race, Class, and Gender in the U.S. Welfare System," 17; Quadagno, *The Color of Welfare*, 126.

43. Quoted in Quadagno, "Race, Class, and Gender in the U.S. Welfare System," 18.

44. Quoted in Sylvia A. Law, "Women, Work, Welfare, and the Preservation of Patriarchy," *University of Pennsylvania Law Review* (May 1983): 1265.

45. Ibid.

46. Quoted in Moynihan, *Politics of a Guaranteed Income*, 409.

47. Ibid., 222; Tom Wicker, "Welfare Reform Crunch," *NYT*, 26 November 1970, 31.

48. Quoted in Jack Rosenthal, "Nixon Signs Welfare Bill and Hails Value of Work," *NYT*, 29 December 1971, 1.

49. "'It Pays to Work': Agnew Explains the President's Welfare Plan," *U.S. News and World Report*, 23 March 1970, 84.

50. Sen. Finance Committee, Hearing on H.R. 16311, 29 April 1970, 169.

51. Roger A. Freeman, "A Wayward Welfare State: The United States, 1970," *Vital Speeches of the Day*, 15 October 1970, 20; Sen. Finance Committee, Hearing on H.R. 1: Social Security Amendments of 1971, 92nd Cong., 2nd sess., 27 January 1972, 1481.

52. Stanley H. Ruttenberg, "The Union Member Speaks," in *Blue-Collar Workers: A Symposium on Middle America*, ed. Sar A. Levitan (New York: McGraw-Hill, 1971), 154.

53. Moynihan, "The Crisis in Welfare," *Public Interest* 10 (Winter 1968), 25.

54. "Welfare: America's Number 1 Problem," *U.S. News and World Report*, 1 March 1971, 39.

55. "Panel Tells Nixon: Welfare Irks 'Excluded and Forgotten' Workers," *Chicago Sun-Times*, 1 July 1970 (reprint), Supplement 2, Box 47, Folder "Ethnicity Conference, May 3–5, 1970," NFS Papers.

56. Quoted in Michelmore, "American Conservatism and the Politics of Welfare Reform," 21.

57. Ibid., 13; Stephen E. Ambrose, *Nixon*, Vol. 2 (New York: Simon and Schuster, 1987), 460.

58. George P. Schultz, "The Family Assistance Act: Welfare Rolls to Payrolls" (Speech to HEW Meeting with Representatives of State and Local Governments, Washington, D.C., 29 January 1970), *Vital Speeches of the Day* 35 (1 March 1970), 295–96; "Welfare Plan Lauded," *NYT*, 10 March 1970, 26.

59. Michelmore, "American Conservatism and the Politics of Welfare Reform," 2.

60. Sen. Finance Committee, Hearings on HR 16311, 29 April 1970, 177.

61. Quoted in Michelmore, "American Conservatism and the Politics of Welfare Reform," 14.

62. Numbers are from HEW estimates released in February 1970, cited in Michelmore, "American Conservatism and the Politics of Welfare Reform," n. 94.

63. Worth Bateman and Jodie Allen, "Income Maintenance: Who Gains and Who Pays?" in Levitan, *Blue-Collar Workers*, 302–5.

64. Agnew, "It Pays to Work," 84.

65. Quoted in Michelmore, "American Conservatism and the Politics of Welfare Reform," 11–12.

66. Quoted in Burke and Burke, *Nixon's Good Deed,* 100.

67. "Deeper and Deeper Still," *National Review,* 24 March 1970, 293.

68. "Work vs. Welfare: Where Nixon Stands," *U.S. News and World Report,* 18 September 1972, 76–78.

69. Michelmore, "American Conservatism and the Politics of Welfare Reform," 25–30. Quote from Nixon's directions to speechwriter William Safire, 27.

70. Testimony of George A. Welsch, Sen. Finance Committee, Hearings on H.R. 1, 26 January 1972, 1320–24.

71. Arch Booth, "Voice of Business," 11 June 1973, Series I, Box 26, U.S. Chamber of Commerce Records, Hagley Museum and Library, Wilmington, Delaware (hereafter Chamber of Commerce Records).

72. Lizabeth Cohen, *A Consumers' Republic: The Politics of Mass Consumption in Postwar America* (New York: Knopf, 2003).

73. Sen. Finance Committee, Hearing on H.R. 16311, 30 April 1970, 370, 223; Ernest Van Den Haag, "Some Modest Proposals: What's Missing in Nixon's Welfare Program," *National Review,* 27 January 1970, 99.

74. Ronald Reagan, "Saving the States from Bankruptcy," *Nation's Business,* May 1971, 60.

75. John A. Hamilton, "Will 'Work' Work?" *Saturday Review,* 23 May 1970, 26.

76. "Welfare Out of Control: Story of Financial Crisis Cities Face," *U.S. News and World Report,* 8 February 1971, 32.

77. Sen. Finance Committee, Hearing on H.R. 16311, 9 September 1970, 2060.

78. "Guaranteed Poverty or Guaranteed Opportunity?" Address by Roger Freeman, Senior Staff Member, Hoover Institution at 73rd Congress of American Industry of the National Association of Manufacturers, 5 December 1968, Series IV, Box 77, Folder "Welfare—Development of NAM Position," NAM Papers, 9.

79. John W. Porter, Jr., to U.S. Chamber of Commerce, 27 July 1971, Series IV, Box 77, NAM Papers. The state was Tennessee. Murray Gruber, "The Welfare-Industrial Complex," *Nation,* 28 June 1971, 809; Mary M. Reynolds, "Welfare Reform Gets Top Priority from League of Women Voters," *Chattanooga Times,* 3 May 1971 (reprint), Series IV, Box 582, Folder "Welfare Reform: Basic Documents, 1971," LWV Papers, 10. Several states had considered similar proposals in the 1950s. Susan L. Thomas, "Race, Gender, and Welfare Reform: The Antinatalist Response," *Journal of Black Studies* 28, 4 (1998), 423–25.

80. "Why the Welfare Bill Is Stuck," *Newsweek,* 7 December 1970, 22; Freeman, "A Wayward Welfare State," 20; "Welfare Out of Control," 30.

81. Sen. Finance Committee, Hearing on H.R. 16311, 9 September 1970, 2060.

82. Sen. Finance Committee, Hearings on H.R. 16311, 24 August 1970, 1329.

83. Quoted in Clint Fair to Andy Biemiller, 9 October 1969, RG21–001, Box 54, Folder 62, Meany Archive.

84. See, e.g., Sen. Finance Committee, Hearings on H.R. 16311, 24–25 August 1970, 1442, 1485–86.

85. Richard Armstrong, "The Looming Money Revolution Down South," *Fortune*, June 1970, 152; Sen. Finance Committee, Hearing on H.R. 16311, 10 September 1970, 2263–65; Sen. Finance Committee, Hearing on H.R. 1, 27 January 1972, 1620–26.

86. First National City Bank Economics Department, "Why Are New York's Workers Dropping Out?" August 1973, Series IV, Box 77, NAM Papers, 12–13.

87. Sen. Finance Committee, Hearing on H.R. 1, 27 January 1972, 1625.

88. Armstrong, "Looming Money Revolution," 66–69, 151–58.

89. Sen. Finance Committee, Hearing on H.R. 16311, 10 September 1970, 2107.

90. Tentative Program, 58th Annual Meeting, Chamber of Commerce of the United States, April 1970, Washington, D.C., Series I, Box 27, Folder "Welfare," Chamber of Commerce Records.

91. "Exclusive Interview with Representative Landrum: 'If the Public Understood This Bill, They Would Oppose It,' " *Washington Report* 9, 7 (n.d.), Series I, Box 27, Chamber of Commerce Records, 2.

92. Freeman, "A Wayward Welfare State," 20; Blanche Bernstein, "Welfare, Work and 'Ambiance'," *Wall Street Journal*, 27 February 1970, 8; "The Great Welfare Debate," *Nation's Business*, April 1970, 59; "What One State Is Doing About the Burden of Relief: Interview with Henry C. White, Commissioner, Connecticut State Welfare Department," *U.S. News and World Report*, 25 October 1971, 67; "Welfare Costs: Sky-High or Down to Earth?" *Nation's Business*, May 1971, 55.

93. Sen. Finance Committee, Hearing on H.R. 1, 26 January 1972, 1310.

94. "Facts About the Chamber of Commerce of the United States," n.d., Series II, Box 28, Chamber of Commerce Records; "Chamber Widens Guaranteed Income Attack: Supports Valid Welfare Reform," *Washington Report* 9, 8 (20 April 1970), Series I, Box 7, Chamber of Commerce Records, 1; "House Vote Nears on Enlarging Welfare Rolls and Starting Guaranteed Income Payments," *Congressional Action* (Special Report on Welfare), 11 March 1970, Series 1, Box 27, Chamber of Commerce Records, 1. See also "National Chamber Steps Up Massive Effort to Defeat Revolutionary Guaranteed Income Plan," 6 April 1970, and "Welfare Reform: Our Crying Need," 6 April 1970 (reprint), both in Series I, Box 27, Chamber of Commerce Records.

95. Earl Steele, "A Communications Campaign on the Guaranteed Income Issue," 26 June 1969, Series I, Box 27, Chamber of Commerce Records, 1.

96. Government Finance Department, "Incentives, Welfare, and the Family Assistance Plan: An Analysis of the Family Assistance Act of 1970 (H.R. 16311) and Comparison with NAM Policy Position," 13 April 1970, and Government Finance Department, "Analysis of H.R. 16311, The Family Assistance Act of 1970," 22 June 1970, both in Series IV, Box 121, Folder "Family Assistance Act of 1970," NAM Papers; Edward Dwyer to E. Trompeter, 5 April 1971, Series IV, Box 77, Folder "Welfare—Correspondence on NAM Position," NAM Papers.

97. Government Finance Department, "Analysis of H.R. 16311," 15; A. L. Bolton, Jr., "Plain Talk on Welfare Reform," *NAM Reports*, 23 August 1971, Series IV, Box 70, NAM Papers.

98. Quadagno, "Race, Class, and Gender in the U.S. Welfare State," 19. The threat of "social decay" was part of HEW secretary Elliot Richardson's presentation

to a meeting with business leaders arranged by NAM. NAM, "Why Welfare Reform?" 15 April 1971, Series IV, Box 77, NAM Papers.

99. NAM Government Operations Subcommittee, "Incentives and the Welfare Program," 26 August 1969, Series I, Box 27, Chamber of Commerce Records, 7–8.

100. "Report on Committee Action: Government Operations/Expenditures Committee on Proposed Position on Welfare and Public Assistance," 2 December 1969, Series IV, Box 77, NAM Papers, 1. NAM changed its position and opposed the FAP in spring 1972 when it became clear that the Nixon administration would not simultaneously eliminate other poverty programs.

101. NAM, "Why Welfare Reform?" 3.

102. Sen. Finance Committee, Hearing on H.R. 16311, 25 August 1970, 1462.

103. Ibid., 1464.

104. "Welfare Reform: Our Crying Need"; "Chamber Widens Guaranteed Income Attack," 1.

105. Bolton, "Plain Talk on Welfare Reform."

106. Sen. Finance Committee, Hearing on H.R. 16311, 1 September 1970, 1895.

107. Earl Steele, "A Communications Campaign on the Guaranteed Income Issue," 1.

108. "Existing Welfare Problems Will Not Be Solved by Adding New Problems of Guaranteed Income," *Congressional Action*, 24 February 1971, Series IV, Box 581, Folder "Welfare Reform Analysis—U.S. Chamber of Commerce 1971," LWV Papers, 1–2.

109. Chamber of Commerce of the United States, "Rehabilitation: The New Direction for Welfare," n.d., Series I, Box 27, Folder "Welfare," Chamber of Commerce Records, 29.

110. Sen. Finance Committee, Hearing on H.R. 1, 27 January 1972, 1392.

111. "House Vote Nears on Enlarging Welfare Rolls and Starting Guaranteed Income Payments," *Congressional Action*, 11 March 1971, Series I, Box 27, Chamber of Commerce Records, 2; "The Great Welfare Debate," *Nation's Business*, April 1970, 60.

112. NAM Government Finance Department, "Analysis of H.R. 16311, The Family Assistance Act of 1970," 22 June 1970, Series IV, Box 121, NAM Papers, 9.

113. "What's the Issue?" Chamber of Commerce of the United States Public Service Radio Program, MBS: "How Can We Solve Our Welfare Problems?" 10 February 1972, Series I, Box 5, Chamber of Commerce Records.

114. Michelmore, "American Conservatism and the Politics of Welfare Reform," 20. For the provisions of Long's bill, see "Payrolls, Not Relief Rolls: Latest Welfare Proposals," *U.S. News and World Report*, 15 May 1972, 71–74.

115. Arch N. Booth, "Voice of Business," 24 May 1971; Booth, "The Ullman Bill: Real Welfare Reform" (Press Release), 21 May 1971, Series I, Box 24, Chamber of Commerce Records; HEW Reply to U.S. Chamber of Commerce, "Here's the Issue" on Welfare Reform, Series IV, Box 581, Folder "Welfare Reform Analysis—U.S. Chamber of Commerce, 1971," LWV Papers.

116. Blanche Bernstein, "Welfare, Work and 'Ambiance'," *Wall Street Journal*, 27 February 1970, 8.

117. Sen. Finance Committee, Hearing on H.R. 1, 26 January 1972, 1354.

118. Arch N. Booth, "Politics, Economics, and the American Business System," *Washington Report*, 17 July 1972, and "National Chamber Launches Stepped-Up Campaign to Put Federal Spending/Budget Under Controls" (news release), 27 March 1972, both in Series I, Box 24, Chamber of Commerce Records.

119. "The Concept of Poverty: Opportunity, Not Guarantee," April 1965, Series I, Box 27, Chamber of Commerce Records, 12; Arch N. Booth, "Voice of Business: Budget Cuts: Welfare Is Ripe," 9 September 1974, Series I, Box 26, Chamber of Commerce Records.

120. U.S. Chamber of Commerce, "Some Serious Questions About the Welfare Reform Bill H.R. 16311," April 1970, Series I, Box 27, Chamber of Commerce Records, 5.

121. For details on the bill's provisions, see National Association of Social Workers, "Summary and Analysis of H.R. 1," 17 June 1971, Box 20, Folder 5, Wiley Papers.

122. Sen. Finance Committee, Hearing on H.R. 1, 27 January 1972, 1491.

123. Center on Social Welfare Policy and Law, "H.R. 1: The Social Security Amendments of 1971: A Critique" n.d., Series IV, Box 580, Folder "Welfare Reform Analysis—CSWP&L, 71," LWV Papers; Lucy V. Katz, "Nixon's Family Assistance Bill," *New Republic*, 18 July 1970, 30–31.

124. Elizabeth Wickenden, "H.R. 1: Welfare Policy as an Instrument of Control," *Welfare Law News* 1, 4 (November 1971), Box 34, Folder 13, Wiley Papers.

125. Ibid; Fern A. Chamberlain, "Statement to the Senate Finance Committee on S. 2081, the Nunn-Talmadge Bill," n.d., and Elizabeth Wickenden, "Statement for Hearings on Child Support Legislation, Sen. Finance Committee, September 25, 1982, prepared on behalf of the National Assembly for Social Policy and Development, Inc.," both in Supplement 2, Box 53, Folder "SIP, Correspondence and Memoranda, 1973," National Social Welfare Assembly Records (hereafter NSWA Records); Wickenden, "Interim Washington Notes #9," 15 October 1973, Supplement 2, Box 57, Folder "SIP: Interim Washington Notes 1973–1974," NSWA Records.

126. Sen. Finance Committee, Hearing on H.R. 16311, 25 August 1970, 1477.

127. League of Women Voters—United States, Human Resources Committee Guide, "Welfare Reform Campaign: A General Action Guide," March 1971, Series IV, Box 601, Folder "Welfare Reform: Vinson, Betty, Chronological File April 1970–71," LWV Papers, 3; "Church Agencies, Civic Groups Press for Welfare Reform," *Christian Century*, 5 May 1971, 551; Mrs. Erwin C. Hannum, "A Summary of League Position, Strategy and Action on Welfare: January–October 1971," Series IV, Box 582, Folder "Welfare Reform: Basic Documents, 1971–72," LWV Papers.

128. For a general statement of liberal demands, see "Campaign for Adequate Welfare Reform Now: Goals and Principles," March 1971, Series IV, Box 582, Folder "Welfare Reform: Campaign for Adequate Welfare Reform Now, 1971," LWV Papers.

129. "The Church and Public Welfare," A Statement adopted by the Executive Council of the Episcopal Church, 29 September 1971, Sen. Finance Committee, Hearing on H.R. 1, 1502.

130. Sen. Finance Committee, Hearing on H.R. 16311, 25 August 1970, 1462.

131. The federal poverty line for a family of four in 1971 was $3,968 a year. The BLS Lower Standard for an urban family of four was $6,960 a year. Sen., Committee on Finance, Hearing on H.R. 1, 1346, 1490–91.

132. The NWRO adjusted its original call for "$5,500 or Fight" to reflect cost of living increases. "White Paper," *Newsweek*, 31 May 1971, 18–19; 26; CSWP&L, "H.R. 1: The Social Security Amendments of 1971: A Critique," Series IV, Box 580, Folder "Welfare Reform Analysis—Center on Social Welfare Policy and Law, 1971," LWV Papers; NWRO 1969 Report (n.d.), Box 13, Folder 23, Wiley Papers, 5; Nadasen, *Welfare Warriors: The Welfare Rights Movement in the United States* (New York: Routledge, 2005), 185.

133. "Ending Poverty," *New Republic*, 7 August 1971, 8.

134. Text of speech (untitled), n.d., Box 18, Folder 2, Wiley Papers, 5.

135. NWRO Notes on FAP, 20 April 1971, Series IV, Box 581, Folder "Welfare Reform Analysis—NWRO 1971–72," LWV Papers.

136. "Church Agencies, Civic Groups Press for Welfare Reform," *Christian Century*, 5 May 1971, 551; Hannum, "A Summary of League Position, Strategy and Action," 3–4; LWV News Release, 18 May 1971, Series IV, Box 581, Folder "WR-Basic Documents, 1970–79," LWV Papers; Betty Vinson to National Board, 2.

137. Ribicoff proposed a higher basic benefit ($3,000 yearly for a family of four with increases to reach poverty level by 1979), a higher earned income disregard, coverage for childless adults, protection of current recipient benefits and no work requirement for mothers with children under age six. Burke and Burke, *Nixon's Good Deed*, 181.

138. Elizabeth Bussiere, *(Dis)Entitling the Poor: The Warren Court, Welfare Rights, and the American Political Tradition* (University Park: Pennsylvania State University Press, 1997); Martha F. Davis, *Brutal Need: Lawyers and the Welfare Rights Movement, 1960–1973* (New Haven, Conn.: Yale University Press, 1993); Nadasen, *Welfare Warriors*, 54–63.

139. National Association of Social Workers, "Summary and Analysis of H.R. 1," 17 June 1971, Box 20, Folder 5, Wiley Papers, 8.

140. Winifred Bell, *Aid to Dependent Children* (New York: Columbia University Press, 1965); Frances Fox Piven and Richard A. Cloward, *Regulating the Poor: The Functions of Public Welfare*, updated ed. (New York, 1993), esp. chaps. 4–5; Joanne L. Goodwin, "'Employable Mothers' and 'Suitable Work': A Re-Evaluation of Welfare and Wage-Earning for Women in the Twentieth-Century United States," *Journal of Social History* 29, 2 (Winter 1995), 253–74.

141. Johnnie Tillmon and George Wiley to Richard Nixon, 6 August 1969, Box 17, Folder 4, Wiley Papers, 3.

142. George Wiley, "The Challenge of the Powerless," Statement at Consultation on Economic Power and Responsibility, 29 March 1968, Box 36, Folder 5, Wiley Papers, 3.

143. "Tape Transcription—Black Perspectives on the News," 1971, Series 4, Box 581, Folder "WR Articles, 74–76," LWV Papers, 1–2.

144. Ibid. For George Wiley's background, see Nick Kotz and Mary Lynn

Kotz, *A Passion for Equality: George A. Wiley and the Movement* (New York: Norton, 1977).

145. One notable exception is the NAACP-LDEF campaign in 1966–67 against abuses in welfare, which included a legal challenge to Georgia's practice of cutting black AFDC recipients off the rolls when local employers needed domestic or agricultural labor. Goodwin, "'Employable Mothers' and 'Suitable Work'," 267.

146. Guida West, *The National Welfare Rights Movement: The Social Protest of Poor Women* (New York: Praeger, 1981), 211–30.

147. Hulbert James to NWRO Second National Convention Program Committee, 18 July 1969, Box 7, Folder 8, Wiley Papers, 1.

148. George Wiley to Charles Diggs, 27 May 1971, and M. Carl Holman to George Wiley, 10 May 1971, both in Box 16, Folder 3, Wiley Papers.

149. Rep. Ronald Dellum, Statement on Welfare Reform, 24 May 1971, Box 16, Folder 3, Wiley Papers.

150. John Conyers to Members of the House, 28 May 1971, Box 16, Folder 3, Wiley Papers, 1–3.

151. Ibid.

152. "Mr. Moynihan Replies," *New Republic*, 18 July 1970, 32.

153. Untitled Welfare Reform Speech, n.d., Series IV, Box 593, Folder "Welfare Reform: League of Women Voters Convention, 1972," LWV Papers.

154. "Washington Letter: The American Jewish Committee," 18 August 1971, Issue 71–5, Series IV, Box 580, Folder "Welfare Reform Analysis: American Jewish Committee, 1971," LWV Papers, 3; Hannum, "A Summary of League Position, Strategy and Action," 4–5.

155. Carl Ericson to Peggy Lampl, 7 March 1972, Series IV, Box 589, Folder "Welfare Reform: General Correspondence, 1971–79," LWV Papers, 1.

156. "Ending Poverty," *New Republic*, 7 August 1971, 8–9.

157. Ibid.

158. Lucy Benson to Ms. Susan S., Cercone, 26 March 1972, Series 4, Box 598, Folder "WR: State and Local-Mich-Wisc, 71–72" and Lucy Benson to Mrs. Elizabeth Chapin Furber, 9 December 1971, Series 4, Box 579, Folder "Welfare Reform Action Letters—October–December 1971," both in LWV Papers.

159. Lucy Wilson Benson (résumé), March 1989, and Stephanie Kraft, "Lucy Benson at Home," *Advocate*, 5 March 1975, both in "Lucy Wilson Benson" File, Series 10, League of Women Voters, Amherst, Massachusetts Records, University of Massachusetts.

160. Quoted in "Washington Letter: The American Jewish Committee," 3.

161. The essay is signed "Dean Swift," but "Bill Pearce, the child Welfare League," is typed at the top. "In Defense of the Liberals and Their Modest Proposal," Box 18, Folder 17, Wiley Papers, 1–2 (my emphasis).

162. "Friends of NWRO," n.d., Box 13, Folder 17, Wiley Papers; George Wiley to Hannah Weinstein (1967), Box 21, Folder 3, Wiley Papers, 2. See Nadasen, *Welfare Warriors*, chap. 5 on recipient efforts to gain control of the NWRO.

163. LWV Kentucky to Lucy Benson, 15 October 1971, Series 4, Box 579, Folder "WR—Action Letters," LWV Papers.

164. Elizabeth Wickenden, "Partial List of Organizations and Individuals Op-

posing Title IV ('Welfare Reform' Provisions) of H.R. 1, Even as Modified by Proposed Ribicoff Amendments," 9 March 1972, Box 34, Folder 13, Wiley Papers. Jennifer Mittlestadt describes the social welfare administration network in which these policymakers operated in *From Welfare to Workfare: The Unintended Consequences of Liberal Reform, 1945–1965* (Chapel Hill, N.C.: University of North Carolina Press, 2005).

165. Paul Minarchenko to Jerry Wurf, 2 September 1971, and *News from AFSCME*, 7 October 1970, Box 75, Folder 19, AFSCME Office of the President: Jerry Wurf Records, Reuther Library (hereafter Wurf Records).

166. National Association of Social Workers, "Memorandum to Chapter Presidents, APAC Chairmen and Elan Team Leaders from Washington ELAN Center," 17 June 1971, Box 20, Folder 5, Wiley Papers, 3.

167. Statement of Mrs. Wayne W. Harrington, Women's Division, United Methodist Church, Sen. Finance Committee, Hearing on H.R. 16311, 10 September 1970, 2299.

168. Cornelia Einsweiler and Barbara Flanigan to Lucy Benson, 8 December 1971, Series IV, Box 579, Folder "Welfare Reform: Action Letters 1971–72," LWV Papers.

169. All the following in LWV Papers: Judith Axler Turner, "Washington Pressures: League of Women Voters Backs Study with Lobbying to Influence Policy," *National Journal* 4, 21 (20 May 1972), Series IV, Box 582, Folder "Welfare Reform: Basic Documents, 1971–72," 860–69; Betty Vinson to National Board, 31 January 1973, Series IV, Box 590, Folder "Welfare Reform: Income Assistance, 1971–73," 2–3; League of Women Voters of Michigan, Statement before Sen. Committee on Health, Social Services and Retirement, 3 October 1968, Series IV, Box 587, Folder "Welfare Reform: Congress—Sen. Finance Committee—League Testimony, State League Background Data, 1971," 1–2.

170. Betty Vinson to Ms. Carol Goerner, 18 April 1972, Series IV, Box 579, Folder "Welfare Reform: Action Letters, March–June 1972," 1, LWV Papers.

171. Mrs. Helen Patterson to Lucy Benson, 24 March 1972, Series IV, Box 579, Folder "Welfare Reform: Action Letters 1971–72," LWV Papers.

172. Maya Miller to LWVUS 1972 Convention delegates, "Re Direct Lobbying Efforts: Oppose H.R. 1 with or without the Ribicoff Amendments," 14 April 1972, Series IV, Box 579, Folder "Welfare Reform: Action Letters, 1971–72," LWV Papers.

173. Mrs. Barbara B. Hauser to Lucy Benson, 7 July 1971, Series 4, Box 579, Folder "Welfare Reform: Action Letters, February–September 1971," LWV Papers; LWV Kentucky to Lucy Benson, 15 October 1971,Series IV, Box 579, Folder "Welfare Reform: Action Letters, 1971–72," LWV Papers.

174. Lester M. Salamon, "Family Assistance: The Stakes in the Rural South," *New Republic*, 20 February 1971, 18.

175. Moynihan, *Politics of a Guaranteed Income*, 73–79, 161; "Welfare and Illfare: The Alternatives to Poverty," *Time*, 13 December 1968, 26; Statement of C. W. Cook, Chairman of General Foods Corporation and Vice President of the Committee on Economic Development Subcommittee on Poverty, Sen. Finance Committee, Hearing on H.R. 16311, 24 August 1970, 1464.

176. Armstrong, "The Looming Money Revolution Down South," argues that Southern blacks distrusted Nixon and that's why they didn't support FAP.

177. "Welfare: Trying to End the Nightmare," *Time*, 8 February 1971, 22.

178. Michael Kazin, *The Populist Persuasion: An American History* (Ithaca, N.Y.: Cornell University Press, 1995), 162. See also Ira Katznelson, "Was the Great Society a Lost Opportunity?" and Nelson Lichtenstein, "From Corporatism to Collective Bargaining: Organized Labor and the Eclipse of Social Democracy in the Postwar Era," in *The Rise and Fall of the New Deal Order: 1930–1980*, ed. Steve Fraser and Gary Gerstle (Princeton, N.J.: Princeton University Press, 1989).

179. The AFL-CIO legislative department attended many meetings with other liberal coalition members and kept abreast of legislative developments. See, e.g., Bert Seidman to Andy Biemiller, RG21–001, Box 54, Folder 63, Meany Archive.

180. Moynihan, *Politics of a Guaranteed Income*, 272.

181. AFL-CIO Executive Council Statement "Toward Eliminating Poverty," 21 February 1969, quoted in George Meany, "AFL-CIO Statement on President Nixon's Messages," reprinted from *AFL-CIO News*, 16 August 1968, Box 19, Folder 13, Wiley Papers, 5.

182. Ibid., 1.

183. American Conservative Union, "The Family Assistance Plan: A Guaranteed Income—What It Means to YOU as a Taxpayer," Series IV, Box 77, NAM Papers.

184. "Toward Eliminating Poverty in America," *AFL-CIO American Federationist*, April 1969, 9–12.

185. Bert Seidman, "The Work Ethic and Welfare Reform," presented to Annual Meeting of the Industrial Relations Research Association, Toronto, 29 December 1972, RG21–001, Box 54, Folder 63, Meany Archive, 5–6; Statement by the AFL-CIO Executive Council on Welfare Reform, Bal Harbour, Florida, 15 February 1971, Box 19, Folder 13, Wiley Papers, 1.

186. Seidman, "Work Ethic and Welfare Reform," 6, 10.

187. Welfare Council of NYC Chapter (NASW), "Mr. Sugarman, What Is This All About?" November 1971, Box 31, Folder 7, Wiley Papers, 1.

188. Welfare rights historian Premilla Nadasen has argued that the NWRO primarily white, male staff accepted the broader culture's assumption that poor single mothers should work, while its largely nonwhite recipient base articulated the culturally radical claim that black women's motherwork represented something of value to society. Nadasen, *Welfare Warriors*, 137–42, 155, 166. Other studies of the movement suggest that some recipient leaders were *more* likely than the male leadership to demand job training and work opportunities. Annelise Orleck, *Storming Caesars Palace: How Black Mothers Fought Their Own War on Poverty* (Boston: Beacon, 2005), 109, 118, 127–28, 247.

189. "Six Myths About Welfare," n.d. (NWRO publication draft), Box 28, Folder 3, Wiley Papers, 3–4, 6–7.

190. "Thought for the Day," n.d., Box 28, Folder 6, Wiley Papers.

191. National Board of the YWCA of USA, Statement on H.R. 1, 15 February 1972, Series 4, Box 595, Folder "WR—Position Statements on Welfare, 1971," LWV Papers.

192. Lucy Benson to Mrs. Beatrice Bibby, 25 February 1972, Series IV, Box 579, Folder "Welfare Reform: Action Letters, January–February 1972," LWV Papers; Cynthia Hannum to Mrs. Barbara Bloy, n.d. Series IV, Box 579, Folder "Welfare Reform: Action Letters, February–September 1971," LWV Papers; Cornelia Einsweiler and Barbara Flanigan to Walter Mondale, 18 October 1971, Series IV, Box 579, Folder "Welfare Reform: Action Letters, October–December 1971," LWV Papers.

193. "Open Letter to Leagues of Women Voters in the U.S.," June 1971, Series 4, Box 595, Folder "WR—Position Statements on Welfare, 1971," LWV Papers.

194. Statement of Mrs. Wayne W. Harrington, 2300.

195. "Why the Welfare Bill Is Stuck," *Newsweek*, 7 December 1970, 23; "In Defense of the Liberals and Their Modest Proposal," 1; Daniel P. Moynihan, "One Step We Must Take," *Saturday Review*, 23 May 1970, 22.

196. U.S. Commission on Civil Rights Statement, Sen. Finance Committee, Hearing on H.R. 16311, 9 September 1970, 1921–26.

197. Lucy V. Katz, "Nixon's Family Assistance Bill," *New Republic*, 18 July 1970, 30–31; *Falling Down on the Job: The United States Employment Service and the Disadvantaged*, prepared by the Lawyers' Committee for Civil Rights Under Law and the National Urban Coalition, 1971, Box 56, Folder "Employment and Unemployment," NFS Records; CSWP&L Statement, Sen. Finance Committee, Hearing on H.R. 16311, 10 September 1970, 2186–99 ; "FAP/OFF—Effects on the South," n.d., Box 18, Folder 2, Wiley Papers.

198. CSWP&L Statement, 2198–99; Katz, "Nixon's Family Assistance Bill."

199. Quoted in U.S. Commission on Civil Rights Statement, 1923–24. See also Minnis, "How the Great Society Solves the Servant Problem," 168–70.

200. "Welfare Reform Bill Inequitable, Woodcock Says," *News from UAW*, 21 May 1971, Box 19, Folder 13, Wiley Papers.

201. "Statement by the AFL-CIO Executive Council on Welfare Reform," 3.

202. Statement of Joseph Wilson, Sen. Finance Committee, Hearing on H.R. 16311, 25 August 1970, 1456–57.

203. Mittlestadt, *From Welfare to Workfare*, chap. 4.

204. "Welfare Is a Women's Issue," n.d., Box 17, Folder 3, Wiley Papers, 1, 5.

205. See Premilla Nadasen, "Expanding the Boundaries of the Women's Movement: Black Feminism and the Struggle for Welfare Rights," *Feminist Studies* 28, 2 (2002), 271–301.

206. Tish Sommers to Merrillee Dolan, 5 June 1971; Mary Vogel to Merrillee Dolan, 10 March 1972; D.C. Family Welfare Rights Organization, Flyer for Welfare Dinner, n.d. (March 1972); "Welfare Dinner—Statement of Purpose and Goals," all in author's possession.

207. *Sisters in Poverty* (Newsletter of the NOW Task Force on Women and Poverty) 3, 1 (June 1972), in author's possession.

208. Merrillee Dolan, "Moynihan, Poverty Programs, and Women—A Female Viewpoint," n.d. (1971), reprinted in Margaret Mason, *Poverty: A Feminist Issue: A Case Study of NOW"s Policies and Actions on Poverty Issues, 1966–1976* (n.d.), Box 45, Folder "Poverty: A Feminist Issue—NOW TF and Newsletters," National Organization for Women Records, Schlesinger Library (hereafter NOW Records), appendix III.

209. Merrillee Dolan, "James Graham, *Enemies of the Poor*," NOW Albuquerque, New Mexico Chapter Newsletter 3, 3 (July 1972): 6–9, in author's possession.

210. Merrillee Dolan to Brenda Feigen Pasteau, 29 March 1970, reprinted in Mason, *Poverty: A Feminist Issue*, appendix III.

211. Report of the Task Force on Women in Poverty submitted by Merrillee Dolan and Jean Temple, n.d. (1970), in author's possession; National Organization for Women, Position Paper: Women in Poverty (n.d.), in author's possession.

212. Statement of W. D. Eberle, co-chair, Common Cause, Sen. Finance Committee, Hearing on H.R. 16311, 24 August 1970, 1371.

213. White, "What One State Is Doing About the Burden of Relief," 68.

214. Sen. Finance Committee, Hearing on H.R. 16311, 24 August 1970, 1354–55, 1371.

215. George Wiley and Johnnie Tillmon to Lucy Benson, n.d., Box 19, Folder 15, Wiley Papers; Lucy Benson to Susan Cercone, 26 March 1972, Series IV, Box 598, Folder "Welfare Reform: State and Local—Michigan-Wisconsin, 1971–72," LWV Papers.

216. Betty Vinson to Ms. Carol Goerner, 18 April 1972, Series IV, Box 579, Folder "Welfare Reform: Action Letters, March–June 1972," 1.

217. Benson to Cercone, 16 March 1972, 3.

218. Hirschel Kasper and Leonard Hausman, "Nixon's Family Assistance Plan," *New Republic*, 28 March 1970, 8.

219. Quoted in Law, "Women, Work, and Welfare," 1311, n. 244.

220. Quoted in Theodore Marmor and Martin Rein, "Reforming 'the Welfare Mess': The Fate of the Family Assistance Plan, 1969–1972," in *Policy and Politics in America*, ed. Allan Sindler (Boston: Little, Brown, 1973), 24.

221. Sen. Finance Committee, Hearing on H.R. 16311, 25 August 1970, 1477.

Chapter 3. Building a New Majority: Welfare and Economic Justice in the 1970s

Epigraph: Tim Sampson, "For Our Own Welfare," *Just Economics* 2, 4 (April 1974), Box 32, Folder 17, Movement for Economic Justice Papers, Wisconsin Historical Society, Madison, Wisconsin (hereafter MEJ Papers), 4.

1. "Workfare" recipients do not have any of the rights or protections of regular workers—they work in exchange for welfare benefits, not a wage. For a thorough discussion of welfare restrictions in the 1970s, see dozens of issues of Washington Notes located in Supplement 2, Box 57, Folder "SIP 'Interim Washington Notes,' 1973–1974" and Box 23, Folder "Washington Notes, 1971–1977," NSWA Records.

2. NCSW, "Centennial Forum and Exposition Program," May 1973, "100 Years of Concern—A Mandate to Shape the Future," National Conference on Social Welfare Records, Social Welfare History Archives, University of Minnesota, Minneapolis (hereafter NCSW Records).

3. James Parks, "Welfare Workers Find U.S. Social Ills Getting Worse," *Milwaukee Journal*, 4 June 1972 (reprint), Box 6, Folder "1972," NCSW Records.

4. Kathryn L. Nasstrom, *Everybody's Grandmother and Nobody's Fool: Frances Freeborn Pauley and the Struggle for Social Justice* (Ithaca, N.Y.: Cornell University Press, 2000), chap. 6, 177–78.

5. Annelise Orleck, *Storming Caesars Palace: How Black Mothers Fought Their Own War on Poverty* (Boston: Beacon Press, 2005).

6. Marie Ratagick to Ms. Carol Ferry, 14 November 1973, Box 31, Folder 10; Arlene Gottlieb, "Mississippeans Rally for Welfare Rights," *Just Economics* 2, 2 (February 1974), Box 32, Folder 17, p. 8; PRO-Wisconsin Stops Welfare Budget Cut," *Just Economics* 3, 6 (June 1975), Box 7, Folder 9, all in MEJ Papers.

7. Orleck, *Storming Caesars Palace*, 3.

8. Between 1970 and 1985, the median value of AFDC benefits declined about one-third, while the value of state/local General Assistance support dropped by about 32%. Michael B. Katz, *The Undeserving Poor: From the War on Poverty to the War on Welfare* (New York: Pantheon Books, 1989), 189. For restrictions placed on AFDC during the 1970s, see Christopher Leman, *The Collapse of Welfare Reform: Political Institutions, Policy, and the Poor in Canada and the United States* (Cambridge, Mass.: MIT Press, 1980), 207, 214–19.

9. Robert Greenstein, "Universal and Targeted Approaches to Relieving Poverty: An Alternative View," in *The Urban Underclass*, ed. Christopher Jencks and Paul E. Peterson (Washington, D.C.: Brookings Institution Press, 1991), 448. On the EITC's origins and development, see Christopher Howard, *The Hidden Welfare State: Tax Expenditures and Social Policy in the United States* (Princeton, N.J.: Princeton University Press, 1997), chaps. 3, 7.

10. Congress expanded the Food Stamp Program in the first third of the decade but—largely in response to vicious political and popular attacks on the program—made it increasingly restrictive during the late 1970s. Nancy Amidei, "On Not Feeding the Hungry," *Commonweal*, 10 April 1981, 205.

11. Irving M. Levine, "A Strategy for White Ethnic America," June 1968, Supplement 2, Box 47, Folder "Ethnicity Conference, May 3–5, 1970," NFS Records, 4; George Wiley, "Building a New Majority: The Movement for Economic Justice," 6 July 1973, Box 41, Folder 4, Wiley Papers, 1.

12. Fred R. Harris, "Hot Under the Blue Collar," in *Blue-Collar Workers: A Symposium on Middle America*, ed. Sar A. Levitan (New York: McGraw-Hill, 1971), 358.

13. Fern Chamberlain to Elizabeth Wickenden, 23 October 1973, and Elizabeth Wickenden to Fern Chamberlain, 25 October 1973, Supplement 2, Box 57, Folder "SIP 'Interim Washington Notes' 1973–1974," NSWA Records.

14. In 1974, Representative Martha Griffiths's Joint Economic Committee proposed a Negative Income Tax plan. In 1975, Representative Bella Abzug introduced a bill to increase federal funding of welfare, and the National Urban League developed its own guaranteed income proposal. In 1976, the NCSW worked with federal welfare administrators to develop "basic principles for an income security system in the United States." None of these proposals garnered broad support or publicity. Meanwhile, some HEW officials and outside welfare experts continued to push for the NIT program, but both the Nixon and Ford administrations rejected such plans. See various documents in Box 54, Folder "SIP Welfare Reform 1975–1977," NSWA

Records, 1–3; Income Maintenance: The National Urban League Position, 15 July 1975, and Jeweldean Jones Londa, "Report to the Board of Trustees on Income Maintenance," 12 May 1975, both in Part III, Box 97, Folder 3, NUL Papers; NCSW, "Principles for an Income Security System for the United States, Final Report," 1976, Supplement 1, Box 33, NCSW Records; "Washington Notes #15," 16 January 1975, "Washington Notes #17," 23 July 1975, and "Washington Notes #20," 11 March 1976, all in Supplement 2, Box 23, Folder "Washington Notes 1971–1977," NSWA Records; Peter Kihss, "A Broader Social Security Plan to Include All Jobless Is Urged," *NYT*, 8 September 1974, 37; "Guaranteed Income," *NYT*, 24 November 1974, 37; Paul Delaney, "Report Foresees Many Welfare Recipients Getting Less Under New System," *NYT*, 12 July 1974, 7.

15. Ad Hoc Coalition on Emergency Aid of NSWA, "Joint Statement on Unemployment and Welfare," Box 53, Folder "SIP, Full Employment 1974–1977," NSWA Records; John Martin to John Hein, 4 June 1973, Box 77, Folder 27, Wurf Records.

16. Nan Waterman to Anne Stephens, 18 October 1976, Series 4, Box 597, Folder "Welfare Reform: State and Local—Michigan-Wisconsin, 1969–1977," LWV Papers. One survey indicated a significant reduction in local and state League action on welfare, as well. While thirty-three states had conducted education and lobbying campaigns around the issue in the late 1960s and early 1970s (with most occurring in 1971, at the height of the FAP battle), by 1976–1977, only three states reported action related to welfare. Sally Laird, "Notes on 6/77 Meeting with Aaron," Series 4, Box 597, Folder "Welfare Reform: State and Local—Michigan-Wisconsin, 1969–1977," LWV Papers.

17. Peter Schrag, "The Forgotten American," *Harper's*, August 1969, 27–35.

18. Dan T. Carter, *From George Wallace to Newt Gingrich: Race in the Conservative Counterrevolution, 1963–1994* (Baton Rouge: Louisiana State University Press, 1996), 28–30; Jon Margolis, "Survival in the Working Class," *Newsday* (1969) (reprint), Box 49, Folder "Ethnicity Conference, May 3–5, 1970," NFS Records, 7.

19. Margolis, "Survival in the Working Class," 3.

20. Bill Moyers, "The Plight of the Not-So-Poor," *Newsday* (1969) (reprint), Box 49, Folder "Ethnicity Conference, May 3–5, 1970," NFS Records, 1.

21. Russell Barta, "Are the Rules Changing?" *America*, 30 October 1971, 345; Thomas H. Clancy, "The Ethnic American—An Interview with Barbara Mikulski," *America*, 26 December 1970, 559.

22. Carter, *From George Wallace to Newt Gingrich*, 4.

23. The description is from the John Birch Society's *Organ*, quoted in Michael Kazin, *The Populist Persuasion: An American History* (Ithaca, N.Y.: Cornell University Press, 1995), 238.

24. Carter, *From George Wallace to Newt Gingrich*, 35; Seymour Lipset and Earl Raab, "The Wallace Whitewash," in Louise Kapp Howe, ed., *The White Majority: Between Poverty and Affluence* (New York: Random House, 1970), 209–28.

25. "Transcripts of Acceptance Speeches by Nixon and Agnew to the G.O.P. Convention," *NYT*, 9 August 1968, 20, and "Excerpts from the Republican Platform Proposed by Committee on Resolutions," 5 August 1968, 25.

26. Carter, *From George Wallace to Newt Gingrich*, 43–44.

27. Kevin Phillips, *The Emerging Republican Majority* (New Rochelle, NY: Arlington House, 1969); Howard L. Reiter, "Blue-Collar Workers and the Future of American Politics," in Levitan, *Blue-Collar Workers*, 127; Jerome Rosow, "The Problems of Lower-Middle-Income Workers" and "Directions for Action" in Levitan, *Blue-Collar Workers*, 76–84, 342–50.

28. Andrew Hacker, "Is There a New Republican Majority?" in Howe, *The White Majority*, 277.

29. Richard M. Scammon and Ben J. Wattenberg, *The Real Majority: How the Silent Center of the American Electorate Chooses Its President* (New York: Coward-McCann and Geoghegan, 1970); "Decades of Progress," *Time*, 16 April 1973, 16. "Reacting Americans in a Time of Anxiety" was the title of a workshop at the NCSW annual forum in 1970. NCSW, 97th Annual Forum and Exposition Program, May 1970, 79, Supplement I, Box 33, NCSW Records.

30. Judith Magidson Herman to Participant, n.d., Box 7, Folder "Ethnicity Conference, May 3–5, 1970," NFS Records.

31. American Jewish Committee, "The Reacting Americans: An Interim Look at the White Ethnic Lower Middle Class," May 1969; Program, The Chicago Consultation on Ethnicity, University of Illinois-Chicago, 17–18 November 1969; "Working in White Ethnic Neighborhoods: A Joint Consultation," May 1970, all in Box 47, Folder "Ethnicity Conference, May 3–5, 1970," NFS Records. Leonard S. Silk, "Is There a Lower-Middle-Class 'Problem'?" in Levitan, *Blue-Collar Workers*, 15–18.

32. Dennis Duggan, "Still Forgotten: The Working Poor," *The Nation*, 9 June 1969, 724–76.

33. Schrag, "The Forgotten American," 30.

34. Levine, "Strategy for White Ethnic America," 1, 12.

35. Howe, *The White Majority*, 4.

36. Carter, *From George Wallace to Newt Gingrich*, 40.

37. Barta, "Are the Rules Changing?" 344; Andrew Levison, *The Working-Class Majority* (New York: Coward, McCann and Geoghegan, Inc., 1974), 234; S. M. Miller, "Sharing the Burden of Change" in Howe, *White Majority*, 287; Moyers, "The Plight of the Not-So-Poor," 1. "We didn't pay enough attention to the concerns of people who were above the welfare line," lamented Mitchell Ginsberg when the FAP battle ended, to "the lower-middle-income worker . . . the guy who feels welfare is taking it away from him." Gareth Davies, *From Opportunity to Entitlement: The Transformation and Decline of Great Society Liberalism* (Lawrence: University Press of Kansas, 1996), 237.

38. For a trenchant critique of this "liberal orthodoxy," see Adolph Reed, "Race and the Disruption of the New Deal Coalition," *Urban Affairs Quarterly* 27, 2 (December 1991), 326–33, and "Introduction: The New Liberal Orthodoxy on Race and Inequality," in *Without Justice for All: The New Liberalism and Our Retreat from Racial Equality*, ed. Adolph Reed, Jr. (Boulder, Colo.: Westview Press, 1999), 1–8.

39. Barta, "Are the Rules Changing?" 342.

40. Levine, "Strategy for White Ethnic America."

41. NCSW, 97th Annual Forum and Exposition Program, May 1970, "Social

Policies for the 1970s: Prospects and Strategies," Supplement 1, Box 33, NCSW Records, 3, 34, 79.

42. Lane Kirkland, "Labor and the Liberal Tradition," AFL-CIO *American Federationist*, December 1969, 13–14.

43. Bayard Rustin, "From Protest to Politics: The Future of the Civil Rights Movement," *Commentary* 39, 2 (February 1965): 25–31; National Black Political Agenda, 1972, Box 29, Folder 6, Wiley Papers, 2–3, 9, 28–29; A. Philip Randolph, Bayard Rustin, and Norman Hill, "The Coalition After the 1972 Election: Working Paper for the Fourth National Conference of A. Philip Randolph Institute Affiliates," 18–20 May 1973, RG98–002, Vertical File, Box 50, Folder 18, Meany Archive, 5.

44. Labor News Conference, Program 6, Series 13, 29 May 1973, RG98–002, Vertical File, Box 50, Folder 18, Meany Archive, 1.

45. Randolph, Rustin, and Hill, "The Coalition after the 1972 Election," 2, 6–8; Bayard Rustin, "The Washington March—A Ten-Year Perspective," *The Crisis*, August–September 1972, 227–28. See also Dr. Vivian W. Henderson, "Race, Economics, and Public Policy," *The Crisis*, February 1975, 52.

46. "Nixon, the Great Society, and the Future of Social Policy: A Symposium," *Commentary*, May 1973, 50.

47. Linda Charlton, "McGregor Mocks McGovern Plans," *NYT*, 11 August 1972, 8.

48. Ronald Reagan, "Welfare Is a Cancer," *NYT*, 1 April 1971, 41; Wallace Turner, "Reagan Answers Unruh on Ethics," *NYT*, 14 September 1970, 11; "Statements from Pre-Election Interview with Nixon Outlining 2d Term Plans," *NYT*, 10 November 1972, 20.

49. Jack Rosenthal, "Large Social Cuts: Reductions Are Aimed at Big Poverty and Education Efforts," *NYT*, 30 January 1973, 1, 22; Alice M. Rivlin, "A Counter-Budget for Social Programs," *NYT Magazine*, 5 April 1973, 33.

50. The meeting was called by the Center for Community Change. CCAP, described in Chapter 1, merged with the Center for Community Change in 1968. *National Priorities Alert*, 14 April 1974, Box 31, Folder 9, Center for Community Change Papers, Reuther Library; Austin Scott, "Rights Forces Map Fight on Budget Slashes," *Washington Post*, 12 March 1973 (reprint), Box 40, Folder 4, Wiley Papers.

51. CHN&BP, Coordinating Committee Meeting, 7 June 1974, Summary Minutes, Box 31, Folder 6, Center for Community Change Papers, Reuther Library; "Coalition for Human Needs and Budget Priorities—Board of Directors" and "Coalition for Human Needs and Budget Priorities—Coordinating Committee," Box 40, Folder 4, Wiley Papers; "Member Organizations of the Coalition for Human Needs," n.d., Box 289, Folder "CHNBP, January–May 1973," NCJW-Washington, D.C., Office.

52. *National Priorities Alert*, 4 May 1973, Box 40, Folder 4, Wiley Papers, 1.

53. CHN&BP, "National Priorities Alert: Kennedy and Mondale Conduct Ad Hoc Budget Hearings Sponsored by Coalition for Human Needs and Budget Priorities: Coalition Chairman Maier Calls Budget 'As Damaging as Watergate'," 14 June 1973, Box 40, Folder 4, Wiley Papers.

54. Jerry J. Berman to Steering Committee of Coalition for Human Needs and Budget Priorities, 14 February 1973, Box 40, Folder 4, Wiley Papers, 1–2.

55. See, for example, "A Call for Action from the Black Economic Summit Meeting," September 1974, Part III, Box 127, Folder 4, NUL Papers.

56. Austin Scott, "Right Forces Map Fight on Budget Slashes," *Washington Post*, 12 March 1973, Box 40, Folder 4, Wiley Papers.

57. Vernon E. Jordan, "Blacks and the Nixon Administration," *Vital Speeches of the Day*, 1 May 1973, 418–20.

58. Testimony by George Wiley, Sen. Ad Hoc Committee on the Budget Versus Human Needs, 14 June 1973, Box 41, Folder 4, Wiley Papers, 1.

59. *National Priorities Alert* did provide occasional updates on food stamp legislation and budgets, but food stamps were primarily targeted to the "working poor." AFDC was rarely mentioned. See multiple issues of *National Priorities Alert* in Box 50, Folder 4, Wiley Papers.

60. Worth Bateman and Jodie Allen, "Income Maintenance: Who Gains and Who Pays?" in Levitan, *Blue-Collar Workers*, 299–30.

61. See, e.g., Margolis, "Survival in the Working Class," 4, 6; Barta, "Are The Rules Changing?" 342; Schrag, "The Forgotten American," 28, 31, 32; Richard Sennett and Jonathan Cobb, *The Hidden Injuries of Class* (New York: W.W. Norton, 1972) 134–38; Hamill, "Revolt of the White Lower-Middle Class," 12; Harvey Aronson, "Life with Cappelli on $101 a Week," *Newsday*, 24 May 1969, 26; Levitan, *Blue-Collar Workers*, xvi, 3; Silk, "Is There a Lower-Middle-Class 'Problem'?" 9; E. E. LeMasters, *Blue-Collar Aristocrats: Lifestyles at a Working-Class Tavern* (Madison: University of Wisconsin Press, 1975), 178–79; Lee Rainwater, "Making the Good Life: Working-Class Family and Life-Styles," in Levitan, *Blue-Collar Workers*, 227; and various contributions to Howe, *White Majority*.

62. Hamill, "Revolt of the White Lower-Middle-Class," 12.

63. Schrag, "Forgotten American," 31.

64. Levison, *Working-Class Majority*, 153; Rainwater, "Making the Good Life," 209; Margolis, "Survival in the Working Class," 2.

65. Levine, "Strategy for White Ethnic America," 2–3.

66. Robert E. Lane, "The Fear of Equality," in Howe, *The White Majority*, 142.

67. Stanley H. Ruttenberg, "The Union Member Speaks," in Levitan, *Blue-Collar Workers*, 160.

68. Rainwater, "Making the Good Life," 207, 209.

69. Levine, "Strategy for White Ethnic America," 3.

70. Charles Hamilton, "The Moynihan Memo and Civil Rights," *America*, 14 March 1970, 262.

71. Glenn W. Olson, "New Approaches to a Hard Right Neighborhood: A Case Example," NCSW, Reacting Americans in a Time of Anxiety, 4 June 1970, Box 47, Folder "Ethnicity Conference, May 3–5, 1970," NFS Records, 4.

72. Quoted in Ben J. Wattenberg and Richard M. Scammon, "Black Progress and Liberal Rhetoric," *Commentary*, April 1973, 35.

73. The Census Bureau reported that 28.9% of African American families were female-headed. Jack Rosenthal, "The 'Female-Headed Household,'" *NYT*, 29 July 1971, 16.

74. Ben J. Wattenberg and Richard M. Scammon, "Black Progress and Liberal Rhetoric," *Commentary*, April 1973, 38, 40, 44.

75. National Urban Coalition (1974), Box 224, Folder 9, UAW President's Office-Leonard Woodcock Papers, 1, 17.

76. National Urban Coalition, "The Welfare Quagmire," n.d., Series IV, Box 581, Folder "Welfare Reform Analysis—National Urban Coalition, 1971," LWV Papers; "Urban Coalition Board Urges President to Act Now on Welfare Reform," 5 November 1971, Box 184, Folder 40, Wurf Records, 1; Statement on National Priorities, Executive Committee Draft, The National Urban Coalition, 4 December 1970, Box 223, Folder 4, Woodcock Papers, 11; Robert M. Smith, "Urban Coalition Praises Welfare Program, But Suggests Ways to Improve It," *NYT*, 15 August 1969, 17.

77. "Revitalizing American Cities: Strategies for the 70s," Leonard Woodcock, president, International Union, UAW, address, National Urban Coalition National Conference, Washington, D.C., 31 May 1973, Box 23, Folder 4, Haener Papers. For the Coalition's increasingly corporate leadership, see National Urban Coalition Leadership, 23 January 1973, Box 184, Folder 39, Wurf Records.

78. Ernest Hollsendolph, "Social Action Hit by Financial Woes," *NYT*, 8 November 1974, 20; Michael T. Kaufman, "Once-Thriving Urban Coalition, Short of Funds, Pares Its Staff," *NYT*, 11 November 1974, 33; Statement to Steering Committee, February 1973, Box 184, Folder 38, Wurf Records, 1.

79. For Gardner's career, and the reference to him as a "pinstripe radical," see the film *John Gardner: Uncommon American*, Twenty-First Century Initiative, www.pbs.org/johngardner.

80. John Herbers, "'Exiles' from Government Head National Urban Coalition," *NYT*, 5 December 1968, 50.

81. John W. Gardner, "The 1970's: Time to Wake Up," delivered at National Press Club, Washington, D.C., 9 December 1969, Box 20, Folder 21, Center for Community Change Papers, Reuther Library, 4.

82. Gardner to Friend, n.d., 1; Lowell R. Beck to Leonard Woodcock, 15 December 1970, Box 195, Folder 5, Woodcock Papers.

83. John Gardner to Friend, n.d. (1970), Box 223, Folder 2, Woodcock Papers, 3.

84. Jack T. Conway, "Opening Up the System," SCAN Annual Forum, Dallas, 1971, Supplement 1, Box 22, NCSW Records, 8–10, 12. A notable exception is Common Cause's opposition to American intervention in Vietnam.

85. "Political Reform Seen Key to Better Social Welfare," *Cincinnati Enquirer*, 22 May 1974 (reprint), Box 6, Folder "1974," NCSW Records.

86. Conway, "Opening Up the System," 3; Common Cause pamphlet, n.d., Box 195, Folder 6, Woodcock Papers.

87. Premilla Nadasen, *Welfare Warriors: The Welfare Rights Movement in the United States* (New York: Routledge, 2005), 200.

88. George Wiley, "The Need for a Taxpayer's Uprising," Keynote Address to the National Council of Churches Conference, 5 March 1973, Statler Hilton Hotel, New York, Box 40, Folder 3, Wiley Papers, 6.

89. George Wiley to Welfare Rights Leaders, Members, Friends and Supporters, December 1972, Box 41, Folder 4, Wiley Papers, 4.

90. Wiley, "Need for a Taxpayer's Uprising," 42; Thomas A. Johnson, "New Power of Welfare clients," *NYT*, 7 August 1971, 20.

91. "Movement for Economic Justice Fundraising Letter," n.d., Box 40, Folder 11, Wiley Papers, 2–3.

92. "Squeeze on America's Middle Class," *U.S. News and World Report*, 14 October 1974, 44.

93. Wiley, "Progress Report on the Planning Phase of the Movement for Economic Justice," 20 June 1973, Box 42, Folder 4, Wiley Papers, 1.

94. Wiley, "Building a New Majority," 6 July 1973, Box 41, Folder 4, Wiley Papers, 5.

95. See multiple issues of *Just Economics* in Box 32, Folder 9, MEJ Papers.

96. Wiley to Friends, 12 April 1973, Box 41, Folder 4, Wiley Papers.

97. The figures are from Robert Lakachman, cited by Alan Gartner, H.R Subcommittee on Equal Opportunities of the Committee on Education and Labor, Hearing on H.R. 50: Equal Opportunity and Full Employment, 94th Cong., 2nd sess., 16 March 1976, 325.

98. "McGovern's Economics," 6 May 1972, *NYT*, 34; John Herbers, "McGovern Forces Shape Planks to Suit Candidate," *NYT*, 13 July 1972, 1, 22; "Excerpts from Proposed Democratic Platform Adopted by Convention Committee," *NYT*, 29 June 1972, 29.

99. Alvin L. Schorr, "Still Waiting for Welfare Reform," *NYT*, 19 January 1974, 31.

100. Wiley, "Need for a Taxpayer's Uprising," 3.

101. Wiley, "Building a New Majority," 7–8.

102. George Wiley to Friends, 12 April 1973, Box 41, Folder 4, MEJ Papers, 1.

103. Testimony by George Wiley before the Ways and Means Committee, 9 March 1973, Box 41, Folder 2, Wiley Papers.

104. Ronald Smothers, "Welfare Activist Plans New Group," *NYT*, 17 December 1972, 49.

105. George Wiley, "Notes on Trip to Milwaukee, Wisconsin," 8 May 1973, Box 42, Folder 4, Wiley Papers, 1, 3.

106. Tim Sampson, "For Our Own Welfare," *Just Economics* 2, 4 (April 1974), Box 32, Folder 17, MEJ Papers, 4–5.

107. Bert DeLeeuw, "Making Us All Less Poor," *Just Economics* 2, 4 (April 1974), Box 32, Folder 17, MEJ Papers, 11.

108. Michael Harrington to Friend, n.d., and The Democratic Agenda, n.d. (1977), both in Box 4, Folder 71, UAW President's Office, Douglas Fraser Records (hereafter Fraser Records).

109. Levison, *Working-Class Majority*, 45.

110. William Spring, Bennett Harrison, and Thomas Vietorisz, "Crisis of the Underemployed," *NYT Magazine*, 5 November 1972, 60.

111. H.R. Subcommittee on Employment Opportunities, Hearing on H.R. 50 and H.R. 2992: The Full Employment and Balanced Growth Act of 1977, 95th Cong., 1st sess., 2 March 1977, 364.

112. "First Full Employment Conference," *Full Employment News Reporter* (from National Committee on Full Employment), September/October 1975, RG98–002, Vertical File, Box 17, Folder 18, Meany Archive.

113. "National Coalition Begins Full Employment Week: Action Planned in 75

Cities September 4–10," *Full Employment Advocate*, Labor Day 1977, and "Millions Turn Out for Full Employment Week," *Full Employment Advocate*, October 1977, in RG98–002, Vertical File, Box 17, Folder 18, Meany Archive.

114. National Committee for Full Employment Membership List, n.d., Box 79, Folder 39, Wurf Records.

115. While the full employment campaign garnered tremendous support from liberal organizations, it does not appear to have been connected to any broader grassroots movement, which may be part of the reason it failed to achieve real reform. As late as 1976, the UAW's Irving Bluestone complained about "apathy surrounding this issue" and Frank Riessman worried that the full employment campaign lacked "large scale demonstrations of [the] unemployed . . . at a grassroots level." Overall, the campaign appears to be a national liberal program with only minimal social movement support, nothing like the kind of mass unemployment movement organized by Communist Party activists in the 1930s. Irving Bluestone to Leonard Woodcock, 5 August 1976, Box 29, Folder 5, Woodcock Papers; Frank Riessman, "Can the Unemployed Be Organized in 1976?" Box 27, Folder 3, MEJ Papers; Irving Bluestone to Douglas Fraser, 9 September 1977, Box 1, Folder 15, Fraser Records, 1.

116. Henry M. Jackson, "Full Employment: The Key to All Goals," *American Federationist*, August 1971, 16.

117. Eli Ginzberg, "The Continuing Search for Jobs and Freedom," *The Crisis*, February 1976, 66.

118. "Wary of Welfare," *New Republic*, 5 June 1976, 3. Rep. John Conyers (D-Mich.) had actually introduced the Full Opportunity Act of 1967, a full employment plan with a job guarantee, much earlier, but such efforts gained little support and little attention. H.R. Subcommittee on Equal Opportunities, Hearing on H.R. 50, 24 March 1975, 25–26. At least one Republican, Jacob Javitz, also introduced a full employment bill. "Javitz Calls for National 'Full Employment Policy'," 17 July 1974, Box 219, Folder 1, Woodcock Papers.

119. For a history of the full employment issue, see Philip Harvey, *Securing the Right to Employment* (Princeton, N.J.: Princeton University Press, 1989).

120. Nancy MacLean, *Freedom Is Not Enough: The Opening of the American Workplace* (New York: Russell Sage, 2006), 40, 105.

121. Dona Cooper Hamilton and Charles V. Hamilton Hamilton, *The Dual Agenda: The African-American Struggle for Civil and Economic Equality* (New York: Columbia University Press, 1997), 66–71.

122. MacLean, *Freedom Is Not Enough*, 5.

123. Bricklayers, Masons, and Plasterers International Union pamphlet of Bayard Rustin, "Black Rage, White Fear: The Full Employment Answer," AFL-CIO Duplicate Pamphlets, Box 1, Meany Archive. See also Richard F. Hamilton, "Black Demands, White Reactions, and Liberal Alarm" in Levitan, *Blue-Collar Workers*, 151.

124. Testimony of Coretta Scott King, H.R. Subcommittee on Equal Opportunities, Hearing on H.R. 50, 4 April 1975, 256.

125. Herrrington J. Bryce, "Toward Full Employment: Minorities and the Cities," National Conference on Public Service Employment, Academy for Con-

temporary Problems, Columbus, Ohio, 1 November 1974, reprinted in H.R. Subcommittee on Equal Opportunities, Hearing on H.R. 50, 18 March 1975, 55.

126. Dale Larson, "The Widening Civil Rights Coalition," *American Federationist*, September 1976 (reprint), RG98–002, Vertical File, Box 6, Folder 7, Meany Archive, 24.

127. H.R. Subcommittee on Equal Opportunities, Hearing on H.R. 50, 26 March 1975, 151; 14 October 1975, 140; and 4 April 1975, 322.

128. Martin Gilens, "How the Poor Became Black: The Racialization of American Poverty in the Mass Media," in *Race and the Politics of Welfare Reform*, ed. Sanford F. Schram, Joe Soss, and Richard C. Fording (Ann Arbor: University of Michigan Press, 2003), 117–18.

129. Susan Hartmann, *The Other Feminists: Activists in the Liberal Establishment* (New Haven: Yale University Press, 1998).

130. H.R. Subcommittee on Equal Opportunities, Hearing on H.R. 50, *H.R. 2276, H.R. 5937*, 94th Cong., 1st sess., 5 May 1975, 3.

131. H.R. Subcommittee on Equal Opportunities, Hearing on H.R. 50, 13 October 1975, 16.

132. Stu Eizenstat and Frank Moore to President Carter, 29 September 1978, Box 104, Folder "9/29/78," Staff Secretary's Office-Presidential Handwriting File, Carter Presidential Library 1; H.R. Subcommittee on Equal Opportunities, Hearing on H.R. 50, 13 February 1976, 17.

133. H.R. Subcommittee on Manpower, Compensation and Health and Safety, Hearing on H.R. 50, 6 April 1976, 183.

134. Quoted in ibid., 2 April 1976, 99.

135. H.R. Subcommittee on Equal Opportunities, Hearing on H.R. 50, 25 February 1975, 90.

136. MacLean, *Freedom Is Not Enough*, 288.

137. "Black Unemployment Rate Rises to Post War High: President Promises Action on Full Employment," *Full Employment Advocate* 2, 3 (October 1977), RG98–002, Vertical File, Box 17, Folder 18, Meany Archive, 2.

138. Norman Hill, "Civil Rights and Full Employment," *American Federationist*, May 1977 (reprint), RG98–002, Vertical File, Box 6, Folder 7, Meany Archive, 3; "Black Unemployment Rate Rises to Post War High," 2.

139. "Black Unemployment Rate Rises to Post War High," 2.

140. Stu Eizenstat and Bill Spring to President Carter, 18 November 1977, Box 60, Folder "11/19/77," Staff Secretary's Office Presidential Handwriting File, 4.

141. Thomas J. Sugrue, "Carter's Urban Policy Crisis," and Hugh Davis Graham, "Civil Rights Policy in the Carter Presidency," in *The Carter Presidency: Policy Choices in the Post-New Deal Era*, ed. Gary M. Fink and Hugh Davis Graham (Lawrence: University Press of Kansas, 1998). Carter opposed guaranteed federal jobs that made the government the "employer of last resort," a long-standing liberal proposal. Stu Eizenstat to President Carter, 17 September 1977, Box 50, Folder "9/19/77[2]," Office of the Staff Secretary-Presidential Handwriting File, 2.

142. James T. McIntyre, Jr., to President Carter, 24 October 1977, Folder "10/25/77[1]," Staff Secretary-Presidential Handwriting File.

143. Mrs. Coretta Scott King Testimony, Sen. Labor Committee, 19 May 1976, Box 219, Folder 5, Woodcock Papers, 6.

144. Murray Finley to Jerry Wurf, 14 August 1974, Box 79, Folder 39, Wurf Records.

145. "Black Unemployment Rises to Post War High," 2.

146. Norman Hill, "Civil Rights and Full Employment," 3.

147. H.R. Subcommittee on Equal Opportunities, Hearing on H.R. 50, 15 March 1976, 167.

148. Ibid.

149. Labor News Conference, Program 18, Series 17, 16 August 1977, RG98–002, Vertical File, Box 17, Folder 18, Meany Archive, 3; H.R. Subcommittee on Equal Opportunities, Hearing on H.R. 50, 16 March 1976, 309, 332; "Why Recovering Economies—A Radical Change in Political Economics," *Business Week*, cited in ibid., 333; H.R. Subcommittee on Manpower, Compensation, and Health and Safety, Hearing on H.R. 50, 8 April 1976, 189.

150. Sen. Committee on Banking, Housing, and Urban Affairs, Hearing on S. 50: Full Employment and Balanced Growth Act of 1976, 94th Cong., 2nd sess., 21 May 1976, 111.

151. Quoted in Helen Ginsberg, "Full Employment: The Necessary Ingredient," *Do It NOW* 9, 7 (1976), Schlesinger Library, 11.

152. H.R. Subcommittee on Manpower, Compensation, and Health and Safety, Hearing on H.R. 50, 14 April 1976, 437; Sen. Subcommittee on Employment, Poverty, and Migratory Labor, Hearing on H.R. 50 and S. 472, May 1976, 572; Sen. Committee on Banking, Housing, and Urban Affairs, Hearing on S. 50, 20 May 1976, 3.

153. H.R. Subcommittee on Equal Opportunities of the Committee on Education and Labor, Hearing on H.R. 50, 18 March 1975, 35–36; Sen. Committee on Banking, Housing, and Urban Affairs, Hearing on S. 50, 20 May 1976, 54–55.

154. Carolyn J. Jacobson, "New Challenges for Women Workers," *American Federationist*, April 1980 (reprint), RG98–002, Vertical File, Box 72, Folder 5, Meany Archive, 2.

155. Sen. Subcommittee on Employment, Poverty, and Migratory Labor, Hearing on S. 50 and S. 472, 19 May 1976, 646–47.

156. Sen. Committee on Banking, Housing and Urban Affairs, Hearing on S. 50, 25 May 1976, 364.

157. Statement of Carl Reinstein, Local 157, UAW, Detroit, in H.R. Subcommittee on Equal Opportunities, Hearing on H.R. 50, 4 April 1975, 337; Statement of Leon Keyserling, 15 March 1976, 272.

158. Hartmann, *The Other Feminists*.

159. Helen R. Parolla, "Full Employment as a Women's Issue," National Women's Agenda Coalition Conference, Washington, D.C., 17 March 1978, Box 318, Folder "Employment-Full Miscellany 1974–76," NCJW Washington, D.C. Office, 1.

160. Cynthia Ellen Harrison, *On Account of Sex: The Politics of Women's Issues, 1954–1968* (Berkeley: University of California Press, 1988), 192–96; MacLean, *Freedom Is Not Enough*, 127–28.

161. Coalition of Labor Union Women, Statement of Purpose, Adopted at the

Founding Conference, 23–24 March 1974, RG98–002, Vertical File, Box 6, Folder 10, Meany Archive.

162. Helen R. Parolla, "Full Employment as a Women's Issue," Speech for National Women's Agenda Coalition Conference, Washington, D.C., 17 March 1978, Box 318, Folder "Employment-Full Miscellany 1974–76," NCJW Washington, D.C., Office, 3.

163. From 1940 to 1972, labor force participation for mothers rose almost fivefold, from 9 to 43%, accompanied by a "sharp rise in the number of mothers with preschool children in the labor force." In 1971, 50% of minority women worked for wages, compared to 43% of white women. Minority women also had higher official unemployment rates. Carolyn J. Jacobson, "Women Workers: Profile of a Growing Force," *American Federationist* (July 1974), Meany Archive, 9–15.

164. "NOW Task Force on Women and Poverty," November 1973, Box 45, Folder "TF: Women and Poverty," NOW Papers; Ann Scott quoted in Helen Ginsberg, "Full Employment: The Necessary Ingredient," *Do It NOW* 9, 7 (1976), NOW Papers, 11.

165. NOW Women and Poverty Task Force, *Commonwealth* (1975), Box 210, Folder 47, NOW Papers.

166. Lynn Darcy, "Full Employment . . . NOW," *Do It Now*, September 1975, NOW Papers, 4.

167. NOW Women and Poverty Task Force, *Commonwealth* (1975), Box 210, Folder 47, NOW Papers, 10.

168. Testimony of Lynn Darcy and Mary Jo Binder of NOW, H.R. Subcommittee on Equal Opportunities, Hearing on H.R. 50, 18 March 1975, 14.

169. H.R. Subcommittee on Equal Opportunities, Hearing on H.R. 50, 14 October 1975, 202.

170. Sen. Subcommittee on Employment, Poverty, and Migratory Labor, Hearing on S. 50 and S. 472, 19 May 1976, 674.

171. H.R. Subcommittee on Equal Opportunities, Hearing on H.R. 50, 18 March 1975, 14.

172. Sen. Subcommittee on Employment, Poverty, and Migratory Labor, Hearing on S. 50 and S. 472, 19 May 1976, 615.

173. H.R. Subcommittee on Equal Opportunties, Hearing on H.R. 50, 14 October 1975, 186.

174. Ibid., 205.

175. Sen. Subcommittee on Employment, Poverty, and Migratory Labor, Hearing on S. 50 and S. 472, 19 May 1976, 617.

176. Ms. Johnnie Tillmon to Friends, 22 March 1973, Box 77, Folder 27, Wurf Records; MacLean, *Freedom Is Not Enough*, 267–79.

177. Maya Miller and Carol Burris to Edie Van Horn, 7 June 1976, Box 15, Folder 18, Haener Papers, 1.

178. H.R. Subcommittee on Equal Opportunities, Hearing on H.R. 50, 4 April 1975, 332.

179. See MacLean, *Freedom Is Not Enough*, 290.

180. Nathan Glazer, " 'Regulating' the Poor—Or Ruining Them," *New York*, 11 October 1971, 58.

181. George Gilder, *Wealth and Poverty* (New York: Basic Books, 1981), 12.

182. The annual earnings for young men ages 25–29 declined by 20% between 1973 and 1986 (28% for black men, 36% for men without a high school diploma). The cause was a decline in both employment and hourly earnings. Paul E. Peterson, "The Urban Underclass and the Poverty Paradox," in Jencks and Peterson, *The Urban Underclass*, 17.

183. Katz, *Undeserving Poor*, 133. For a longer-term analysis of the "urban crisis," see Thomas J. Sugrue, *The Origins of the Underclass: Race and Inequality in Postwar Detroit* (Princeton, N.J.: Princeton University Press, 1996).

184. Katz, *Undeserving Poor*, 137. At the same time, non-metropolitan and suburban poverty rates fell significantly. Peterson, "The Urban Underclass and the Poverty Paradox," 7.

185. Harry Anderson, "Is Poverty Dead?" *Newsweek*, 9 October 1978, 85–86; "War on Poverty Created New Dependent Class," *USA Today*, December 1978, 9.

186. Robert Greenstein, "Universal and Targeted Approaches to Relieving Poverty: An Alternative View," in Jencks and Peterson, *The Urban Underclass*, 439.

187. Martha Hill, "The Changing Nature of Poverty," *Annals of the American Academy of Political and Social Science* 479 (May 1985): 43–45. By the early 1970s, the official American poverty rate leveled off (despite occasional fluctuations) at about 13% of the population. The changing composition of the poverty population, though, suggests how important transfer policies were in keeping that rate low in the 1970s, when poverty among the aged declined significantly while the poverty rate for young families (whose social safety net contained many more holes) increased. Paul E. Peterson, "The Urban Underclass and the Poverty Paradox," 6–7.

188. "America's Rising Black Middle Class," 17 June 1974, 26–27.

189. Quoted in Roger Wilkins, "The Sound of One Hand Clapping," *NYT Magazine*, 12 May 1974, 43.

190. Charles W. Bowser, Philadelphia Urban League, "Federal Revenue Sharing: Reform or Retrenchment?" in 101st Annual Forum (NCSW), Cincinnati, May 1974, SCAN 310-013399-974 to 310-01434-974, Box 23, NCSW Records, 2, 6.

191. James D. Williams to Vernon Jordan, 25 March 1977, Box 42, Folder 7, Part III, NUL Papers, 2. See also Oorde Combs, "Three Faces of Harlem," *NYT Magazine*, 3 November 1974, 36.

192. "After Twenty Years: The New Turn in Black Revolution," *U.S. News and World Report*, 20 May 1974, 29.

193. "The American Underclass: Destitute and Desperate in the Land of Plenty," *Time*, 29 August 1977, 14–27.

194. Susan Sheehan, "Profiles: A Welfare Mother," *New Yorker*, 29 September 1975, 42–99.

195. Quoted in "The March to Equality Marks Time," *Time*, 3 September 1973, 75.

196. Auletta, *The Underclass*, xvi, 68.

197. Godfrey Hodgson, *The World Turned Right Side Up: A History of the Conservative Ascendancy in America* (Boston: Houghton Mifflin, 1996); Lisa McGirr, *Suburban Warriors: The Origins of the New American Right* (Princeton, N.J.:

Princeton University Press, 2001); David Farber and Jeff Roche, eds., *The Conservative Sixties* (New York: Peter Lang, 2003).

198. Andrew E. Busch, "Ronald Reagan and Economic Policy" in *The Reagan Presidency: Assessing the Man and His Legacy*, ed. Paul Kengor and Peter Schweitzer (Lanham, Md.: Rowman & Littlefield, 2005), 26.

199. David Brian Robertson, "Introduction: Loss of Confidence and Policy Change in the 1970s," *Journal of Policy History* 10, 1 (1998), 5.

200. S. M. Miller, "Can the Poor Solve America's Problems?" *Society* (September–October 1978): 7.

201. Burt F. Raynes, "Letter to NAM Members 1973: Some New Directions" in "Industry Speaks Out: NAM 1972 Annual Report to Board Members," Series IV, Box 70, NAM Papers, 2–3.

202. Between 1970 and 1983, the budgets of the conservative American Enterprise Institute and Heritage Foundation grew tenfold, while the Hoover Institution's budget quadrupled. At the same time, the mainstream/liberal Brookings Institution's budget only doubled. One scholar estimates that conservative think tanks had four times the funding of liberal think tanks. Ellen Reese, *Backlash Against Welfare Mothers Past and Present* (Berkeley: University of California Press, 2005), 151–52.

203. Text of Pamphlet in Edward A. Sprauge to GO/EC, 6 September 1972, Series IV, Box 70, NAM Papers.

204. Glenn Tinder, "Defending the Welfare State," *New Republic*, 10 March 1979, 22.

205. Lawrence W. Reed, "The Fall of Rome and Modern Parallels: The Respect for Life and Property," *Vital Speeches of the Day*, 1 August 1979, 629–31.

206. Gilder, *Wealth and Poverty*, 67.

207. Tom Bethall, "Treating Poverty,"*Harper's*, February 1980, 24.

208. See, e.g., M. S. Forbes, Jr., "Would You Take a New Job?" *Forbes*, 30 October 1978, 43.

209. Flyer for Industry Week's Closed-Circuit Teleconference, "How to Restore the Will to Work," 14 November 1972; "Background Memorandum for GO-EC Meeting, 29 February 1972," 1; and "Industry Speaks Out: NAM 1972 Annual Report to Members," all in Series IV, Box 70, NAM Papers, and GO/EC Committee to Bolton Re: Welfare and Family Assistance for Board of Directors Meeting, 17 May 1972, Series IV, Box 77, NAM Papers.

210. "Why Are New York's Workers Dropping Out?" August 1973, Series IV, Box 77, NAM Papers.

211. "How Welfare Keeps Women from Working," *Business Week*, 7 April 1973, 51; "Points to Be Made on 'Work Ethic vs. Welfare Ethic'," for "The Will to Work," 2 November 1972, Series IV, Box 77, NAM Papers, 2.

212. GO/EC, "Welfare Reform—AFDC Program" (Analysis of HR 5133 and S 1719), 18 June 1975, Series IV, Box 77, NAM Papers, 3003.

213. Sen. Finance Committee, Hearings on H.R. 1: Social Security Amendments of 1971, 92nd Cong., 2nd sess., 27 January 1972, 1413; "Welfare Reform: What Government Can Do," 2 November 1972, Series IV, Box 77, NAM Papers, 1.

214. Oscar Lewis, *The Children of Sanchez: Autobiography of a Mexican Family*

(New York: Random House, 1961), and *La Vida: A Puerto Rican Family in the Culture of Poverty—San Juan and New York* (New York: Random House, 1966).

215. Edward C. Banfield, *The Unheavenly City: The Nature and Future of Our Urban Crisis* (Boston: Little, Brown, 1970), 46, 53.

216. "Two Possible Alternatives for NAM Input to Congressional Budget Office on Budget Options for Fiscal 1977," 25 April 1975, Series IV, Box 49, Folder "Fiscal 1975 Budget Study Task Force," NAM Papers, 1.

217. "Points to be made on 'Work Ethic vs. Welfare Ethic'," for "The Will to Work," 2 November 1972, Series IV, Box 77, NAM Papers, 1.

218. "Summary: The National Welfare Reform Act of 1975: A Proposal for Meaningful Reform of the Nation's Aid to Families with Dependent Children Program, March 1975," Accession 1411, Series IV, Box 128, Folder "HEW Proposed Regulations re: Eligibility for AFDC-UF Benefits in Labor Disputes," NAM Papers, 1.

219. Gilder, *Wealth and Poverty*, 71.

220. George Gilder, *Sexual Suicide* (New York: Quadrangle/ NYT, 1973), 98, 173.

221. Gilder, *Wealth and Poverty*, 12, 115.

222. Ibid., 126–27, 98, 159, 169.

223. Between 1945 and 1973, the average weekly earnings of forty-year-old American men increased by 2.5 to 3.0% annually. After 1973, those wages stagnated and declined. Between 1973 and 1980, despite an increase in working wives, the average family income declined by 7%. Katz, *Undeserving Poor*, 129.

224. Melinda Beck, "Welfare: A Surprising Test," *Newsweek*, 27 November 1978, 33–34.

225. Stephen Chapman, "Poor Laws," *New Republic*, 2 December 1978, 8; Robert Moffitt, "The Negative Income Tax: Would It Discourage Work?" *Monthly Labor Review*, April 1981, 23–27.

226. Bethall, "Treating Poverty," 23. Other antiwelfare conservatives argued that experimenter bias and experimental design probably greatly understated the NIT work disincentive. Martin Anderson, *Welfare: The Political Economy of Welfare Reform in the United States* (Stanford, Calif.: Hoover Institution Press, 1978), 100–101.

227. The Seattle and Denver experiment tested eleven different NIT plans, with benefits ranging from 90 to 140% of the federal poverty level and with various tax rates applied to earnings. Marital dissolution appeared to increase in families receiving lower benefit levels but not higher benefit levels, complicating the findings. Laurence E. Lynn, Jr. and David deF. Whitman, *The President as Policymaker: Jimmy Carter and Welfare Reform* (Philadelphia: Temple University Press, 1981), 247; Meg Greenfield, "Policy Without People," *Newsweek*, 23 October 1978, 140.

228. "Welfare Reform, Family Breakups," *National Review*, 8 December 1978, 1526–27; Donald C. Bacon, "America's War on Poverty—Is It a No-Win Struggle?" *U.S. News and World Report*, 22 January 1979, 22; Memo from Russell Long to President Carter, n.d., Box 319, Folder "Welfare Reform 8/77," Domestic Policy Staff-Stuart Eizenstat File, Carter Library (hereafter DPS-Eizenstat File), 2–3.

229. Chapman, "Poor Laws," 8.

230. Andrew Cherlin, "Divorcing Welfare from Marriage," *Psychology Today*, July 1979, 92.

231. Moynihan, quoted in Lynn and Whitman, *President as Policymaker*, 248–49.

232. Gilbert K. Steiner, *The Futility of Family Policy* (Washington, D.C.: Brookings Institution Press, 1981), 108–9.

233. Gilder, *Wealth and Poverty*, 114–15.

234. Ibid., 120.

235. J. David Hoeveler, "Populism, Politics, and Public Policy: 1970s Conservatism," *Journal of Policy History* 10, 1 (1998), 84.

236. For an overview of the rise of neoconservatism and a discussion of the neoconservative political ideology, see Gary Dorrien, *The Neoconservative Mind: Politics, Culture, and the War of Ideology* (Philadelphia: Temple University Press, 1993); Mark Gerson, *The Neoconservative Vision: From the Cold War to the Culture Wars* (Lanham, Md.: Madison Books, 1996); Murray Friedman, *The Neoconservative Revolution: Jewish Intellectuals and the Shaping of Public Policy* (Cambridge: Cambridge University Press, 2005).

237. Friedman, *Neoconservative Revolution*, 189–90.

238. Gerson, *Neoconservative Vision*, 96.

239. Herbert Gutman, *The Black Family in Slavery and Freedom, 1750–1925* (New York: Pantheon, 1976); Nathan Glazer, "On the Gutman Thesis," *Current*, December 1976, 10.

240. Gerson, *Neoconservative Vision*, 91; Friedman, *Neoconservative Revolution*, 34.

241. Irving Kristol, "The Poverty of Equality," *Wall Street Journal*, 12 July 1976, 10. Kristol as a "disillusioned liberal" is from Friedman, *Neoconservative Revolution*, 116.

242. John A. Davenport, "The Welfare State Versus the Public Welfare," *Fortune*, June 1976, 37.

243. M. Stanton Evans, "Dark Horses," *National Review*, 23 June 1978, 793; "Is Real Welfare Reform an Impossible Dream?" *Nation's Business*, January 1979, 36–37; Bethall, "Treating Poverty," 16.

244. Kenneth Y. Tomlinson, "We *Can* Clean Up the Welfare Mess," *Reader's Digest*, April 1980, 85; Evans, "Dark Horses," 793; "Is Welfare Reform an Impossible Dream?" *Nation's Business*, January 1979, 30; Bethall, "Treating Poverty," 16; George Gilder, "The Welfare Trap," *Washington Monthly*, September 1978, 47–52.

245. Jencks, "Is the American Underclass Growing?" 28.

246. Nicholas Lemann, *The Promised Land: The Great Black Migration and How it Changed America* (New York: Vintage, 1991), 351.

247. Martha S. Hill, "The Changing Nature of Poverty," *Annals of the American Academy of Political and Social Science* 479 (May 1985): 31–47; Robert Reinhold, "Poverty Is Found Less Persistent But Wider Spread Than Thought," *NYT*, 15 July 1977, 1, 36.

248. Katz, *Undeserving Poor*, 130.

249. Rone Tempest, "Welfare Not Used to Avoid Working, U-M Study Claims," *Detroit Free Press*, 22 July 1973 (reprint), Box 13, Folder 23, Haener Papers.

250. For a summary of the research, see Greg J. Duncan, Martha S. Hill, and Saul D. Hoffman, "Welfare Dependence Within and Across Generations," *Science* n.s. 239, 4839 (29 January 1988): 467–71.

251. Diana Pearce, "Welfare Is Not *for* Women: Why the War on Poverty Cannot Conquer the Feminization of Poverty," in *Women, the State, and Welfare*, ed. Linda Gordon (Madison: University of Wisconsin Press, 1990), 265–79.

252. Thomas Powers, "The Night the Lights Went Out," *Commonweal*, 19 August 1977, 531.

Chapter 4. Debating the Family Wage: Welfare Reform in the Carter Administration

NCSW, "Principles for an Income Security System for the United States, Final Report," 1976, Supplement 1, Box 33, NCSW Records, x.

1. Gilbert K. Steiner, *The Futility of Family Policy* (Washington, D.C.: Brookings Institution, 1981), 99.

2. For an overview of *Califano v. Westcott*, see Clare Cushman, ed., *Supreme Court Decisions and Women's Rights: Milestones to Equality* (Washington, D.C.: Congressional Quarterly, 2001), 81–82.

3. Abigail McCarthy, "The Ideal and the Issue: Facing Reality in Helping Families," *Commonweal*, 25 April 1980, 233; Linda Greenhouse, "High Court Holds Jobless Mother Equal to Father on Welfare Right," *NYT*, 26 June 1979, 9; Susan K. Blumenthal, "Court Extends AFDC Benefits in Westcott Decision," *National NOW Times*, August 1979, Schlesinger Library, 3; Center on Social Welfare Policy and Law, Memorandum to Welfare Specialists, 19 July 1979, Series IV, Box 589, Folder "Welfare Reform: General Correspondence, 1977–79," LWV Papers, 2.

4. Blumenthal, "Court Extends AFDC Benefits in Westcott Decision," 3.

5. Arlene S. Skolnick and Jerome H. Skolnick, "Introduction: Family in Transition" in *Family in Transition: Rethinking Marriage, Sexuality, Child Rearing, and Family Organization*, ed. Arlene S. Skolnick and Jerome H. Skolnick, 6th ed. (Glenview, Ill.: Scott, Foresman, 1989), 1.

6. The term "degendered family wage" is Dorothy Sue Cobble's. Cobble, *The Other Women's Movement: Workplace Justice and Social Rights in Modern America* (Princeton, N.J.: Princeton University Press, 2004).

7. Cushman, *Supreme Court and Women's Rights*, 81.

8. Quoted in George E. Jones, "Can Carter Revitalize the American Family?" *U.S. News and World Report*, 28 February 1977, 35.

9. Joan Cook, "The Family Could Become a Relic by 2000, Sociologists Say," *NYT*, 2 June 1977, II, 25.

10. "To Fulfill These Rights: Remarks of the President at Howard University, June 4, 1965," in Lee Rainwater and William L. Yancey, *The Moynihan Report and the Politics of Controversy* (Cambridge, Mass.: MIT Press, 1967), 130.

11. Urie Bronfenbrenner, "The American Family in Decline," *Current*, January 1977, 42; Steiner, *Futility of Family Policy*, 12.

12. Marshall Berman, "Family Affairs," *NYT*, 15 January 1978, Section 7, 6.

13. "Study Sees Changes in the Family by 1990," *NYT*, 23 May 1980, 18; Steven V. Roberts, "The Family Fascinates a Host of Students," *NYT*, 23 April 1978, Section IV, 20; Steven V. Roberts, "Studying Government Role in Family," *NYT*, 24 June 1978, 12; Linda Asher, "Uncle Sam's Family Budget," *Psychology Today* 13, 7 (December 1979), 34; "Panel Urges Move to Shore Up Family and Protect Poor Children," *NYT*, 15 December 1976, Section IV, 29; Donald Tinder, "Family Life Begins at Home," *Christianity Today*, 7 November 1975, 62–63; Nadine Brozan, "Mondale: Family's Man in the Senate," *NYT*, 26 February 1974, 32.

14. Bronfenbrenner, The American Family in Decline"; "Saving the Family," *Newsweek*, 15 May 1978, 63–73; "The American Family: Bent—But Not Broken," *U.S. News and World Report*, 16 June 1980, 48–61.

15. George E. Jones, "Can Carter Revitalize the American Family?" *U.S. News and World Report*, 28 February 1977, 35; Charles Mohr, "Carter, in New Hampshire, Promises to Seek to Restore Respect for Family," *NYT*, 4 August 1976, 12; Steiner, *Futility of Family Policy*, 3, 14.

16. "Poll Finds People Feel Family Life on Decline," *NYT*, 3 June 1980, II, 12.

17. "Study Sees Changes in the Family, by 1990," *NYT*, 23 May 1980, 18.

18. Stephanie Coontz, *The Way We Never Were: American Families and the Nostalgia Trap* (New York: Basic Books, 1992), 3; Daniel P. Moynihan, Timothy M. Smeeding, and Lee Rainwater, "The Challenge of the Family System: Changes for Research and Policy" in *The Future of the Family*, ed. Daniel P. Moynihan, Timothy M. Smeeding, and Lee Rainwater (New York: Russell Sage, 2004), 8–9.

19. Andrew Cherlin, "Recent Changes in American Fertility, Marriage and Divorce,"*Annals of the American Academy of Political and Social Science* 510, 1 (1990): 145–54, 146; Coontz, *The Way We Never Were*, 3. To put the statistics another way: between 1960 and 1984, the proportion of American households headed by women increased from 9 to 12% for whites and from 22 to 23% for African Americans. Michael B. Katz, *The Undeserving Poor: From the War on Poverty to the War on Welfare* (New York: Pantheon, 1990), 219.

20. Quoted in Jean Bethke Elshtain, "Hard Times for the American Family," *Progressive*, May 1981 (reprint), RG98–002, Vertical File, Box 16, Folder 6, Meany Archive, 18.

21. Ibid.

22. Steven V. Roberts, "Studying Government Role in Family," *NYT*, 24 June 1978, 12.

23. See, for example, "The American Family: Can It Survive Today's Shocks?" and "As Parents' Influence Fades—Who's Raising the Children?" *U.S. News and World Report*, 27 October 1975, 30–31, 41–43.

24. Boylan quoted in "Street Crime Tied to Broken Homes," *NYT*, 23 March 1975, 71.

25. Armand M. Nicholi II, "The Fractured Family: Following It into the Future," *Christianity Today*, 25 May 1979, 14.

26. Kimberly Morgan, "A Child of the Sixties: The Great Society, the New Right, and the Politics of Federal Child Care," *Journal of Policy History* 13, 2 (2001), 240.

27. The Free Congress Foundation continues to define itself as a think tank focused on cultural issues like family. http://www.freecongress.org/, accessed 26 September 2006.

28. Sara Diamond, *Spiritual Warfare: The Politics of the Christian Right* (Boston: South End Press, 1989), 85.

29. Kristin Luker, *Abortion and the Politics of Motherhood* (Berkeley: University of California Press, 1984); Jane Sherron De Hart, "Gender on the Right: Meanings Behind the Existential Scream," *Gender & History* 3, 3 (1991); Dierdre English, "The Fear That Feminism Will Free Men First," in *Powers of Desire: The Politics of Sexuality*, ed. Ann Snitow, Christine Stansell, and Sharon Thompson (New York: Monthly Review Press, 1983).

30. Nancy MacLean, *Freedom Is Not Enough: The Opening of the American Work Place* (New York: Sage, 2006), 246–47.

31. Coontz, *The Way We Never Were*, 30.

32. For an overview of workers' declining standard of living after 1973, see Bennett Harrison and Barry Bluestone, *The Great U-Turn* (New York: Basic Books, 1988). See also Marsha Garrison, "The Goals and Limits of Child Support Policy," in *Child Support: The Next Frontier*, ed. J. Thomas Oldham and Marygold S. Melli (Ann Arbor: University of Michigan Press, 2000), 36, n. 21.

33. Coontz, *The Way We Never Were*, 260.

34. Barbara Bergman, "The Economic Risks of Being a Housewife," *American Economic Review* 71, 2 (1982), 81–86.

35. " 'The Traditional Family Will Make a Comeback': Interview with Dr. Lee Salk, Child Psychologist," *U.S. News and World Report*, 16 June 1980, 60.

36. " 'Throwaway Marriages'—Threat to the American Family," *U.S. News and World Report*, 13 January 1975, 44; " 'Why Marriages Turn Sour—And How to Get Help,' Interview with psychiatrist E. James Lieberman, M.D., director of Family Planning Project for the American Public Health Association," *U.S. News and World Report*, 27 October 1975, 44.

37. William V. Shannon, "Our Lost Children," *NYT*, 10 September 1975, 45.

38. Carter promised a White House Conference on the Family in a speech to the National Conference of Catholic Charities in the fall of 1976. For an overview of the WHCF's disastrous planning process, see Steiner, *Futility of Family Policy*, 32–45.

39. National Commission on Families and Public Policies, "Families and Public Policies in the United States, Final Report of the Commission," 1978, Supplement 1, Box 33, NCSW Records, 1.

40. Walter F. Mondale, "Introducing a Special Report: The Family in Trouble," *Psychology Today* 10, 12 (May 1977), 39.

41. "Alabama Will Bypass the Conference on Families," *NYT*, 12 February 1980, II, 6.

42. The change to the plural was at the urging of HEW officials. Steiner, *Futility of Family Policy*, 35. In 1980, the U.S. Census also discarded its automatic denomination of the adult male as "head of household." Jessie Bernard, "The Good-Provider Role: Its Rise and Fall," in Skolnick and Skolnick, *Family in Transition*, 143.

43. Nadine Brozan, "Carter, Opening Family Conference, Calls for Creative Solutions," 6 June 1980, II, 4; "Catholics Quit Family Coalition," *NYT*, 27 June 1980, 20; Diane Ravitch, "In the Family's Way," *New Republic*, 28 June 1980, 19.

44. Steiner, *Futility of Family Policy*, 21, 45.

45. "Alabama Will Bypass the Conference on Families," 6; John Maust, "The White House Feud on the Family," *Christianity Today* 24, 9 (2 May 1980), 47–50.

46. Melinda Beck, "A Family Meeting Turns into a Feud," *Newsweek*, 16 June 1980, 31; Maust, "The White House Feud on the Family," 47–50; "All in the Family," *Time*, 16 June 1980, 30; Brozan, "Carter Calls for Creative Solutions."

47. *The Right Woman: Congressional News for Women & the Family* 3, 2 (November 1979), ed. Jo Ann Gasper, Box 415, Folder "White House Conference-Families Correspondence and Minutes 1979," NCJW Washington, D.C., Office Records.

48. John L. Kater, Jr., *Christians on the Right: The Moral Majority in Perspective* (New York: Seabury, 1982), 83–84.

49. "The Family: Cornerstone of America's Strength," NCAC *ALERT*, November 1979, Box 415, Folder "White House Conference-Families Correspondence and Minutes 1979," NCJW Washington, D.C., Office Records, 1.

50. Rosalind Pollack Petchesky discusses the relationship between the New Right's family ideology and its ideology of "privatism" in "Antiabortion, Antifeminism, and the Rise of the New Right," *Feminist Studies* 7, 2 (Summer 1981): 206–46.

51. M. Stanton Evans, "Saving the Family," *National Review*, 25 January 1980, 101.

52. "One-Parent Families Singled Out for Trouble," *Dollars & Sense*, September 1983 (reprint), RG98–002, Vertical File, Box 16, Folder 6, Meany Archive, 12.

53. Quoted in J. David Hoeveler, Jr., *The Postmodernist Turn: American Thought and Culture in the 1970s* (New York: Twayne, 1996), 147.

54. See, for example, Midge Decter, *The New Chastity and Other Arguments Against Women's Liberation* (New York: Coward McCann, 1972); Rita Kramer, *In Defense of the Family: Raising Children in America Today* (New York: Basic Books, 1983); and Peter Berger and Brigitte Berger, *The War Over the Family: Capturing the Middle Ground* (New York: Anchor, 1983).

55. Nina Roth, "The Neoconservative Backlash Against Feminism in the 1970s and 1980s: The Case of *Commentary*" in *Consumption and American Culture*, ed. David E. Nye and Carl Pederson (Amsterdam: VU University Press, 1991), 83–98. While neoconservatives did not reject the entire New Deal social welfare state, their increasingly hostile attacks on a variety of social programs and taxation "became increasingly difficult to distinguish from traditional conservative rhetoric against social engineering." Gary Dorrien, *The Neoconservative Mind: Politics, Culture, and the War of Ideology* (Philadelphia: Temple University Press, 1993), 17. Despite some veiled anxieties about the "cultural contradictions of capitalism," neoconservatives by the late 1970s maintained a strong belief "that the free market system allows everyone an opportunity to rise out of poverty," provided they adopted bourgeois values and the government stayed out of the way. Mark Gerson, *The Neoconservative Vision: From the Cold War to the Culture Wars* (Lanham, Md.: Madison Books, 1996), 224–27.

56. John W. Donohue, "Family Trouble," *America* 142, 13 (5 April 1980): 288–89.

57. Steiner, *Futility of Family Policy*, 42–43; Roger Wilkins, "U.S. Family Conference Delayed Amid Disputes and Resignations," *NYT*, 19 June 1978, 1.

58. Steiner, *Futility of Family Policy*, 43; Donohue, "Family Trouble," 289. For Carr's background and antipoverty work, see http://pewforum.org/events/0605/carrbio.htm, accessed 15 April 2009.

59. "Topical Statement: White House Conference on Families," 22 June 1978, Series I, Box 33, Folder "NCJW Board Meeting 6/78," NCJW National Office Papers.

60. LWV-US to Joseph Califano, 24 February 1977, Series IV, Box 589, Folder "Welfare Reform: General Correspondence, 77–79," LWV Papers, 2.

61. Quoted in Anne-Marie Schiro, "Interfaith Support Asked for Family Panel," *NYT*, 26 March 1980, III, 18; Leslie Bennetts, "Family Parley: Balance a Goal," *NYT*, 1 June 1980, 23, 1.

62. Nadine Brozan, "Second Day of Family Conference: Workshops and a Walkout," *NYT*, 7 June 1980, 46; "Family Conference Rejects Anti-Abortion Amendment," *NYT*, 22 June 1980, 24; Sharon Johnson, "After Heated Debates, Family Parley Ends Quietly," *NYT*, 14 July 1980, 2, 12.

63. "Catholics Quit Families Coalition," *NYT*, 27 June 1980, 20; "Family Conference Ends in Agreement on Ten Goals," *NYT*, 23 June 1980, II, 8.

64. James P. Corner, "The Hidden Costs of Unemployment," *NYT*, 9 June 1975, 31.

65. Steiner, *Futility of Family Policy*, 25.

66. Thomas A. Johnson, "Urban League Finds 25.4% of Blacks Are Still Jobless," *NYT*, 3 August 1976, 22.

67. "Panel Urges Move to Shore Up Family and Protect Poor Children," *NYT*, 15 December 1976, IV, 29; National Commission on Families and Public Policies, "Families and Public Policies in the United States, Final Report of the Commission," 1978, Supplement 1, Box 33, NCSW Records; Bishop J. Francis Stafford, "An Agenda for a National Family Policy," *America* 142, 23 (14 June 1980), 495–98; "The American Family: Labor's View," *American Federationist*(April 1980), 9–18. Also see the following, all in RG98–002, Vertical File, Box 16, Folder 6, Meany Archive: Lane Kirkland to Sir and Brother, 28 January 1980; Labor News Conference, Mutual Broadcasting System, Program 41, Series 19, 22 January 1980; Alan Bosch, Written Statement Submitted to The White House Conference on Families by the AFL-CIO, 20 November 1979, 1.

68. Steiner, *Futility of Family Policy*, 22–23; Kenneth Kenniston and the Carnegie Council on Children, *All Our Children: The American Family Under Pressure* (New York: Harcourt Brace, 1977); John W. Donohue, "Family Ecology," *America*, 24 December 1977, 456–59; Pamela G. Hollie, "Study Urges a U.S. Family Policy," *NYT*, 12 September 1977, 1.

69. Kater, *Christians on the Right*, 82–83.

70. Nicholi, "Fractured Family," 12.

71. Coontz, *The Way We Never Were*, 42. This is a primary contention in Alice O'Connor, *Poverty Knowledge: Social Science, Social Policy, and the Poor in*

Twentieth-Century United States History (Princeton, N.J.: Princeton University Press, 2001).

72. Ralph E. Smith, ed., with Nancy S. Barrett, Nancy M. Gordon, Sandra L. Hofferth, Kristin A. Moore, and Clair Vickery, *The Subtle Revolution: Women at Work* (New York: Urban Institute, 1979); "Working Women: The Subtle Revolution," UFCW Action (1980) (reprint), RG98–002, Vertical File, Box 72, Folder 5, Meany Archive; Suzanne Schiffman, "Making It Easier to Be a Working Parent," *NYT*, 24 November 1980, 27.

73. "Norman Rockwell and the GOP," *NYT*, 10 July 1980, 18.

74. Jane Fleming and Avril Madison, Testimony before the Senate Labor and Human Resources Committee, 28 January 1981, Box 11, Folder "Testimony," Wider Opportunities for Women Records, Schlesinger Library (hereafter WOW Records), 5.

75. Women's Work Force, "The Feminization of Poverty: Issue Brief," December 1981, Box 10, Folder "Mobil Action—Minutes and Meeting Correspondence," Downtown Welfare Advocacy Center Records, Social Welfare History Archives, University of Minnesota, Minneapolis, (hereafter DWAC Records), 1.

76. In the mid-1970s, women's poverty rate was 12.2% compared to 7% for men; women headed only 14% of all families but 48% of poor families; and poor women outnumbered poor men by more than four million, making up 60% of America's poor. In 1976, the median earnings for a woman who worked full-time, year-round were 60% of those of a similarly situated man, making the gender gap in wages greater than it had been when Congress passed the Equal Pay Act in 1963. Kathleen Riordan, "Women and Work, Women and Poverty: A Look at a Women's Bureau Project," Supplement 1, Box 26, Folder "SCAN Manuscripts, 105th Annual Forum-Los Angeles (1978)," NCSW Records, 1.

77. Heather L. Ross and Isabel V. Sawhill, *Time of Transition: The Growth of Families Headed by Women* (Washington, D.C.: Urban Institute, 1975), 3.

78. Margaret H. Mason, *Poverty: A Feminist Issue*, 1966, Box 98, Folder 23, NOW Papers, 24, 18.

79. Personal Communication with Merrillee Dolan, 16 May 2005.

80. Mason, *Poverty*, 72.

81. Albuquerque NOW Chapter Report, 1972, in author's possession.

82. Johnnie Tillmon, "Welfare Is a Women's Issue," *Ms.*, Spring 1972, 111–16; Mary Vogel to Merrillee Dolan, 10 March 1972, and Tish Sommers to Merrillee Dolan, 5 June 1971, both in author's possession, and personal communication with Merrillee Dolan, 16 May 2005.

83. Personal communication with Dolan.

84. Patricia Huckle, *Tish Sommers, Activist, and the Founding of the Older Women's League* (Knoxville: University of Tennessee Press, 1991).

85. See Transcript of interview with Catherine Day Jermany, n.d., Box 25, Nick Kotz Papers, Wisconsin Historical Society, Madison; Premilla Nadasen, *Welfare Warriors: The Welfare Rights Movement in the United States* (New York: Routledge, 2005), 134–35.

86. Mason, *Poverty*, 18.

87. The Women, Work and Welfare Project surveyed lawmakers on welfare-

related issues and lobbied for more generous federal policies for poor women. Maya Miller to Joseph Califano, 24 February 1977, Series IV, Box 590, Folder "Welfare Reform—Income Assistance," LWV Papers, 1.

88. "Women, Welfare and Poverty," Resolutions Adopted by Delegates to the National Women's Conference, Box 104, Folder "Women and Family Issues 11/77–4/78," and National Commission on the Observance of International Women's Year, "After Houston: Update 9," February 1978, both in Box 104, Folder "Women's and Family Issues 11/77–4/78," Public Liaison Papers, Carter Library; Statement of the NWPC by Ms. Lupe Anguiano, Chairperson, Welfare Reform Task Force to Welfare Reform Subcommittee, House of Representatives on "Better Jobs and Income Act—H.R. 9030," 31 October 1977, Box WE-4, Folder "WE 12/1/78–4/30/78," General Subject File, Carter Library, 3.

89. Nadasen, *Welfare Warriors*, 208–22.

90. Becky Alexander to DWAC, 1 March 1975, Box 15, Folder "Correspondence/Other Groups—Abraham & Straws to Center on Social Welfare Policy and Law"; List of Welfare Recipients, Organizers, and Advocates, n.d., Box 1, Folder "DWAC/RAM Meetings—to 1978"; various documents in Boxes 15–16 demonstrating DWAC's Theresa Funiciello's speaking engagements at a variety of feminist events; Diana Autin, "Women and Children Last: Welfare," n.d., Box 17, Folder "Press Clippings—n.d.; 1977–78"; DWAC Press Advisory: Feminists Unite with Welfare Women: Announce New Drive Against Albany, n.d., and "Women and Children Last," n.d., both in Box 16, Folder "Press Releases/Advisories, 1978–82," all in DWAC Records.

91. Maureen Whalen, "Women, the Poorer Sex: A Report of the National Council on Women, Work and Welfare," May 1978, Box 412, Folder "Welfare Reform Printed Matter, 1972–79, n.d.," NCJW Washington, D.C., Office Records; "Welfare Reform Is a Women's Issue," *Women's Agenda* (newsletter of the Women's Action Alliance, Inc.) 3, 1 (March 1978), Series IV, Box 595, Folder "Welfare Reform-Position Statements-Welfare, 1977–78," LWV Papers, 8; Nancy Cornblath-Moshe, ed., "Sex and Poverty: An Intimate Relationship," A Report of the National Council on Women, Work and Welfare, Box 56, Folder 19, Women's Equity Action League Records, Schlesinger Library (hereafter WEAL Records), 1.

92. Leonore J. Weitzman and Ruth B. Dixon, "The Transformation of Legal Marriage Through No-Fault Divorce," in Skolnick and Skolnick, *Family in Transition*, 324–35; Terry Arendell, "Mothers and Divorce: Downward Mobility," ibid., 328–40; "One-Parent Families Singled Out for Trouble," *Dollars and Sense*, September 1983 (reprint), RG98–002, Vertical File, Box 16, Folder 6, Meany Archive, 13; Ann Crittenden, "Nearly Half of All Fatherless Families Said to Live in Poverty," *NYT*, 18 April 1977, 26.

93. Women's Lobby, Inc., "Notes on the Administration's Welfare Reform Plan, The Better Jobs and Income Act, HR 9030 and S 2084," prepared for Congressional Women's Caucus by Maya Miller and Pam MacEwan, 13 October 1977, Series IV, Box 585, Folder "Welfare Reform-Congress-House of Representatives, Welfare Reform Subcommittee, 1977," LWV Papers.

94. Congress passed child support enforcement legislation in 1950, 1965, and 1967. The 1975 legislation (Title IVD of the Social Security Act) provided additional

federal assistance, financial and technical, to help states provide child support services to both welfare and nonwelfare mothers, though states had a much greater interest in (and tendency to) target AFDC applicants and recipients. Alfred J. Kahn and Sheila B. Kamerman, "Child Support in the United States: The Problem," in *Child Support: From Debt Collection to Social Policy*, ed. Alfred J. Kahn and Sheila B. Kamerman (Newbury Park, Cal.: Sage, 1988).

95. Marian P. Winston and Trude Forsher, "Non Support of Legitimate Children by Affluent Fathers as a Cause of Poverty and Welfare Dependence," December 1971, Box 4, Folder "AFDC Fathers Calif. Study," NOW Papers, iii; Testimony of Elizabeth C. Spalding at Child Support and Work Bonus Hearing Before the Sen. Finance Committee, S. 1842 and S. 2081, 25 September 1973, Sen. Finance Committee, Hearing on Child Support and Work Bonus, 93rd Cong., 1st sess., 25 September 1973, 180; Claire Spiegel, "Most Absent Fathers Give No Aid to Kin, Study Finds," *Los Angeles Times*, 24 May 1978 (reprint), Box 6, Folder "1978," NCSW Records.

96. Lowell H. Lima and Robert C. Harris, "The Child Support Enforcement Program in the United States," in Kahn and Kamerman, *Child Support: From Debt Collection to Social Policy*, 22.

97. Ann Crittenden, "Nearly Half of All Fatherless Families Said to Live in Poverty," *NYT*, 18 April 1977, 26.

98. "It's Not Pop Who Pays," *NOW Acts*, December 1970, NOW Papers, Schlesinger Library, 14.

99. Irwin Garfinkel, "The Limits of Private Child Support and the Role of an Assured Benefit," in Oldham and Melli, *Child Support: The Next Frontier*, 185; Greg J. Duncan, Martha S. Hill, and Saul D. Hoffman, "Welfare Dependence Within and Across Generations," *Science* n.s. 239, 4839 (29 January 1988): 470; Marsha Garrison, "The Goals and Limits of Child Support Policy," also in Oldham and Melli, 16–45.

100. Mary Jo Bane is responsible for demonstrating this discrepancy. See Coontz, *The Way We Never Were*, 251.

101. Fern A. Chamberlain, "Statement to the Senate Finance Committee on S. 2081, the Nunn-Talmadge Bill," n.d., and Elizabeth Wickenden, "Statement for Hearings on Child Support Legislation, Sen. Finance Committee, September 25, 1973," both in Supplement 2, Box 53, Folder "SIP, Correspondence and Memoranda, 1973," NSWA Records; Sen. Finance Committee, Hearing on Child Support and Work Bonus, 25 September 1973, 212–17.

102. Mason, *Poverty*, 36–37; Task Force on Women and Poverty to National Board Members, 1 December 1975, Box 8, Folder "Poverty," NOW Papers, 1–2.

103. Testimony of Elizabeth C. Spalding, Sen. Finance Committee, Hearing on Child Support and Work Bonus, 25 September 1973, 176–212; Betty Spalding to Eleanor Smeal, 16 January 1976, Box 8, Folder "Poverty," NOW Papers, 3.

104. Adele Blong, "Federal Intervention in Child Support: Boon or Betrayal," *Common Wealth*, Newsletter of the Women and Poverty Task Force; Task Force on Women and Poverty to National Board Members, 1 December 1975; and "Proposed Resolution on Child Support," all in Box 8, Folder "Poverty," NOW Papers, 1–2. Recent research revealed that as many as 60% of TANF recipients had experienced domestic violence. See Sharmila Lawrence, "Domestic Violence and Welfare Policy: Research Findings That Can Inform Policies on Marriage and Child Well-Being,"

National Center for Children in Poverty, Mailman School of Public Health, Columbia University, December 2002, http://www.researchforum.org/media/DomVio.pdf, accessed 20 April 2009.

105. Mason, *Poverty*, 36–37; Spalding, Card, Binder, and Day-Jermany to James S. Dwight, Jr., 30 May 1975, in author's possession.

106. Margaret Mason and Nancy Duff Campbell, "Announcement of Women and Poverty Meeting," 8 November 1978, and Nancy Duff Campbell, "Women and Poverty Meeting," 22 January 1979, both in Box 290, Folder "Coalition for Women and Poverty, 1979," NCJW Washington, D.C., Office Papers, 1–2; Nancy Duff Campbell, "Women and Poverty Meeting," 22 January 1979, Box 55, Folder 14, WEAL Records; Carol Oppenheimer to Women and Poverty Meeting Participants, 8 February 1979, Box 55, Folder 13, WEAL Records.

107. Statement of Ann Scott (Vice President for Legislation, NOW), Sen. Subcommittee on Employment, Manpower, and Poverty of the Committee on Labor and Public Welfare, Hearing on Comprehensive Manpower Reform Legislation, 92nd Cong., 2nd sess., 29 March 1972, 1425.

108. Labor News Conference, Mutual Broadcasting System: Women in the Labor Movement, Program 5, Series 19 (15 May 1979), RG98–002, Vertical File, Box 72, Folder 5, Meany Archive, 3; Christina Robb, "Learning a Skill, Earning a Future," *Boston Globe Magazine*, 2 August 1981 (reprint), RG98–001, Vertical File, Box 72, Folder 1, Meany Archive, 1.

109. Jane F. Fleming and Betsy Cooley to Augustus Hawkins, 16 October 1979, Box 199, Folder 20, Women's Action Alliance Records, Sophia Smith Collection, Smith College, Northampton, Massachussetts (hereafter WAA Records), , 1.

110. Carolyn J. Jacobson, "New Challenges for Women Workers," *American Federationist*, April 1980 (reprint), RG98–002, Vertical File, Box 72, Folder 5, Meany Archive, 2.

111. Robb, "Learning a Skill, Earning a Future."

112. NCJW, "Better Jobs and Income Act (H.R. 9030)—Welfare Reform," 16 January 1978, Box 414, Folder "Welfare Reform Statements and Testimony, 1978–79, n.d.," NCJW Washington, D.C., Office Records.

113. LWV-US to Califano, 24 February 1977, Series IV, Box 589, Folder "Welfare Reform: General Correspondence, 1977–79," LWV Papers, 5.

114. Nancy Seifer, "Big Losers in the Hot Stove League," *NYT*, 10 April 1974, 41.

115. Karen DeCrow, "The First Women's State of the Union Address," 13 January 1977, in Joint Economic Committee, Subcommittee on Economic Growth and Stabilization, Hearing on American Women in a Full Employment Economy, 95th Cong., 1st sess., 16 September 1977, 31.

116. "Every Mother Is a Working Mother" and "From Soweto to New York," *Safire* (Black Women for Wages for Housework-USA) 1, 1 (Fall 1977), Box 1, Folder 7, Minorities Collection, Smith College, 1–2.

117. Statement to Democratic Platform Committee by Maya Miller on behalf of National Women's Political Caucus and Women's Lobby, Inc., Atlanta, 17 April 1976, Box 15, Folder 18, Haener Papers, 1, 4–5; Alice S. Rossi, *Feminists in Politics: A Panel Analysis of the First National Women's Conference* (New York: Academic Press,

1982), 407; Nan Robertson, "The Martha Movement: Growing Advocate for Home-makers," *NYT*, 29 October 1977, 17.

118. Cobble, *Other Women's Movement*, 117.

119. *Sisters in Poverty* 3, 1 (June 1972), in author's possession.

120. Theresa Funiciello, "W.O.W. (Women on Welfare) Now!" n.d., Box 12, Folder "Speeches/Testimony by DWAC Personnel," DWAC Records 1, 5.

121. DWAC to All Welfare Coalition Folks Who Attended the April 5th Working Meeting for May 11th Action, n.d., Box 12, Folder "Miscellaneous Actions, 1978–82," DWAC Records, 1–2.

122. Summons from Supreme Court of the State of New York, County of New York, 24 March 1979, Box 14, Folder "DWAC/RAM Litigation—General"; "Class Action Suit Asks Court to Direct State to Increase State Welfare Grant," 20 November 1979, Box 16, Folder "Press Releases/Advisories, 1978–82"; and numerous documents in Box 15, Folder "RAM v. Blum—Press Material," all in DWAC Records.

123. DWAC Press Release, May 1978, and Bert Splain to Theresa, et al., 12 November 1978, both in Box 12, Folder "Miscellaneous Actions, 1978–82," DWAC Records; Testimony of Eve Dembaugh, Box 5, Folder "Outreach Welfare-Chicago 7/22/80," Records of President's Commission for National Agenda for the Eighties-General Communication File, Carter Library.

124. Resumé, Ms. Lupe Anguiano, November 1977, Box 22, Folder 18, East Papers; Statement of the NWPC by Ms. Lupe Anguiano, Chairperson, Welfare Reform Task Force to Welfare Reform Subcommittee, H.R., on "Better Jobs and Income Act—H.R. 9030," 31 October 1977, Box WE-4, Folder "WE 1/1/78–4/30/78," General Subject File, Carter Library; Radio-TV Monitoring Service, Inc., "60 Minutes: Getting Off Welfare," 20 November 1980, Box 20, Folder 56, AFSCME President's Office, Wurf Records.

125. Resumé, Ms. Lupe Anguiano.

126. Biography of Alexis Herman, http://www.thehistorymakers.com/biography/biography.asp?bioindex=548, accessed 15 April 2009.

127. U.S. Department of Labor/Employment Standards Administration, *Women in the Economy: Full Freedom of Choice*: A Conference Marking the 55th Anniversary of the Women's Bureau and International Women's Year, 11–13 September 1975, Washington, D.C., Box 191, Folder 1, WAA Records.

128. U.S. Department of Labor (DOL), Office of the Secretary, Women's Bureau, *Employment and Economic Issues of Low-Income Women: Report on a Project*, 1978, RG98–002, Vertical File, Box 72, Folder 3, Meany Archive, iii, 1–5.

129. DOL, *Employment and Economic Issues of Low-Income Women*, iii.

130. LWV-US to Califano, 24 February 1977, Series IV, Box 589, Folder "Welfare Reform: General Correspondence, 77–79," LWV Papers, 6.

131. The report went on to recommend the creation of additional jobs for "welfare recipients and *low-income fathers*." To Women's Bureau economist Kathleen Riordan, this last statement suggested the problem. "Most federal programs (welfare, employment and training, youth)," she complained, "continue to stress the unemployed/underemployed male youth or male head of household without recognition that only half the problem is thereby solved." Kathleen Riordan, "Women and Work, Women and Poverty: A Look at a Women's Bureau Project,"

Supplement 1, Box 26, Folder "SCAN Manuscripts, 105th Annual Forum-Los Angeles (1978)," NCSW Records.

132. Untitled document, Box 61, Folder 3; Wanda Wooten, Draft-General Support Proposal, 29 October 1991, Box 71, Folder 7; "Women in Poverty, Final Report, n.d., Box 61, Folder 5; and Dutchess County Community Action Agency, Inc., "Women in Poverty Project," July 1980, Box 61, Folder 1, all in National Congress of Neighborhood Women Papers, Smith College.

133. "Low Income Women at City Hall to Demonstrate the Need for Accessible Job Training Programs in Brooklyn," National Congress of Neighborhood Women Press Release, n.d., Box 56, Folder 8, National Congress of Neighborhood Women Papers.

134. Cornblath-Moshe, "Sex and Poverty."

135. Brenda M. Morton (coordinator, Montgomery, Alabama, Low-Income Women's Project) to Women's Bureau, 24 June 1977, Box 6, Folder "Low Income Women, 4/77–10/77," Staff Offices-Costanza File, Carter Library, 1–2.

136. "Partial List of Recommendations Concerning Federal Policy and Women," prepared for Meeting with President Carter, Vice President Mondale and the Ad Hoc Coalition for Women, 10 March 1977, Special Projects-Mitchell, Box 25, Folder "Women 10/76–7/78," Carter Library, 2, 4; "The Five Top Priorities," n.d., and "Brief Description of the Accomplishments, Priorities and Problems of the Women's Bureau," n.d., Box 6, Folder "Low Income Women, 4/77–10/77," Assistant for Public Liaison-Costanza File.

137. National Council on Women, Work and Welfare, "Women and Poverty," n.d., Box 290, Folder "Coalition for Women and Poverty, 1979," NCJW Washington, D.C., Office, 2.

138. Walter Mondale, "Introducing a Special Report: The Family In Trouble," *Psychology Today* 10, 12 (May 1977): 39.

139. "Remarks of the President and Informal Question and Answer Session at the Department of Health, Education, and Welfare," 16 February 1977, Staff Offices-Speechwriter's Office, Chronological File, "2/16/77-HEW Visit," Carter Library, 2; Laurence E. Lynn and David D. Whitman, *The President as Policymaker: Jimmy Carter and Welfare Reform* (Philadelphia: Temple University Press, 1981), 36.

140. "Message from President John Turner," *Conference Bulletin* 80, 4 (Summer 1977), Box 4, Folder "NCSW Conference Bulletin, 1975–77," NCSW Records, 2.

141. William E. Leuchtenburg, "Jimmy Carter and the Post-New Deal Presidency," in *The Carter Presidency: Policy Choices in the Post-New Deal Era*, ed. Gary M. Fink and Hugh Davis Graham (Lawrence: University Press of Kansas, 1998), 11–12.

142. National Conference on Social Welfare, "Principles for an Income Security System for the United States, Final Report," 1976, Supplement 1, Box 33, NCSW Records.

143. Regina O'Leary to Selected State League Presidents, 20 October 1977, Series 4, Box 589, Folder "Welfare Reform-General Correspondence, 1972–78," and Sally Laird to Organizations with an Interest in Welfare Reform, 12 August 1977, Series 4, Box 579, Folder "Welfare Reform Action Letters, 1977–79," both in LWV Papers.

144. Center for Community Change, "Welfare Reform: Alternative Strategies," April 1977, Series IV, Box 585, Folder "Welfare Reform-Congress-House of Representatives Legislation-Welfare Reform Bill (HR 9030, 1977)," LWV Papers.

145. David E. Rosenbaum, "Carter Would Scrap Welfare Programs for a New System; But Sees Delay of Four Years," *NYT*, 3 May 1977, 1.

146. Thomas J. Sugrue, "Carter's Urban Policy Crisis" in Fink and Graham, *The Carter Presidency*, 137.

147. Joseph Califano to President Carter, 30 November 1977, Box WE-2, Folder "WE 11/1/77–12/31/77," Executive Subject File, Carter Library, 4; Jack Watson to President Carter, 7 October 1977, and "County Officials Present 'Welfare Reform' Postcards to President Carter," NACO Press Release, 11 October 1977, both in Box WE-2, Folder "WE 10/1/77–10/31/77," Executive Subject File, Carter Library.

148. Meg Greenfield, "Making Sense of Welfare," *Newsweek*, 9 May 1977, 116.

149. Michael B. Katz, *In the Shadow of the Poorhouse: A Social History of Welfare in America*, 10th anniversary ed., rev. and updated (New York: Basic Books, 1996), 261–72.

150. "Social Welfare Spending—Can Anyone Bring It Under Control?" *U.S. News and World Report*, 14 March 1977, 41; Donald E. Bacon, "Another Go at the Welfare Mess: Will It Work?" ibid., 9 August 1977, 45.

151. Califano quoted in Bacon, "Another Go at the Welfare Mess," 40–41; Elliott Currie, "A Piece of Complicated Gimmickery," *Nation*, 17 September 1977, 230.

152. Lynn and Whitman, *President as Policymaker*, 91; "Announcement of Welfare Reform Package," 6 August 1977, Box 25, Folder "Welfare Reform: Program for Better Jobs and Income," DPS-Eizenstat File, 1–2.

153. "Carter Says Plans of Government Should Keep Families Together," *NYT*, 16 June 1977, 16.

154. President Carter to the Congress of the United States, 6 August 1977, Box 319, Folder "Welfare Reform: Program for Better Jobs and Income 8/77," Presidential Handwriting File, Carter Papers, 2; Lynn and Whitman, *President as Policymaker*, 91.

155. "Suggestions from Jerry Rafshoon," 5 August 1977, Box 319, Folder "Welfare Reform (Message Working Papers) and Backup," DPS-Eizenstat File.

156. Tom Joe, "Designing a Three-Tiered Approach to Welfare Reform," 12 January 1977, Box 317, Folder "Welfare Reform 1/77," DPS-Eizenstat File.

157. Jack Watson and Jim Parnham to Jimmy Carter, 23 May 1977, Box 318, Folder "Welfare Reform 5/77," DPS-Eizenstat File, 1.

158. Statement by the AFL-CIO Executive Council on Welfare Reform, 29 August 1977, RG4–006, Executive Council. AFL-CIO Executive Council Minutes, 1955–, Volume 22, 1977, Meany Archive, 26–31; Watson and Parnham to Carter, 23 May 1977, 1.

159. "Transcript of Education and Domestic Policies Press Briefing, Plains, Georgia," 16 August 1976, Box 319, Folder "Welfare Reform 8/77," DPS-Eizenstat File, 2.

160. Marian Wright Edelman to Stu Eizenstat, 2 May 1979, Box WE-5, Folder "WE1–1 1/20/77–1/20/81," General Subject File, Carter Library, 6.

161. H.R. Welfare Reform Subcommittee, Committees on Education, Labor,

and Ways and Means, Joint Hearings on H.R. 9030: A Bill to Replace the Existing Federal Welfare Programs, 95th Cong., 1st sess., 22 November 1977, 115–16.

162. Joe, "Designing a Three-Tiered Approach to Welfare Reform."

163. Lynn and Whitman, *President as Policymaker*, 51.

164. Ibid., 102–3.

165. Bert Lance to President Carter, 27 July 1977, Box 318, Folder "Welfare Reform 7/77," DPS-Eizenstat File, 1, 5–7.

166. Elizabeth Wickenden, "Public Policy Papers #1: Welfare Reform," 12 May 1977, Box 54, Folder "SIP, Welfare Reform, 1975–1977," NSWA Records, 2.

167. James T. Patterson, "Jimmy Carter and Welfare Reform," in *The Carter Presidency: Policy Choices in the Post-New Deal Era*, ed. Gary M. Fink and Hugh Davis Graham (Lawrence: University Press of Kansas, 1998), 129. Byrd quoted in Center for Social Welfare Policy and Law to Welfare Specialists, 2 May 1977, Series IV, Box 582, Folder "Welfare Reform: Center on Social Welfare Policy and Law, 1977," LWV Papers.

168. Alvin Schorr, "Welfare Reform, But Not Alone," *NYT*, 7 June 1977, 35.

169. Joseph Califano to President Carter, 25 July 1977, Presidential Handwriting File, Box 40, folder "Welfare Reform Plan 7/25/77," Carter Library, 41–42; H.R. Welfare Reform Subcommittee, Joint Hearings on H.R. 9030, 21 September 1977, 479.

170. Califano to Carter, 25 July 1977, 42; President Carter to the Congress of the United States, 6 August 1977, Box 25, Folder "Welfare Reform: Program for Better Jobs and Income," Presidential Handwriting File, 12.

171. Bert Lance to President Carter, 1 August 1977, Box 42, Folder "8/2/77[1]," Staff Secretary-Presidential Handwriting File, 2. HEW wanted to index all recipients' benefits, but DOL and OMB advised against it, and Carter refused the request. Charlie Schultz to President Carter, 27 July 1977, Box 319, Folder "Welfare Reform 8/77," DPS-Eizenstat File, 3.

172. Joseph Califano to President Carter, 25 July 1977, 56–59.

173. Testimony of Louise Brookins, chair, Pennsylvania State Welfare Rights Organization, H.R. Welfare Reform Subcommittee, Hearings on H.R. 9030, Part IX: Public Witnesses, 95th Cong., 1st sess., 22 November 1977, 180.

174. Richard P. Nathan, "Building on Existing Programs," Center for Community Change, "Welfare Reform: Alternative Strategies," April 1977, Series IV, Box 585, Folder Welfare Reform-Congress-House of Representatives Legislation-Welfare Reform Bill (HR 9030, 1977), LWV Papers, 22.

175. Lynn and Whitman, *President as Policymaker*, 81–82.

176. President Carter to the Congress of the United States, 6 August 1977, Box 25, Folder "Welfare Reform: Program for Better Jobs and Income," Special Assistant to the President-Martha (Bunny) Mitchell Papers, Carter Library, 1, 2.

177. Lynn and Whitman, *President as Policymaker*, 83; Charlie Schultz to President Carter, 27 July 1977, Box 319, Folder "Welfare Reform 8/77"; Joseph Califano to President, 8 November 1977, Box 318, Folder "Welfare Reform 8/77"; and Stu Eizenstat and Frank Moore to President Carter, 25 January 1978, Box 318, Folder "Welfare Reform 8/77," all in DPS-Eizenstat File. Joseph Califano to President, 30 November 1977, Box WE-2, Folder "WE 11/1/77–12/31/77" Executive Subject File,

4–5; President Carter to the Congress of the United States, 6 August 1977, Box 25, Folder "Welfare Reform: Program for Better Jobs and Income," Presidential Handwriting File, 7, Carter Library.

178. Statement by the AFL-CIO Executive Council on Welfare Reform, 29 August 1977; William B. Welsch to AFSCME Leadership, 12 August 1977, Box 31, Folder 5, MEJ Papers, 1–3.

179. Tom Joe to Stu Eizenstat, 2 August 1977, Box 319, Folder "Welfare Reform 8/77," DPS-Eizenstat File, 2.

180. Stu Eizenstat, Bert Carp, Bill Spring, and Frank Raines to President Carter, 3 August 1977, Box 319, Folder "Welfare Reform 8/77," DPS-Eizenstat File, 1.

181. Joseph Califano to President Carter, 30 November 1977, Box WE-2, Folder "WE 11/1/77–12/31/77," Executive Subject File, Carter Library, 6.

182. Briefing by Ray Marshall and Joe Califano, 6 July 1977, Box 319, Folder "Welfare Reform 8/77," DPS-Eizenstat File, 7.

183. Eizenstat et al. to Carter, 3 August 1977.

184. Stu Eizenstat and Bert Carp to President Carter, 4 August 1977, 1–3; President Carter to the Congress of the United States, 8; Joseph Califano to President Carter, 1 August 1977, Box 319, Folder "Welfare Reform 8/77," DPS-Eizenstat Papers, 1.

185. Memorandum from Russell Long to President Carter, n.d., Box 319, Folder "Welfare Reform 8/77," DPS-Eizenstat File, 3.

186. Joseph Califano to President Carter, 25 July 1977, Box 40, Folder "Welfare Reform Plan 7/25/77," Office of Staff Secretary-Presidential Handwriting File, Carter Library, 59. Lobbyists from women's organizations may have played a role in pressing this issue. Women's Lobby insisted that "the words 'day care' did not appear in the proposals until the women lobbyists" at welfare reform planning sessions "fought for them." "Welfare Reform Is a Women's Issue," *Women's Agenda*, 8.

187. Eizenstat et al. to Carter, 3 August 1977, 2–3.

188. Susan M. Hartmann, "Feminism, Public Policy, and the Carter Administration," in Fink and Graham, *The Carter Presidency*, 225–27, 230–31; Jan Peterson to Lupe Anguiano (NWPC), 18 May 1977, Executive Subject File, Box WE-1, Folder "WE 5/1/77–5/31/77," Carter Library.

189. Hartmann, "Feminism, Public Policy, and the Carter Administration," 228.

190. Zillah Eisenstein, "Antifeminism in the Politics and Election of 1980," *Feminist Studies* 7, 2 (Summer 1981): 191–92.

191. Jimmy Carter to Joseph Califano, 3 February 1977, and Joseph Califano to President Carter, 5 February 1977, in Box 317, Folder "Welfare Reform 2/77," DPS-Eizenstat File; Elizabeth Wickenden, Washington Notes #23, 31 March 1977, Supplement 2, Box 23, Folder "Washington Notes 1971–1977," NSWA Records, 2–3; Statement of Secretary Joseph Califano, Jr., on Welfare Reform, 25 March 1977, Box 318, Folder "Welfare Reform 5/77," DPS-Eizenstat Papers, 2; Lynn and Whitman, *President as Policymaker*, 63–64.

192. Lynn and Whitman, *President as Policymaker*, 54–56; "Participants for Working Session on Women's Perspective on Issues of Welfare Reform," 27 June 1977, Box 412, Folder "Welfare Reform-Lists and Notes, 1972–77, n.d.," NCJW

Washington, D.C., Office Papers; Jan Peterson to Margaret Costanza, 28 July 1977, Box WE-1, Folder "WE 7/1/77–7/31/77," Executive Subject File, Carter Library; LWV-US to Califano, 24 February 1977, Series IV, Box 589, Folder "Welfare Reform: General Correspondence, 1977–79," LWV Papers.

193. "Welfare Reform Is a Women's Issue," 6; Maya Miller to Joseph Califano, 24 February 1977, Series IV, Box 590, Folder "Welfare Reform-Income Assistance, 1977," LWV Papers, 1; LWV-US to Califano, 24 February 1977, Series IV, Box 589, Folder "Welfare Reform: General Correspondence, 1977–79," LWV Papers.

194. "Better Jobs and Income?" n.d., Series IV, Box 589, Folder "Welfare Reform: Position Statements on Welfare, 1977–78," LWV Papers.

195. "Welfare Reform Is a Women's Issue," 6.

196. Warren Brown, "Activists Denounce Carter's Welfare Revision Plan," *Washington Post*, 26 October 1977 (reprint), and Faith Evans, "The Carter JIP Proposals—A Step Backwards," n.d., both in Box 28, Folder 1, Wiley Papers.

197. H.R. Welfare Reform Subcommittee, Joint Hearings on H.R. 9030, 22 November 1977, 177.

198. Ruth Petajan to National Ofice, 9 December 1977, Series IV, Box 579, "Action Letters, 1977–79," LWV Papers.

199. H.R. Welfare Reform Subcommittee, Joint Hearings on H.R. 9030, 31 October 1977, 1682; 30 September 1977, 804.

200. "Welfare Reform Is a Women's Issue."

201. H.R. Welfare Reform Subcommittee, Joint Hearings on H.R. 9030, 29 September 1977, 664.

202. "Power to the Sisters!" *Safire* 1, 1 (Fall 1977), Box 1, Folder 7, Minorities Collection, Smith College, 3.

203. Warren Brown, "Activists Denounce Carter's Welfare Revision Plan," *Washington Post*, 26 October 1977 (reprint), and Faith Evans, "The Carter JIP Proposals—A Step Backwards," n.d., both in Box 28, Folder 1, Wiley Papers; Ruth Petejan to National Office, 9 December 1977, Series IV, Box 579, Folder "Action Letters, 1977–79," LWV Papers.

204. H.R. Welfare Reform Subcommittee, Joint Hearings on H.R. 9030, 22 November 1977, 68.

205. Carol Payne to Executive Officers, 11 May 1977, Series IV, Box 595, Folder "WR-Payne, Carol-Human Resources Dept. Staff Specialist 77–78," LWV Papers, 2.

206. Marian Wright Edelman to Stu Eizenstat, 2 May 1979, General Subject File, Box WE-5, Folder "WE1–1/20/77–1/20/81," Carter Library, 6.

207. Arnold Packer, quoted in Lynn and Whitman, *President as Policymaker*, 63.

208. Lupe Anguiano to Peg Cass, 19 July 1977, Box 22, Folder 18, East Papers.

209. H.R. Welfare Reform Subcommittee, Joint Hearings on H.R. 9030, 22 November 1977, 60, 78.

210. That support was expressed at the NWPC 1977 convention. Statement of Lupe Anguiano, H.R. Welfare Reform Subcommittee, Joint Hearings on H.R. 9030, 31 October 1977, 1707.

211. Barb Splain to Theresa Funiciello et al., 12 November 1978, and DWAC

Press Release, May 1978, both in Box 12, Folder "Miscellaneous Actions, 1978–82," DWAC Records, 1.

212. Welfare Action Coalition Press Release, n.d., and DWAC Press Advisory, n.d., Box 16, Folder "Press Releases/Advisories, 1978–82," DWAC Records.

213. Carmen Delgado Votaw to Margaret Costanza, 14 September 1977, Box WE-2, Folder "WE 9/1/77–9/30/77," Executive Subject File, Carter Library.

214. Cornblath-Moshe, "Sex and Poverty," 3–4.

215. LWV-US to Califano, 24 February 1977, Series IV, Box 589, Folder "Welfare Reform: General Correspondence, 1977–79," LWV Papers, 5; Jo Freeman, No Title, n.d., Box 12, Folder "Miscellaneous Actions 1978–82," DWAC Records, 3.

216. H.R. Welfare Reform Subcommittee, Joint Hearings on H.R. 9030, 12 October 1977, 1103–22.

217. National Women's Agenda, 1978, Box 196, Folder 12, WAA Records, 95.

218. National Council on Women, Work and Welfare Statement, 16 September 1977, Series IV, Box 595, Folder "Position Statements 1977–1978," LWV Papers, 1–2.

219. Carol Payne to Executive Officers, 11 May 1977.

220. H.R. Welfare Reform Subcommittee, Joint Hearings on H.R. 9030, 22 November 1977, 114.

221. National Urban League Position on Jobs and Welfare, 25 July 1977, Part III, Box 41, Folder 6, NUL Papers, 12.

222. Quoted in "Welfare Reform Is a Women's Issue," 7–8.

223. H.R. Welfare Reform Subcommittee, Joint Hearings on H.R. 9030, 14 October 1977, 1194–1215.

224. Helen R. Parolla, "Full Employment as a Women's Issue," National Women's Agenda Coalition Conference, Washington, D.C., 17 March 1978, Box 318, Folder "Employment-Full Miscellany 1974–76," NCJW Washington, D.C., Office, 1.

225. Freeman, No Title, 2.

226. NCWWW Statement, 16 September 1977, 2.

227. Freeman, No Title, 3.

228. Lynda Johnson Robb to Stu Eizenstat, 24 May 1979, Box WE-3, Folder "WE 7/1/79–9/30/79," Executive Subject File, Carter Library, 2.

229. Mason, *Poverty*.

230. H.R. Welfare Reform Subcommittee, Joint Hearings on H.R. 9030, 22 November 1977, 110, 114.

231. Ibid., 21 November 1977, 264.

232. Ibid., 22 November 1977, 16.

233. Ibid., 19 September 1977, 248.

234. Ibid., 22 November 1977, 70.

235. Patterson, "Jimmy Carter and Welfare Reform," 129.

236. Ballard C. Campbell, "Tax Revolts and Political Change," *Journal of Policy History* 10, 1 (1998), 153–78; David O. Sears and Jack Citrin, *Tax Revolt: Something for Nothing in California* (Cambridge, Mass.: Harvard University Press, 1985).

237. Joseph A. Califano, *Governing America: An Insider's Report from the White House and the Cabinet* (New York: Simon & Schuster, 1981), 362.

238. William E. Leuchtenburg, "Jimmy Carter and the Post-New Deal Presi-

dency," and Bruce J. Schulman, "Slouching Toward the Supply Side: Jimmy Carter and the New American Political Economy," both in Fink and Graham, *The Carter Presidency*, 7–28, 51–71.

239. Stu Eizenstat, Frank Moore, Jack Watson, and Anne Wexler to President Carter, Box 317, Folder "Welfare Reform [CF, O/A 732][1]," Domestic Policy Staff-Eizenstat File, , 1–2; Stu Eizenstat to the Vice President, Hamilton Jordan, Frank Moore, Jody Powell, Jerry Rafshoon, Phil Wise, Anne Wexler, and Jack Watson, 22 May 1979 and Stu Eizenstat, Jim McIntyre, Charlie Schultz, Joe Califano, and Ray Marshall to President Carter, 15 May 1979, both in Box 132, Folder "5/21/79[3]," Staff Secretary-Presidential Handwriting File, 4, 12.

240. Patterson, "Jimmy Carter and Welfare Reform," 119.

Chapter 5. Relinquishing Responsibility for Poor Families: Reagan's Family Wage for the Wealthy

Testimony of Preston Kayanagh before the President's Commission for a National Agenda for the Eighties, 22 July 1980, Box 5, Folder "Outreach Welfare-Chicago 1/22/80," Records of President's Commission for National Agenda for the Eighties-General Communications Files, Carter Library, 2.

1. Remarks, Annual Meeting of the National Alliance of Business, 5 October 1981, Public Papers of the Presidents: Ronald Reagan, 882.

2. Ibid.

3. R. Kent Weaver, *Ending Welfare as We Know It* (Washington, D.C.: Brookings Institution Press, 2000), 68; Ann Orloff, "Ending the Entitlements of Poor Single Mothers: Changing Social Policies, Women's Employment, and Caregiving in the Contemporary United States," in *Women and Welfare: Theory and Practice in the United States and Europe*, ed. Nancy J. Hirschmann and Ulrike Liebert (New Brunswick, N.J.: Rutgers University Press, 2001), 151.

4. David Steigerwald, *The Sixties and the End of Modern America* (New York: St. Martin's, 1995), 243.

5. Ronald Reagan, "Saving the States from Bankruptcy," *Nation's Business*, May 1971, 56–57.

6. John Osborne, "Reagan's Welfare Deal," *New Republic*, 15 May 1971, 11–15; Lawrence T. King, "Governor Reagan's Private War: The Battle of the Bar in California," *Commonweal*, 9 July 1971, 358–59; William Schultz, "California Cleans Up Its Welfare Mess," *Reader's Digest*, August 1973, 67–70; Charles D. Hobbs, "How Ronald Reagan Governed California," *National Review*, 17 January 1975, 28–42.

7. "'Welfare: America's No. 1 Problem': Interview with Ronald Reagan," *U.S. News and World Report*, 1 March 1971, 36–39.

8. On Reagan's political evolution, see John Ehrman, *The Eighties: America in the Age of Reagan* (New Haven, Conn.: Yale University Press, 2005).

9. Richard Schweiker, HHS secretary, quoted in "What Reagan Has in Mind for Welfare, Health Care," *U.S. News and World Report*, 27 April 1981, 35.

10. Robert Carleson and Kevin Hopkins, "Principles of Responsible Welfare

Reform," n.d. (1981), Robert Carleson Files, OA9590, Folder "Welfare Reform II," Ronald W. Reagan Presidential Library, Simi Valley, California, 8–9.

11. Medicaid was down 6%, housing assistance 4%, compensatory education 17%, child nutrition 28%, and public service employment was eliminated altogether. In all, while defense spending was up nearly 50% in real dollars by the end of the first Reagan administration, federal nondefense spending for programs other than OASDI and Medicare were down 12.5%. Michael Nelson, "Elections and Achievement: Campaigning and Governing in the Reagan Era," in *The Reagan Presidency: Assessing the Man and His Legacy*, ed. Paul Kengor and Peter Schweitzer (Lanham, Md.: Rowman and Littlefield, 2005), 18.

12. J. Richard Munro, "Executive Dissent: Against the Budget Cuts," *NYT*, 15 November 1981 (reprint), Box 17, Folder "Press Clippings-1981," DWAC Records.

13. H.R., Subcommittee on Public Assistance and Unemployment Compensation of the Committee on Ways and Means, Hearing on the Administration's Fiscal Year 1983 Legislative Proposals for Unemployment Compensation and Public Assistance, 97th Cong., 2nd sess., 21 April 1982, 313.

14. H.R., Committee on Ways and Means, Hearings on the Administration's Fiscal Year 1983 Economic Program, 97th Cong., 2nd sess., 18 February 1982, 6; 19 February 1982, 107; Jules Tygiel, *Ronald Reagan and the Triumph of American Conservatism*, 2nd edition (New York: Pearson Education, 2006), 154–55, 158.

15. See, e.g.. "Welfare Fraud: The Backlash," *Newsweek*, 31 January 1972, 58; "Welfare Mess: Any Hope of Solution," *U.S. News and World Report*, 7 June 1976, 33–38; Marvin Stone, "Can't We Do Better?" *U.S. News and World Report*, 11 April 1977, 104; Kenneth Y. Tomlinson, "Which Way Out of the Welfare Mess?" *Reader's Digest*, December 1977, 149–54; "Working While on Welfare," *Time*, 13 February 1978, 73; Don Bacon, "Mess in Welfare—The Inside Story," *U.S. News and World Report*, 20 February 1978, 27–31; Lawrence D. Maloney, "The Great National Rip-Off," *U.S. News and World Report*, 3 July 1978, 27–31; "Fraud and Abuse Are the Twin Plagues of Welfare," *Nation's Business*, January 1979, 38.

16. Tomlinson, "We *Can* Clean Up the Welfare Mess," *Reader's Digest*, April 1980, 84.

17. Jerry Rafshoon, Greg Schneiders, and Rick Hertzbert to President Carter, 24 November 1978, Staff Offices-Speechwriters Chronological File, Folder "12/13/78—Luncheon Remarks—HEW National Conference on Fraud, Abuse, and Error in Social Programs RH[1]," Carter Library.

18. "Remarks by the President at the HEW Conference on Fraud, Abuse, and Error," 13 December 1978, Staff Offices-Speechwriters Chronological File, Folder "12/13/78—Luncheon Remarks," Carter Library, 1.

19. Jim McIntyre to President Carter, 27 October 1978, Box 108, Folder "11/1/78," Staff Secretary-Presidential Handwriting File, 1; "Remarks of Secretary Joseph A. Califano, Jr., HEW, before the National Press Club," Washington, D.C., 29 November 1978, Staff Offices-Speechwriters Chronological File, Folder "12/13/78—Luncheon Remarks," Carter Library, 8–9.

20. Greg Schneiders, Bonnie Aronson, and Rick Hertzbert to President Carter, n.d., and Joseph Califano to President Carter, 5 October 1978, in Staff Offices-Speechwriters Chronological File, Folder "12/13/78—Luncheon Remarks."

21. "Remarks by the President at the HEW Conference on Fraud, Abuse, and Error," 1–2.

22. "Remarks of Secretary Joseph A. Califano, Jr.," 29 November 1978, Staff Offices-Speechwriters Chronological File, Folder "12/13/78—Luncheon Remarks," 2–5, 26–77.

23. Tygiel, *Ronald Reagan and the Triumph of American Conservatism*, 120–21. "Remarks at a Question-and-Answer Session on the Program for Economic Recovery at a Breakfast for Newspaper and Television News Editors," 19 February 1981, 133, and "Remarks at a Question-and-Answer Session on the Program for Economic Recovery at a White House Luncheon for Congressional Women," 16 March 1981, 251, both in Public Papers of the Presidents: Ronald Reagan, 1981.

24. Center for Social Welfare Policy and Law, "Proposed AFDC Budget Cuts," n.d., Box 61, Folder 15, National Congress of Neighborhood Women Records, Smith College (hereafter NCNW Records), 1–2; H.R., Subcommittee on Public Assistance and Unemployment Compensation, Hearing on Administration's Fiscal Year 1983 Legislative Proposals, 21 April 1982, 315–16. Congress agreed to most of the administration's proposed administrative changes.

25. "Fact Sheet: Aid to Families with Dependent Children," n.d., Martin Anderson Files, FFOA83, Folder "Entitlement Programs," Reagan Library, 1–2.

26. "Other Points on the Economy," n.d., Martin Anderson Files, CFOPA83, File "Economic Recovery Package," Reagan Library, 1.

27. Robert Carleson, "The Working Poor," n.d. (1982), Robert Carleson Files, OA9590, Folder "Welfare Reform II," 1; and Robert Carleson to Martin Anderson and Ed Gray, 26 October 1981, Robert Carleson Files, OA9590, Folder "Welfare— Welfare Reform," 1 (both in Reagan Library).

28. Center for Social Welfare Policy and Law, "Proposed AFDC Budget Cuts," n.d., 1–2; Sen. Finance Committee, Hearing on Spending Reduction Proposals, 97th Cong., 1st sess., 19 March 1981, 227.

29. Fact Sheet attached to Bobbi Felder to President, 23 December 1982, Elizabeth Dole Files, Box 6393, Folder "Women: Gender Gap," Reagan Library, 1.

30. For a description of OBRA work program provisions, see Sylvia Law, "Sex Discrimination and Federal Welfare Policy," n.d., Box 38, Folder 4, Frances Fox Piven Papers, Smith College (hereafter Piven Papers), 8–9

31. Theresa J. Flynn, "State Work and Welfare Initiatives: Trends and Innovations," in *Ladders Out of Poverty*, ed. Jack A. Meyer (Washington, D.C.: American Horizons, 1986), 88–89.

32. Sen. Finance Committee, Hearing on Administration's Fiscal Year 1983 Budget Proposal, 97th Cong., 2nd sess., 10 March 1982, 340.

33. "Welfare: America's No. 1 Problem," 39.

34. Robert Carleson and Kevin Hopkins, "Principles of Responsible Welfare Reform," 11. Reversing his earlier proposals to cut child support enforcement spending, Reagan supported a law that pressed states to step up their collection efforts. Wendy Sarvasy, "Reagan and Low-Income Mothers: A Feminist Recasting of the Debate," in *Rethinking the Welfare State: Retrenchment and Social Policy in America and Europe*, ed. Michael K. Brown (Philadelphia: Temple University Press, 1988), 262.

35. "'Welfare State Promotes What It Is Supposed to Cure': A Conversation with George Gilder," *U.S. News and World Report*, 6 April 1981, 53; Testimony of George Gilder, Joint Economic Committee, Hearing on the 1981 Economic Report of the President, 97th Cong., 1st sess., 28 January 1981, 112.

36. Remarks at a National Black Republican Council Dinner, 15 September 1982; Remarks at the Annual Meeting of the American Bar Association in Atlanta, Georgia, 1 August 1983; Remarks Accepting the Presidential Nomination at the Republican National Convention in Dallas, Texas, 23 August 1984, all in Public Papers of the Presidents: Ronald Reagan, 1163, 1166, 1115, 1176.

37. Mike Horowitz to David Stockman and Ed Harper, 19 July 1982, Robert Carleson Files, OA9593, Folder "Fairness," Reagan Library, 1–3, 9, 24–25.

38. Quotation from Douglas Muzzio's review of Charles Murray, *Losing Ground*, for *The American Political Science Review* 79, 4 (December 1985), 1199.

39. Charles Murray, *Losing Ground: American Social Policy, 1950–1980* (New York: Basic Books, 1984), 9, 160, 183.

40. Muzzio, Review of *Losing Ground*, 1199; Alice O'Connor, *Poverty Knowledge: Social Science, Social Policy, and the Poor in Twentieth-Century United States History* (Princeton, N.J.: Princeton University Press, 2001), 248–49.

41. O'Connor, *Poverty Knowledge*, 249–50.

42. Zillah Eisenstein, "Sexual Politics of the New Right: Understanding the 'Crisis of Liberalism' for the 1980s," *Signs* 7 (Spring 1982): 576; Muzzio, Review of *Losing Ground*, 1199.

43. Carleson and Hopkins, "Principles of Responsible Welfare Reform," 8.

44. Mike Uhlmann to Craig L. Fuller, 1 September 1982, Michael Uhlmann Files, OA9442, Folder "Women's Issues: Memo to Fuller re Memo to President 9/1/82," Reagan Library, 2.

45. Adam Clymer, "Male-Female Split on Politics Found Decisive in Some Polls," reprint, William Barr File, OA9095, Folder "Women's Issues," Reagan Library.

46. Lee Atwater to James A. Baker III, 23 November 1982, and Lee Atwater, "The Gender Gap: A Post-Election Assessment," n.d., both in Elizabeth Dole Files, Box 6393, Folder "Women: Gender Gap," Reagan Library, 1.

47. "The Gender Gap," n.d., Michael Uhlmann Files, OA9422, "Women's Issues: 1/18/83 Meeting of the Women's Coordinating Council," Reagan Library, 2.

48. Hinckley, "Propositions and Conclusions," 6, 8, 11.

49. "Women's Strategy: A Two-Year Plan," n.d., Elizabeth Dole Files, Box 6411, Folder "Women's Strategy, July–November 1982," 1.

50. Hinckley, "Propositions and Conclusions," 3.

51. Lenora Cole-Alexander to Mel Bradley, 8 June 1982, Elizabeth Dole Files, Box 6471, Folder "Women's Strategy, January–June 1982," 2–3.

52. Hinckley, "Propositions and Conclusions," 6–7.

53. "The Feminization of Poverty—Press Guidance," 17 September 1982, William Barr Files, OA9095, Folder "Women's Issues," Reagan Library, 2–3.

54. "Two Year Gender Gap Strategy," 17 November 1982, William Barr File, OA9095, Folder "Women's Issues: Gender Gap," Reagan Library, 3, 5.

55. Lee Atwater, "The Gender Gap: A Post-Election Assessment," Elizabeth Dole Files, Box 6393, Folder "Women: Gender Gap," Reagan Library, 7.

56. "Women's Strategy: A Two-Year Plan," 6.

57. Evan Witt, "What the Republicans Have Learned About Women," *Public Opinion*, October–November 1985 (reprint), Linda Arey File, OA15056, Folder "Women," Reagan Library, 49.

58. "The Two Feminisms," *National Review*, 31 December 1981, 19.

59. "Executive Summary," "Federal Equity Project," and "50 States Project," Michael Uhlmann Files, OA9442, Folder "Women's Issues: 1/18/83 Meeting of the Women's Coordinating Council," Reagan Library.

60. Bobbi Felder to President Reagan, 23 December 1982, Elizabeth Dole Files, Box 6393, Folder "Women: Gender Gap," Reagan Library, 1.

61. Atwater, "Gender Gap," 10.

62. "Tax Reform and Other Economic Initiatives," n.d., Michael Uhlmann Files, OA9442, Folder "Women's Issues: 1/18/83 Meeting of the Women's Coordinating Council," Reagan Library, 2.

63. See the following, all in Reagan Library: White House Office of Policy Information, "Issue Update Number 7: Economic and Legal Equity for Women," 17 September 1982, William Barr Files, OA9095, Folder "Women's Issues," 2; Women's Bureau, "Economic Recovery Tax Act: Selected Provisions of Interest to Women," August 1982, Judi Buckalew Files, OA10225, Folder "Women's Bureau (Packet) (2)," 1. U.S. Women's Bureau Fact Sheet No. 85–4, July 1985, "Working Mothers and Their Children," Linda Arey File, OA15056, Folder "Women," 1; Atwater, "Gender Gap," 10.

64. Abbie Gordon Klein, *The Debate over Child Care, 1969–1990: A Sociohistorical Analysis* (Albany, N.Y.: SUNY Press, 1992), 39.

65. Sonya Michel, "Childcare and Welfare (In)Justice," *Feminist Studies* 24, 1 (Spring 1998): 49.

66. "Child Care," n.d., Michael Uhlmann Files, OA9442, Folder "Women's Issues: 1/18/83 Meeting of the Women's Coordinating Council," Reagan Library, 1; Atwater, "The Gender Gap," 14. At the same time, Reagan cut the Equal Employment Opportunity Commission's budget, supported Department of Labor guidelines to rein in affirmative action policies, and presided over a conservative turn at the Justice Department's Civil Rights Division, responsible for enforcing antidiscrimination laws. Marilyn Power, "Falling Through the 'Safety Net': Women, Economic Crisis, and Reaganomics," *Feminist Studies* 10, 1 (Spring 1984): 44–46.

67. Klein, *Debate over Child Care*, 38, 63–64.

68. Klein, *Debate over Child Care*, 64; Madeline H. Kimmich, *America's Children, Who Cares? Growing Needs and Declining Assistance in the Reagan Era* (Washington, D.C.: Urban Institute Press, 1985), 12; H.R., Subcommittee on Oversight of the Committee on Ways and Means and Subcommittee on Health and Environment of the Committee on Energy and Commerce, Joint Hearing on the Impact of the Administration's Budget Cuts on Children, 97th Cong., 2nd sess., 3 March 1982, 137.

69. The poorest paid little in taxes, while even the more economically secure among the poor could rarely afford the advanced planning and flexibility needed to

take advantage of tax-free child care accounts. Sonya Michel, "Childcare and Welfare (In)Justice," 48–49; Klein, *Debate over Child Care*, 39–40; Inge Holloway and Maxine Forman, "Women Maintaining Families Alone: Obstacles to Self-Sufficiency," n.d., Box 56, Folder 20, WEAL Records, 7.

70. Barbara Ehrenreich and Karin Stallard, "The Nouveau Poor," *Ms.*, July/August 1982, 219.

71. Kimberly Morgan, "A Child of the Sixties: The Great Society, the New Right, and the Politics of Federal Child Care," *Journal of Policy History* 13, 2 (2001), 238.

72. Wendy Borscherdt to Elizabeth Dole, 6 July 1982, Elizabeth Dole Files, Box 6411, Folder "Women's Strategy, July–November 1982," Reagan Library, 1.

73. White House Office of Policy Information, "Issue Update, No. 15: Legal and Economic Equity for Women," 19 September 1983, Judi Buckalew Files, OA10227, Folder "Women's Issues(2)," Reagan Library, 2.

74. White House Office of Policy Information, "Issue Update No. 7: Economic and Legal Equity for Women," 17 September 1982, William Barr Files, OA9095, Folder "Women's Issues," Reagan Library, 2.

75. "Suggested Remarks for President Reagan to Make to Eagle Forum, September 20, 1985," Linda Arey Files, OA 15026, Folder "Eagle Forum (Phyllis Schlafly)(1)," Reagan Library, 3.

76. "Significant Women's Rights Legislation from the 66th to the 97th Congress," n.d., Elizabeth Dole Files, Box 6411, Folder "Women's Strategy 7–11/82," and "Suggested Talking Points for Meeting with the Eagle Forum Leadership Conference," n.d., Linda Arey Files, OA15026, Folder "Eagle Forum (Phyllis Schafly) (1)," Reagan Library, 2.

77. "Remarks of Faith Ryan Whittlesey, Assistant to the President for Public Liaison, Republican Women's Leadership Conference, Indianapolis, IA, 4 June 1983," Michael Uhlmann Files, OA 9443, Folder "Women's Issues: Faith Whittlesey Speech (6/4/83), Reagan Library, 5.

78. Mike Horowitz to David Stockman and Ed Harper, 19 July 1982, Robert Carleson Files, OA9593, Folder "Fairness," Reagan Library, 25.

79. "Remarks of Faith Ryan Whittlesey," 14. See also White House Office of Policy Information, "Issue Update Number 7," 1–2.

80. Quoted in Zillah Eisenstein, "Sexual Politics of the New Right," 575.

81. *The Family: Preserving America's Future*, Report to the President from the White House Working Group on the Family (1986), 1–2, 3, 4, 6, 15, 23, 31. For a discussion of the working group and its report, see Nina Roth, "The Politics of Federal Family Policy in the U.S., 1965–1988: The American Family as Contested Rhetorical Terrain," diss., University of Kansas, 1993, 221–26.

82. "Dear Friends," n.d., Box 10, Folder "Mobil Action—Minutes and Meeting Correspondence," DWAC Records, 1.

83. Nelson Lichtenstein, *State of the Union: A Century of American Labor* (Princeton: Princeton University Press, 2002), 248.

84. Eric Pianin and Warren Brown, "250,000 March to Protest Reagan's Policies: Crowd Proclaims Labor's Solidarity," *Washington Post*, 20 September 1981, 1.

85. "A Powerful Expression of Protest: Text of a Resolution Adopted by the

AFL-CIO General Board, August 1981 in Chicago," *American Federationist* 88, 10 (October 1981); Seth S. King, "260,000 in Capital Rally for Protest of Reagan Policies," *NYT*, 20 September 1981, 1, 34; David Shribman, "A Potpourri of Protesters," *NYT*, 20 September 1981, 1, 34; Judith Valente and Tom Sherwood, "Protesters Give Voice to Their Anger and Fears," *Washington Post*, 20 September 1981, 20; David S. Broder, "AFL-CIO Leader Riding a Big Bet," *Washington Post*, 20 September 1981, 1, 21.

86. Thomas Ferguson and Joel Rogers, *Right Turn: The Decline of the Democrats and the Future of American Politics* (New York: Hill and Wang, 1986); Thomas Byrne Edsall, *The New Politics of Inequality* (New York: Norton, 1984).

87. George J. Church, "Are There Limits to Compassion?" *Time*, 6 April 1981, 17.

88. Cited in Richard J. Margolis, "Strained Mercy of the Truly Rich," *New Leader*, 9 March 1981, 9; "Don't Just Stand There and Kill Us (A People's Report on AFDC)," May 1982, Box 166, Folder 8, Part III, NUL Papers, 32.

89. "Joint Statement of the Budget Coalition" in Joint Economic Committee, Hearing on the 1981 Economic Report of the President, 97th Cong., 1st sess., 24 February 1981, 112–15.

90. "Call for a National Jobs with Peace Week, April 10–16, 1982," Box 12, Folder "Miscellaneous Actions, 1978–82"; FRAC to Friend, 16 November 1981, Box 14, Folder "Food Stamp Advocacy, 1980–83"; "Jobs with Peace . . . A Healthy Economy in a Peaceful World," n.d., Box 12, Folder "Miscellaneous Actions, 1978–82," all in DWAC Records.

91. Children's Defense Fund, *A Children's Defense Fund Budget: A Response to President Reagan's Black Book*, Sen. Finance Committee, Hearings on Spending Reduction Proposals, 19 March 1981, 224; "Don't Just Stand There and Kill Us"; Vernon Jordan, Jr., "The Surrender of Federal Programs to the States: The Rights of the Poor Would Be Abused," *Vital Speeches of the Day*, May 1981, 421.

92. For example, see "Wage Activities and Victories, 1982," Box 16, Folder "WRO's: North Shore to W.A.G.E.," DWAC Records; "Philadelphia Citizens in Action" and "Mississippi Coalition for Mothers and Babies," n.d., Box 56, Folder 29, WEAL Records.

93. White House Office of Policy Information, "Fairness Issue: A Briefing Book on Individual Programs and General Perspectives," 1 June 1982, J. Upshur Moorhead Files, OA 10626, Folder "Notebook of White House Office of Policy Information on 'Fairness Issue': A Briefing Book on Individual Programs and General Perspectives, June 1, 1982 (1)," Reagan Library, 1.

94. Frances Fox Piven, Richard Cloward, Fred Block, and Barbara Ehrenreich, *The Mean Season: The Attack on the Welfare State* (New York: Pantheon, 1987), xv.

95. Steve Max, "Reagan's Economics and the Destruction of His Popular Support in the Middle Class," August 1981, Box 16, Folder "Correspondence/Other Groups: MacPherson to New World," DWAC Records, 1, 11.

96. See, e.g., "How the Poor Will Be Hurt," *Newsweek*, 23 March 1981, 32–34; Michael Harrington, "The Lower Depths," *New Republic*, 9 June 1982, 26; Arthur I. Blaustein, "Moral Responsibility and National Character," *Society*, May–June, 1982,

28; John E. Jacob, "If the New Federalism Gets Off the Ground: Racism Still Lives in America," *Vital Speeches of the Day*, 1 June 1982, 497.

97. "The Budget Cutters Ball, "*New Republic*, 28 February 1981, 8; Philip Green, "Redeeming Government," *Nation*, 12 December 1981, 644.

98. For transcripts of Solidarity Day speeches, see *American Federationist* 88, 10 (October 1981).

99. Ibid.

100. Joint Economic Committee, Hearings on the 1981 Economic Report of the President, 13 March 1981, 201.

101. Ibid., 201, and 24 March 1981, 409.

102. Theresa Funiciello, *Tyranny of Kindness: Dismantling the Welfare System to End Poverty in America* (New York: Atlantic Monthly Press, 1993), 108, xvi; DWAC Annual Report, July 1, 1979–June 1, 1980, Box 1, Folder "RAM Meetings—1979, 1980"; "Current Sources of Funding, Fiscal Year 1980–81," and "Cash Received," Box 3, Folder "DWAC/RAM Funding History, 1979–83," DWAC Records.

103. RAM, Minutes of Meeting, 22 October 1979, Box 1, Folder "RAM Meetings—1979, 1980," DWAC Records, 1–2.

104. "Working Committee of April Fools Action, 18 December 1981 Minutes" and "Dear Friends," n.d., Box 10, Folder "Model Action—Minutes and Meeting Correspondence," DWAC Records.

105. Many of these actions are described in DWAC "Narrative Report, 1982," Box 1, Folder "DWAC/RAM Annual Reports, 1978–79," DWAC Records.

106. "Don't Just Stand There and Kill Us." 4.

107. Ibid., 4, 8, 19.

108. Testimony of Sheldon Danziger, Institute for Poverty Research, Congress, Joint Economic Committee, Hearing on the 1981 Economic Report of the President, 28 January 1981, 97.

109. Sen. Finance Committee, Hearing on Spending Reduction Proposals, 19 March 1981, 283; H.R., Subcommittee on Public Assistance and Unemployment Compensation, Hearing on Administration's Fiscal Year 1983 Legislative Proposals, 21 April 1982, 408.

110. Testimony of Bert Seidman of the AFL-CIO, H.R., Subcommittee on Public Assistance and Unemployment Compensation, Hearing on Administration's Proposed Savings in Unemployment Compensation, Public Assistance, and Social Service Programs, 97th Cong., 1st sess., 12 March 1981, 197.

111. Leslie Bennetts, "Federal Cuts Frustrate 'Working Poor' Mother," *NYT*, 10 April 1982, reprinted in *Welfare: A Documentary History of U.S. Policy and Politics*, ed. Gwendolyn Mink and Rickie Solinger (New York: New York University Press, 2003, 463–65.

112. "'Welfare Reform' Forever," *The Progressive*, September 1981, 11–12.

113. David E. Rosenbaum, "Study Shows Planned Welfare Cuts Would Hurt Poor Who Work," *New York Times*, 20 March 1981 (reprint), Martin Anderson File, CFOA91, Folder "Welfare," Reagan Library.

114. Arthur I. Blaustein, "Moral Responsibility and the National Character," *Society*, May–June 1982, 29.

115. Edwin L. Dale, Jr., of the OMB, quoted in Rosenbaum, "Study Shows

Planned Welfare Cuts Would Hurt Poor Who Work"; Kevin Hopkins, "Draft Refutation Points," 30 March 1981, Martin Anderson File, CFOA91, Folder "Welfare," Reagan Library.

116. Rosenbaum, "Study Shows Planned Welfare Cuts Would Hurt Poor Workers the Most."

117. "Why Welfare Rolls May Grow," *Business Week*, 29 March 1982, 165–66.

118. Sen. Finance Committee, Hearings on Spending Reduction Proposals, 19 March 1981, 221, 226.

119. H.R., Subcommittee on Public Assistance and Unemployment Compensation, Hearing on Administration's Proposed Savings, 12 March 1981, 331.

120. Women's Work Force Issue Brief, December 1981, Box 56, Folder 29, WEAL Records, 4. See also Women's Work Force, "Against the Welfare of Women and Children: The Impact of Reagan Cuts on AFDC," April 1981, Box 64, Folder 12, NCNW Records.

121. "The Women's Campaign for Jobs and Economic Justice," n.d. (1982), Box 16, Folder "Correspondence/Other Groups: MacPherson to New World," DWAC Records; "All in Her Power: Twenty Years of Wider Opportunities for Women: A Review of the People, Programs, and Principles That Make WOW Work," Linda Arey File, OA15024, Folder "WOW(1)," Reagan Library, 16; Women's Work Force, "Against the Welfare of Women and Children: The Impact of Reagan Cuts on AFDC," April 1981, Box 64, Folder 12, NCNW Records; Wider Opportunities for Women, "Make Women and Kids Victors—Not Victims—of Welfare Reform," 5 February 1986, Box 56, Folder 20, WEAL Records.

.   122. Marlene Cimons, "Proposed Budget Cuts Rile Women," *Los Angeles Times*, 27 March 1981 (reprint), Box 61, Folder 14, NCNW Records, emphasis added.

123. Mary Rubin, Research Summary Series 4, "Women and Poverty," 1981, Economics Collection, Box 1, Folder 6, Smith College, 3; Sylvia Law, "Sex Discrimination and Federal Welfare Policy," n.d., Box 38, Folder 4, Piven Papers, 7.

124. H.R., Subcommittee on Public Assistance and Unemployment Compensation, Hearings on Administration's Fiscal Year 1983 Legislative Proposals, 21 April 1982, 390–91, 398.

125. DWAC Press Release, n.d., Box 16, Folder "Press Releases/Advisories, 1978–82," DWAC Records, 2.

126. *American Federationist* 88, 10 (October 1981), 12; Joyce D. Miller, Speech at Solidarity Day, 19 September 1981, Box 23, Folder 21, Coalition of Labor Union Women Records, Reuther Library, Reuther Library, 2.

127. Coalition on Women and the Budget, *Inequality of Sacrifice: The Impact of the Reagan Budget on Women*, 16 March 1983, Box 77, Folder 20, WEAL Records.

128. National Consultation on Economic Justice for Women Who Are Poor, Washington, D.C., January 1984, and "Inequality of Sacrifice, January 1984 Address by Yvonne V. Delk, Economic Justice for Women Who Are Poor Consultation, Washington, D.C.," both in Box 83, Folder 4, WAA Records.

129. Nita M. Lowey to Committee, 24 April 1984, Box 66, Folder 11, NCNW Records, 1; Ronnie Feit, "Preliminary Report and Recommendations for State Follow-Up to the New York Department of State and Gail Shaffer, Secretary of State

from the National Congress of Neighborhood Women," Box 65, Folder 15, NCNW Records, 3–5.

130. National Congress of Neighborhood Women to Honorable Miriam Friedlander, 17 January 1984, Box 66, Folder 12, NCNW Records, 1–3.

131. C.O.U.R.T., n.d., Box 56, Folder 29, WEAL Records.

132. Feit, "Preliminary Report and Recommendations for State Follow-Up," 5.

133. Funiciello, *Tyranny of Kindness*, 77.

134. H.R., Subcommittee on Public Assistance and Unemployment Compensation, Hearing on Administration's Fiscal Year 1983 Legislative Proposals, 22 April 1982, 624–25.

135. ACORN, "A People's Platform," 1980, Box 15, Folder "ACORN/The Institute: Training Materials, Notes, 1980," DWAC Records, 1, 7–8, 14; Women for Economic Justice, "Feminist Economic Agenda," n.d., Box 34, Folder 14, Piven Papers, 3–5.

136. H.R., Subcommittee on Public Assistance and Unemployment Compensation, Hearing on Administration's Fiscal Year 1983 Legislative Proposals, 21 April 1982, 295.

137. Ibid., 107–10; 165–66; 179–87; 22 April 1982, 426–431, 636–40, 911–13, 1137–45.

138. Testimony of Rep. Henry Waxman, using the words of the Children's Defense Fund, H.R., Subcommittee on Oversight of the Committee on Ways and Means and Subcommittee on Health and the Environment, Joint Hearing on the Impact of the Administration's Budget Cuts on Children, 3 March 1982, 4.

139. Ibid., 112.

140. H.R., Subcommittee on Public Assistance and Unemployment Compensation, Hearing on Administration's Fiscal Year 1983 Legislative Proposals, 21 April 1982, 305, and 22 April 1982, 595, 759–83.

141. Testimony of Reverend Timothy McDonald of Georgia's Public Assistance Coalition, H.R., Subcommittee on Public Assistance and Unemployment Compensation, Hearing on Administration's Proposed Savings, 12 March 1981, 313.

142. Julie Kosterlitz, "Reexamining Welfare," *National Journal*, 16 December 1986 (reprint), RG98–002, Vertical File, Box 46, Folder 19, Meany Archive, 2927.

143. George Gilder, "The Coming Welfare Crisis," Sen. Finance Committee, Subcommittee on Public Assistance, *How to Think About Welfare Reform for the 1980's: Hearings Before the Subcommittee on Public Assistance*, 96th Cong., 2d sess., 1980, in Mink and Solinger, *Welfare*, 444.

144. Sarvasy, "Reagan and Low-Income Mothers," 267. Moynihan's proposal is described in the *NYT*, 24 January 1987, A1, A7.

145. O'Connor, *Poverty Knowledge*, 243–44. The members of the Ford Foundation's Project on Social Welfare and the American Future and the American Horizons Foundation's Project on the Welfare of Families represented individuals and groups allied with the moderate, liberal element of the 1960s antipoverty coalition.

146. Michael Novak, *The New Consensus on Family and Welfare: A Community of Self-Reliance* (Washington, D.C.: American Enterprise Institute, 1987), vii, xiv.

147. Charles Murray, "Losing Ground Two Years Later," *Cato Journal* 6, 1

(1986), 20; Paula Roberts and Rhonda Schultzinger, "Toward Reform of the Welfare System: Is Consensus Emerging?" *Connections*, Women's Work Force National Network Newsletter, May 1987, Linda Arey Papers, OA15024, "WOW(2)," Reagan Library, 11; Reischauer quoted in Julie Kosterlitz, "Reexamining Welfare," *National Journal*, 16 December 1986 (reprint), RG98–002, Vertical File, Box 46, Folder 19, Meany Archive, 2931.

148. Falwell quoted in Eisenstein, "The Sexual Politics of the New Right," 575; *The Family: Preserving America's Future*, 44.

149. O'Connor, *Poverty Knowledge*, 257.

150. *The Common Good: Social Welfare and the American Future, Policy Recommendations of the Executive Panel*, Ford foundation Project on Social Welfare and the American Future (New York: Ford Foundation, 1989), 62.

151. *A New Social Contract: Rethinking the Nature and Purpose of Public Assistance*, Report of the Task Force on Poverty and Welfare, Submitted to Governor Mario M. Cuomo, December 1986, 6, 7.

152. Quoted in Novak, *New Consensus*, 52.

153. Sarvasy, "Reagan and Low-Income Mothers," 253.

154. Ibid., 254, 259, 271.

155. Nancy A. Naples, "The 'New Consensus' on the Gendered 'Social Contract': The 1987–1988 U.S. Congressional Hearings on Welfare Reform," *Signs* 22, 4 (1997), 914; Vanessa Sheared, *Race, Gender, and Welfare Reform: The Elusive Quest for Self-Determination* (New York: Garland Publishing, 1998), 39.

156. Brenner, "The Politics of Welfare Reform" reprinted in *Women and the Politics of Class* (New York: Monthly Review Press, 2000), 142.

157. Ibid., 134. On the Family Support Act, see Weaver, *Ending Welfare*, 70–78; Michael B. Katz, *Price of Citizenship: Redefining the American Welfare State* (New York: Holt, 2001), chap. 3; Naples, "The 'New Consensus'."

158. "WOW Summary: Program for Minority Single Female Parents," August 1982, Box 17, WOW Records, 1.

159. Ibid, 1 "Changing Welfare: An Investment in Women and Children in Poverty," The Proposal of the National Coalition on Women, Work, and Welfare Reform, April 1987, and "Welfare Reform in the 100th Congress," *Connections*, May 1987.

160. Robert Curvin, "The Family Is Crucial Indeed," *NYT*, 15 January 1982, 22.

161. *Investing in Poor Families and Their Children: A Matter of Commitment.* A Policy Development Project of the American Public Welfare Association and the National Council of State Human Service Administrators, Final Report Part I: One Child in Four (1986), 13.

162. WEAL Facts: Families Maintained by Single Women, April 1985, Box 46, Folder 47, WEAL Records, 1–2.

163. David Ellwood, *Poor Support: Poverty in the American Family* (New York: Basic Books, 1988), 110.

164. Michael Harrington, *The New American Poverty* (New York: Holt, Rinehart, 1984), 250.

165. Economic Self-Sufficiency for Women: A National Priority, Testimony Before the Joint Economic Committee of the U.S. Congress, 3 April 1984 by Avril

J. Madison, Executive Director, WOW, Box 11, Folder "Testimony," WOW Records, 3.

166. *The Common Good*, 7.

167. *New Social Contract*, 9–11, 13–14.

168. O'Connor, *Poverty Knowledge*, 252–53.

169. Meyer, *Ladders Out of Poverty*, 2, 3.

170. *The Common Good*, 63–64.

171. Ellwood, *Poor Support*, 181.

172. O'Connor, *Poverty Knowledge*, 253.

173. Lawrence Mead, *Beyond Entitlement: The Social Obligations of Citizenship* (New York: Free Press, 1986) 13.

174. Novak, *New Consensus*, 5, 13, 62, 116.

175. Meyer, *Ladders Out of Poverty*, 1.

176. *New Social Contract*, 9, 33.

177. *Investing in Poor Families and Their Children*, 6–7; Meyer, *Ladders Out of Poverty*, ix–x; New York State, Task Force on Poverty and Welfare, *A New Social Contract*, 9, 74–80; *The Common Good*, 62–3.

178. Blanche Bernstein, *Saving a Generation* (New York: Priority Press Publications, 1986), 13.

179. Ibid, 45.

180. Eleanor Holmes Norton, "Restoring the Traditional Black Family," *NYT Magazine*, 2 June 1985.

181. *Investing in Poor Families and Their Children*, 63.

182. Julie Kosterlitz, "Reexamining Welfare," *National Journal*, 16 December 1986, 2927.

183. O'Connor, *Poverty Knowledge*, 272, 276–280. The SSRC program's historical volume, edited by Michael Katz, is a notable exception. Michael Katz, ed., *The "Underclass" Debate: Views from History* (Princeton, N.J.: Princeton University Press, 1993).

184. "Bill Moyers Examines the Black Family," *Newsweek*, 27 January 1986, 58.

185. Robert J. Samuelson, "The New Candor on Race," *Newsweek*, 10 February 1986, 64.

186. John Corry, "TV: 'CBS Reports' Examines Black Families," *NYT*, 25 January 1986, 49; Michael Novak, "The Content of Their Character," *National Review*, 28 February 1986, 47; "Bill Moyers Examines the Black Family," 56; Sheared, *Race, Gender, and Welfare Reform*, 48.

187. Mickey Kaus, "The Work Ethic State" (1986) in Mink and Solinger, *Welfare*, 484.

188. Norton, "Restoring the Traditional Black Family."

189. Walter Goodman, "Blacks' Meeting Stirs Mixed Mood," *NYT*, 3 May 1984, I, 19; Dorothy J. Gaiter, "Blacks See Blacks Saving the Family," *NYT*, 7 May 1984, I, 14.

190. Norton, "Restoring the Traditional Black Family."

191. Novak, *New Consensus*, 110.

192. Chuck Hobbs to James Hooley, 26 May 1988, Peter Germanis Files, Box

3, Folder "White House Workshop on Self-Help Efforts and Welfare Reform, 6/9–10 (2)," Reagan Library.

193. Robert B. Hill, "Proposal to Establish a Welfare Reform Idea Exchange," 15 April 1988; "Background/Issues/Recommendations," n.d.; and "Information Exchange," n.d., all in Peter Germanis File, Box 3, Folder "White House Workshop on Self-Help Efforts and Welfare Reform, 6/9–10 (2)," Reagan Library.

194. O'Connor, *Poverty Knowledge*, 258.

195. Novak, *New Consensus*, xiii–xiv, 25, 45; Bernstein, *Saving a Generation*, 18.

196. Ellwood, *Poor Support*, 218.

197. Leslie Lenkowski, "The Federal Government and the Family," 10 November 1985, Office of Policy Development, OA10488, Folder "Federal Policies-Effects on Families," Reagan Library, 7–10.

198. Novak, *New Consensus*, 74.

199. Cited in Roth, "The Politics of Federal Family Policy," 257.

200. Ellwood, *Poor Support*, 22, 42. Ellwood noted that "no highly regarded study has indicated that welfare has played more than a minor role in the changing patterns of families" (57).

201. "Welfare Reform: Meeting with Howard Baker and White House Staff, July 28, 1987," White House Office of Records Management (WHORM) Subject File, WE010, Poverty Programs [509352–512337]," Reagan Library, 2–3.

202. Presidential Remarks: Welfare Reform Signing Ceremony, 13 October 1988, WHORM Subject File, WE010, Poverty Programs [601139], Reagan Library, 1.

203. *Up from Dependency: A New National Public Assistance Strategy: Report to the President by the Domestic Policy Council Low Income Opportunity Working Group*, December 1986 (Washington, D.C.: Government Printing Office, 1987), 1.

204. Ibid., 33; White House Issue Brief: "The President's National Welfare Strategy: 'Up From Dependency'," 5 February 1987, WHORM Subject File, WE Welfare [470569(1)], Reagan Library, 2.

205. Presidential Remarks: Welfare Reform Signing Ceremony, 13 October 1988, WHORM Subject File, WE010, Poverty Programs [601139], Reagan Library, 1.

206. Quoted in Sheared, *Race, Gender, and Welfare Reform*, 43.

207. Judith M. Gueron, "Work and Welfare: Lessons on Employment Programs," *Journal of Economic Perspectives* 4, 1 (Winter 1990), 84–85, 96–97. FSA did not mandate states to provide education, training, and job placement: most services optional; states required only to provide less costly job search and "workfare" programs; child care mandates for only 9 and 12 months of Medicaid, automatic child support deductions from wages of absent fathers.

Conclusion: Beyond the Family Wage

1. Carmen DeNavas-Walt, Bernadette D. Proctor, and Jessica Smith, *Income, Poverty and Health Insurance Coverage in the United States: 2006* (Washington, D.C.: U.S. Census Bureau, August 2007), 11, 14; Joel F. Handler and Yeheskel Hasenfeld, *Blame Welfare, Ignore Poverty and Inequality* (Cambridge: Cambridge University

Press, 2008), 17, 20; Robert D. Plotnick, Eugene Smolensky, Eirik Evenhouse, and Siobhan Rielly, "Inequality and Poverty in the United States: The Twentieth-Century Record," *Focus* 19, 3 (Summer–Fall 1998), 8, 12; Carmen DeNavas-Walt, Bernadette D. Proctor, and Jessica C. Smith, *Income, Poverty, and Health Insurance Coverage in the United States: 2007*, August 2008 (U.S. Census Bureau), 12, http://www.census.gov/hhes/www/poverty/poverty07.html, accessed 20 April 2009.

2. DeNavas-Walt, Proctor, and Smith, *Income, Poverty, and Health Insurance Coverage*, 15.

3. Roberta Spalter-Roth, Beverly Burr, Heidi Hartmann, and Lois Shaw, *Welfare That Works: The Working Lives of AFDC Recipients—A Report to the Ford Foundation* (Washington, D.C.: Institute for Women's Policy Research, 1995), 53, 59–60.

4. Frances Fox Piven, Joan Acker, Margaret Hallock, and Sandra Morgan, eds., *Work, Welfare, and Politics: Confronting Poverty in the Wake of Welfare Reform* (Eugene: University of Oregon Press, 2002); Kuttner, *Making Work Pay*; Handler and Hasenfeld, *Blame Welfare*.

5. Kim Moody, *Workers in a Lean World: Unions in the International Economy* (London: Verso, 1997), 185–93; Jacob S. Hacker and Elisabeth Jacobs, "The Rising Instability of American Family Income, 1969–2004: Evidence from the Panel Study of Income Dynamics," Economic Policy Institute Briefing Paper #213, 29 May 2008, http://www.epi.org/content.cfm/bp213, accessed 20 April 2009; Louis Uchitelle, *The Disposable American: Layoffs and Their Consequences* (New York: Knopf, 2006); David Stoesz, *A Poverty of Imagination: Bootstrap Capitalism, Sequel to Welfare Reform* (Madison: University of Wisconsin Press, 2000), 105–6.

6. Daniel Patrick Moynihan, "Social Justice in the *Next* Century," *America*, 14 September 1991, 132–37.

7. The Earned Income Tax Credit (EITC) now brings more children out of poverty than any other government program—in part because Congress expanded it sixfold between 1980 and 1996 and in part because of declining effectiveness among other income support programs, like the minimum wage (whose value declined significantly) and Unemployment Insurance (which reached a declining proportion of workers). Ann Orloff, "Ending Entitlements of Poor Single Mothers: Changing Social Policies, Women's Employment, and Caregiving in the Contemporary United States," in *Women and Welfare: Theory and Practice in the United States and Europe*, ed. Nancy J. Hirschmann and Ulrike Liebert (New Brunswick, N.J.: Rutgers University Press, 2001), 78–84, 139–40; Piven et al., *Work, Welfare, and Politics*; Robert Reich, "Introduction: Working Principles—From Ending Welfare to Rewarding Work," in *Making Work Pay: America After Welfare: A Reader from the American Prospect*, ed. Robert Kuttner (New York: New Press, 2002), x.

8. For Democratic candidates' positions and proposals, see http://www.johnedwards.com/issues/poverty/, accessed 20 April 2009; http://www.barackobama.com/issues/poverty/, accessed 20 April 2009; Tim Harper, "Clinton Promises to Battle Poverty," *Toronto Star*, 5 April 2008.

9. Stephen Luce, "'The Full Fruits of Our Labor': The Rebirth of the Living Wage Movement," *Labor History* 43, 4 (2002): 401–9; Bruce Nisson, "Living Wage Campaigns from a 'Social Movement' Perspective: The Miami Case," *Labor Studies Journal* 25, 3 (2000): 29–50; Vanessa Tait, *Poor Workers' Unions: Rebuilding Labor*

from Below (Boston.: South End Press, 2005); Ruth Milkman, *L.A. Story: Immigrant Workers and the Future of the U.S. Labor Movement* (Ithaca, N.Y.: ILR Press, 2006); Harold Meyerson, "A Clean Sweep: The SEIU's Organizing Drive for Janitors Shows How Unionization Can Raise Wages," in *Making Work Pay*, 1–20.

10. Jon Gertner, "What Is a Living Wage?" *NYT Magazine*, 15 January 2006.

11. Nancy MacLean, "From the War on Poverty to 'The New Inequality': The Fight for a Living Wage," *American Quarterly* 59, 1 (2007): 230.

12. See, e.g., Gwendolyn Mink, "Feminist Poverty Scholars Intervene in Welfare Debate," *Social Justice* 30, 4 (2003), 108n. In Piven et al., *Work, Welfare and Politics*, see Randy Albelda, "What's Wrong with Welfare-to-Work?" 73–79; and Stephanie Limoncelli, "'Some of Us Are Excellent at Babies': Paid Work, Mothering, and the Construction of 'Need' in a Welfare-to-Work Program," 81–94. In Hirschmann and Liebert, *Women and Welfare*, see Martha Albertson Fineman, "Dependencies," 23–37; Eva Feder Kittay, "From Welfare to a Public Ethic of Care," 38–64; Joan C. Tronto, "Who Cares? Public and Private Caring and Rethinking of Citizenship," 26–83; and Nancy J. Hirschmann, "A Question of Freedom? A Question of Rights? Women and Welfare," 84–107. In *Feminist Studies* 24, 1 (Spring 1998), see Eva Feder Kittay, "Dependency, Equality, and Welfare," 32–43; Gwendolyn Mink, "The Lady and the Tramp (II): Feminist Welfare Politics, Poor Single Mothers, and the Challenge of Welfare Justice," 59; and Felicia Kornbluh, "The Goals of the National Welfare Rights Movement: Why We Need Them Thirty Years Later," 65–79.

13. Limoncelli, "Some of Us are Excellent at Babies"; Joan Acker and Sandra Morgen, "The Impact of Welfare Restructuring on Economic and Family Wellbeing," in *Work, Welfare, and Politics*, 255; Tilly and Albelda, "Toward a Strategy for Women's Economic Equality"; Ann Orloff, "Ending Entitlements of Poor Single Mothers: Changing Social Policies, Women's Employment, and Caregiving in the Contemporary United States," in *Women and Welfare*, 133–159; Barbara Bergmann and Heidi Hartmann, "A Welfare Reform Based on Help for Working Parents," *Feminist Economics* 1 (Summer 1995), 85–89; Piven et al., "Toward a New Politics," in *Work, Welfare, and Politics*, 349–57: Spalter-Roth et al., *Welfare That Works*, 4.

14. Even universal child care, a program that fits well with progressive Democrats' "make work pay" philosophy, is virtually absent from contemporary political debate. Jonathan Cohn, "Child's Play: Why Universal, High-Quality Day Care Should Be Elementary," in *Making Work Pay*, 78–89; Janet C. Gornick, "Support for Working-Class Families: What We Can Learn from Europe About Family Policies," in *Making Work Pay*, 90–107; Gail Collins, "None Dare Call It Child Care," *NYT*, 18 October 2007.

Index

Acknowledgments

For a seemingly solitary endeavor, writing a book is in fact a social activity. It is a reminder that, contrary to the myth of "independence" so often touted during debates about federal income support, we are all dependent upon one another. I often found myself engaging more actively than I expected with the subjects of my research—at turns questioning them, arguing with them, and cheering them on. More tangibly, I relied on assistance, advice, criticism, and support from a broad group of individuals. I hope my words can, in some small measure, repay them.

I could not have completed the research stage of this work without the generosity of a number of individuals and institutions. Grants from the Hagley Museum and Library, the Arthur and Elizabeth Schlesinger Library at Radcliffe, the Social Welfare History Archive at the University of Minnesota, and Oregon State University's Valley Library funded crucial research trips. A Northwestern University Alumnae Association Dissertation Fellowship and, later, an Oregon State University Center for the Humanities Fellowship provided vital time to write, as did generous and timely assistance from Jane Chappell and Alan and Cyndy Schreihofer. A number of friends offered lodging during my many research excursions; thanks to Elizabeth DeBray, Lise Shapiro and Eric Sanders, Anne-Marie Chang and Orfeu Buxton, and the Kolker and Kolker/Spencer family for their hospitality. The members of the History Department at Oregon State have been ideal colleagues, both intellectually and personally. I am particularly grateful to Bob Nye, Mary Jo Nye, Jeff Sklansky, and Ben Mutschler for their wise counsel and consistent encouragement. Paul Farber and Jon Katz have been exceptionally supportive chairs, going out of their way to ensure that I had the support I needed to complete this book.

As any historian knows, librarians and archivists provide the critical expertise that enables our work. Many thanks to all those who assisted me at the Library of Congress Manuscript Reading Room; the Walter P. Reuther Library, Archives of Labor and Urban Affairs at Wayne State University; The George Meany Memorial Archives; the Schlesinger Library at

Radcliffe; the Sophia Smith Collection, Women's History Archives at Smith College; the Social Welfare History Archives at the University of Minnesota; the Hagley Library; the Carter Presidential Library; the Reagan Presidential Library; and the Wisconsin Historical Society. A number of individuals went out of their way to help me obtain images and copyright permissions; I'm grateful to David Klaassen, Yuning Zhou, Lynda DeLoach, James Bruno, Lisa Marine, Roy Doty, Bob Adelman, Janie Eisenberg, Eileen Betit, Linda Stinson, Margaret Jessup, and Doris Hansen. Merrillee Dolan was kind enough to share her memories and papers with me.

My intellectual debts are great. My graduate student colleagues at Northwestern University helped me think through the project in its earliest stages and provided critical moral support. My thanks to Leslie Dunlap, Wallace Best, James Burkee, David Johnson, Anastasia Mann, Karen Leroux, Michele Mitchell, Seth Jacobs, Charlotte Brooks, and Chris Front. Fellow panelists and audiences at numerous conference presentations pushed my thinking and challenged me to sharpen my argument. Thank you to fellow panelists and contributors at the 27th and 30th Annual Berkshire Conference on the History of Women, the 2003 Organization of American Historians Annual Meeting, the 28th Annual Meeting of the Social Science History Association, the University of California Santa Barbara Department of Feminist Studies colloquium, and the "End of Welfare as We Know It: A Decade Later" conference at Trinity College. Michael Sherry, Henry Binford, and Ann Orloff were ideal graduate committee members and provided feedback that greatly improved the manuscript. Eileen Boris has proven a dedicated mentor; not only has her own research and writing taught me a great deal, but her insightful critiques and warm encouragement have been invaluable. Jennifer Mittlestadt, Premilla Nadasen, Ellen Reese, Stephanie Gilmore, and Annelise Orleck have offered conversation, suggestions, and encouragement, and Bryant Simon, Tom Sugrue, and Dorothy Sue Cobble have proven astute readers of portions of this manuscript. The introduction and conclusion are immeasurably improved thanks to Jeff Sklansky's sharp reading and insightful advice, and the prose is much cleaner thanks to Bob Nye, who read the entire manuscript. Thank you, as well, to the anonymous readers for the press, whose thorough reading of two drafts helped direct my revisions and improved the book immensely. My deepest intellectual debt is to Nancy MacLean, who directed the dissertation upon which this book is based. She taught me more than I can express: about the welfare state, the political economy of race and gender in modern America, the labor movement, and so much more. Nancy never let me get away with easy answers; she pushed me to think big and to trust that I had something important to say. I will always be grateful.

Finally, thank you to the people in my life whose contributions to this project are less tangible but no less important. My mother and father, Cyndy and Alan Schreihofer, gave me a foundation of love, learning, and achievement that carries me forward. My friends provided necessary distraction and much-needed emotional support, especially Jennifer Gonzalez, Jennifer Roberts, Susan Andrews, and Malissa Larson. Everett Chappell, whose life has paralleled the life of this book, kept me grounded, reminded me about the truly important things in life, and taught me—more than any archival research or book could—about the joys and challenges of parenting in contemporary America. Lastly, Patrick Chappell has been my partner, my sounding board, my cheerleader, my travel agent, and my best friend. His support and encouragement, and his willingness to sacrifice to ensure that we are both fulfilled in our jobs as well as our family, have made this book possible. This book is for him, with love and gratitude.